A Different Shade of Colonialism

COLONIALISMS

Jennifer Robertson, General Editor

A Different Shade of Colonialism

Egypt, Great Britain, and the Mastery of the Sudan

EVE M. TROUTT POWELL

University of California Press

BERKELEY   LOS ANGELES   LONDON

Some of the material in this book appeared earlier in the following articles: "Brothers Along the Nile: Egyptian Concepts of Race and Ethnicity, 1895–1910," in Israel Gershoni and Haggai Erlich, eds., *The Nile: Histories, Cultures, Myths* (Boulder, Colo.: Lynne Rienner Publishers, 2000); "Burnt-Cork Nationalism: Race and Identity in the Theater of ʿAlī al-Kassār," in Sherifa Zuhur, ed., *Colors of Enchantment: Theater, Dance, Music and the Visual Arts of the Middle East* (Cairo: American University in Cairo Press, 2001); "The Silence of the Slaves" in John Hunwick and Eve M. Troutt Powell, eds., *The African Diaspora in the Mediterranean Lands of Islam* (Princeton, N.J.: Markus Wiener Press, 2002); and "Slaves or Siblings: ʿAbdallah al-Nadim's Dialogues about the family," in Israel Gershoni, Hakan Erdem, and Ursula Wokock, eds., *Histories of the Modern Middle East: New Directions* (Boulder, Colo.: Lynne Rienner Publishers, 2002).

University of California Press
Berkeley and Los Angeles, California

University of California Press, Ltd.
London, England

© 2003 by
The Regents of the University of California

Library of Congress Cataloging-in-Publication Data
Powell, Eve Troutt.
   A different shade of colonialism : Egypt, Great Britain, and the mastery of the Sudan / Eve M. Troutt Powell.
      p.   cm.—(Colonialisms ; 2)
   Includes bibliographical references and index.
   ISBN 0-520-23316-6—ISBN 0-520-23317-4 (pbk.)
   1. Egypt—Relations—Sudan.   2. Sudan—Relations—Egypt.
3. Egypt—History—19th century.   4. Sudan—History—19th century.
5. Slavery—Egypt—History—19th century.   6. Slavery—Sudan—History—19th century.   I. Title.   II. Series.

DT82.5.S8 P69 2003
325'.362'09624—dc21   2002151313

10   09   08   07   06   05   04   03
10   9   8   7   6   5   4   3   2   1

To the memory of my parents,
who showed me all the colors
that lie between black and white

Contents

Illustrations

Acknowledgments

My mother, Dr. Bobbye Troutt, died very suddenly in 1998. Her absence makes bittersweet the victory of finishing this book. So much of it is based on questions she raised and even more on her encouragement and love. She read page after page as this project moved from seminar paper to dissertation to its first draft as a manuscript. I am more grateful to my mother than words can say.

A project that begins as a dissertation and grows into a book requires tremendous help along the way. I was very lucky to have a wonderful dissertation committee: Roger Owen, Zachary Lockman, and John Voll, all three of whom read and discussed chapters with me quickly and profoundly and, even more important, taught me how to become a historian. I also had the ear of Stanley Hoffman, whose unending support and friendship I will always cherish. I found encouragement among other faculty and staff at the Center for Middle East Studies, Harvard University, such as Cemal Kafadar and Susan Miller. My friend and colleague William Granara was always there to help with his sense of humor, his thoughtful questions, and the permanent offer of a place for my family to stay. I also could not have finished without the help of the Foreign Language and Area Studies Grant, the Whiting Fellowship, and the Dorothy Danforth Fellowship at Harvard University. Much-needed financial aid was also provided by a fellowship from the Ford Foundation.

Many of the ideas for this book were suggested to me during my year of study at the Center for Arabic Studies Abroad (CASA). I am very grateful to Nabila al-Assiouti, ʿAbbas al-Tunsi, Zaynab Taha, and Raghda al-ʿIssawi for their encouragement and their imaginative teaching. And many thanks go to my friend Marsa Deng Magok, who took me along with her through

Cairo and showed me what it felt like to live as a refugee from the southern Sudan.

Twice the American Research Center in Egypt gave me not only financial support but a place in Cairo to rest my feet. My thanks go to Terence Walz, who taught me many ways to research the history of Egypt's relationship to the Sudan. Many deep thanks to Ibrahim Sadeq, who helped me in so many ways, particularly with his jokes. Ibrahim was kind enough to introduce me to Isma'il al-Mahdi, and after that doors kept opening. This book could never have been written without them or Nawal Muhammad 'Abdallah, a friend who with grace and kindness frequently set me straight.

With the help of the Social Science Research Center I was able to conduct research in London and in Oxford several times. In London I was lucky enough to meet often with the late Albert Hourani. One summer with him was worth semesters of lectures. I also had the opportunity to work with Anthony Pagden, whose work on early racial hierarchies in Spain and the New World proved very helpful (and provocative) to my own research.

Gabr Asfur of Cairo University and the Higher Council of Egyptian Culture offered suggestions that deepened my work, and the staff of the Archives of the Egyptian National Theater took the time to explain jokes to me that would otherwise have remained mysterious. The staff of the National Library made themselves dusty finding old newspapers for me, and Mme. Sawsan of Egyptian National Archives made my life as a researcher much easier.

The faculty and staff of the Department of History at the University of Georgia helped me endlessly: they babysat, read my papers, and listened to my harangues. David Schoenbrun and Kearsley Stewart changed my entire perspective on the historiography of Africa, among other things. My deep thanks go to my mentor, John Morrow, and my friend Diane Batts Morrow. Miranda Pollard, Robert Pratt, Joshua Cole, Bryant Simon, and John Inscoe all listened to or read more versions of chapters than they care to remember. David Roberts and Jim Cobb were instrumental in finding ways to help keep my research and writing going.

The University of Georgia also supported me with a Center for Humanities Grant, through the office of Dr. Betty Jean Craige, and the Sarah Moss Fellowship. My thanks go also to all the members of RRALL, particularly Dwight Reynolds and Kristen Brustad.

At the Institute for Advanced Study, I relearned the art of debate, had the opportunity to do research in Princeton's formidable Firestone Library, and met a ferocious cohort of other members. In particular I thank Claire Kim, Xiaorong Li, Mary Louise Roberts, Anat Biletski, Moshe Shokeid, Ken

George, and Danilyn Rutherford. I am also most appreciative of Joan Scott's honesty and help. While in Princeton, I participated in an amazing seminar of scholars who studied modern Egypt. For their comments, their help, and all the laughter, I thank in particular Samah Selim, Bob Vitalis, Ellis Goldberg, Ron Shacham, Khaled Fahmy, and Bob Tignor.

Without the help of my friend Magda al-Nowaihi, I would not have understood my readings of Arabic literature or appreciated the emotion and beauty to be found there. Without the help of my friend Beth Baron, who organized that wonderful seminar at Princeton, I would have missed much in the history of gender and slavery. Without the help of Israel Gershoni, John Hunwick, and Everett Rowson, I would be a historian bereft of sensitivity to the people I study.

I am grateful to the anonymous reader at the University of California Press for such careful attention and to Marilyn Booth, whose insights into the manuscript have proven so helpful. My thanks go also to Lynne Withey, who made the entire process easy.

My indebtedness extends to my in-laws, David and Lucia Powell, who helped keep me sane through this process; my sister, Margot Troutt Keys, who has faith when I have none; and my brother, David Troutt, who set the model as the first published author in our family.

Most of all, I thank my husband, Timothy Powell. Sometimes I am not sure where one of us ends and the other begins. The help and love he gives me has no name. It has taken us years, but we make each other productive in so many ways. And I thank my beautiful son, Jibreel, who came at the end of the dissertation, and my baby boy, Gideon, who arrived with the end of this book.

Introduction

In August 1894, a Bedouin slave dealer named Muḥammad Shaghlūb led a small caravan to a stop in the village of Kerdessa, within sight of the Great Pyramids of Giza. The caravan consisted of six Sudanese women, purchased hundreds of miles to the south, who had walked slowly and barefoot with Shaghlūb and three other traders along the Forty Days' Road, the old and well-traveled trade route that ended in lower Egypt. All were exhausted upon reaching Kerdessa, but Shaghlūb persevered, acting quickly to find an accommodating friend who agreed to hide the women on the top floor of his house. While the six women waited in this room, under admonition to be silent in the hot, cramped quarters, Shaghlūb went on to Cairo to negotiate for buyers for the six women.[1]

Shaghlūb and the other traders were only too aware that being caught with six African women by the authorities of the Slave Trade Bureau would mean imprisonment. Trade in African slaves had been abolished in Egypt in 1877, and the bureau had been created to search for unlawful caravans and to enforce the abolition. Nervously, Shaghlūb left Kerdessa to scout the streets of Cairo and, through inquiries whispered in a coffee shop, found a carriage driver who dealt with the servants of elite households, a man in a position to know which families were eager to buy a Sudanese slave woman or two. Within several days, Shaghlūb had found four wealthy buyers, and the six women were placed in new homes. The most prominent of these buyers was ʿAlī Pasha Sharīf, the head of the Egyptian Legislative Assembly. Ironically, ʿAlī Pasha had recently committed an act that would make this a cause célèbre: only weeks before, he had used the floor of the Legislative Assembly to petition the government to close down the many offices of the Slave Trade Bureau, saying that the practice had been discontinued for so long that Egyptians had forgotten the very meaning of the term *slave trade*.

The authority to whom 'Alī Pasha appealed was the government of Egypt, but he was well aware that this was not a government run by Egyptians. Instead of sending his petition to the Egyptian khedive 'Abbas Hilmī II, 'Alī Pasha sent it to Lord Cromer, the British consul-general who had run the economic and political infrastructure of the country since the British military occupation of 1882. 'Alī Pasha questioned the high salaries of British civil employees, comparing them to the very low wages paid to their Egyptian equivalents, and made a particular example of the bloated incomes of the British agents who worked for the Slave Trade Bureau, a commission set up in 1884 to manumit African slaves. Why were there so many officials, 'Alī Pasha complained to Cromer, when there were hardly any slaves?

Unfortunately for 'Alī Pasha, Cromer did not agree with this line of reasoning, and ordered the Slave Trade Bureau to be doubly vigilant for illicitly purchased slaves. One can only imagine the expression on Cromer's face when he learned from Schaefer Bey head of the bureau, that an informant had alerted his office to Shaghlūb's activities in Kerdessa and that the bureau had traced all six slave women, two of whom had been discovered in the spacious Cairo villa of none other than 'Alī Pasha himself. Three of the four purchasers were immediately arrested and jailed along with the Bedouin traders, and their trial was set for early September, to be conducted in a military tribunal and presided over by a British magistrate. 'Alī Pasha, however, escaped arrest by claiming Italian citizenship and seeking asylum in the Italian consulate.

The trial began on 4 September 1894 in a hail of publicity. The popular Egyptian nationalist and writer Muṣṭafa Kāmil quickly condemned the proceedings, and a diverse array of Egyptian newspapers sent correspondents to the courtroom and published daily accounts of the trial. The *Times* and the *Manchester Guardian* also sent reporters, as did Italian and French newspapers. The trial of the pashas, or *bāshawāt*, as it became known, was a scandal of international proportions. On one side were the defenders of the elite slave buyers, their lawyers, and other nationalists who believed that the case was meant to punish 'Alī Pasha Sharif for his petition and that there was no crime in buying Sudanese slaves. These nationalist writers insisted that purchasers of Sudanese slaves were actually conduits of a civilizing mission that taught uneducated and unkempt Sudanese girls the finer arts of domestic life and brought to them a sense of Islam not to be found in the Sudan itself. On another side were British officials and abolitionists, who saw in the purchase of the slave women another example of the barbarity and despotism that kept Egyptians from being able to govern themselves, which justified the British presence in Egypt.

All the parties connected to the trial adopted their own discourse to discuss slavery, each of which revealed the social and political complexities of slavery in the late nineteenth century. This was easily discernible in the ways in which the six women were characterized. The traders, trying to exonerate themselves, claimed that the six women were actually their wives. The pashas' lawyers claimed that the women were beneficiaries of generous and educational domestic employment. For men like Frith Bey, the slave women could only be described as victims, innocent and ignorant prey to marauding slave raiders and unscrupulous Muslim elites. One Egyptian writer, a Copt, used his editorials to question how Egyptians could sanction slavery, while others wrote of the singular gentleness of Islamic slavery compared to its counterpart in the colonies of western Europe and in the United States. One of the women, Zanūba, testified before the court that she came from Islamic territory in the Sudan, an assertion that implied her identity as a Muslim and disputed the legality of her status as a slave. Her assertion undermined many of the assumptions of the judges, lawyers, and reporters in the courtroom, yet it seemed difficult for them to hear her. She had trouble raising her eyes to meet those of her interlocutors, perhaps having been taught to avert her gaze from those considered her social superiors. Perhaps the pressure was too great to face directly: the entire trial, with its ramifications for the political sovereignty of Egypt, rested on the significance of her physical presence on Egyptian soil.

The bodies of the six slave women were, thus, rendered into legal texts that signified very different political arguments for all the claimants in the slavery trial. Their identity as Sudanese women bore special importance to each of the parties. To the pashas, slavery was part of an ages-old trade relationship between Egypt and the Sudan that symbolized the special connection between the two countries, a connection often framed as a domestic exercise in a national "civilizing mission." This intimate bond was also based on the fact that since 1821 the Sudan had been an Egyptian colony. In 1884, only ten years before the slavery trial, this bond had been severed by a powerful rebellion that occurred almost simultaneously with the British occupation of Egypt. To many of the British officials, including Frith Bey, the black bodies of the six Sudanese women aroused indignation; they were living reminders of the perceived antiquity of the Egyptian slave trade and vivid proof that, without British vigilance, Egypt would relapse into despotism. For these two opposing sides, the Sudanese women embodied the question of Egyptian capability for self-government and the need for continued British occupation. But as the trial demonstrated, the issue of Egyptian sovereignty could not be decided without determining who controlled the Sudan as well. Mastery of the Sudan was the pivot—yet few Sudanese were ever consulted. Though Zanūba's assertion of Islamic origins undermined many of the assumptions about Egyptian colonization of the Sudan and British colonization of Egypt, unfortunately, in 1894, the Sudan was hotly contested and little understood, and indigenous interpretations of its political geography did not yet count for much.

The trial ended within ten days. Following Lord Cromer's recommendations, Frith Bey and the other judges decided that the trial itself had taught Egypt a humiliating lesson. The pashas were freed, with the exception of the one buyer who had confessed to purchasing a slave; he was sentenced to five months' imprisonment. The court sentenced Shaghlūb and the other Bedouin slave traders to five years' hard labor. Zanūba and the five other slave women were placed in the Cairo Home for Freed Slaves, to be trained in domestic work so they could find gainful employment afterward. 'Alī Pasha's appeals to the Italian government were denied, and his image in the Egyptian nationalist press was severely tarnished by his claimed citizenship in another, European country. He died of a heart attack two years later. The Legislative Assembly made no more appeals to close the Slave Trade Bureau.

The immediate fates of the defendants were resolved fairly quickly by the trial, but the issues of race, slavery, and colonialism that the tribunal had raised were not summarily dispensed with. The trial revealed Egyptian nationalism at a peculiar nexus: Egypt was colonized by the British and yet often eager to recolonize the Sudanese in some way or another. The racial constructions inherent in these circumstances were also complex. Shaghlūb, the Bedouin slave trader, could claim a slave as his wife with none of the taboo of racial miscegenation that a similar marriage would have borne in Great Britain or the United States. Still, she was a slave. Higher up the economic and social ladder, the pashas and their defenders reformulated the intimacy of their connections to the slave women in a more paternalistic and political framework, in which the boundaries of difference are bridged by the civilizing mission. But the slaves were incorporated into the households neither as equals nor as children but as blank beings, in whom proper conduct and behavior would be instilled. For many of the British observers, the six slaves were victims, made vulnerable by their skin color. And the women knew themselves to have been purchased, and they considered themselves wrongly enslaved. If they were Muslims, then their religion removed them from the categories of the enslaveable, where polytheistic religious practices were nearly the equivalent of racial distinction.

TRIANGULATED CONQUEST

The scandal of the slavery trial arose at the height of British imperialism in the Middle East, of which Egypt was a focal point. The British had occupied Egypt in 1882, shortly after the emergence of the first Egyptian patriotic rebellion, known as the ʿUrābī rebellion after its leader, Colonel Aḥmad ʿUrābī. Although the incorporation of Egypt into the British empire was informal, it was efficiently executed. Two years later, a Sudanese religious leader known as the Mahdī completed his revolt, seizing Khartoum and evicting Egypt from territory it had ruled since 1821. The British occupation remained confined to Egypt until 1898, when British-led armies invaded the regions of the Sudan held by the Mahdist government and again annexed them to Egypt. British officials continued to run or supervise the administrations of both countries for decades. In response to these crises, important ideologies of race, empire, and nation were formed.

The Egyptian colonial experience in the Sudan was an encounter that took place in two territories: in the Sudan and in Egypt itself (just as Egyptian travelers to Europe reexperienced a sense of empire). It is true that the administration of the Sudan was known as the Turkīya by generations of Sudanese, because the Sudan initially had been conquered by Turkish-speaking officers for Muḥammad ʿAlī (also known as Mehemet ʿAlī), the Albanian Ottoman officer who was acting as a governor of Egypt for the Ottoman Empire in the early nineteenth century. But the characterization of the administration as Turkish by people unfamiliar with the ethnic nuances of Egypt's population also disguises the fact that native-born, Arabic-speaking Egyptians participated in the colony's administration, more prominently as decades passed and the administration strengthened its roots. As I will discuss in later chapters, many Egyptians served in the army stationed in the Sudan, finding there opportunities for promotion impossible to duplicate in Egypt itself in the 1860s and 1870s. Muhammad ʿAlī and his successors tried periodically to create Sudanese battalions in the army. Although these efforts met with varying success, they continued for decades and resulted in many regiments of Egyptian soldiers training alongside Sudanese in Upper Egypt.[2] Egyptian notables often feared being posted to the Sudan, as if it were exile, yet continued to regard the region as an intrinsic part of Egypt. With the expansion of Egypt's educational system, Egyptians traveled there as teachers, part of the government's project to "civilize" the Sudanese. Others traveled in the opposite direction: thousands of Sudanese doormen and wagon drivers, servants and slaves, in addition to the rich caravans of Sudanese traders, entered Egypt. Those groups of Sudanese who worked in Cairo and Alexandria often belonged to their own guilds and were well-integrated into urban economic life. Since the early days of Muḥammad ʿAlī's reign, Sudanese students too had made the trip to Cairo to study at al-Azhār University. There were therefore many ways for Sudanese in Egypt to earn their livelihoods and participate in urban culture, and they were a familiar part of the demographic landscape. Given the Sudan's political significance at this time, it is crucial to explore how the Sudanese in Egypt became the source of many jokes, stereotypes, and caricatures. As we shall see, in popular and print culture the Sudanese were often portrayed as no more than an empire of domestics.

However they were represented, the Sudanese were clearly considered by many Egyptians to be a part of Egypt, and this connection developed into a pronounced sense of possessiveness about the Sudan by the late nineteenth century. In an article published in Paris several years after the famous slavery trial of the pashas, the charismatic nationalist leader Muṣṭafa Kāmil wrote that "the Sudan, as is clear to the reader, is a piece of Egypt and has been stripped from her without legal right." Voicing his fear that the British were ready to conquer the Sudan, a fear shared by many in Egypt and soon to be proven correct, Kāmil characterized the country as "Egyptian property" to which the British had no right. So as not to leave doubts about the forcible nature of Egypt's potential reconquest of the region lost to the Mahdī, Kāmil announced that "our army, even less than our whole army, would have been enough to accomplish this result."[3] Surely, Kāmil's remarks assume a knowledge of and power over the Sudan similar to those of Lord Balfour regarding Egypt. At the same time, Kāmil's article is stamped by anger and defiance toward the British. This is the language of colonialism as well, but unique in the simultaneity of its aggression toward the Sudan and defensiveness toward Great Britain.

What Kāmil and many other theoreticians of Egyptian nationalist ideals expressed was the perspective of the colonized colonizer. This duality gave these men a Janus-like view of the world in which they lived, and of the nation they wished to bequeath the next generation of Egyptians: an Egypt whose past greatness and regional power could be grasped once again in the Sudan, free of the political and economic control of the British government. During the slavery trial, the pashas' defenders spoke from this vantage point when they condemned the trespass of the British authorities into Egyptian households and when they upheld the custom of domestic slavery as a civilizing mission that saved the Sudanese, women in particular, from the supposed barbarity into which they had been born. Kāmil's views on the Sudan also emanated from this dualism: the Sudan was Egypt's by right and by nature, and British control of Egypt was all the more tyrannical in its denial of Egyptian rights to independence and to sovereignty over the Sudan.

This dualistic nationalism did not begin in 1894 with the slavery trial, nor did it reach its culmination with the untimely death of Kāmil in 1908. It was not a static movement but one that changed with people and events in Egyptian history. The outlook of the colonized colonizer began to take shape in the last decade of Muḥammad ʿAlī's reign and emerged full-blown by the 1870s. Nationalists developed these themes throughout the rest of the nineteenth century but especially from 1898 to 1899, the period of the British reconquest of the Sudan. By 1919 there was a well-established slogan that called for "the unity of the Nile Valley." Although there were important exceptions—nationalist writers or leaders who disliked the idea of colonizing the Sudan or who feared colonization's implications of racial discrimination—most of the nationalists examined in this study agreed that what made the Egyptian struggle for independence irrepressible was Egypt's unique claim to mastery over the Sudan.

By the late nineteenth century, Egypt had experienced imperialism on many levels. Conquered by Sultan Selim I in 1516, Egypt in the early nineteenth century was a country steeped in the traditions of the Ottoman Empire, with a ruling class of Ottoman governors, officials, and descendants—an Ottoman-Egyptian elite. Although many of these elite had been born in Egypt, they were often most comfortable speaking and writing in Turkish. Muḥammad ʿAlī himself was a member of this group, and he and his successors did not identify themselves as Egyptians.[4] But Muḥammad ʿAlī succeeded in making the rule of Egypt the dynastic right of his family, and his successful conquest of the Sudan incorporated it under Egyptian auspices. The new class of bureaucrats he created thus grew up perceiving the Sudan as an Egyptian colony. His grandson, the khedive Ismaʿīl, pursued both policies: the expansion of Egyptian control of the Sudan, and the institutionalization of a native-born bureaucracy. But his expansionism exceeded his budget, and, having drawn loans from British, French, and other European banks that he could not repay, Ismaʿīl made Egypt vulnerable to the economic, and then the political, control of foreign governments, which eventually led to his deposition in 1879 and the British occupation in 1882.

Egypt's vulnerability to external control brought on by Ismaʿīl's debts incurred the wrath of a group of army officers, who led Egypt's first patriotic rebellion in 1881. At the same time, Egyptian control of the Sudan, often enforced by high-ranking European army officers, provoked the rebellion of the Sudanese Mahdī, who took control of almost all the Sudan by

1884. In just four years, Egypt had become a de facto colony of Great Britain and had lost its own colony in the Sudan, all during a period when certain pivotal groups of Egyptians were beginning to distinguish themselves culturally and ethnically from the Ottoman-Egyptian elites who occupied the highest posts in the country. The resulting triangle of colonialism marked by Great Britain, Egypt, and the Sudan thus had a profound imprint on the development of Egyptian nationalism. Thus my study differs from other explorations of Egyptian nationalism: I examine not a Manichean binary relationship between colonizer and colonized, but a more fluid relationship, in which the colonizer came from more than one continent, and the colonized could aspire to be a colonizer not only by adopting the tools of the British, or the traditions of the Ottomans, but also by making the Sudan a part of what defined Egypt as truly Egyptian.

DEFINING THE IMPACT OF EMPIRE

Perhaps no work has forced more attention on imperialism in the Middle East, or provoked more criticism, than Edward Said's *Orientalism*, first published in 1978. Said focused attention on a wide spectrum of media, political works, novels, poetry, and art to show how Europeans had created a virtual, textual reality of the "Orient" that both served and was engendered by the process of imperialism. Such themes are replete in one example of an official statement:

> You may look through the whole history of the Orientals in what is called, broadly speaking, the East, and you never find traces of self-government. All their great centuries—and they have been very great—have been passed under despotisms, under absolute government. All their great contributions to civilization—and they have been great—have been made under that form of government. Conqueror has succeeded conqueror; one domination has followed another; but never in all the revolutions of fate and fortune have you seen one of those nations of its own motion establish what we, from a Western point of view, call self-government. That is the fact.[5]

Using examples like this, taken from a 1910 speech made by Lord Balfour—the former British prime minister, experienced member of Parliament, and colonial administrator in India, Egypt, and southern Africa—Said demonstrated how deeply the themes of knowledge and power ran within the imaginations of the men working to create and maintain the British empire. This knowledge, acquired by the study of the Orient and its people, assumed a great distance between the knower and the known, a cold binary relationship that created its own reality for Europeans, or "a political vision of reality whose structure promoted the difference between the familiar (Europe, the West, 'us') and the strange (the Orient, the East, 'them')."[6] This construction of cultural difference engendered a vocabulary that was powerful enough to become a reality, in both literary and political form, for the bureaucrats of colonial administrations, writers, painters, composers, and European tourists to the Middle East, who were convinced they "knew" the truth about Oriental lives and thus "knew" how to deal with them. And *Orientalism* proceeded to explore the works of European novelists and politicians across a century, to illustrate the tenaciousness of these presumptions and the dehumanization of the East and its people.

Orientalism opened doors through which literary scholars, theorists of postcolonialism, historians, and any academics writing about the modern Middle East must pass; as Aijaz Ahmad remarked about Edward Said, "I can scarcely find my own thought without passing through [his]."[7] Although Ahmad admits his profound loyalty to the ambitions of Said's work, he and others have brought to light an important criticism of *Orientalism:* the trap set by the seductive binary "us" and "them" that Said challenges when observing it within the writings of Western authors about the East, but into which he himself falls. In his brilliant critical chapter on Said's work, Ahmad examines very closely how Said creates the same binary relationship for Western writers; but for our purposes here, what is most revealing is Said's omission of a similar binary relationship, one that bears different ramifications for the concept of "knowledge as power" that could exist within the discourse of the colonized as well. Ahmad writes,

> And if one steps out of the Euro-American traditions, one is struck by the fact that neither the architecture of *Orientalism* nor the kind of knowledge the book generally represents has any room in it for criticisms of colonial cultural domination of the kind that have been available in Latin America and even India, on an expanding scale, since the late nineteenth century. In fact, it is one of the disagreeable surprises in *Orientalism* that it refuses to acknowledge that vast tradition, virtually as old as colonialism itself, which has existed in the colonized countries as well as among the metropolitan Left traditions, and has always been occupied, precisely, with drawing up an inventory of colonial traces in the minds of people on both sides of the colonial divide.[8]

And with this refusal to see the same Foucauldian awareness of knowledge-as-power active in the imaginations of those people colonized by western Europe, Said's analysis freezes them into a curious passivity, in worlds in which the only prime movers are British or French or German. They remain either faceless victims or idle mannequins possessing the statuesque still-ness of the odalisques of European Orientalist art, and always turned toward Europe.

When Said published *Orientalism* in the late 1970s, he was, of course, writing within a context of cultural analysis made famous decades earlier by the politically charged works of Jean-Paul Sartre, Frantz Fanon, and Albert Memmi. Their works of the late 1950s and 1960s were the first to portray the lives led by those subjected to European colonialism, which only recently had collapsed. The power of books like Fanon's *Black Skins, White Masks* and Memmi's *The Colonizer and the Colonized* created a canon for postcolonial studies. But, as Robert Young writes, since the appearance of these books "postcolonial criticism has constructed two antithetical groups, the colonizer and the colonized, self and Other, with the second only know-able through a necessarily false representation, a Manichean division that threatens to reproduce the static, essentialist categories it seeks to undo."[9]

This is not to deny the victimization that people in Asia and Africa in general, and Egypt in particular, experienced as a result of the policies and presumptions of European imperialist politicians, administrators, and offi-cers; they did indeed suffer and their descendants continue to struggle with the legacies of such treatment. Nor does this deny the pervasiveness or the longevity of the Western images of the "Orient" that Said discusses. What my study challenges in Said's work is the idea that Egyptians suffered in silence, the idea that many in Egypt did not themselves engage in a dis-course of stereotypes and fantasies about the Sudan specifically and Africa in general, a discourse that paralleled Orientalist imagery. Although he wrote many pages on the objectification of Egypt in European literature, Said did not include in *Orientalism* a single sample of Egyptian literature or a discussion of Egyptians' long history of creative and eventually successful response to the British occupation. Even had he included such material, Said would have had to address other levels of often contradictory discourse, par-ticularly in reference to the Sudan. As Ania Loomba writes, "'Colonialism' is not just something that happens from outside a country or a people, not just something that operates with the collusion of forces inside, but a ver-sion of it can be duplicated from within."[10]

This question of the response to imperialism has in turn inspired many important, often universalizing, interpretations. For example, Eric Hobs-bawm characterizes the response of the "dependent countries" as an effort to incorporate the model of the West: "For all governments and elites of countries faced with dependency or conquest, it had been clear for several decades that they had to westernize or go under." Even those who resisted

British or French imperialism and the totalizing transformations of culture that westernization implied did so by "Westernizing to some extent."[11] More specifically, Albert Hourani has shown that westernization worked in the Middle East through the expansion of secularized schools—from primary levels to highly specialized professional institutions—and books, periodicals, and newspapers that eventually came to be called a cultural awakening, or *nahḍa,* in the Levant and Egypt. This awakening created new arenas in which the most sensitive issues of the time could be discussed among a small but increasingly literate audience, setting the stage for nationalist discourse as print media expanded.[12]

What is troubling in these otherwise seminal studies of imperialism and Middle Eastern nationalism is the resurfacing of a narrowly constructed cause-and-effect analysis, in which Egyptian nationalists look only toward western Europe, even when shaping their resistance to it. Timothy Mitchell explores this issue of colonialism and the response to it even further in his book *Colonising Egypt* in ways that are both helpful and problematic for my purpose here. As Mitchell declares in his introduction, his book is "a study of the power to colonise." By this he means not only the establishment of a European presence in Egypt but also "the spread of a political order that inscribes in the social world a new conception of space, new forms of personhood, and a new means of manufacturing the experience of the real."[13] These are curiously passive sentences, in which the amorphous "power to colonise" is never quite situated yet possesses an incredible transformative power. In *Colonising Egypt,* Egyptian bureaucratic and political elites appear to be as responsible as the British administrators for the act of ordering Egypt into a colonial, eventually modern, shape. In fact, as represented in this book, most of the processes of colonialism—the intensive reordering of the military, the classification of the population into a census, the widening of streets in Egyptian towns, the reliance on Jeremy Bentham's Panopticon as an architectural model for Egyptian schools, towns, and prisons—all occurred well before the British occupation of 1882. Thus, with the title of his book, Mitchell raises a provocative question: exactly who is doing the colonizing here?

Mitchell begins his study by examining how various Egyptian visitors to world exhibitions in Europe in the late nineteenth century confronted the displays of Egyptian streets and customs. The system of representations in these exhibitions, a panoptic vision of the same kind of literary Orientalism so well described by Edward Said, horrified and disgusted many of the Egyptian visitors with its contradictory ability to immerse the onlooker in an Egyptian "scene" while enabling the same viewer to stand far apart.[14] But as Mitchell argues, Egyptians had experienced a similar process of ordering in their own country beginning in the early nineteenth century with the reign of Muḥammad ʿAlī. To further his ambition to make Egypt a peer to the Ottoman Empire (in whose name he ruled), France, and Great Britain, Muḥammad ʿAlī had undertaken a series of economic and social reforms that in turn created a new class of Egyptian bureaucrats, many of whom demonstrated—in literature that Mitchell analyzes—as deep a commitment to the restructuring of Egypt as that exhibited by Lord Cromer.

Mitchell thus introduces an important new element into the Manichean canon of colonizer and colonized: the actively self-colonizing colonized. In his account we see men of tremendous energy and great commitment attempting to revamp their country during periods when European imperialism seemed the only answer. By identifying their responsibility in this project, Mitchell reveals that the source of colonialism was diffuse, the result of a collaborative effort. Perhaps another reason colonialism in Egypt should be attributed to more than one source, as Mitchell presents it, is that, during much of the nineteenth century, Egypt was nominally the province or dependency of two empires, the Ottoman and the British. But Mitchell's account neglects the fact that, for much of the nineteenth century, Egypt also attempted to establish its own empire, in the Sudan. He acknowledges that, for a brief time in the early part of the century, Egypt controlled territories as far east as the Hijaz, as far west as the Morea, as far north as Syria, and as far south as the Sudan. But he dismisses this in the next sentence, writing that the empire was forcibly dismantled by local revolt and foreign intervention.[15] It is certainly true that Egypt lost control of most of these territories by the 1840s, but the Sudan remained under Egyptian authority from 1821 until 1884. These six decades (almost the length of the British occupation of Egypt) affected the lives of many Egyptians—differently than their encounter with western Europe but in ways just as profound and complicated. Even the famous and decisive rebellion of the Mahdī, which lasted from 1881 to 1898 and effectively ended direct Egyptian control of the Sudan, could not put a stop to the calls made for its reconquest, by men whose books Mitchell himself analyzes in *Colonising Egypt*. And the omission of these views further ignores the fact that the world of Egyptian bureaucrats and nationalists was not simply a bipolar path between London or Paris and Cairo. This observation, then, complements Ahmad's point about Said not addressing the existence of colonialist tendencies in the colonized, and it adds another transitive meaning to the verb in the title Mitchell chose for his book: colonizing Egypt—a country that was both object and subject.

Although not exclusively reliant on them, my study examines in detail the books, speeches, plays, poems, journals, newspapers, and songs of several generations of nationalist elites for what they wrote about the Sudan and its people. It is true that such literature often bears a top-down imposition of ideologies, and many historians have lately and often rightly criticized methodological dependency on the writing of elites. On this issue, my study takes up a gauntlet that Hobsbawm threw at the feet of social historians exploring nationalism:

> That view from below, i.e., the nation as seen not by governments and the spokesmen and activists of nationalist (or non-nationalist) movements, but by the ordinary persons who are the objects of their action and propaganda, is exceedingly difficult to discover. Fortunately, social historians have learned how to investigate the history of ideas, opinions and feelings at the sub-literary level, so that we today are less likely to confuse, as historians once habitually did, editorials in select newspapers with public opinion.[16]

This is an awareness further developed in the historiography of modern Egypt by Zachary Lockman, who suggests the dangers of privileging "the written over the spoken word." This privileging prevents historians from accounting adequately "for the ways in which nonliterate subaltern groups may appropriate and construct nationalism through orally transmitted indigenous discourses of individual and collective identity and agency, sometimes drawing on nonhomogeneous and nonlinear conceptions of time."[17]

Joel Beinin suggests that the historical dichotomies between classical, standard Arabic and several colloquial dialects complicated "the establishment of a national language" in Egypt. As he explains, colloquial Egyptian Arabic has been the sole vernacular of illiterate Egyptians, yet it has often been disparaged by educational reformers, Muslim scholars, and certain nationalist leaders for being "a perversion of the language of the Koran" or a "threat to the linguistic unity of the Arab world." This disparagement meant that writing in colloquial Egyptian Arabic, as several of the important nationalist writers discussed in this study chose to do, could be perceived as a political act, a "poetic anti-canon which, through its language, subject matter, and mode of publication, constitutes a discourse of popular opposition to the hegemonic form of Egyptian national literary culture expressed in standard Arabic."[18] Some of these important writers cannot, as Beinin asserts, be considered unproblematically as representatives of the "voice of the disenfranchised masses." Either their writings were aimed at elite audiences or they themselves ended their careers as bureaucrats for the uppermost echelons of Ottoman society. Throughout their careers they were familiar with "the world of elite politics and foreign cultures."[19]

Keeping these important issues in mind, I return to the political discourse of the elites of Egyptian nationalism to explore *this* particular perspective of the colonized colonizer, their sense of empire, and their ideas of who was to be included within the ambitious reach of their nationalist ideologies; whenever possible, I incorporate nonelite discourses of nationalism as well. This is crucial in response to the imperative that diverse Sudanese reactions to Egyptian colonialism and Egyptian nationalism be included. But by reexploring the literature of elite or "bourgeois" nationalists, my study investigates the complicated matter of ethnicity as discussed by influential, nationalist Egyptians in the late nineteenth century. It also addresses the question that Beinin raises about who represents the voice of the "disenfranchised masses" by exploring how caricatured voices of Sudanese characters were used in articulations of Egyptian nationalism. If, as Hobsbawm writes, the "populations of large territorial nation-states are almost invariably too heterogeneous to claim a common ethnicity," then how did Egyptian nationalist leaders develop a position for the Sudanese?[20] Here, after all, were people once considered a subject population, a people who, after 1884, had, almost alone in the conflictual world of the British empire, fought and triumphed over British-led armies, a people who, after 1898, were again fellow victims of British imperialism. Without denying their often lofty perches, these nationalists were leaders in shaping Egyptian identity as a nation, and their literary works helped promote nationalist *policy* in the Sudan (or toward the Sudan), Egypt's oldest colony. Ironically, these elite members of the colonized population of Egypt thus reinforce Said's demonstration of the power of certain kinds of imperial language.

The works of Egyptian writers in my study also reflect many of the important themes about nationalist language that Benedict Anderson describes in his work *Imagined Communities,* a book that, like Said's *Orientalism,* has become part of the canon for scholars of colonialism and nationalism. Anderson portrays the historical and economic processes that define nations in the minds of their citizens, and the rapidity with which nationalist ideas have taken hold. His point is to situate the self-conscious political ideologies of nationalism within "the large cultural systems that preceded it, out of which—as well as against which—it came into being." The pivotal element in all of these cultural systems is language, and great changes were brought by the divorce, initiated by print capitalism, between sacral and vernacular languages in Europe that created both new means of publishing, new voices, and new audiences. In communities of "sacred scripts," where "readers were, after all, tiny literate reefs on top of vast illiterate oceans," those with the power to read were "adepts, strategic strata in a cosmological hierarchy of which the apex was the divine." But the power of such monks and clerics changed—as did notions of historical time—with the advent of the modern clock and calendar. Print capitalism went a long way in helping people see themselves in simultaneity, as transversing time in the company of other people speaking or reading the same language. In other words, a novel of the late nineteenth century empowered its reader to imagine himself or herself "temporally coinciding" not only with the novel's characters but also with other readers who could be envisioned as belonging to the same "community."[21]

Anderson situates the origin of this linguistic evolution in Europe in the late eighteenth and early nineteenth centuries, but he finds its real impact in nationalist movements in societies colonized by western European nations. The work of "imagining the community" was performed by "pilgrim creole functionaries and provincial creole printmen." Through them, a model "of the independent national state was available for pirating," a model which privileged the ideas that specific groups of people owned their languages and that "these groups, imagined as communities, were entitled to their autonomous place in a fraternity of equals." Thousands of colonized bureaucrats made their way to the colonial metropole, in search of this fraternity, and found themselves excluded by the uglier, more racist fact that imperialism and its instruction in the language of the empire, did not guarantee one the right to belong to the imperial nation—to what Anderson calls the "official nationalism." And so the new intelligentsia, created by the schools and bureaucratic needs of the empire, became central to the development of nationalism in the colonial regions, their "bilingual literacy" giving them a "vanguard role." This bilingualism "meant access, through the European language-of-state, to modern Western culture in the broadest sense, and, in particular, to the models of nationalism, nation-ness, and nation-state produced elsewhere in the course of the nineteenth century."[22] Through this bilingual ability, these nationalists were able to create and disseminate their own imagined communities.

This construction of nationalism is relevant to the situation of Egyptian nationalists in the late nineteenth and early twentieth centuries and their conscious efforts, as outlined by Mitchell, to wield the power of the pen as a means of instilling nationalism and inciting patriotic feeling for the new, modern Egypt. But by problematizing the limits of his still bipolar geographical perspective, we can see, in his chapter on patriotism and racism, where Anderson floats painfully adrift. Here, Anderson challenges those who insist that the roots of nationalism grow from "fear and hatred of the 'Other' and its affinities with racism," and he reminds his readers that "nations inspire love, and often profoundly self-sacrificing love." Anderson continues,

> Where racism developed outside Europe in the nineteenth century, it was always associated with European domination, for two converging reasons. First and most important was the rise of official nationalism and colonial "Russification." As has been repeatedly emphasized[,] official nationalism was typically a response on the part of threatened dynastic and aristocratic groups—upper *classes*—to popular vernacular nationalism. Colonial racism was a major element in that conception of "Empire" which attempted to weld dynastic legitimacy and national community. It did so by generalizing a principle of innate, inherited superiority on which its own domestic position was covertly (or not so covertly) conveying the idea that if, say, English lords were naturally superior to other Englishmen, no matter: these other Englishmen were no less superior to the subjected races.[23]

In terms of racism, with its implications of discrimination and biological difference, Anderson's position is appropriate to the discourse of non-European colonized and European colonizer. But his presentation of racism is an over-simplification of the term, one that deserves more complicated questioning. As Etienne Balibar has written in partial answer to Anderson, "There is not merely a *single* invariant racism but a number of *racisms*, forming a broad, open spectrum of situations." Racism, then, can be as unique as any virus or, as Balibar puts it, "a determinate racist configuration has no fixed frontiers; it is a stage in a development which its own latent potentialities, as well as historical circumstances and the relations of force within the social formation, will shunt around within the spectrum of possible racisms."[24] Balibar justifies his criticism of Anderson's chapter by enumerating the "plethora of devastating racisms, both institutional and popular, *between* 'nations,' 'ethnic groups,' and 'communities' in Africa, Asia and Latin America."[25]

Is this level of inquiry into the presence of racism anachronistic, to borrow a term frequently leveled at late-twentieth-century historians of race? Does the very term itself seem too rooted in images of the Ku Klux Klan or the Nazis? Labeling nineteenth-century Egyptians with such a term clouds the discussion and attributes power that simply did not exist; by keeping his discussion of race limited to the idea of racism, Anderson avoids a much more complicated investigation. However, it is just as anachronistic to deny race consciousness in cultures confronting British or French or German imperialism in the late nineteenth century, when political, cultural, and scientific definitions of the word *race* were being coined. In terms of construction of race, or even consciousness of race, the very system of racial identification that Anderson rightly ascribes to Europe did not simply melt into a broth of political love when confronted by indigenous, colonized nationalists. The appellations and categories of race imposed by the empire were either accepted, denied, translated, or redirected, but they were always provocative. In late-nineteenth-century Egypt, writers and nationalists were acutely aware of the discourse on race being conducted in western Europe, and they used it to frame their various perspectives about the Sudan and its people. This should not be interpreted to mean that they were themselves racists, or even that they held the power to discriminate racially, but analysts of race and nationalism should take care not to assume that nationalists in Egypt were deaf and blind to the very charged issue of race in the late nineteenth and early twentieth centuries. There were many nuances to certain terms: *ʿabīd* (slave), *barbarī* (Berber or barbarian), *nūbī* (Nubian), *ʿarabī* (Arab), and *sūdānī,* to name a few that bore particular significance in the hierarchy of political and economic relations from one end of the Nile Valley to the other.

Within the literature of Egyptian nationalism, especially the literature of writers of colloquial Arabic who paid particular attention to nuances, such words were immensely controversial. Moreover, these words were not simple impositions by Egyptians on Sudanese. As Anders Bjorkelo shows, such words could also be found in the language of Sudanese traders and religious leaders, people as sensitive to difference and community as the nationalists of Egypt.[26] These were words of the market and the slave trade, and were of grave importance in identifying who could be sold and who could not. One Sudanese tribe could identify another with such words and could reveal a kinship based on shared religion or trade networks. And as the colonial relationship between Egypt and the Sudan became politicized as a result of the British occupation, the meanings changed. Eventually, words signifying "slave" or "black," even the word for Sudanese, would be used in the Sudan itself to identify who was considered suitable by a certain kind of educated Sudanese to speak of the Sudanese nation. According to Peter Woodward, in Khartoum in the 1920s, for example, Sudanese leaders were also involved in an often angry debate over these racial attitudes.[27] The linguistic history of particularly sensitive words connoting race in the Nile Valley should therefore complicate our reading of Benedict Anderson's account of the relationship between race, patriotism, and nationalism.

Concepts of race require textual and literary analyses as rich as historical ones. Here, it makes sense to draw from Mikhail Bakhtin's concept of heteroglossia in the novel, because a tapestry of signifiers was woven from the threads of ideas and vocabulary about race in the late-nineteenth and early-twentieth-century Nile Valley that must be examined in order to gauge the unique articulations of Egyptian nationalism. In *The Dialogic Imagination,* Bakhtin intended to rewrite the history of the novel by challenging formalist, linguistic analyses of language that, in his view, denied "the problem of alterity in language." As his translators note, for Bakhtin "there is no such thing as a 'general language,' a language that may be divorced from a specific saying, which is charged with particular overtones." In this sense, heteroglossia means that "at any given time, in any given place, there will be a set of conditions—social, historical, meteorological, physiological—that will insure that a word uttered in that place and at that time will have a meaning different than it would have had under any other conditions; all utterances are heteroglot in that they are functions of a matrix of forces practically impossible to recoup, and therefore impossible to resolve." In other words, there can be no analysis of literary expression that truly separates the ideological from the formal, because such a separation denies the idea that "verbal discourse is a social phenomenon." Every literary artist lives and writes from a sense of "social life," which he or she experiences "in the open spaces of public squares, streets, cities and villages, of social groups, generations and epochs."[28]

I substitute the political and literary arena of nationalism for Bakhtin's novel, because the concept of heteroglossia fits well into the historical and social context of the Egyptian nationalists. These were people wrestling publicly and self-consciously with the establishment of a national language for Egypt and using terms to describe their sense of national, cultural, and racial identity that were, as they knew, replete with layers of meaning collected from Europe, the Ottoman Empire, and Africa. Egyptian nationalists confronted something similar to what Bakhtin describes as the prerequisites for the modern novel: the complications brought by "the internal stratification of any single national language into social dialects, characteristics, group behavior, professional jargons, generic languages, languages of generations and age groups, tendentious languages, languages of the authorities, of various circles and of passing fashions." In their efforts to create a language that would unify Egypt, nationalists had to incorporate social and political contradictions in order to offer a centralizing method of expression. This was necessary in an environment in which words like *nation* had only recently been translated into Arabic, words whose viability within an Egyptian context were continuously contradicted by the British occupying forces. As Bakhtin writes, "Between the word and its object, between the word and its speaking subject, there exists an elastic environment of other, alien words about the same subject, the same theme." Through the lived process of this kind of interaction, in this kind of environment, "the word may be individualized and given stylistic shape."[29]

When addressing the issue of the Sudan, nationalist writers often created characters who spoke with a certain kind of Sudanese voice or accent and who discussed important themes of the time, like companionate marriage or slavery or the unity of the Nile Valley. This type of heteroglossia, according to Bakhtin, "is another's speech in another's language, serving to express authorial intentions but in a refracted way." Bakhtin calls this "double-voiced discourse," in which the intentions of the character are expressed at the same time as the "refracted intention of the author." These two voices, although written by one, seem to "actually hold a conversation with each other." But this conversation occurs within a specific historical context of struggle: "it deals with discourse that is still warm from that struggle and hostility, as yet unresolved and still fraught with hostile intentions and accents." For Egyptian nationalists, the argument with the British remained heated in such dialogues, as did the effort to convince the Sudanese of Egyptian rights to sovereignty over them. And this last effort, which I see in the many stereotypes of Sudanese figures in the humorous articles and dialogues of certain Egyptian nationalist writers, fits Bakhtin's idea that heteroglossia includes "the tendency to assimilate others' discourse" in the formation of "an individual's ideological becoming," a tendency he calls "an internally persuasive discourse." All the efforts to include the voices of others thus enable the author to know his own language "as it is perceived in someone else's language, [and thereby to come] to know one's own belief system in someone else's system."[30]

Bakhtin was describing the carnival of voices and worldviews that European novelists, beginning in the eighteenth century, incorporated in the miniature worlds that their novels encapsulated. The journalists, writers, politicians, and actors that this book analyzes were not novelists in the way Bakhtin imagined, but their work encompassed a parallel cultural linguistic effort as they tried to put a similar carnival of voices onto paper and into the imaginations of their audiences. I explore these themes later in the book, but here it is important to highlight Bakhtin's relevance to the liberation from simple binary relationships in the study of cultural history, particularly in the construction of non-European nationalism. And the idea of a multiplicity of meanings and voices will further deepen our understanding of the definitions of race, as expressed by nationalists in the Egypt of the late nineteenth and early twentieth centuries.

ZANŪBA'S HISTORICAL IMPORTANCE

How would any of this have mattered to the six Sudanese slave women seated in the courtroom of the military tribunal in September 1894? The slavery trial, with its unfamiliar crowds and officials and angry speeches, must have seemed carnivalesque to these six bewildered witnesses. What matters is that they themselves, the circumstances that brought them there, the darkness of their faces, and most of all, their unknown place of origin were simultaneously familiar and yet a mystery to the judges, audience, defendants, lawyers, and journalists in the courtroom. They were the ciphers who inspired another heteroglossia. Few of their contemporaries sitting near them were certain of the geography of the Sudan or the differences among the many tribes and kingdoms still thriving along the White Nile and Blue Nile in the late nineteenth century. The newspaper accounts of the trial reveal a constant conflation of the terms *Nubian, Barbari, Sudanese,* and even *habashī* (Ethiopian) when referring to darker-skinned people of the south, whether slaves, servants, or soldiers. When we explore how Egyptian nationalists defined the nation of Egypt culturally, ethnically, and sometimes racially, we see that many attitudes about Nubia and the Sudan were legacies of not only Ottoman culture but also older Islamic cultures. This widespread geographic and cultural uncertainty about what and where the Sudan actually was represents a phenomena of Bakhtinian irony, one that coexisted during the height of Egyptian colonial activity in the Sudan with increasing amounts of "valuable empirical evidence" about sub-Saharan East Africa that was gathered by explorers and traders and published (in Arabic).[31] Here is another example of the inherent volatility of words connoting the Sudan and the Sudanese that Bakhtin's concept of heteroglossia explains so well: "free-floating classificatory labels" to describe actual places and people took on entirely new significance within the environment of a colonial military courtroom.[32] This conflict of meaning created an even larger silence during the trial when the slaves asserted that they were from *bilād al-'arab* (land of the Arabs; Islamic territory) and not *bilād al-sūdān* (land of the blacks). Until that assertion, they had been six tabula rasa: innocents from unknown Africa who could be adopted into the Egyptian family on many levels; orphans from Africa who could be saved by the British abolitionists and the imperial administrators who maintained the Slave Trade Bureau.

The controversy over the six slaves occurred at a time when British abolitionists, colonial officials, and Egyptian nationalists were debating important questions about the nature of the "home" and the "household" in Islamic societies and the role of women in Egypt itself. Lord Cromer considered the seclusion of Muslim women and their lack of education a major obstacle to Egyptian self-government. As a result, British efforts to establish schools for girls were central to the empire's civilizing mission in Egypt.[33] A French-educated Egyptian lawyer named Qāsim Amīn published *Taḥrīr al-mar'a* (The Liberation of Women) in 1899, a revolutionary book at the time that advocated education for women and equated women's low social status with the status of the Egyptian nation.[34] After the slavery trial, a few upper-class women in Egypt published newspapers aimed at women readers that featured articles about model ways in which to conduct a proper household.[35] As the household became a metaphor for Egypt's engagement with "modernity," the presence of domestic servants and slaves had somehow to be addressed, and the other six Sudanese women thus served as "boundary markers" (as Anne McClintock labels the role of domestics in Victorian culture) in that they were examples of "evolutionary belatedness evidenced by their 'feminine' lack of history, reason and proper domestic arrangements."[36] Although the British opponents and the Egyptian defenders of the slave-buying pashas were divided about the boundaries between Egypt and the Sudan, it is ironic that on this boundary of slave women they were in agreement: the civilizing mission would enable slave women to be trained differently and brought into a new, modern era. As McClintock states, writing of Victorian England, "The family offered an invaluable trope for figuring *historical time*. . . . Imperial intervention could thus be figured as a linear, nonrevolutionary progression that naturally contained hierarchy within unity: paternal fathers ruling benignly over immature children. The trope of the organic family became invaluable in its capacity to give state and imperial intervention the alibi of nature."[37] These women were vortexes for Victorian conceptions of race, colonialism, and the "family of man." This is one of the important reasons why fictionalized Sudanese slaves appeared so often in the writings of nationalists in Egypt throughout the late nineteenth and early twentieth centuries.

Given the layers of meaning surrounding these women, there is great irony in the fact that the six slaves left the courtroom and were placed in the Cairo Home for Freed Slaves, an institution created by the British as a sort of training and employment clearinghouse, where manumitted black women could find paying jobs, as domestics, keeping their connection to the institution of the family respectable. Once they left the auspices of this idealizing home, Fatima, Saʿīda, Ḥalīma, Marāsila, and Maryam also left the historical record and disappeared into, one hopes, better and more stable lives. But the issues they raised for Great Britain's civilizing mission in Egypt, and Egypt's civilizing mission for the Sudan, were far from over.

COLONIZED COLONIZERS

By revealing the intrinsic alterity of the "colonized colonizer" theme in important articulations of Egyptian nationalism, my study challenges many accepted tenets of the binary relationship between European empires and non-European colonies still prevalent within the fields of postcolonial, cultural, African, and Middle Eastern studies. Drawing from sources traditionally studied in the historiography of Egyptian nationalism, as well as from popular literature and African history, and using alternative methodologies of literary criticism, this book sheds new light on the unique position in which Egyptian nationalists found themselves in the late nineteenth and early twentieth centuries. And through my investigation of the cultural ramifications of the African slave trade in Egypt, my book offers a rigorous reexamination of the political significance of the slave trade and of the slaves themselves within Egyptian political culture.

In an article on black slavery in Egypt, Terence Walz discusses the puzzle presented by what he calls the "minimal impact black Africans have had on the biological make-up of Egyptians." Walz asks, "If it is true that as many as 800,000 Africans were forcibly settled in the country during the eighteenth and nineteenth centuries, why is there so little 'African' imprint on the general population?"[38] The purpose of this book is not to identify a biological imprint of black slaves in Egypt (for how could it be proven that such an imprint exists?) but instead to reveal other imprints: how deeply the relationship with the Sudan and the Sudanese affected Egyptian nationalism and cultural identity. It is my hope that this study returns Zanūba and the other five slave women to the witness stand and shows that their presence in Egypt was not so ephemeral as previously thought.

Chapter 1 offers a historical background to the relationship between Egypt and the Sudan, from the conquest launched by Muḥammad ʿAlī Pasha in 1821 to the beginning of the reign of his grandson, Khedive Ismaʿīl. It explores the motivations and nature of this conquest and the subsequent sense of the cultural and political geography of the Sudan that developed within a growing bureaucracy of native-born Egyptians, a geography that was heavily politicized by the end of Muḥammad ʿAlī's reign. By looking at the works of Muḥammad al-Tunisī, Selim Qapudan, Rifaʿah Rafiʿ al-Ṭahṭawī, and ʿAlī Mubārak, prominent men all writing at different points during Muḥammad ʿAlī's reign, this chapter examines how definitions of the relationship between Egypt and the Sudan changed as the latter became more effectively colonized. It also looks at concepts of "blackness" as described by each of these men, and how constructions of race hardened after the middle of the century, particularly in the work of Shaykh al-Ṭahṭawī. Universally considered to have sown the first seeds of an Egyptian sense of nationalism, al-Ṭahṭawī also set down on paper important tropes about the Sudan, a place he despised yet considered intrinsic to the territorial and historical integrity of Egypt. On one hand, al-Ṭahṭawī made his concept of *waṭan* (homeland) legendary with his historical perspective on Egypt's place in the Nile Valley. On the other, his disparaging remarks about the "blackness" of the Sudanese offer an important introduction to the racial constructions of the Sudanese that influenced many writers after his time.

Chapter 2 investigates the era of Khedive Ismaʿil (1863–1879), Muḥammad ʿAli's grandson and successor to a program of expansionism into East Africa and to his specific ambitions for the Sudan. It was during Ismaʿil's reign that the question of slavery became politically explosive, culminating in the antislavery convention of 1877. This chapter analyzes the writings of the early Egyptian nationalists, Yaʿqūb Ṣanūʿa and ʿAbdallah al-Nadīm, one a playwright, both journalists, who came of age under Ismaʿil. Both writers adopted colloquial Egyptian Arabic for their famous journals, in which they had much to say about the status of the Sudanese in Egypt.

Chapter 2 also explores how Egyptian nationalism was affected by the almost simultaneous uprising of the Mahdīya in the Sudan in 1881 and the military rebellion in Egypt, led by Colonel Aḥmad ʿUrābī, which occurred the same year. This context shows how triangular colonialism became in Egypt by the end of the century. Egypt was simultaneously affected by its identity as the province of an increasingly weak Ottoman Empire, its own confrontation with the British occupation of 1882, and its loss of the Sudan to the superior strategy of the charismatic Mahdī. And the challenge presented by the Mahdī raised important questions for Islamic reformers and nationalists who envisioned Egypt as a Muslim nation. Thus this chapter explores the articles of the roaming Islamic reformer Jamāl al-Dīn al-Afghānī and his Egyptian disciple, Muḥammad ʿAbduh, that discuss the problems posed by the Mahdī for Egypt, which they published in their journal *al-ʿUrwa al-Wuthqa* (the Indissoluble Bond) while in exile during the Mahdīya. I also analyze Yaʿqūb Ṣanūʿa's journal, *Abū Naẓẓara Zarqa* (The Man with the Blue Glasses), also published in exile from Paris, and how the Mahdīya affected Ṣanūʿa's presentation of Sudanese characters.

Chapter 3 explores the narrative of a prominent Egyptian soldier, Ibrāhīm Fawzī Pasha, who more than any other lived the contradictions of Egyptian nationalism and the idea of recolonizing the Sudan. No one seems to have understood the transparencies of the Egyptian flag as intimately as this famous Egyptian patriot, a fighter for ʿUrābī as well as the right-hand man to General Charles Gordon when the latter was employed by Khedive Ismaʿīl in the Sudan. He endured the Mahdī's siege of Khartoum with Gordon, only to spend the next fourteen years of his life as a prisoner of the Mahdī and the Mahdī's successor, known as the Khalifa. This chapter compares Fawzī Pasha's account of the political meaning of his life with that of the infamous Sudanese slave trader, al-Zubayr Raḥman Pasha, who was held under house arrest in Cairo for almost as long as Fawzī languished in the Sudan, and who also sought ways to publicize his unique experience with Egyptian nationalism.

Chapter 4 delves in greater detail into the ramifications of the slavery trial of 1894 and what the explosive issue of slavery meant to Egyptian society by the end of the century. It examines the ways in which two critical leaders of the nationalist movement in the early decades of the twentieth century, Mustafa Kāmil and Aḥmad Luṭfī al-Sayyid, articulated—in discussions of the important slogan of the "unity of the Nile Valley"—ideas about how the Sudanese and their land should be incorporated into Egypt. It also investigates their discussion of race and racial discrimination, showing how important to these leaders concepts of racial identity had become, and how conscious they were of the racializing language and policies of the British administration.

My final chapter looks at the era of the 1919 revolution in Egypt, when demonstrations against the British grew widespread enough to win Egyptians a nominally independent parliament. It also analyzes the thinking of Huda Shaʿrawī—the first Egyptian feminist, founder of the Egyptian Feminist Union, and a significant leader of the 1919 revolution—and how she treated the subject of the Sudan and the Sudanese, a subject she took seriously to heart. The chapter also examines how proponents of popular culture, such as the popular songwriter Sayyid Darwīsh and the vaudevillian star ʿAlī al-Kassār, used the question of the Sudan and the Sudanese to direct Egyptians of different classes to the cause of Egyptian unity against the British. Looking at Darwīsh's songs, which were intended to be sung in a variation of Sudanese Arabic dialect, and at ʿAlī al-Kassār's portrayal, in blackface, of the half-Nubian, half-Sudanese ne'er-do-well Osman ʿabd al-Baṣit, this chapter considers the ways in which caricatures of the Sudanese became central to Egyptian articulations of national identity. At the same time that these two performers were making Cairene audiences laugh, another revolution was emerging in the Sudan, led by a group known as the White Flag League, who protested the British government of the Sudan (known as the Anglo-Egyptian Condominium). This chapter explores the goals and experiences of the young ʿAlī ʿabd al-Laṭīf, a Muslim descendant of Dinka tribespeople and leader of the White Flag League, and how his political goals and eventual imprisonment affected other Sudanese leaders while conflicting with popular images of the Sudanese then current in Egypt. The chapter concludes with the ways in which Sudanese figures debated the issue of unity with Egypt under the watchful eyes of British administrators in the Sudan, and a discussion of how the dualism of the colonized colonizer was viewed by people in the Sudan, nominally colonized by both Great Britain and Egypt.

1 Journeys from the Fantastic to the Colonial

It was another country, whose excitable gestures I knew but could not connect with my mind.

DEREK WALCOTT, Omeros

Although born in a prosperous realm, we did not believe that its boundaries should limit our knowledge, and that the lore of the East should alone enlighten us.

MONTESQUIEU, Persian Letters

Medieval Arabic geographers of Africa defined the continent with a paradoxical mixture of fact, legend, and mystery. Some, like Ibn Baṭuṭa and al-Mas'ūdī, visited different parts of Africa; others, like al-Kazwinī and al-Idrisī, synthesized the information of other voyages into their geographical work. Most were indebted to the works of the Greek geographers, sometimes including Greek views of African cannibalism and savagery unquestioningly in their own accounts; others were deeply struck by the differences between African societies and their own Islamic cultures.[1] By the end of the fourteenth century, the map of Black Africa reflected a combination of mythical and empirical knowledge or, in the words of Paulo Fernando de Moraes Farias, "the interplay of the ideological and the cognitive." This kind of map illustrated certain categories by which Africans in general were known, and where cultural boundaries were drawn between more specific areas, like Egypt and neighboring African kingdoms.[2] Merchants and traders also contributed to the mapping of the frontier to Egypt's uppermost south, the vast territory known as *bilād al-sūdān*. But in the early nineteenth century, the identity of Egyptians traveling to sub-Saharan Africa began to change. Traders and merchants, who had long before charted the *darb al-arba'īn*, or Forty Days' Road, from Assiout in Egypt to Dārfūr in the Sudan, were now joined by explorers (foreign and indigenous), soldiers, and engineers who journeyed much farther south and west. As the mix of travelers changed, so too did the maps and charts of the Sudan in order to answer the need for a new kind of information.

What caused these changes? In 1820, the Egyptian ruler Muḥammad 'Alī Pasha launched a military campaign to conquer the Sudan. That push,

26

that striving for an Egyptian empire, established a new kind of mapping of the Sudan: one created by officially employed government agents, geographers, explorers, engineers, and scholars. They projected new images of the Sudan with their carefully drawn maps and their ethnographic accounts of the African people of the Nile Valley. But this mapping was more than merely technologically correct cartography. Their works also reveal the other layers of mapping that occurred as this empire literally began to take shape. Travel narratives, too, delineated Africa, and these literary mappings joined with cartography. As J. B. Harley writes, "So the surveyor, whether conscious or otherwise, replicates not just the 'environment' in some abstract sense but equally the territorial imperatives of a particular political system. Whether a map is produced under the banner of cartographic science—as most official maps have been—or whether it is an overt propaganda exercise, it cannot escape involvement in the processes by which power is deployed."[3] As these maps described the Sudan in increasingly precise detail, so too did their creators chart a more defined map of Egypt geographically, politically, and culturally. The process of conquering and studying the Sudan would create among Egyptians, by the last quarter of the century, a much stronger sense of the state and nation—of what Egypt meant. This small empire was drawn by its colonies.

In the past decade, scholars, particularly geographers, have drawn from the works of Michel Foucault and Edward Said to explore the meaning of empire and its impact on geographical knowledge in Western thought. Anna Godlewska, Felix Driver, and J. B. Harley, to name a few, have examined how mapmaking in Asia and Africa was affected by and informed by European imperial campaigns.[4] This literature is important for its exploration of geographical knowledge and the processes by which power is enforced and represented in colonial encounters; but this literature remains situated in one definition of empire—European—which limits the definition of geographical knowledge. Muḥammad ʿAlī's Egypt also experienced an exercise in imperial imagination, an exercise that proved to be highly influential on successive generations. Although ultimately Muḥammad ʿAlī's manpower and other resources proved far less effective than those of Great Britain or France, his attempts to colonize the Sudan had great impact on the future of the Nile Valley and on how Egyptians came to draw boundaries in their sense of nationhood and nationalism.

The layers of mapping and their influence become clearer when we look at the narratives of journeys into the Sudan written by four men, all born as subjects of Muḥammad ʿAlī Pasha. These men owed their social preeminence to Muḥammad ʿAlī's reforms and policies. Muḥammad al-Tunisī, who as his name suggests was of Tunisian origin, was a trader who eventually became a prominent translator of medical texts in one of the medical colleges established by the viceroy in Cairo. Selim Qapudan was a naval officer under Muḥammad ʿAlī, commissioned by the viceroy to explore the uppermost regions of the Nile Valley and bring back details about the origins of the Nile River. Shaykh Rifaʿah Rafiʿ al-Ṭahṭawī also accepted many commissions from Muḥammad ʿAlī, from his appointment as imam to the first delegation of young Egyptian students to Paris to his appointment as director of the School of Languages. He also translated foreign literature and other works into Arabic. The sojourn in the Sudan represented, in fact, the end of these great assignments; it was an exile imposed by ʿAbbas I, Muḥammad ʿAlī's successor. Al-Ṭahṭawī's influential views on the Sudan and the Sudanese reflect the changes in perception about that land that had occurred during the rule of Muḥammad ʿAlī and are, in many ways, a narration of that ruler's colonial map. The writer ʿAlī Mubārak represents an important bridge between men like al-Tunisī and al-Ṭahṭawī and the next generation of nationalists to emerge in Egypt. Born twenty years after al-Ṭahṭawī, ʿAlī Mubārak would never have become a highly educated teacher and civil engineer had it not been for the secular schools created by Muḥammad ʿAlī. In an engineering curriculum, ʿAlī Mubārak found an intellectual freedom that his training at al-Azhār University—the premier Islamic university in Cairo—had not provided him. As a member of a delegation similar to the one supervised by al-Ṭahṭawī, he traveled to Paris and returned with a zeal for reform in public works and education. Like al-Ṭahṭawī, ʿAlī Mubārak chronicled the society around him. But unlike the other travelers mentioned in this chapter, ʿAlī Mubārak never made the voyage up the Nile into the Sudan. His long narrative of travel in the Sudan is a striking and often thoughtful combination of hard geographical fact and of myths and legends against whose stubborn repetitiveness Egyptians increasingly defined their own civilization.

The first of the four voyagers, al-Tunisī, was the youngest to make the trip. He arrived in Dārfūr in 1803, two years before Muḥammad ʿAlī became the viceroy of the Ottoman province of Egypt. Selim Qapudan traveled to the Sudan in 1839, almost twenty years after Egypt first conquered the Sudan; he was the first explorer to journey so far south along the Nile by boat. The third man, al-Ṭahṭawī was older; he had been exiled to Khartoum in 1850 at the age of 49, ostensibly to establish a school of languages there similar to the one he had created in Egypt. The timing of their voyages contributes to the importance of their narratives, for both Selim Qapudan and al-Ṭahṭawī were in the Sudan at a time of profound change in Egypt's political and cultural geography. The neighboring territories known as *bilād al-sūdān* also played a vital role in the definition of this new map. However, the fourth man, ʿAlī Mubārak, the one chronicler with no African experience, most influenced that map. Thus, his book *ʿAlam al-Dīn,* about a mythical encounter—written in 1857 but published in 1882, just before Egypt's first nationalist rebellion—is not only one of a series of books "dealing with the theme of 'Arab re-discovery of Europe,' " as has been claimed, but also is part of a much different tradition of representing Africa.[5]

The narratives of these four men, when viewed together, reveal the interplay between personal experience and memory, popular myths, and the changing constructions of racial identity that occurred in Egyptian society after the official conquest of the Sudan. They demonstrate how this society came to privilege certain kinds of information over other traditions of knowledge transmission. This privileging occurred on many levels as Muḥammad ʿAlī tried to reform the military system of the country, which led to increasing state involvement in the development of education. Many areas of public life were affected: schools, hospitals, factories, and ministries of public works were created within the largest Egyptian cities, and new canals and agricultural methods were developed in the countryside.[6] Similar changes took place in the Sudan, after Muḥammad ʿAlī's armies conquered it in 1820. As Terence Walz has shown, prior to the viceroy's conquest there had existed a long tradition of trade between Egyptians and Sudanese of different kingdoms and sultanates.[7] When Muḥammad al-Tunisī traveled to the sultanate of Dārfūr, for example, the most concrete knowledge of the Sudan was owned by merchants, most notably the slave traders who regularly traveled the famous *darb al-arbaʿīn* trail. These traders communicated recent events that had occurred throughout the vast regions of the Sudan once they arrived at the *wikalat al-jāllaba* (slave market) in Cairo, which is how Muḥammad al-Tunisī was able to discover important facts about his own father in Darfur. But with the official Egyptian expansionist campaigns into the Sudan in 1820, Muḥammad ʿAlī institutionalized the relationship between Egypt and the Sudan. Selim Qapudan's fact-finding mission was completely different from Muḥammad al-Tunisī's. It was the means by which Muḥammad ʿAlī hoped to discover the origins of the Nile, whether Sudanese gold existed, and whether the inhabitants of the uppermost regions of the Nile would be suitable as slaves for his increasingly modernized military. Selim Qapudan's voyage Jowas an important and officially sanctioned postscript to the conquest of the Sudan, and a preamble to a new way of knowing about the Sudan and the Sudanese. Compared to al-Tunisī's account, where some of the Sudanese were family, even if they were not familiar, Selim Qapudan's account narrated an experience with colonized subjects, or those whom Egypt expected to colonize.

Shaykh al-Ṭahṭawī inherited his view of the Sudan and its people, who not only were burdened with the ages-old stereotype of them as wild and savage but also were the subjects of many explorations and studies and were conceptualized as a subject people. He was the most politicized of the four voyagers of this study, because of his particularly energetic participation in Muḥammad ʿAlī's program of social reform for Egypt, and because of the perspectives about national community and identity that he gained from his experiences in France, which he promoted eloquently and forcefully in Egypt. From Paris, al-Ṭahṭawī brought home a new lexicon to describe his own country, the most powerful being *al-waṭan*, his complicated word for the nation and its community and the bond that had to be forged between the two. His deep and abiding love for Egypt was rivaled only by his profound disgust with the Sudan and the Sudanese. His long poem about the Sudan imparts a kind of knowledge different from that shared by the other three voyagers. His master work, *Manāhij al-albāb al-miṣriya fī mabāhij al-ʿadāb al-ʿasriya*, offers a more politicized sense of Egypt's cultural geography. His particular poem about the Sudan and its people also demonstrates how the process of colonialism and nationalism came to be racialized, and how an increasing sense of racial difference could be incorporated into a sense of political and cultural boundaries.

An incident that confronted ʿAlī Mubārak's consciousness of racial differentiation also prodded him to reevaluate his personal ambitions and may have informed how he later identified certain Sudanese attributes with those of pre-Islamic Arabs. The experience of meeting a dark-skinned yet high-ranking functionary shocked the young ʿAlī Mubārak, upsetting his conceptions about the hierarchy of culture and order in Egypt and inspiring his deep wish to profit from the same new educational and bureaucratic order in Egypt, created originally by Muḥammad ʿAlī.

In fact, race is an important marker of difference for all four writers, who painstakingly noted racial differences in skin color, sexual behavior, and religious attitudes among the Sudanese. Sometimes the writers seem to have plucked these concepts from medieval literature about blacks and Sudanese, but more often they mixed stereotypes about blacks with new terminology about power and concepts of civilization translated from European texts. As this chapter shows, however, al-Ṭahṭawī's perceptions were different from those of the other three writers, reflecting, I think, a hardening perspective of Egyptian intellectuals about the nature of Egyptian identity and its measure against African societies. Racial differentiation sharply defined the contrast between Egypt and others. Egyptian society was bound to the South both by memories of conquest and by increasing sensitivity to its own vulnerability to western Europe.

MUḤAMMAD AL-TUNISĪ IN DĀRFŪR: FOLLOWING IN FATHER'S FOOTSTEPS

> I am but too certain that my father is no more; but I will go
> down to the infernal regions in quest of him.
>
> TOBIAS SMOLLETT, *The Adventures of Telemachus*

Bilād al-sūdān, where al-Tunisī first traveled at the age of fourteen, has had a long history in the geographic imaginations of Arabs from further north, although its exact place on maps seems to have shifted over the centuries.[8] P. M. Holt and M. W. Daly write that, when medieval Muslim geographers referred to *bilād al-sūdān,* they meant all African territory south of the Sahara. Many of their maps and literary mappings of Africa were taken at face value for centuries; al-Idrisī and al-ʿUmari depicted the Nile River as having continental length and expanse, a mythological span that added to its great mystery. De Moraes Farias has suggested that these medieval "mistakes" of geographical knowledge are "much more complicated than the word 'mistake' implies," that in them can be found ideologies of classification that led to further mythification of Africans' identities:

> On the one hand, they were caused by insufficiency of empirical knowl-
> edge about the real world; on the other hand, they were caused by a
> fixed scheme of categories, according to which the world was divided
> into "temperate" and "extreme" climates; one of the "extreme" climates
> was the torrid zone, in which life was only possible along the banks
> of great rivers; it follows, logically, that (a) if there was agriculture and
> urban life in Kanem, and (b) if Kanem indeed was situated in the torrid
> climate, then it was to be expected that there was a "Nile" flowing
> across Kanem.[9]

This process of fitting the Sudan into paradoxical categories of fact and fiction also occurred in Egypt, but by the early nineteenth century a new kind of map, informed by different investigations, was needed to reinforce trade and changing political circumstances. After 1820, Egyptians concentrated more on the Sudan, the region south of Egypt from the Red Sea coast up to the western provinces of Dārfūr, including Nubia.[10] Dārfūr itself was also known to medieval Arabs, and it is clear that, by the early sixteenth century, Egyptian merchants were traveling back and forth between Cairo and

Dārfūr as a sultanate formed in this region of the western Sudan under the aegis of Sultan Suleiman.[11] As R. S. O'Fahey describes it, by the end of the seventeenth century the caravan route of *darb al-arbaʿīn* between Dārfūr and Assiout in Upper Egypt was well-established.

The merchants regularly went back and forth across great distances of desert, and learned to find or create homes at either end of their journeys. In a way, this was true of the ʿulamāʾ too. These were learned men who crossed the Islamic world in wide swathes from Mecca to West Africa, and who traveled to Dārfūr to work as judges or in other capacities for the sultan. Many of them came from North Africa, Arabia, or Egypt. They had credentials from al-Azhār University and spoke an impressive classical Arabic that raised their importance in the eyes of the Fur sultans, who were themselves looking to Islamize both court and country.[12] The ʿulamāʾ brought with them to Dārfūr a wider sense of the world. As Mary Helms writes, "It was this wider experience, conjoined with their mystical divinatory talents and literate-magical abilities, that made them valued associates, particularly of ruling elites."[13] This was the case for Muḥammad al-Tunisī's grandfather Suleiman, who left Tunis for the hajj in the late eighteenth century, never to return. In Mecca, Suleiman met other traders from Sennār who invited him to join them when they returned home, an offer he accepted. There, the Sennāri *mek*, or king, honored him for his learning with a fine home and a beautiful Ethiopian slave, with whom Suleiman fell in love and began another family. As his grandson remembered it many years later, "He forgot his family in Tunis and all of his young children."[14]

Impoverished by this abandonment, Suleiman's son ʿUmar al-Tunisī traveled to Sennār with his uncle to bring his father back to Tunis. Suleiman had become a prominent slave trader. When found, he told his son he would return but that first he had to sell his slaves in Cairo. His plan was to sell them off, return to Sennār for his family, and meet his son and brother in Cairo. In agreement with this plan, ʿUmar and his uncle themselves went on the hajj. His uncle Muḥammad, however, died in Mecca, and ʿUmar traveled on to Cairo alone. While waiting for his father to keep his promise, he enrolled in al-Azhār University. Time dragged on, and, losing patience, ʿUmar returned to Sennār to see what had become of Suleiman. He found him back with his Sennāri family, apparently having forgotten his promise to return to his other children. Suleiman also claimed that debts in Sennār kept him from leaving, and he invited his son to stay. ʿUmar did so for six months, then left by caravan, angry with his father for wasting his time and keeping him from his studies. Three days after his departure, Suleiman caught up with him and offered him slaves and camels in addition to supplies of water and food. Like the promises of his father, the slaves and camels died along the way, and ʿUmar al-Tunisī returned to Cairo as poor as he had left it.[15]

In Cairo, he reentered al-Azhār and married. After two years he returned to Tunis, bringing his pregnant wife and his mother-in-law with him, and there his son Muḥammad was born, in 1789. Three years later, ʿUmar fell out with his brothers and made another angry departure, again to Cairo and to al-Azhār. In 1796, ʿUmar received a letter from his half brothers in Sennār informing him of Suleiman's death. Leaving enough money with his family to last six months, ʿUmar rushed to Sennār to deal with his father's affairs. But he stayed a long time, and Muḥammad's mother was forced to sell all her jewelry.[16]

In his book, Muḥammad ibn ʿUmar al-Tunisī included many other personal details about the difficulties of fatherless life in Cairo (all of which occurred during the French invasion of the country) that led to his becoming the head of the family at age fourteen. He too studied at al-Azhār, but the family was so impoverished that he abandoned his studies to learn a trade. At this disillusioning juncture, he heard that a caravan from Dārfūr was coming to Cairo, and he went to the slave market to inquire about opportunities and about his father, whom he had learned was in Dārfūr. He met the caravan and found an acquaintance of ʿUmar, who informed him that his father had become a very important advisor to Muḥammad al-Faḍl, the sultan of Dārfūr. This acquaintance persuaded Muḥammad to return with the caravan to Dārfūr, and so, following in the footsteps of his father and grandfather, he left for the Sudan shortly thereafter.

In Muḥammad al-Tunisī's memoirs of his earlier life, it is clear how complicated a site the Sudan was for him and how personal was his sense of its geography. The Sudan was a treasure chest for learned young Arabs like his grandfather, his father, and eventually himself. It offered a last resort when all other financial possibilities had been exhausted, again as made clear by the examples of his father and his grandfather. It extended to them privileged social standing and luxuries they could not easily have afforded in either Tunis or Cairo. But there was a harsher side to the Sudan as well. Dārfūr was not a center of learning; it could not itself offer a marketable education, and the circumstances that brought enterprising young scholars there removed them from opportunities like completing their studies at al-Azhār. The Sudan may have presented great opportunity, but it also stole fathers. It was a distant place from which forgetful parents had to be dragged, or where it would be discovered they had died. Finally, the Sudan was a place where half siblings lived, where there was family, which further complicated its geography for al-Tunisī. It was part of the wide-ranging expanse where his family resided: Tunis, Cairo, Mecca, Sennār, Dārfūr. It was thus foreign and intimately familiar to al-Tunisī.

CHARTING HIS OWN MAP: MUḤAMMAD AL-TUNISĪ AND THE EXPERIENCE OF TRAVEL

> No man can enter this island without being punished for his rashness; and even the circumstance of your shipwreck should not screen you from my resentment, if I did not love you.
>
> TOBIAS SMOLLETT, *The Adventures of Telemachus*

Dārfūr was in a strange and complicated way a homeland for Muḥammad ibn ʿUmar al-Tunisī, but the physical act of voyaging there across the frightening expanse of *darb al-arbaʿīn* caused Muḥammad to experience himself as a foreigner for the first time. He became very sick along the way, finding "myself among those not of my tribe *[maʿa ghayrī abnā jinsī]*, but instead between tribesmen whose language I could understand only a little; I did not see among them one face that was pleasing to me." This feeling of alienation was powerful enough to bring tears to his eyes, and all he saw reinforced his terror: the faces surrounding him were "blackness in blackness in blackness *[sawādan fī sawādin fī sawādin]*." He regretted having exposed himself to the danger presented by these "sons of Ham" *(abna Ham)*. He remembered what he had heard of their hostility to the "sons of Shem," and "a feeling of dread possessed me that I cannot describe, to the point where I almost demanded that we return." At this moment of abandoning himself to his fears, Muḥammad al-Tunisī took refuge in the texts of his studies at al-Azhār and noted how they praised the benefits of travel, saying that travel could provide one with new kinds of sustenance, and that "as the learned men said, 'The voyage uncovers the morals of men.' "[17]

As told in *Tashḥīdh al-adhhān bi-sirat bilād al-ʿarab wal-sūdān* (Sharpening the Intellect with Travel in the Country of the Arabs and the Blacks), the book he would later write about his voyage, Muḥammad al-Tunisī first made himself a foreigner, or confirmed his foreignness, by dividing the new world he was entering into that of the wild "Other," the sons of Ham, and his own community, the sons of Shem. But when this became too overwhelming, too frightening, he situated himself in another collective, one of scholars, and, using the perspective of these teachers, envisioned himself as part of a greater community of voyagers. The terror of finding himself suddenly thrust into an entirely unfamiliar adventure with people who looked unlike him and spoke so differently was ameliorated by his reliance

on textual knowledge, on traditions of scholarship that validated his otherwise alienated position. It is interesting also that al-Tunisī relied on texts to
identify those around him as sons of Ham, giving them a universalist, timeless (and timelessly accursed) identity that resituated them in their legendary, scriptural origins.

But Muḥammad al-Tunisī could not sustain such metaphysical distance
through the entire narrative. Nor could he always be identified as a total
stranger—as the caravan advanced on Dārfūr, a man approached him with
gifts of pearls and gold as a token of his esteem and gratitude, a response to
kind acts bestowed on him by 'Umar, Muḥammad's now powerful father in
Dārfūr. Even at first footfall, the Sudan was a complicated network of connections and family. Then he found his father, who immediately brought
him to the sultan. And there, 'Umar asked the sultan for permission to
return to his family, offering to leave Muḥammad in Dārfūr to oversee his
affairs. The formerly frightened young son of Shem became his father's
representative, a man with connections and valuable roots in the area.

This position gave Muḥammad al-Tunisī a perspective as an eyewitness
and shaped the rest of his long narrative about his years in Dārfūr. For
example, he was present during a dramatic struggle for power between the
sultan Muḥammad al-Faḍl and his successor, 'abd al-Raḥman al-Yatīm, and
for the fall from grace of the great eunuch general Muḥammad Karra. Such
accounts make al-Tunisī's book essential reading for students of Sudanese
history; the events he recounts reveal a complicated history among the
tribes of Dārfūr. He presents vibrant Dārfūri cultures and people, with
heroes and passions and tragedies of their own—accounts that alternate
with much more objectifying presentations of Dārfūris as primitives. With
these descriptions comes a sense of the geography of Dārfūr, but not only
the one delineated by maps. This is a moral geography, with a topography
defined by skin color, sexual behavior, and religious practices. For instance,
Muḥammad al-Tunisī includes a map in *Tashḥīdh al-adhhān* to help his
readers see where the different tribes of Dārfūr were located, along with a
code for interpreting that map:

> I know that the more cultivated, populated part of the northern country
> is the region of the Bartī and the Zaghawa, due to their sheer numbers.
> And notice the wisdom of God: the two tribes live on one land, but the
> Bartī are purer of heart and prettier of face, with more beautiful women:
> the Zaghawa are the opposite.
>
> Just as the Dago and the Baqū share the same area, and the Baqū
> girls are more beautiful than the Dago girls. You find among the Birqid
> and the Tunjur the beautiful and the ugly. But the Birqid are treacher-
> ous and, stealing night and day, unafraid of God and his prophet, while

the Tunjur have some religion and some restraint. As for the people of
the mountain, they are all equal in wickedness and savagery. But if you
went to Dar Abadima [nearby], you would find men and women of
beauty, praise be upon the Creator.[18]

What authority gave Muḥammad al-Tunisī the ability to travel around
the vast regions of Dārfūr and document the behavior of its inhabitants?
Unlike Selim Qapudan and al-Ṭahṭawī, Muḥammad al-Tunisī did not travel
to the Sudan under the orders of the Egyptian ruler. Once situated there,
however, he did gain the permission of the sultan of Dārfūr, to travel around
the region of Jebel Marra, permission that he carried with him, signed and
sealed, throughout his journeys. This authority, and the guards that came
with it, shielded him from violence and gave him a layer of protection when
he encountered hostile tribes in the market town of Numliyya. Visiting the
market with his servants and guards, he had his first encounter with "people of deep blackness, red of eye and teeth."

> When they saw me they gathered around me, much struck by the red-
> ness of my color. They came upon me in droves, because they had never
> before seen an Arab. They wanted to kill me out of mischief—and at
> that time I did not know one word of the Furi language. They frightened
> me except for when I saw my companions unsheath their weapons and
> thrust them in the faces of the crowd. They put themselves between me
> and the crowd. I asked them why this was happening and they replied,
> They wish to murder you. Then I asked why? And the guards replied,
> Their minds are so small that they are saying that someone like you
> could not be born from the womb of his mother. Others are saying, If
> I brought down the tip of my spear [or sword, *dhubāba*] on him, blood
> would come out. Another said, Be patient, and I'll stab him with my
> spear and we'll see what, if any, blood comes out of him. When we heard
> that we were afraid for you and surrounded you.[19]

This passage reveals many layers of translation and identity. Al-Tunisī could
not know what the crowd was saying about his color without the mediating
translation of his guards, who could not have revealed that information to
him until the hostile encounter had resolved itself. Writing some forty years
after his original voyage, al-Tunisī thus brings into sharp relief the immediate color consciousness that both he and these Furis instigated in each
other. The authority of the sultan, however, shielded him, in the form of the
guards and servants he sent along. By his very person and presence, al-
Tunisī defined the boundaries between the land of the Arabs, *bilād al-'arab*,
and the land of the blacks, *bilād al-sūdān*.

That is how the rest of his narrative mapped the landscape around him as he moved farther east and south: his personal sense of honor and identity defined which area was civilized and which area was not. After the dramatic encounter in the market of Numliyya, he charted, with the yardsticks of customs, skin color, and sexual mores, which tribes he encountered belonged to the more civilized Dārfūr (those acknowledging Sultan Muḥammad al-Faḍl as ruler) and which were beyond the pale of civilization. Civilization existed where the honor code was similar to al-Tunisī's, where he felt less like a foreigner. If race is one marker of cultural difference and boundaries, then women are the signposts of civilization in al-Tunisī's account. Their beauty, their chastity, their dress all serve as codes for who is wild and who is not. After a long discussion of the harem of Sultan Muḥammad al-Faḍl and how royal women evaded the eunuch guardians, al-Tunisī listed reasons for the perversions of the women of the region:

> Know that the women of the Sudan are much more lustful and wanton than other women for the following reasons:
>
> 1. the excessive heat of the region;
> 2. their frequent mingling with men;
> 3. The lack of chastity and not settling in the house; for you see women among them who are not married and who have more than one lover.

He then adds to this list two more reasons for these pathologies among not just Dārfūri women but all women of the Sudan. First was the lack of restrictions on the number of times they could marry and, when married, the fact that they could mingle with unrelated men. According to al-Tunisī, men also behaved with a similar lack of restraint, conducting relations with numerous women and thus offering no example on which women could model themselves. Second was that Sudanese women customarily had socialized with men since their childhood, "and if custom is reinforced [istiḥkamat] it becomes nature."[20] The geographical spread of this behavior not only loses all specific reference to area, becoming the entire Sudan, it also explains the "nature" of the Sudan's people. Chastity directly figures into his sense of beauty, and so al-Tunisī's map is marked by the changing nature of beauty along the Nile Valley, with particular tribes and the faces of their women becoming landmarks in the geography of Dārfūr in particular and the Sudan in general.

In a place where the boundaries are unclear, where the kingdom or state exists simultaneously with large tribes of varying loyalties, where tribes share the same stretch of land, where communications are oral and languages abound, Muḥammad al-Tunisī created boundaries out of the physical features of people, sexual practices, and the public behavior of women. Each of these helped him to distinguish one tribe from another, as noted earlier in his comparison of the women of the Dago and the Baqū, for example. Other behaviors or customs enabled al-Tunisī to distinguish the land of the blacks *(bilād al-sūdān)* from the land of the Arabs *(bilād al-'arab)*. It is important to remember, however, that although al-Tunisī reviled the "uncivilized" behavior of women, usually black women, in his account, these racial distinctions are not based on a hatred of blacks. Perhaps remembering the Sudanese families of his father and grandfather, Muḥammad al-Tunisī includes a number of interesting excerpts from different poems in his narrative, in which he explains the beauties of blackness and how one could love a brown- or black-skinned woman.[21]

Al-Tunisī's perspective on the Sudan was written through the filter of hindsight. The text of *Tashhīdh al-adhhān* was not published in Arabic until 1845, several years before the death of Muḥammad 'Alī and forty years after al-Tunisī had completed his travels to Dārfūr. He dedicated the work to the viceroy, who is also mentioned in appendices attached by al-Tunisī's French colleague and translator, M. Perron. But even though the narrative was written during Muḥammad 'Alī's reign, well after the pasha had launched his campaign of expansionism into the Sudan, and even though he was encouraged to set it on paper by a French doctor and scholar who had also journeyed often to the Sudan, al-Tunisī never himself experienced the political changes that the conquest stirred in the Sudan.[22] He never saw the Dārfūris and the Sudanese in general as people subject to Egypt, even though he considered them to be drowning in a sea of wildness and barbarian behavior. He was too personally implicated, and sometimes too personally involved. The voyage charted his reactions to the people and their strong reactions to him, and with those reactions he gauged where he and they were culturally. The map he wrote down offers a geography of the self, not of the state.

MUḤAMMAD 'ALĪ AND THE QUESTION OF THE EGYPTIAN EMPIRE

When Muḥammad 'Alī assumed control of Egypt as *walī*, or viceroy, for the Ottoman Empire in 1805, the conditions that had enabled a merchant-voyager like Muḥammad al-Tunisī to explore a more personal geography in the Sudan changed drastically. Muḥammad 'Alī's ambition to expand the boundaries of the Ottoman province of Egypt fit a pattern of expansionism established by previous Ottoman governors, such as ʿAlī Bey al-Kabīr in the eighteenth century. Unlike his predecessors, however, Muḥammad ʿAlī sought more than the quasi autonomy that came from occupying neighboring countries and controlling their trade routes through Egypt.[23] As Afaf Lutfi al-Sayyid Marsot describes it, Muḥammad ʿAlī took Egypt steps toward seceding from the Ottoman Empire and becoming an independent empire on its own.

But Egypt's long-held and tenuous position as a province of the Ottoman Empire makes it difficult to define Egyptian expansionism under Muḥammad ʿAlī. While it is easy to identify and date all of Muḥammad ʿAlī's expansionist expeditions (to the Hijaz, 1811–1818; the Sudan, 1820–1822; the Morea, 1824–1827; and Syria, 1831–1840), many scholars of Egyptian history are much more ambivalent about the nature of these conquests, especially with regard to the Sudan. Part of the ambiguity stems from what many scholars consider the changing nature of Egypt's own national identity that, in turn, altered the shape of its expansionism. Egypt conquered the Sudan, for example, long before achieving independence from the Ottoman Empire. Because of this relationship with Istanbul and the fact that the language spoken by Egypt's administrators and generals was Turkish, the administration of the "Egyptian Sudan" region was known for generations in the Sudan as the Turkīya.[24] So, although the Sudan was conquered by the ruler of Egypt, the "Arabic-speaking Egyptian nation-state with its national army did not then exist." The contradictions between this political truth and the goals Muḥammad ʿAlī entertained for Egypt and the Sudan make it difficult to situate the source of authority for Egypt's conquest of the Sudan or to find "a convenient designation for the conquest."[25]

Muḥammad Sabry, writing in 1930, resolved this ambiguity by effacing the "Turkish" nature of Muḥammad ʿAlī's armies in the Sudan and identifying them as completely Egyptian. Sabry considers the invasion to have been an essential part of the *walī's* imperialistic ambitions; once the invasion was completed, he writes, "l'empire égyptien est, d'orès et déjà, constitué."[26] But even with this unambiguous statement, Sabry's narrative reveals his doubts, when he writes of Muḥammad ʿAlī that "il était entrainé comme par un idéal, bien que le but immediat de son expedition soudanaise fut de ramener de l'or et des ésclaves."[27] These fruits of invasion seem not to have dignified it, even for Sabry.

Other historians incorporate a different kind of equivocation in their studies of Muḥammad ʿAlī. For instance, in his exploration of the relationship between domestic political conflict in early-nineteenth-century

Egyptian society and Egyptian military expansionism, Fred Lawson argues that the struggle between Egypt's dominant social forces left the ruling members no choice but to adopt military expansionism as a means of preserving their control of domestic society.[28] Because they controlled the local armed forces and had "concentrated capital," "Egypt's dominant coalition of state administrators, rich import-export merchants and—later on—large-scale commercial estate-holders succeeded in carrying out a program of imperialist expansion during the first third of the nineteenth century."[29] But Lawson's descriptions of these campaigns inexplicably exclude the Sudan. What follows his interesting analysis of the first Egyptian campaign into the Hijaz is an exploration of the expeditions into the Aegean, with hardly any mention of the invasion of the Sudan that occurred between the two. Lawson offers no reasons for the exclusion and so excludes the African campaign from the rubric "imperialist expansion." Is such an omission historically defensible? How can one then characterize this conquest (which lasted much longer than any of Muḥammad ʿAlī's other campaigns)?

Like Lawson, Afaf Lutfi al-Sayyid Marsot concludes that, under Muḥammad ʿAlī, the Egyptian campaigns were imperial enterprises that do not fit the model of the Ottoman Empire. Marsot believes Egypt needed to expand because of the paucity of markets within its own borders. Had there been a more equitable distribution of wealth, Egyptians could have created markets for their own products. The struggle for economic and political control that Lawson describes as having occurred among the dominant elites of Egyptian society prevented this from occurring, thus leaving Muḥammad ʿAlī with only one option, according to Marsot: "an imperialist one that fitted in with mercantile thought with its imperialist flavour."[30] And so the viceroy "followed the practice of earlier European mercantile countries like England and France who had sought to build colonies in the New World, and for the same reasons. That is why he regarded military expansion and imperialist designs as essential to his economic development, and his economic development as essential for independence." Marsot includes the Sudan invasion as part of this process; although not a complete success, it left the *walī* "with an empire that was half the size of Europe."[31]

Holt and Daly, looking specifically at the impact of Egypt's conquest on the Sudan, also cite the influence of European ideas of conquest on Muhammad ʿAlī and his intentions for the Sudan, which they see as a political instrument for strengthening his power and gaining economic control of important trade routes. But with much more emphasis than the other historians mentioned above, Holt and Daly point out the attraction that the Sudan's slave trade held for Muḥammad ʿAlī, and the potential for creating a docile and loyal slave army trained by Europeans.[32] Robert Collins goes even further in his discussion of the significance of slavery in the Sudan campaign, saying that, although many men had been enlisted in Egyptian armies since the time of the Pharaohs, it was not until the conquest of the Sudan that "the slave trade became an organized function of an Oriental colonial government."[33]

Not all historians see Egypt's invasion of the Sudan as imperialism. In a collection of articles he edited that debate the very use of the term *imperialism* in the context of the Nile Valley, 'Abd al-'Azim Ramadan writes that this conquest was not an example of one foreign country's raiding of another, like "England's invasion of Egypt, or France's invasion of Algeria or Tunisia or Morocco, or Italy's invasion of Libya." The conditions that characterized European imperialism were not present in the historical relations between Egypt and the Sudan, or in the political culture of Egypt at this time. There was no sense of Egyptian identity—thus precluding the creation of the colonized Other in Egyptian society—nor was the Sudan a unified country (Dārfūr was not annexed until 1874). And perhaps in response to Holt and Daly, Ramadan also discounts the idea that slavery attracted Muḥammad 'Alī to the Sudan and that the invasion amplified the trade. Rather, the trade in slaves existed long before the Egyptians conquered the Sudan, and that trade was only one of the resources Muḥammad 'Alī hoped to exploit. Finally, Ramadan negates the possibility of imperialism because, unlike in Europe, there was no bourgeoisie in Egypt, no class of capitalists who could really generate markets for Sudanese goods at the time of the invasion.[34] Like Lawson omitting mention of the Sudan from his model, Ramadan thus excludes Egypt from the definition of imperialism.

When discussing the political jargon of Egyptian nationalists debating the identity of the Sudan three generations after its conquest, Ramadan contextualizes terms like *imperialism* and *colonialism* carefully and observes that this terminology was fashionable in both Egypt and Europe at the end of the nineteenth century.[35] His methodology is helpful to this study as well, if we draw from his exploration of the historical context of certain terms and examine the words used in the middle of the nineteenth century to describe Selim Qapudan's voyages up the Nile into the Sudan. These voyages were commissioned at an important juncture, when the conquest of the Sudan was almost twenty years old and Muḥammad 'Alī was trying to sort out what these vast territories should mean to Egypt. What, then, was the context of meaning for such voyages? In whose hands lay the authority to draw the map of Egypt and the Sudan?

SELIM QAPUDAN AND THE SHIPS OF STATE

> "Let us see," said Mentor, "what number your people may
> amount to, both in the town and country; let us take an exact
> account of them. Let us enquire too what number of peasants
> and husbandmen there may be among them, and how much
> wine, oil, and other fruits your lands produce, one year with
> another."
>
> TOBIAS SMOLLETT, *The Adventures of Telemachus*

It is important to remember that Muḥammad ʿAlī employed Europeans to help him chart out the recently conquered Sudan immediately after its conquest, a point that Dr. Frederic Bonola Bey, secretary general of the Khedivial Geographic Society, stressed in 1889 when discussing what he considered to be the half-backward, half-modernized liminality of Muḥammad ʿAlī's empire. This may seem strange, Bonola Bey conceded, yet he considered the situation understandable, given the political circumstances of Egypt upon Muḥammad ʿAlī's ascension to power. As a result of the internecine wars that had ravaged Egypt in the aftermath of the French invasion (1798–1801), the new dynasty found that Egypt "had fallen into a state close to barbarity. The Egyptians, absorbed in the struggle of progressive transformation that was being accomplished under the power of their sovereigns, found themselves insufficiently prepared to undertake scientific explorations."[36] Because of this, Muḥammad ʿAlī sought recourse in the geographic experience of Europeans very early, one result of which was the first official map of Kordofan, in the western part of the Sudan, drawn by M. Ruppel in 1829.[37] Muḥammad ʿAlī also allowed Europeans to journey up the Nile into the Sudan to gather zoological and geographical information for their own countries fairly early in the history of the Egyptian administration of the Sudan, as shown by the trips taken by M. Georges Thibaut into Dongola and Sennār to buy giraffes for the Zoological Society of London in 1834.[38] And, acting on accounts of the gold to be found in the Blue Nile region of the Sudan, near Ethiopia, Muḥammad ʿAlī sent a Franco-Italian team of engineers and geologists to the area to begin what was hoped would be large-scale extractions of gold.[39]

Clearly, then, the viceroy himself relied deeply on Europeans to help him define the geography of the Sudan and, consequently, what should and could be done with the region and its diverse peoples. But his employing a dependable Turkish-speaking naval officer known as Selim Qapudan to journey up the Nile to find its source also suggests that Muḥammad ʿAlī hoped to diversify the group of people who were to categorize and classify the Sudan in his name. Was this then a means of personalizing Egypt's control of the resources of the Sudan? Prior to Selim Qapudan's trip, Muḥammad ʿAlī had tried to enlist his commander, or *ḥikimdar*, of the Sudan, Khurshid Pasha, to lead another expedition up the Nile. In a letter to Khurshid Pasha, Muḥammad ʿAlī wrote that "each of the greatest of men who have come to this world and then left it, left a trace on which their name lies, or their highest hopes, or their fame." To that lofty end, he instructed Khurshid Pasha to prepare for the exploration of the Nile's origins, not only for the promise of promotion and personal fame this would guarantee Khurshid Pasha but also for Egypt, in its new state of "fluorescence": "It is incumbent upon you to extend the greatest of your efforts to heighten and augment her situation."[40]

Even with these grandiloquent encouragements, Khurshid Pasha was unable to muster the forces to achieve these goals, and so Muḥammad ʿAlī commissioned Selim Qapudan some years later to launch an expedition, in the course of which the source of the White Nile was discovered. The viceroy provided the officer with three large boats *(dhahabīyāt)*, soldiers, and the following orders:

> What is incumbent upon you, Captain Selim, is to request whatever you need and all will be delivered to you. We are not going to these territories as raiders or conquerors. Be judicious and offer gifts that would be worthy of me. Work hard to conciliate these uncivilized peoples *[tilk al-shuʿūb al-mutarbira]* that you encounter. Attain their confidence and their affection with gifts that you present to their leaders. The soldiers will accompany you not to attack or to raid but to protect your welfare.[41]

The historian Nissim Maqqar concludes that documents like the above affirm the scientific goals of the expedition: to bring home geographic knowledge of the White Nile and to civilize *(tamdīn)* the tribes and uncivilized groups living along the river. In many instances, Maqqar takes Muḥammad ʿAlī at his word, but it may be helpful to problematize the word *tamdīn*, loaded with meanings that changed with every decade of the viceroy's reign.

Selim Qapudan led three expeditions up the Nile during the years 1839–1842, accompanied by four hundred soldiers. The captain painstakingly noted many of the details of the third and most successful voyage. When parts of this journal were published in French in 1842, the expedition was heralded by M. Jomard, the head of the French Geographic Society, as one of the greatest moments in Egyptian history.[42] Selim Qapudan's journal was widely celebrated in France, where it was quickly translated from the original Turkish (it was not translated into Arabic until 1922). The journal is very different from the memoirs of Muḥammad al-Tunisī; as an official document that would have been sent immediately to the viceroy, it excludes personal experience and narrations of cultural alienation. Instead, Selim Qapudan diligently describes his daily efforts to enforce the journey's mission, efforts that were sometimes quite difficult to achieve in the expedition's encounters with tribes along the banks of the White Nile. This was new territory for the expedition, deep into the south where tribes were infamous for their lack of monotheistic religion. Selim Qapudan and his men were also new to the people they encountered. They came face to face with tribes who had never seen men in uniform, or Europeans, and who constructed very different meanings for the expeditions when they saw the huge ships and the armed soldiers camping on their shores. Each encounter, as narrated by Selim Qapudan, required an explanation that would make sense to the leaders of the tribe. With armed soldiers surrounding and protecting the mission, the message of scientific inquiry was not always clearly conveyed.

The expedition left Khartoum on 16 November 1839 (9 Ramadan A.H. 1255) and began the journey up the Nile following earlier charts of the river (charts that Selim Qapudan did not identify). Five days after their departure, the expedition encountered a man from the Shilluk tribe. Ten members of the crew surrounded him, and, presumably with the help of a translator, Selim Qapudan asked him where they could find his chief. After learning the chief's whereabouts, the captain informed him of why the expedition had come: "We did not come here to harm anyone but instead in hopes of finding the source of the White Nile. There is no need to fear us, as we will just continue on our path in hopes of fulfilling our goals. Our leader, the viceroy, has ordered us to gather only what we require, like wood, and we will present to all the tribes who agree to meet us gifts and curiosities." Selim Qapudan continues, "Then I sent to the shaykh of the Shilluk two of my men, accompanied by two Shilluk, to arrange an appointment for the next day at eight o'clock."[43] But the Shilluk did not respond as Selim Qapudan had hoped, and the people ran from the sight of Selim Qapudan and his men. Such fear was in fact mutual, as Selim Qapudan recounts shortly after that the Shilluk were themselves renowned for their inclination to slaughter their enemies, an idea made more concrete by their destruction of some of the expedition's small boats. But these fearful meetings continued, giving Selim Qapudan several more chances to use gifts to persuade the Shilluk of his peaceful intentions.

The gifts he offered were important currency, because the expedition depended on the tribes for provisions—for the gifts of meat and other foods the tribes offered in exchange for his presents of trinkets and glass. But such exchanges were themselves fraught with many levels of meaning and interpretation, as the expedition learned when they approached the territory of the White Nile where the Kik tribe lived. The people of the Kik began to worship them, heralding them as messengers sent by the gods. Selim Qapudan sent his translator, a converted Dinka soldier named Muḥammad, to explain to them that the expedition came by order of Allah to punish rebellious tribes and protect obedient ones. In response to Muḥammad's message, the Kik left a number of cows; the expedition gave glass trinkets to a delegation of Kik elders.[44]

But the exchange deteriorated when the tribe shortly thereafter mobilized to fight the soldiers, who quickly killed a number of them:

> We saw their leaders signal for them to escape from us, and we chased them off right up to their huts; where we took eight of their women and girls and a large measure of their embroidered fabrics. But we hastily freed the young girls because we realized that enslavement went against the intentions of His Highness our leader, and we gave to these women some gifts and explained to them that we wanted them to treat us as we treated them.[45]

The violent encounters continued between the Kik and the expedition. Despite the volume of gifts being exchanged, the fear would not evaporate. And Selim Qapudan was still trying to determine his response to the alternating attacks and worship by the Kik. His narrative suggests that different Kik villages responded differently to the expedition, which only further complicated Selim Qapudan's sense of how the expedition was being interpreted. And on top of this confusion, the expedition was enduring either difficult weather conditions or shallow water in which their boats ran aground. Frequent repairs were required, sometimes with nearby villagers coming to help and bring food, or responding more ambivalently. One tribe approached the expedition, but Selim Qapudan noticed that there were no children among them. He asked about this, and they responded that they had hidden the children out of fear; yet they said they considered the soldiers to be sent from God.[46]

Then the expedition discovered two tributaries of the Nile that had not been drawn on the maps they were following, and they had to decide which of the two would be the most passable. The officers of the group (including two Europeans) all met with Selim Qapudan, well aware of the importance of this moment to their entire campaign. They decided to venture farther along the eastern estuary, but as it grew shallower they agreed to turn back, recording a statement in the ship's journal that outlined their reasoning.[47] After an arduous return trip, they arrived in Khartoum on 16 Muharram, announcing themselves with a twenty-one-gun salute and then immediately sending off their report to Muḥammad ʿAlī in Cairo.[48]

Selim Qapudan's narrative describes more than these troubling encounters. He observed the depths of the Nile very carefully, almost daily, and added important details in his journal about changes in vegetation and aquatic life. The length of the river they followed was mapped, as were villages of the different tribes. Some of the people they encountered were very instructive, and from them the expedition learned the locations of mountains they themselves could not find, where it might be possible to extract copper or iron. Still, no landmarks were more closely evaluated than the people living along the White Nile.

For Jomard, himself an experienced traveler to Egypt and the Sudan, that was where the value of Selim Qapudan's trip lay. Certainly, within the discourse of western Europe in the early to mid–nineteenth century, the gathering of geographical information was a labor performed in the service of understanding "the world and its contents."[49] And the techniques of geographical study enhanced the power of the explorer-observer on important levels: "To map hitherto 'unknown' regions (unknown, that is, to the European) using modern techniques in triangulation and geodesy was both a scientific activity dependent on trained personnel and state-of-the-art equipment and also a political act of appropriation which had obvious strategic utility to occupying military forces."[50] Muḥammad ʿAlī was keenly aware of this discourse and, in his turn, tried to channel this force of geographical expertise by hiring noted European experts for Selim Qapudan's expedition, one of whom, Thibaut, had earlier scouted the Sudan for giraffes for the Zoological Society of London. And so, on a journey reminiscent of the French expedition to Egypt under Napoleon, Muḥammad ʿAlī sent a group of scientists and engineers into the Sudan accompanied by military might.

The expedition was an act of empire, mimicking acts of other empires—but in the name of which empire? Here lies the mystery. Although the expedition brought great glory to Egypt and to its ruler, it remains unclear how many native-born, Arabic-speaking Egyptians took part in the expedition. Its leader himself was a Turkish-speaking officer, and his journal was not translated into Arabic until 1922. Some Egyptian historians, like Maqqar, have claimed Selim Qapudan as an Egyptian pioneer or an Egyptianized hero. But this leads back to the opacity that continues to surround Muḥammad ʿAlī's African empire. Selim Qapudan endured the hardships of his voyages out of duty to Muḥammad ʿAlī, but which community was he claiming as his own? In the name of which nation, if any, was he exploring?

The answer lies in the different ways in which the expedition was interpreted. For Selim Qapudan, the expedition had been sent by Muḥammad ʿAlī as a means of gathering information and offering the Nilotic tribes a glimpse of the civilization that was extending its authority over their territories. For the Shilluk and the Kik, it was an act of conquest by armed men sent without warning to their land by a nameless authority. For European geographers and scientists interested in the Nile Valley, it was a knowledge-seeking campaign that opened new pathways into the "mysteries of Africa."[51] And for Muḥammad ʿAlī, the real author of the expedition, it was a gesture that would dignify Egyptian control of the Nile Valley with European ideals about the values and uses of such scientific information. More than that, it was an investment in the future. Muḥammad ʿAlī's language and practice of imperialism planted the seeds of a future Egyptian empire to which future generations would be able to lay claim. In this construction, both the Sudan and Egypt represented a wished-for place, a dream empire. The expedition helped to define each for the future. By absorbing the Sudan into Egypt's borders, Muḥammad ʿAlī distinguished Egypt from the Sudan and brought Egypt a little closer to Europe.

Too often scholars of nationalism and imperialism collapse the historical complexities into overly simplistic theoretical binary relationships such as colonizer/colonized. This particular moment in 1840 shows Egypt standing at empire's edge, where meanings of empire were no longer being formed in the Ottoman model, but along a new European pattern. In the Egyptian case, the word *imperialism* fits this temporal limbo; this imperialism was embarked upon in the name of a future state. Selim Qapudan's expedition fit into this desired legacy, a projection of Egypt into the future, the making of a nation whose geographic and cultural shape would emerge from its imperial extensions.

RIFAʿAH RAFIʿ AL-ṬAHṬAWĪ IN THE SUDAN: A BLACKNESS IN A BLACKNESS IN A BLACKNESS

> From the provincial edge of an atlas, from the hem of a frayed
> empire, a man stops.
>
> DEREK WALCOTT, *Omeros*

It would take the literary skill of Shaykh Rifaʿah Rafiʿ al-Ṭahṭawī, Egypt's brilliant scholar, Muḥammad ʿAlī's loyal official, the master teacher and translator of foreign words and meanings, to bring this envisioned Egypt into sharper focus by using the Sudan as a boundary. His map of Egypt is not the work of a cartographer but is instead a literary construction, a powerful set of images that served to memorialize Muḥammad ʿAlī's dream of Egypt's future. It is universally recognized among scholars of Egyptian history and literature that al-Ṭahṭawī was the originator of the concept *waṭan* (nation, patrie) in Egyptian society and the first to articulate a sense of Egypt as a culturally and politically unified community. In his important historical works, al-Ṭahṭawī's emerging sense of nationalism helped create a map of Egyptian civilization. For the purpose of this study, two factors make al-Ṭahṭawī's literary mapping interesting: his idealization of the Sudan as a conquered and dependent territory whose resources could help Egypt achieve Muḥammad ʿAlī's goals, and his horror of the Sudan itself, when he was sent to live in Khartoum in 1850, eight years after Selim Qapudan had completed his final expedition up the Nile.

As Hourani states, "Ṭahṭawī lived and worked in a happy interlude of history, when the religious tension between Islam and Christendom was being relaxed and had not yet been replaced by the new political tension of east and west."[52] Born in 1801, al-Ṭahṭawī came from a family from Upper Egypt. He began his intellectual career at al-Azhār University when he was sixteen years old. He studied there with Shaykh Hassan al-ʿAttar, one of the first Egyptian scholars to engage the French sciences at Napoleon's Institut d'Égypte. Nine years later, al-Ṭahṭawī was appointed the imam of the first delegation of students that Muḥammad ʿAlī sent to Paris in 1826. Al-Ṭahṭawī stayed there for five years, learning French and the art of translation and, with these skills, delving deeply into ancient history, philosophy, and French literature. Upon returning to Egypt, he published a description of Paris, the celebrated *Takhlīṣ al-ibriz fī talkhīṣ Bārīz* (Refinement of Pure Gold in the Summary of Paris). Soon Muḥammad ʿAlī appointed him the director of the new School of Languages, an institution created to train Egyptian students for new secular professions. He also worked as a school inspector and editor of the government's newspaper, *al-Waqāʾiʿ al-miṣrīya*.

When the School of Languages was enlarged to include a bureau of translation under his direction, al-Ṭahṭawī had clearly become something of a cultural institution in Egypt. Heading a team of translators, al-Ṭahṭawī himself published twenty translations of French geographical, historical, and scientific works, all commissioned by Muḥammad ʿAlī and reflecting the viceroy's interest in the history and "lives of great rulers and soldiers."[53] But after Muḥammad ʿAlī's death in 1849, al-Ṭahṭawī's fortunes changed. The viceroy ʿAbbas Hilmī I sent him to Khartoum to open a school of languages there, and he closed the Egyptian school shortly afterward. Al-Ṭahṭawī considered this new commission to be a banishment, an exile brought about through the machinations of a high-ranking and jealous rival.[54] While in the Sudan, al-Ṭahṭawī translated Fenelon's *Télémaque.* When he returned home in 1854, he was restored to prominence, becoming the director of a new school of languages and translation and working on commissions to plan Egypt's new educational system. He published original works as well on education, the most important, for the purposes of this study, being *Manāhij al-albāb al-miṣriya fī mabāhij al-'adāb al-'asriya* (which Hourani elegantly translates as "The Paths of Egyptian Hearts in the Joys of the Contemporary Arts").[55]

In his description of al-Ṭahṭawī's life, Hourani repeats the word *new* many times: leaving his home in Tahta, al-Ṭahṭawī "found himself pushed by circumstances from the old world into the new"; at al-Azhār he "had his first glimpse of a new world"; he was the imam of the regiment of "the new Egyptian army," and "the new army was the nucleus of a new Egypt"; in France he encountered, through the works of Voltaire and Montesquieu, "new ideas" of the nation.[56] Al-Ṭahṭawī thus presented was a man on the cusp of two traditions, well-trained in Islam scholarship and open to the European Enlightenment. This liminal position has been immortalized by many scholars of history and Arabic literature, who see al-Ṭahṭawī as "the first Egyptian intellectual who thoroughly understood Western ideals which he transmitted to his conservative society without prejudice."[57] Al-Ṭahṭawī symbolizes an entire generation of Egyptians who lived during a time when "men's minds were undergoing the same transformation as their cities and their history."[58]

This cultural bridge on which al-Ṭahṭawī and his descendants stood spanned Europe and Egypt, and it offered a new vista from which to view one's homeland. Charles Wendell discusses the impact of this kind of travel for Egyptians' (and others') sense of political geography and development: "As everywhere in the East, the sudden drops in the level of culture from capital to provincial town to village still existed, and in an even more exaggerated fashion than heretofore. The contrasts were now so great as to be tantamount to differences of 'culture time.'"[59] For Sabry Hafez, who saw a similar discordance within the different strata of Egyptian culture, a map created by literature was the means of guiding oneself home. Hafez states that, with his concept of *waṭan*, al-Ṭahṭawī had to change an idea into a reality, to make a new sense of time fit the place, the site of the nation. Al-Ṭahṭawī's books, particularly *Manāhij al-albāb*, were analogous to the work of translators, and eventually to the work of creative writers, in that they had "to utilize the strategies of traditional narrative in vindicating the new narrative discourse and endorsing its novel ways"; and of these novel ways, the most important "is the change in the concepts of time and place."[60]

The Sudan constituted another, crucial aspect of the bridge being constructed by al-Ṭahṭawī in the service of Muḥammad ʿAlī and his successors. In the middle of the nineteenth century, Egyptian rule in the Sudan was changing. After twelve years (1826–1838) of effective administration on the part of Khurshid Pasha (the *ḥikimdar* of the Sudan, who Muḥammad ʿAlī had encouraged to make the expedition that eventually was completed by Selim Qapudan), Khartoum had transformed into a city: an international community of merchants had settled there, as had the consuls of European governments; permanent barracks for the military had been constructed and dockyards built along the Nile.[61] By 1842, the Egyptian administration extended to the ports of Suakin and Massawa, thus reaching as far as the Red Sea coast, and, thanks to Selim Qapudan, a route was opened up to the southern Sudan along the White Nile.[62] During the last years of Muḥammad ʿAlī's reign, the administration in the Sudan tottered from the viceroy's increasingly confused orders (as Holt and Daly point out, Muḥammad ʿAlī had become senile at this late point in his life). His son Muḥammad Said Pasha, who became viceroy in 1854, almost gave up completely on the Sudan, before changing his mind and seeking ways to integrate the administration of this vast territory more closely with Cairo.[63]

The middle of the century was thus an important time for rethinking the Sudan's importance to Egypt, and the region became a geographic and political symbol of great ambiguity to Egyptian administrators, officers, and intellectuals. The mines designed to extract the Sudan's mineral wealth, crucial to the success of this colonial enterprise, were also places to which Egyptian convicts were sentenced for hard labor.[64] Even though the exploitation of the Sudan was intended to help reform Egypt economically and politically, reforms, like the building of schools and hospitals, did not reach the Sudan. Even for those officials not sent to the mines or prisons, "service there came to be regarded by Egyptian elites as a sort of exile."[65] Yet reassertions of the connection between Egypt and the Sudan began to crystallize national identity, at least for elites. As Ehud Toledano describes the situation:

> The reassertion of Egyptian power in the Sudan, it is suggested, should be seen also within an Ottoman-Egyptian context. That is, as part of the emerging identity of the elite, as it was trying to negotiate a regional role for the autonomous, though still Ottoman, Egypt. This is what I termed the notion of "mini-empire." Together with a loyalty to the House of Mehmet Ali, a commitment to live and serve in Egypt, and

a sense of belonging to Ottoman culture and an Ottoman Empire, this notion formed a distinct Ottoman-Egyptian identity.[66]

In other words, the Sudan helped Egyptians identify what was Egyptian about Egypt, in an idealized, burgeoning nationalist sense; yet one's presence in the Sudan was an exile, a detachment from home in Egypt, a disgrace.[67]

Al-Ṭahṭawī is a perfect emblem of this powerful geographic push-and-pull between Egypt and the Sudan. It seems, from his writings and from descriptions of him living in the Sudan, that no one could have felt more alienated and foreign or more miserable than al-Ṭahṭawī. In 1852, Bayard Taylor, the first American tourist to visit the Sudan, met al-Ṭahṭawī at a dinner given at the home of the governor-general, Laṭīf Pasha. Taylor was struck by this "intelligent Egyptian" drinking claret, "Rufaa Bey (whose Moslem principles had been damaged by ten years' residence in Paris)."[68] After dinner, Taylor and other guests walked home with al-Ṭahṭawī, "who detained us an hour by the narration of the injuries and indignities which had been inflicted upon him by order of ʿAbbas Pasha." Al-Ṭahṭawī made his own sense of banishment clear to Taylor. He asserted that he was not truly on a mission to create a school of languages in Khartoum; after all, a year and a half had passed and "no order had been received from Cairo relative to the College." The uncertainty, the inactivity, and the climate, Taylor wrote, contributed to the deaths of two of the other professors exiled with al-Ṭahṭawī, who foresaw for himself a similar fate. Hearing this, and having it later confirmed, Taylor understood "the bitterness of the curses which the venerable old Bey heaped upon the head of his tyrannical ruler."[69]

Such direct expression of anger at ʿAbbas Pasha may have been appropriate for conversation with this American, but al-Ṭahṭawī chose another way to sublimate his distress at displacement from Egypt. He turned to translating Fenelon's *Télémaque,* and "found an allegory which perfectly fitted his case and the injustice done to him."[70] Telemachus was the son of Ulysses. In the company of his tutor, Mentor (the goddess Athena in disguise), he sails to faraway lands in search of his father. While Telemachus sees a great deal of heroic action, Mentor gives wise advice to the different rulers they encounter, thus offering lessons in public virtue and decent, uncorrupted government. Fenelon, too, had that sense of being torn away from home. When the book was first published in France in 1699, many considered *Les Aventures de Télémaque* (The Adventures of Telemachus) to be a veiled criticism of Louis XIV, who quickly had it banned. Fenelon had already fallen into disgrace in 1697 for his religious practices, and had gone into temporary exile. With the controversy over *Télémaque* two years later, Louis XIV declared his banishment permanent. Fenelon never returned to France, but his book became a tremendous success, translated into many languages.[71]

Al-Ṭahṭawī did return to Egypt after completing his translation, which was published in Beirut in 1867. It was titled *Mawāqiʿ al-aflak fī waqāʾiʿ Telemaque* (The Accordance of the Planets in the Adventures of Telemachus). In the introduction to his translation, al-Ṭahṭawī described the heat and the terrible conditions under which he lived in the Sudan, a country he considered very far away from Egypt.[72] The Sudan was not only far geographically, but its distance from Cairo seems to have been temporal as well. He intended his translation to be a bridge over time, enabling Egyptian students to understand important lessons from the world outside of Egypt. He writes, "I thank God for having put me in this era," when such brilliant books were available.[73] Al-Ṭahṭawī situated many of Telemachus's adventures in ancient Egypt as well, to provide a context he felt would help contemporary Egyptians understand Fenelon's lessons, but this also gave al-Ṭahṭawī the opportunity to recapture for himself his Egypt while so far away in exile in the Sudan. He states that he "created in the book the picture of beloved Egypt which unlocked the reins of my pen."[74] He wrote himself a map that, at least in his imagination, could lead him closer to home.

The Sudan itself is lost here, serving only as the anathema to Egypt, the darkness against which Egypt is better drawn in contrast. But two years after publishing *Mawāqiʿ al-aflak,* al-Ṭahṭawī published his masterpiece on Egyptian history and geography, *Manāhij al-albāb al-miṣriya fī mabāhij al-ʿadāb al-ʿasriya,* in which the Sudan serves a much more complicated purpose. This, too, al-Ṭahṭawī intended to be a guide for Egyptian students of the new secular schools, from which they would "deduce a theory of politics and of the nature and destiny of Egypt."[75] In *Manāhij al-albāb,* al-Ṭahṭawī presents Egypt as a natural community, using the word *waṭan* and the phrase *ḥubb al-waṭan* (love of the nation, patriotism) to discuss both the unity that bonded Egyptians to Egypt and their duty to their country.[76] This community was not an Arab one, as Hourani points out, but specifically an Egyptian one.[77] To inculcate this sense among his readers, al-Ṭahṭawī drew sharp lines along Egypt's borders. Israel Altman suggests that this increased sense of geographic and national specificity was al-Ṭahṭawī's response to European colonialism, which he realized was beginning to target Islamic countries. Al-Ṭahṭawī's proposed remedy was "that each Islamic country integrate, on an individual basis, in the European political structure."[78] But European colonialism was less a threat to al-Ṭahṭawī and more a model, offering great promise for Egypt's future colonial expansion in its natural site, the Sudan.

The idea of Egyptian control of the Sudan also added a sense of timelessness to Egypt's geography, as the movement of Egyptian armies and power southward was "the direction taken by her earliest imperial armies as far back as the Old Kingdom." It was thus an affirmation of Egypt's ancient identity and borders, and "the first step toward the realization of a politically unified Nile Valley."[79] Wendell calls this a "unified picture of Egypt's manifest destiny in Africa." He states that, "as one of the civilized nations of the world, Egypt takes her place alongside Europe, and the less developed peoples of the southern Sudan especially, are held up to criticism as examples of improvidence, shiftlessness, and technical and social backwardness."[80] So, in its passivity as the object of Egyptian imperialism, the Sudan played a crucial role in helping Egyptians define and maintain their cultural, historical, political, economic, and geographic integrity. The dreamed-of Egypt, in its active domination of the Sudan, was therefore as much an ancient state as it was a state that would be realized in the future, when it was to achieve parity with Europe. A new geography was created, based on measurements of time and development.

Because he understood the importance of this geographic unity, al-Ṭahṭawī considered Muḥammad ʿAlī to be one of the greatest of Egyptian rulers. It was Muḥammad ʿAlī, al-Ṭahṭawī wrote, who connected all the waters of the Nile, from the uppermost Saʾid to the ocean at Alexandria. Al-Ṭahṭawī narrated the history of irrigation reform from the north of Egypt to the south, city by city, area by area. The utilization of the Nile was thus an important means by which to unify Egypt, and from which the ruler could chart his own country. This unity offered the inhabitants of the Nile Valley the opportunity to travel in their own country, by boat up the Nile, and provided the government with easy access to all Egyptian territory. It was a logical extension of his argument for al-Ṭahṭawī to praise Selim Qapudan's expedition for its exploration (and subsequent inclusion within Egyptian auspices) of the lands of the White Nile.[81]

Al-Ṭahṭawī also wished for the extraction of the Sudan's mineral resources, particularly its fabled gold deposits, to help Egypt gain entry into the international metals market, then dominated by Russia, Austria, and South America. This was important to Muḥammad ʿAlī, al-Ṭahṭawī wrote, who took it upon himself to visit Fazughlī in the Sudan in 1838 to see how the gold mines he had commissioned were functioning. Al-Ṭahṭawī compares Africa to America—"li bilādin ifriqiyatin laha shibhun bi-amrīka"— in its resources, and it was for its resources generally that Muḥammad ʿAlī invested so much manpower and money.[82] But it all came to nothing. The French engineers hired by the viceroy could not agree on the right system of extraction, there was little gold, and the inhabitants of the Fazughlī region repeatedly and successfully attacked the enterprise. The raids of these *'abid* (slaves), as al-Ṭahṭawī called them, finally caused the enterprise to be abandoned.

In al-Ṭahṭawī's book, the Sudanese were ultimately most important as targets of Egyptian colonialism. After his return to Egypt from the Sudan, Muḥammad 'Alī began to bring the children of Sudanese shaykhs and leaders to Cairo, to educate them in the basics of agriculture or in the language schools. The point of this, wrote al-Ṭahṭawī, was "to give them a taste of the food of learning and civilization, so that they could then spread this in their country."[83] As they became increasingly "civilized," these Sudanese children offered proof of Egypt's political and cultural hegemony. Upon them was written the text, therefore, of Egyptian achievement.

Al-Ṭahṭawī, while still suffering exile in the Sudan, had intended to send his lament in the form of a *qaṣīda* (a rhymed praise poem) to the *katkhuda* of Egypt, Hassan Pasha. This *qaṣīda* was never sent, so al-Ṭahṭawī decided to include it in the text of *Manāhij al-albāb*. In it, he complained that "the Sudan is never a place for someone like me, not the place for my safety or my happiness" *(wa ma al-sūdān, qat maqamun mithl[im]—wa lā salāmī fīhi wa la su'adī)*. As he described it, half of its inhabitants were like beasts and others like stones. The men of the Sudan forced their women into prostitution, and they accepted the progeny of these unions, despite the prohibition of Islamic law. They taught the women to fornicate like beasts. If it had not been for the white Arabs—*law la al-bayda min al-'arab la kānu*—they would have been blacker and blacker and blacker, nothing but blackness—*sawādan fī sawādin fī sawādin*. He should not have been sent there, the *qaṣīda* stated, a man who had served his country for so long. He could not accomplish the impossible there in the Sudan. His hopelessness was underscored by his plaintive and beautiful phrase "lā hayāta li man tunadi" (there is no hope—all is done for), although he implores the *katkhuda* to help a "prisoner in the jail of the Zanj."[84]

Al-Ṭahṭawī's *qaṣīda* continues for many pages, echoing the sadness of his position but also offering stark images of hateful Sudanese, to whom he attributed no tribe, no religion, no language, no identity except that of slave or "a blackness in a blackness in a blackness." The lessons of detailed geographical knowledge that much of *Manāhij al-albāb* discussed were lost on al-Ṭahṭawī when he himself looked at the Sudanese. At the end of the poem, al-Ṭahṭawī resumed writing in prose, expressing his deprivation of the benefits of his nation—*waṭanī*—and devoting much of his time to the translation of *Télémaque*.[85] He did tutor some of the Sudanese teachers in readings of the Qur'an, and, in his last nine months, he established a small school for the children of Egyptians serving in Khartoum. Thus he contributed to the civilizing mission begun by Muḥammad ʿAlī and continued by Muḥammad ʿAlī's grandson, Ismaʿīl, who had become ruler of Egypt in 1863. In some part as a result of al-Ṭahṭawī's activities, the Sudanese were learning to become modern.

This prose summation of the *qaṣīda* and al-Ṭahṭawī's experience in the Sudan offers an interesting opposition of feelings. He made it clear in the *qaṣīda* that the only reason he had been sent to the Sudan was the slander of rivals, which resulted in his banishment from his country. Yet he followed that with praise for the work done there by Egyptian intellectuals like himself. This he supported with the assertion that the new school built for the children of Egyptians, the establishment of the first mosque, the introduction of Europeans to the area, and the building of railroads all helped bring the Sudan into modern civilization.

His personal sense of geography was striking: the Sudan, he states, when one is actually living there, does not at all feel like a part of Egypt. Al-Ṭahṭawī felt himself terribly oppressed in his exile so far from home, living near people who were basically inanimate objects or wild barbarians to him, unable or unwilling to participate in the culture that al-Ṭahṭawī had brought with him. But his sense of nationalist connection to Egypt was powerful enough for him to argue that bringing the Sudan closer into the Egyptian sphere created one country, with links to both the glories of the ancient Egyptian past and the future power of Europe. Still, the Sudan never felt like home.

ʿALĪ MUBĀRAK: OUT OF AFRICA, MANY DREAMS

In al-Ṭahṭawī's work, it is interesting to note how synecdochical Khartoum becomes for the entire region of the Sudan. Ahmad Sayyid Ahmad, writing respectfully of al-Ṭahṭawī, laments that the latter did not travel outside of Khartoum, for had he done so, he could have familiarized himself with the customs of different tribes and shaykhs. He might well have come across beautiful stories, like "Tajuj wa Mihlaq," a love story told across the Sudan and well-known in al-Ṭahṭawī's time.[86] If he had been in circumstances more customary, he might have analyzed with greater sensitivity the claims made by many about the harm that the Egyptian administration was actually doing the Sudan. Or he might have appreciated the rise of new cities, seeing them as part of the cultural harvest Egypt had sown. Al-Ṭahṭawī, so interested in geography, might have taken a deeper interest in the exploration of the White Nile and the increase in trade with the southern Sudan. But Ahmad attributes al-Ṭahṭawī's weak vision (a weakness he calls uncharacteristic of this great scholar) to his absorption in the translation of Fenelon's *Télémaque*.[87] This absorption, or rather immersion, in this French text removed al-Ṭahṭawī from the work he was assigned to carry out, work that would have placed him in greater contact with Sudanese contemporaries and the vibrant Sudanese culture.

'Alī Mubārak's textual approach to the Sudan led him along a different path, although to the same conclusion. If the Sudan crystallized into a racially inferior but absolutely necessary colony of Egypt for al-Ṭahṭawī, 'Alī Mubārak saw it as a landscape of savagery, but one whose immaturity represented a past only recently shared by Egypt. The connection was much more intimate. For Mubārak, the alleged practices and customs of Africans and the Sudanese were not unlike those of pre-Islamic Arabs. Within them lay as much potential and possibility as in any child. When he wrote about the Sudan and Africa in his fictional narrative *'Alam al-Dīn* in 1857, it was with an almost Montesquieu-like empathy. But the Sudan served also as a warning: Egypt had to beware that, unless it actively pursued knowledge of the outside world, it would be as easily marginalized and as vulnerable as he considered the Sudan to be.

This extraordinary engineer, historian, and educator had a difficult time finding either his calling or the right path to a solid education. As Mubārak describes it, his first *mu'alim* (teacher), who taught him and other local children in his home, filled him with such fear that he could barely learn the Qur'an, and his difficulties resulted in terrible beatings. This situation lasted for two years, until he could tolerate no more and returned to his father's house in the village of Birnabal. When his father, fearful that 'Alī Mubārak would lose what little education he had gained, tried to return his son to the same teacher, the boy refused and threatened to run away for good. In his account of his childhood, 'Alī Mubārak describes himself turning this way and that, making new choices, with his father at wit's end trying both to please and raise his willful, intelligent son. Conceding that a traditional education would not work, his father agreed to apprentice him to a local clerk. 'Alī Mubārak's father paid for his keep, and he lived with the clerk and his family. But this, too, went badly. The clerk verbally abused him in public and punished him severely for small indiscretions, and young 'Alī ran away again, this time for days.[88]

After several more unsatisfactory experiences working as an assistant here and there, 'Alī found a position with a fiscal agent whom he suspected of not paying him his full salary. Given his suspicions, he took for himself what he thought he was owed. This landed him in prison for several weeks, where he learned to negotiate his way with his jailers and, through them, to appeal to a visiting civil officer *(ma'mur)* from the Ministry of Agriculture for a job as a clerk. This high-ranking commissioner freed him from prison and hired him, and opened the young boy's eyes to a different kind of future.[89]

Very much to 'Alī Mubārak's surprise, the high-ranking commissioner, 'Anbar Effendi, was black. In his own words, 'Alī Mubārak could not wrap his mind around this inversion of social and cultural hierarchies:

> I looked at him and saw that he was black, Abyssinian, as if he were a Mamluk's slave. Yet he was both magnanimous and dignified. I saw how the shaykhs and judges of the area stood before him, and how he counseled them. I stayed around until they had gone, and then entered his chamber and kissed his hand.
>
> He then spoke to me in elegant classical Arabic: "Would you like to work for me as a clerk, for daily meals and a salary of 75 piasters a month?"
>
> "Yes," I responded. Then I moved back and sat down with the servants, and I recognized that the shaykhs who stood before him were a group of the most powerful, with great fortunes and servants and retinues and slaves. I was shocked by their behavior in his presence. I never would have imagined nor even heard of such a thing. I had always thought that the ruling classes only included Turks; this was the custom during those days. So, I remained shocked and confused that these dignitaries stood before a slave and kissed his hand.[90]

This apparent social upheaval upset 'Alī Mubārak deeply. He turned to his father for answers about how a dark-skinned African could ever achieve so high a position. They mulled over it together:

> "This *ma'mūr* is not a Turk, since he's black," I said.
> My father answered, "Maybe he is a freed slave."
> "Can a slave become a government official when even provincial notables cannot, and even less so slaves?"
> My father searched for answers but still could not satisfy me. He said, "Perhaps the cause of his rise is his morality and his knowledge?"
> "What kind of knowledge could that be?"
> "Perhaps he studied at al-Azhār," my father replied.
> "Do the lessons one learns at al-Azhār help one to work for the government? Do graduates of al-Azhār become officials?"
> My father answered, "My son, we are all slaves of God, and God raises whomever He chooses."
> "I agree," I said, "but there have to be reasons." My father continued to recite stories and poems that still did not convince me."[91]

Absorbed by this mystery and still at an educational crossroads himself, 'Alī researched the source of 'Anbar Effendi's power and found out that he was indeed a manumitted slave, and that his last owner had enrolled him in the recently established Qaṣr al-ʿAynī School, now identified as "the road to wealth and power."[92] ʿAlī Mubārak decided, finally, that if this school, established by the government, could enable a former slave to achieve so much, then it was the path for him too, and so at the age of twelve he enrolled in Qaṣr al-ʿAynī. He continued in the new schools of the government, and was sent on an educational delegation (similar to the kind for which al-Ṭahṭāwī served as imam) to the L'École Militaire Égyptienne in Paris.[93] Thirteen years after meeting ʿAnbar Effendi, ʿAlī Mubārak returned to Egypt to embark on a brilliant career as civil engineer, historian, professor, government minister, and founder of the national library, which in his own telling was launched by the miracle of seeing a black man in power.

STRANGERS IN A STRANGE LAND

> People fail to understand why you should forsake your wives,
> your relations, your friends, your native country, to visit lands
> about which Persians know nothing.
>
> MONTESQUIEU, Persian Letters

ʿAlī Pasha Mubārak, as he was to become known, is famous for many works, particularly his multivolume geographical history of Cairo, *Al-Khiṭaṭ al-tawfīqiya al-jadīda* (New Guide to the Districts Ruled by Tawfīq), first published in 1886–1889. But for his ideas about the Sudan, we have to turn to his extraordinary text, the fictional narrative titled *ʿAlam al-Dīn*, written much earlier, in 1857, when the author was just reaching a position of real authority. *ʿAlam al-Dīn* is the story of an intellectually gifted but very poor al-Azhar scholar named ʿAlam al-Dīn, who is engaged by an Englishman (known throughout the fifteen-hundred-page work only as al-Inklīzī) to work with him on a volume called *Lisān al-ʿArab* (The Languages of the Arabs),on the condition that ʿAlam al-Dīn travel with him to Alexandria, Marseilles, and Paris. ʿAlam al-Dīn decides, with his wife's full support, to go and to bring his young son, Burhan al-Dīn, with him.

ʿAlam al-Dīn meets much more resistance from his students at al-Azhar. Their fears are multiple: Is it for money that he will leave his country and his people? How could he put himself into a subservient position to someone from a different religion? How would he not lose himself in this immersion in another culture? ʿAlam al-Dīn replies that he is not traveling to serve but to help edit a volume important to Egyptians as well, and that the pursuit of knowledge in other parts of the world was not synonymous with betrayal of one's country, religion, or people.[94] This dialogue reflects much of ʿAlī Mubārak's own confrontation with standard Islamic education, described in his more personal memoirs. ʿAlam al-Dīn is a respectable, well-trained religious scholar who retains his curiosity despite his long education in a tradition "which made the East satisfied with the answers it found, contented with what it had to the point of killing every sense of curiosity in it and of suffocating every desire of exploring the unknown."[95]

Wadad al-Qadi convincingly argues that this narrative fits into a genre of "the Arab rediscovery of Europe—books quite in fashion in the second half of the nineteenth century," as the success of al-Ṭahṭawī's *Takhlīṣ al-ibrīz* in 1834 had shown. But Mubārak, unlike al-Ṭahṭawī, did not just inform his Egyptian readers about affairs and customs in the West. Instead, *ʿAlam al-Dīn* "put the East in a direct situation of actual confrontation with the West, so that the East, before the West, knows its proper place in world civilization."[96] This is why Africa was so important, for it too was in confrontation with the West and the East. Only through the strengthening process of confronting Africa through scientific exploration, reform of education, and colonialism could Egyptians possibly maintain themselves in what had become a new world order.

The narrative is constructed so that ʿAlam al-Dīn and his son are constantly in the act of discovery—about trains, steam engines, hotels, different countries—in a manner similar to that of the two Persians, Rica and Usbek, created in 1724 by Montesquieu to analyze the rights and wrongs of French culture. Like Montesquieu's *Persian Letters*, *ʿAlam al-Dīn* represents a fictional journey that mimics the narratives of geographers and explorers. The two Egyptian characters ask for help and information from their European friends, and they pull together to share their feelings about the unfamiliar world into which they step. The chapters *(mūsamarāt)*, which revolve around long lectures and explanations, are shot through with surprising moments of emotion. The lectures given by the Inklīzī, and questions that ʿAlam al-Dīn and his son ask, relate immediately, materially, to each stage of the trip: the steam-powered train they take to Alexandria, the mechanics of the ship to Marseilles, the nature of the Industrial Revolution. Travel and discovery reveal the secrets of progress.[97]

No wonder, then, that travel to Africa takes on such mythical status in this book, idealized to the point of legend. ʿAlī Mubārak never traveled to Africa, and so the two hundred or so pages devoted to the continent are a story of shipwreck and adventure, as told to the Egyptian characters by a young British sailor named James (Yaʿqūb), whom they encounter in Marseilles. This fictionalized travel narrative seems to be a camouflaged act of confronting Egypt and the Islamic East, reminiscent of Montesquieu's own literary disguises in the form of two Persians in Paris during the reign of Louis XIV. Disguised as "true accounts of the discovery of unknown lands [these narratives] were the pretexts for the construction of an Ideal State in which, of course, the evils of European civilization were obviated or suppressed."[98] As Montesquieu's creation, the Persians' views on European civilization in general and French culture in particular were reflections from "a civilized European's critical intellect."[99] In *'Alam al-Dīn*, James the storyteller and his listeners all represent the views of an educated Egyptian intellect and as such offer valuable insights into how deeply 'Alī Mubārak had internalized the idea of a civilizing mission in the Sudan discussed earlier by al-Ṭahṭawī.

James tells his story to cheer up his cotravelers, after Burhan al-Dīn describes a heartbreaking experience at the theater in Marseilles, where a group of women ogled him for hours during a performance. His self-consciousness touches his father and makes the entire group thoughtful, until James tries to distract them with his entertaining tale. Apologizing for the weakness of his Arabic vocabulary, James begins, with al-Inklīzī translating for him. As an orphan in London working as an apprentice, he overhead Egyptian merchants discussing how to get rich from overseas travel. All agreed that the best method of self-enrichment was in overseas trade. James was entranced and hastily decided to leave his job and his sister, who worked as a domestic; he found a position on a ship heading to Africa. There was a terrible shipwreck (here the beauty and danger of sea voyage is gracefully narrated by 'Alī Mubārak), and James found himself washed ashore.[100]

James tried for weeks to survive on his own, but loneliness so overwhelmed him that he finally forced himself to approach some nearby huts, bringing his gun with him. A visiting chief took a liking to him and conducted him through miles and miles of territory,

> until the fourth day, when we finally arrived at a small village. All of the people were black and lived in huts, and we spent the night. I found myself surrounded by slaves [*'abīd*], who rushed around me like I was some kind of miracle or strange being; they came from every corner and quarter—young, old, male, female—they all came to stare at me. Women came even closer than the men, and a group surrounded me speaking their foreign language that I couldn't understand. At first I was scared, but then I got used to it and tolerated it for the rest of the day and the night.[101]

James's experience with the Africans echoes what Burhan al-Dīn endured during his harrowing evening at the theater in Marseilles, when he was better entertainment for the spectators than the stage itself. But despite James's claims of patience and tolerance with his African observers, he continued to feel trapped within the village and deeply regretful of his earlier wanderlust. Time only worsened his alienation. The more he got to know the people, the further he wanted to be from them. "Knowing" them could not mean joining them or identifying with them: "They all cared about me and I got used to this situation and to their mentality. Very quickly I learned their language and could speak with them and was drawn into their way of life; something of a sense of ease entered me and I remained among them, as if I were one of them, until I was able to get out of their clutches." As the text makes clear, James could not, would not, be assimilated into African life. The subsequent debate problematized this idea of assimilation. For al-Inklīzī, assimilation seems a wonderful progress-wielding instrument for Africans, but one with little real promise. Even those Africans who have had a long history of trade with the British, French, and Portuguese, and whose customs have been somewhat altered by close contact with Europeans, still follow the "corrupt" superstitions of their fathers and ancestors.[102]

There remained the threat of being absorbed into this culture, a pull that James fought daily and with difficulty while shipwrecked. As he learned the local language and customs, he became "like one of them" except for his skin color. The whiteness that had at first so amazed the visitors lost its difference. As time passed they still called him "the white one" *(al-abyaḍ),* but out of habit, since "my color had changed after all the time I spent outside in the sun."[103] People truly liked him and accepted him, a fact that is immediately followed in the text by his learning that a group of foreign explorers had arrived, thus providing him with his chance to escape. True kinship feelings were restored by Europeans, never Africans. As James got ready to leave, the chief told him he would miss him dearly but did nothing to stop him. There never was a real prison, or a threat.

James and al-Inklīzī continue to comment on the strange ways of the Africans, traversing the continent with examples of this or that tribe's barbaric behavior. The worst custom, al-Inklīzī says, is slavery. Although acknowledging that the trade worsened considerably with the arrival of Europeans on the coastlines of Africa, al-Inklīzī says that abolition of the trade is impossible as long as Africans remain ignorant, uneducated, and without religion. Only when they accept true religion and learn the skills of civilized countries will they be able to give up a trade that has become second nature. Until such a time, al-Inklīzī says, it is better that they enslave each other than massacre each other.[104] For many more pages, they debate the relative benefits of slavery to the generalized savagery of an entire continent, uniformly benighted and blackened.

There are so many examples of these attitudes among European writers and explorers of the mid–nineteenth century that one wonders about their identities. Is it possible that the speakers are European but created by an Egyptian? Was Mubārak merely spouting the same hardening racialist thinking so prevalent at the time? My reading of *'Alam al-Dīn* leads me to think that 'Alī Mubārak was not so dismissive of Africans. There is a stronger identification with Africans within the text, and the narrative finds interesting links between Africans and Egyptians. For example, after many pages of excoriation, 'Alam al-Dīn himself notes that the "ugly practices" of the Africans were once practiced also by Arabs in the pre-Islamic era. A similar litany of uncivilized and terrible customs formerly practiced by Arabs emerges in 'Alam al-Dīn's account, customs he is grateful that the prophet Muḥammad abolished. But 'Alam al-Dīn's own discussion ends with him encouraging Europeans to take a greater role in bringing the tools of progress to Africa and thereby helping Africans toward civilization. There is no debate when al-Inklīzī tells his friends that there are Europeans, the French in particular, who insist that nothing should be or even can be done about the trade in slaves. This British observer accuses them of collaborating in the slave trade. Although there are many British antislavery outposts on the continent, many of the agents died from climactic conditions. Finally, he says, African values have a corrupting influence on some, and fraternizing too closely only loosens the values of Europeans.[105]

It is important to remember that, of all the authors mentioned in this chapter, only 'Alī Mubārak lived to see Egypt itself colonized by the British. Although he wrote the book in 1857, he published it in 1882, soon after the British occupied Egypt. According to Wadad al-Qadi, this explains why he chose British voyagers instead of French ones.[106] It certainly helps to understand the irrevocability of colonialism in 'Alī Mubārak's account, or, if not irrevocability, the necessity for it. Had it not been for the presence of Europeans, Egyptians could easily have fallen into the same abyss that Mubārak saw engulfing the Africans. But in adopting their ways, this text seems to assert, Egyptians could gain the same power as Europeans and, like them, colonize other lands.

As the texts of Muḥammad al-Tunisī, Selim Qapudan, Rifa'a Rafi' al-Ṭahṭawī, and 'Alī Mubārak demonstrate, the process of conceptualizing and mapping the Sudan was shadowed by European thinkers and explorers and their texts. Each text was heavily influenced by a European with prior experience in geographic exploration (and, thus. the basic mechanics of empire) in the Sudan. Until urged on by Perron, Muḥammad al-Tunisī had kept his memories of the Sudan to himself for over thirty years; it was his French friend and colleague who translated his narrative into French *(Voyage au Darfour)* and made it an important guide for European travelers who followed.[107] Selim Qapudan relied on the expertise and judgment of the French explorer and geologist G. Thibaut throughout his expeditions up the Nile. Al-Ṭahṭawī most intimately related himself to the fictional hero Telemachus, adopting Fénélon's epic and words to articulate his own sense of alienation when exiled to the Sudan. Mubārak's European characters express, in Arabic, the need for cultural self-improvement and the civilizing process of colonialism; that they do so upon Egypt's own colonization is even more telling. These authors welcomed and sometimes invited the participation of different French men or sought the influence of different French texts. Quite self-consciously, intellectuals and elites in Egypt viewed the French as guides, and, just as self-consciously, many in France were aware of this.

When Napoleon's armies invaded Egypt in 1801, the geographers of the expedition entertained the idea of instilling in Egyptians a sense of empire, and not only a passive one. As M. P. S. Girard, a French geographer, explained in his journal of the expedition, "Already our expedition in Egypt has familiarized its inhabitants with ways of life other than theirs; it has expanded their ideas, and weakened their prejudices; they have seen the superiority that the practice of our modern arts gives us[,] and they are better disposed to practice these themselves than they were."[108]

Girard was correct, if a little vainglorious. Although the process took years to develop under Muḥammad ʿAlī's rule, Egyptians learned to translate definitions from French and other European texts and to appreciate a sense of belonging to a particular culture. They learned well the lessons of empire. And as they learned these lessons, they drew different maps of the Sudan, ones with a single, increasingly defined borderline around the two territories, even as they drew ever harsher distinctions between their cultures.

2 Black Servants and Saviors

The Domestic Empire of Egypt

> To be in someone else's power is a conscious experience which
> induces doubt about the ordering of the universe, while those who
> have power can forget it, or can assume that it is part of the natural
> order of things and invent and adopt ideas which justify their posses-
> sion of it.
>
> ALBERT HOURANI, *A History of the Arab Peoples*

An ordered world for the powerful, a disordered one for the powerless—
this was the geographic binary model (with its implied political threat)
whose resolution was entrusted to ʿAlī Mubārak during the twenty-five
years that passed between his writing *ʿAlam al-Dīn* and its publication in
1882. He was remarkably busy. During those years, he immersed himself in
careers as Minister of Schools and Minister of Public Works, jobs that made
him the architect of both a secular educational system and the reorganization of the streets and landmarks of Cairo. With the full support of the state
behind him, ʿAlī Mubārak became a primary agent of modernization. As
Timothy Mitchell describes it, "Laying out the streets of a city and planning
institutions of learning did not come together only by accident, by some
chance in the career of an exceptional individual." This conjunction of
opportunity and need "indicated the concerns of his age."[1] As the intensive
rebuilding of Cairo and the equally significant founding of schools showed,
he constructed his life and the lives of many others around the connectedness between "spatial order and personal discipline."[2]

Working under the orders of Khedive Ismaʿīl, with like-minded and
extremely capable colleagues such as Rifaʿah Rafiʿ al-Ṭahṭawī (who returned
to public service in 1863), ʿAlī Mubārak set up bureaus of public works,
instruction, and religious endowments in the center of the city. He opened
the School of Administration and Languages, the School of Surveying and
Accounting, the School of Ancient Languages, and a teacher training school.
A new railway station was built and, under his authority, an entire new
boulevard was dug through the middle of the old city.[3] Not only Cairo but
other cities, like Alexandria and Ṭanṭa, were reconstructed, and a new one,
Ismāʿīlīya, was built near the Suez Canal (completed in 1869).

64

As Mitchell explains, these great efforts were intended to make the state responsible for the education of its people and to create new generations of Egyptians nurtured in a Westernized, "ordered" system whose pragmatic training would enable them to become effective bureaucrats and officials of a more powerful and modern nation. Mubārak and al-Ṭahṭawī were thus projecting a new order onto a protonationalist ideal, one that envisioned a future community whose unity and identity had not yet been defined by either man. They worked for a ruler, Khedive Ismaʿīl (1863–1879) who envisioned making Egypt part of Europe under his leadership and who also entertained expansionist ambitions concerning the Sudan and other territories of East Africa. Though this ruler did employ certain native-born Egyptians like Mubārak and al-Ṭahṭawī as part of his effort to redefine Egypt as a political entity, he relied strongly on a bureaucratic system in which "access to the centre of power was determined by origin, personal connections and relations with the dynasty" of his grandfather, Muḥammad ʿAlī. Egyptians only rarely joined the ranks of the ruling classes of Ottoman Egyptians,[4] and when they did, they were "confined to jobs for which, according to Ismaʿīl, they showed special aptitude."[5] Ismaʿīl's discriminatory dreams would raise the issue of who should lead Egypt, while his expansionism into Africa would raise the issue of what form of the Egyptian empire should take. Ironically, both would provoke rebellions.

NEGOTIATING AN AFRICAN EMPIRE

Casting his ambitious gaze over the increasingly detailed maps of Egyptian Africa, which extended inch by inch up the Nile, and treaty by treaty along the Red Sea coast, Ismaʿīl stood poised over the Sudan, controlling territory as far east as ports in Abyssinia and as far south as Equatoria by 1874. But though he was ready to extend Egypt's reach into Africa, Ismaʿīl could not afford to be brash in disclosing his ambition. He told British diplomats that his intentions for Africa were not imperial but were of a reformist nature: to end the trade in slaves and to open new forms of trade with the East African heartland, thus civilizing peoples long excluded from international markets.[6] But in the eyes of many British observers, particularly members of the British and Foreign Anti-Slavery Society, Ismaʿīl's attempts at empire represented no civilizing mission, no opening of the dark continent to free trade, but instead were an extension of what seemed to them the notoriously despotic rule of Islam. For these abolitionists, a religion that sanctioned the seclusion of women and the trading of slaves could never encourage progress among other peoples.

The farther south Isma'il moved, therefore, the more vigilant the influential members of the Anti-Slavery Society became. Not only did they petition the khedive directly to abolish the slave trade, but they also had the ear of many individuals in Parliament and the Foreign Office. So loud were their voices that, by 1877, Isma'il signed the Anglo-Egyptian Slave Trade Convention. Under the terms of this treaty, Isma'il committed Egypt to abolition of the trade in African slaves, particularly those from the Sudan and Abyssinia. The treaty also permitted the participation of British forces in this campaign to end the slave trade.[7] This treaty was to be enforced by proclamation throughout the Sudan by officials hired by the khedive and with the assistance of the British government. An infrastructure of bureaus was created in all the provinces of Egypt, including the Sudan, to oversee the prohibition of all trade in African slaves and to arrest all offenders.[8]

Isma'il then decided that the employment of British officials in the Egyptian administration of the Sudan would silence his doubters in Exeter Hall, the London headquarters of the Anti-Slavery Society, and add the desired legitimacy to his consolidation of the Nile Valley.[9] He hired independent European military men, most of them English, to explore the uppermost regions of the Nile and to establish administrative outposts there. Men like Sir Samuel Baker and General Charles Gordon made their international reputations in the khedive's employ as they cemented his rule in east Africa. Isma'il hoped these English soldier-explorers would lend credibility to his projects in the Sudan in the eyes of European governments grown increasingly watchful and competitive over Africa. Political equality with Europe was crucial to Isma'il. He intended that reforms like the abolition of the African slave trade in Egypt and in the Sudan would promote Egypt's equality with the most advanced nations. And meanwhile, his internal reforms—building railways through Egypt, extending the telegraph service, creating more schools, even the opening of Cairo's first opera house and the promotion of native drama troupes—were intended to propel Egyptian society to greater parity with European culture.[10]

But his dreams outweighed his finances. The Egyptian treasury alone could not support the weight of these projects. The completion of the Suez Canal had necessitated getting the legal permission and financial assistance of several governments: France, Great Britain, the Ottoman Empire, and Egypt. For his part, Isma'il had had to negotiate with the French emperor and the Suez Canal Company for Egypt to be granted ownership of the land crossed by the canal. Isma'il paid 130 million francs for this right.[11] The many miles of railway and canals were built at tremendous expense, and Isma'il borrowed heavily, on unfavorable terms, from British, French, and

German banks. By 1876, the khedive had become so financially desperate that he was forced to sell 44 percent of Egypt's Suez Canal shares to the British government.[12] The situation was worsened by the fact that, since 1875, the Ottoman Empire had been facing bankruptcy, and, as a province of the empire, even with virtual political autonomy, Egypt's credit was intimately connected to that of the empire. By the spring of 1876, all hope was exhausted and Isma'il declared the Egyptian Treasury bankrupt (it was followed seven months later by the Ottoman Empire). The British and French governments, in support of their bondholders, reached an agreement in which an independent Anglo-French commission would assume the task of consolidating and administering the Egyptian government's debt repayments. Thus, by 1876, direct European control of Egyptian finances had begun. Isma'il struggled with this commission, known as the Caisse de la Dette Publique, or Dual Control, for three years, and used the unpopularity of the European commissioners to garner support for a pro-Isma'il Nationalist Party. The governments of Britain and France, encouraged by Germany and Austria, finally forced the Ottoman sultan to depose Isma'il in 1879. They installed Isma'il's son, Tawfiq, as the new khedive.

Before this, challenges to Isma'il's authority had emerged in the African arena as well. In 1877 the Egyptian army was still fighting an expensive and unresolved war against the Abyssinian king Menelik, begun in 1869.[13] Demoralized by their lack of success over the Abyssinian troops and stung by the government's financial difficulties that impeded the sending of reinforcements, many Egyptian officers blamed the incompetent strategies of their Circassian superiors for the defeats. Still, authority remained unshakably in the hands of these Turkish-speaking members of the ruling classes.[14] Egyptian soldiers were also losing their commissions as the strained budget dictated shrinking the army. Since the unsympathetic khedive was beholden to European creditors, he dismissed the appeals of Egyptian officers for their rights to promotion, back pay, and pensions.[15] In their anger and frustration, groups of officers gathered under Colonel Aḥmad 'Urābī and asked the khedive for the long-delayed back pay, for adequate pensions, increases in the number of enlisted soldiers, and an end to the monopoly on senior positions long held by Turco-Circassian officers. When they were turned down, the officers rebelled against their Turco-Circassian commanders.

During the same months of 1880 and early 1881 in which Colonel 'Urābī was gathering support for his protest of military conditions, a young religious leader named Muḥammad Aḥmad rallied the Sudanese with his call to evict what he called the "Turkish" administration from the Sudan. Muḥammad Aḥmad soon became known more popularly as the Mahdi, the "rightly guided one," and he attracted thousands with his promises to relieve Sudanese Muslims from overtaxation by the Egyptian administration and to end the government's attempts at abolition of the slave trade.

In September of 1881, 'Urābī Pasha's loyal officers staged a huge demonstration in front of 'Abdin Palace, the khedive's residence in Cairo, in which all the regiments of the army were represented. Khedive Tawfīq discovered that 'Urābī's popularity was even greater than he had estimated, and he was forced to listen to the new, expanded demands of the rebels.[16] 'Urābī assumed the powerful position of war minister. As 'Urābī's rebellion gained power in Cairo and Alexandria, the Mahdī's popularity fanned eastward across the Sudan. But 'Urābī and other ministers were preoccupied by their struggle with the khedive, even as telegraph after telegraph from increasingly desperate commanders communicated the spreading success of the Sudanese Mahdī.

By the end of May 1882, British naval forces had arrived in the Mediterranean and had trained their guns on the port city of Alexandria. In June, the gunboats bombarded Alexandria, provoking riots and causing great destruction and loss of life. As rumors of the massacres of Europeans in Alexandria reached the British, the British commander acted to put down what seemed a bloodthirsty, terrorist rebellion. Over the next three months, 'Urābī and his officers struggled to maintain order against the encroaching British forces and the machinations of the khedive, but all came to nothing in the fall of 1882, when the British navy occupied Alexandria, moved into Cairo, and arrested 'Urābī Pasha and his men. By the end of the year, Britain had occupied Egypt. With a haste just as ruthless, the Mahdī was circling the city of Khartoum, and in early 1883, he had control of almost all the Sudanese territory once held by the Egyptian government.

With the British occupation, all the goals of the "Egypt for the Egyptians" movement were lost, and so was the political autonomy of the Ottoman Egyptian ruling classes. Now, with their own authority to govern slipping through their fingers, Tawfīq's ministers awakened to the imminent loss of Egypt's long-held territory in the south. They pleaded with the British authorities to intercede on Egypt's behalf and put down the Mahdī's rebellion, but the new consul-general and agent, Lord Cromer, refused. He and his counterparts in the Foreign Office in London officially recognized Egypt's claims to the Sudan and the source of the Nile, yet the bankruptcy of Egypt's finances precluded the organization of any military campaign. In effect, the Egyptian bankruptcy meant that an empire that could not support itself lost its right to the name.[17]

Every Egyptian felt the impact of these quickly evolving and wrenching dramas: the humiliation of the British occupation replaced the cultural pride and nationalism that the 'Urābī rebellion had helped to inspire, and the uprising in the Sudan shocked Egyptians who considered themselves to be much more sophisticated, militarily and culturally, and more civilized than the Sudanese. The Mahdī and his success in the Sudan also became news items at a time when news traveled faster and in more sophisticated ways. Newly founded wire services like Reuters took full advantage of the expansion of the telegraph system between Cairo and Khartoum and quickened the spread of stories about the Sudan and its people. News of battles and maneuvers that would previously have taken weeks to arrive in Egypt's big cities was now announced immediately. The Sudan thus dramatically entered the emerging public discourse of Egyptians, a discourse fueled by an exploration of language, identity, and the symbols of shared culture then taking place among a new generation of writers and intellectuals, the inheritors of Isma'īl's ambitious attempts to redefine Egyptian education.[18] And with perhaps unintentional irony, these newspaper accounts reinforced the idea of the Sudan as part of Egypt even while the Mahdī's armies forcibly removed the region from Egyptian authority; just as it was lost to Egypt, the Sudan became a part of Egypt's idea of itself.

But what was this Sudan? Until 1884, the Sudan and Nubia were ostensibly united under the Egyptian aegis, yet throughout the nineteenth century the majority of Egyptians had little idea about real life in these two regions, and instead entertained highly romanticized and vague fantasies about life in Nubia or along the White Nile. Meanwhile, the Egyptian government had only recently completed the extension of its authority in Upper Egypt and Lower Nubia, a project it had begun a few decades previously, thereby establishing a modern administrative system where tribal authority had for so long dominated.[19] These provinces had a long history of trade and relations with the Sudan, but again, this fact was unknown to urban Egyptians, especially the intellectual heirs of 'Alī Mubārak and al-Ṭahṭawī, who were starting their newspapers and secret literary societies in Cairo and Alexandria. Years earlier, their ignorance about the region and its people would have made little difference, but by the 1870s, more and more Sudanese and Nubian people had moved into the cities of Lower Egypt, sometimes as slaves but increasingly as merchants and traders or doormen and gatekeepers.[20] This meant that just as Isma'īl's attempt at colonizing the Sudan reached its apogee, these subjects of the Egyptian empire began to create for themselves a presence in Cairo and Alexandria. They were an active part of the increasingly diverse mosaic of the Egyptian population.

As the writers that I examine in this chapter demonstrate, the presence of the Sudanese and the Nubians in Egypt during the late nineteenth century was crucial for the development of Egyptian national identity and for situating where Egyptians stood culturally in relation to Africa and Europe. Writers from this period repeatedly show their sensitivity to ethnic and racial differences among the residents of Egypt as they endeavor to define who was Egyptian and who was a foreigner. Increasingly, *foreigner* implied one of those closest to the ruling circles. Foreigners could be the pashas who surrounded the khedive and served as his ministers and highest officers. They could also be the increasing number of Europeans hired by the khedive for military service or as consultants, or the representatives of banks. They could be the Greek factory owners in towns. More and more, Egyptians were growing resentful of these "foreigners," particularly the Ottoman Egyptians, who were frequently open in their disdain for native Egyptians.[21] But black people fell into a different and much vaguer category. Whether they were Nubian or Sudanese, a single identity was projected onto them: that of *al-barbarī*, or the Nubian, whose color, customs, and accent Egyptian writers sketched out in numerous essays, dialogues, and stories. It is important to note here the distinction between Nubians and Sudanese. In the nineteenth century, the native homelands of Nubians extended from Upper Egypt to the northern Sudan, in the Wadi Halfa-Dongola region. Many Nubians did not speak Arabic at home, and they picked up what vocabulary they could when working in the cities of Egypt. Many Sudanese from the North came to Cairo as native speakers of Arabic. It was rare indeed for such a distinction to be made, so that in the work of most Egyptian writers of the period it is hard to find a Sudanese eloquent in spoken classical Arabic.[22]

It is easy, therefore, to understand why the issue of race was both volatile and intimate; it is also not surprising that this topic inspired some of the finest, most innovative writing in Arabic to have yet emerged in Egypt. In particular, Yaʿqūb Ṣanūʿa, a playwright and journalist, dedicated many articles and plays to his exploration of these questions, but he was not unique. The journalist and orator ʿAbdallah al-Nadīm and the Islamic reformers Shaykh Jamāl al-Dīn al-Afghānī and Shaykh Muḥammad ʿAbduh all had their say about the Sudanese and the Sudan. These writers scrutinized the complications of empire and its implications for Egypt, as the British moved closer toward occupation of their country and as the Sudan was dramatically lost to the Mahdī. They created for their readers small, meaningful literary portraits of Egypt. They all felt affected by the Sudan and the Sudanese. On this issue, Ṣanūʿa best expressed the idea that Egypt was a part of three empires—the Ottoman Empire, the British empire, and its own domestic empire in the Sudan—although all four writers conveyed a sense of this division of empire in their work.

ṢANŪ'A'S TWO SUDANS

The man considered by many scholars to have been the father of modern Egyptian playwrights was not a simple mouthpiece of "the people." Ṣanū'a was born into a well-educated Jewish family in 1839. As a child he was educated in both Hebrew and Arabic. Reportedly very precocious, he impressed a member of the royal family with his intelligence and his gift for languages and was sent to Italy to study. Soon after his return to Egypt, his father died, and he was compelled to take a job as a tutor to children of the relatives of Viceroy Muḥammad 'Alī. In 1863, the same year that Isma'īl became ruler of Egypt, Ṣanū'a began teaching at the Polytechnic School, one of Muḥammad 'Alī's original schools, which was organized on a European curriculum to educate soldiers and officers of the Egyptian army.[23] Interestingly, this school fell under the authority of 'Alī Mubārak and included students who, years later, would become prominent supporters of 'Urābī.

Ṣanū'a began writing plays in 1870, supported with great enthusiasm by Khedive Isma'īl. Ṣanū'a's plays were performed in colloquial Arabic, and often in front of audiences that included the khedive's circle, foreign dignitaries, and the highest echelons of Egyptian society.[24] Ṣanū'a's dramatic troupe enjoyed success for only a few years, however. Whether due to the malicious jealousy of 'Alī Mubārak, or to the machinations of certain British officials as Ṣanū'a later claimed, or to the khedive's anger at one play deemed too critical of polygamy, Ṣanū'a lost the khedive's support in 1872.[25] He then founded two literary groups: Maḥfil al-taqaddum (the Circle of Progress), followed by Jam'at Muḥibbi al-'ilm (The Society of Lovers of Knowledge). Both were dedicated to intellectual discussions among Egyptians, no matter their religion. Reformist-minded '*ulamā*' from al-Azhar joined, as did officers of the army. But these societies were short-lived. The khedive closed them in 1874, even exiling some of their members to the south of the Sudan.[26] For years Ṣanū'a was deprived of an outlet for his political views, which had become increasingly critical of Isma'īl's policies. Although he continued to socialize in the elite circles of the khedive's ministers, he declared himself to be angry with the khedive's policies. Finally, in 1877, he sought the protection of the Italian consulate and, with that protection secured, founded his satirical newspaper, *Abū Naẓẓara Zarqa* (The Man with the Blue Glasses), in early 1878 (see fig. 1).[27]

The humor and wit of Ṣanūʿa's journal, and its publication in the colloquial Arabic of urban Egypt, made it a successful and enduring organ of political dissent, even after Ṣanūʿa was exiled to Paris in 1878 (for the journal's critiques of the khedive). He continued to publish the journal in France, smuggling it into Cairo. The journal was popular, to the point where it was considered by many of his contemporaries to be one of the most important organs of the ʿUrābī rebellion.[28] Ṣanūʿa thus provides a reliable example of a duality around which Egyptian nationalism was beginning to take shape. This dichotomous approach to empire was articulated in racial terms. Although Ṣanūʿa was fiercely critical of Great Britain's imperialism in India and feared the same fate for Egypt, his work reveals an intimate empire, in which the Sudanese were the servants, guards, and doorkeepers of Egyptian society. Although the Sudan itself was depicted as a wild and untamed land, Sudanese residents in Egypt were often portrayed as docile, fearful, and in need of Egyptian guidance. As the following two excerpts show, Ṣanūʿa saw more than just a geographic border between the Sudan and Egypt: he saw a bridge of dependency as well.

In the first excerpt, which appeared in 1878, Ṣanūʿa offers a humorous glimpse of his fictional servant Muḥammad:

MUḤAMMAD THE NUBIAN *[in dialect]:* Please listen to me, sir, please keep your eyes wide open because, I swear by the Prophet and our Lady Zaynab, some of the khedive's men *[awlād al-haram]* are right behind you. I've seen them when you leave here, one guy wearing pants, the other a suit.

ABŪ NAẒẒARA: Stop talking that nonsense, boy. Are you afraid?

THE NUBIAN: Me, scared? No, by God, we Nubians fear nothing except God and His prophet; as for fearing other men, we are not like the Egyptian peasants. But see here, sir, yesterday after you went out, a gentleman came here and asked us "Where's your master, boy?" I said he was at the store. He said, "No, I'm asking about Monsieur James." I said to him, "He's not here." So he said to me, "OK, then where's his room?" I asked him what did he want with it. He said, "I want to see it, and bring me a cigarette." But we Nubians are stubborn. . . . He said, "Okay, give me the papers in the box and I'll pay you two pounds."

ABŪ NAẒẒARA: You weren't convinced, clever one.

THE NUBIAN: I wasn't convinced and I stepped back and closed the door, but still, keep your eyes on the khedive's men.

[Knocking heard at the door. The Nubian jumps at the sound.].

ABŪ NAẒẒARA: Go see who is knocking at the door.

1.   Self-portrait of Ya'qūb Ṣanū'a, published in Paul de
Baignières, *L'Égypte satirique: L'Album d'Abou Naddara*
(Paris: Imprimerie Lefebvre, 1886).

THE NUBIAN: Don't open it, sir!

ABŪ NAẒẒARA: Go open it, my boy, don't be afraid. I'm right here.[29]

As the servant of Abū Naẓẓara, Muḥammad guards his employer against
the aggressive surveillance of the government's men sent by a khedive who
has become deeply suspicious of Ṣanū'a's involvement in clandestine political activities. Muḥammad and Abū Naẓẓara stand at more than just the
doorway of the latter's rooms: they stand at the threshold of Ṣanū'a's actual
exile—this was the first issue of *Abū Naẓẓara Zarqa* to be published after
the writer's banishment to Paris. Despite the Nubian's claims that such
emotions were foreign to him, he is clearly afraid, and Abū Naẓẓara pater-

2. Caricature of the Sudanese Mahdī, from *Abū Naẓẓara Zarqa*, 1883.

nalistically comforts him and exhorts him to calm down. Ṣanū'a allows Muḥammad's fear and naïveté to cloak his own. Muḥammad also raises the question of Egyptian identity again, with his purported ignorance and Ṣanū'a's manipulation creating a pun, in Arabic, on the idea of *awlad al-haram*. In the 1870s, this term was an epithet for Egyptians and also bore another meaning: "sons of filthy hags." I am interpreting Muḥammad the Nubian's expression as an articulation of Ṣanū'a's epithet for the khedive and his minions, the official "Egyptians" worthy only of his contempt. Although directly related to the dramatic turn Ṣanū'a's political life was taking, Muḥammad's fear also provided comic relief. Drawn upon the familiar lines of Sudanese and Nubians represented in early Egyptian drama, this Nubian buffoon's fears and mispronunciations made him a sympathetic, unthreatening, and infantile character for Egyptians, a comfortable gatekeeper of domestic life during a time of great political upheaval.

In his drawings of the Sudanese Mahdī, published several years later, the miraculously successful rebellion in the Sudan against British and Egyptian forces forced Ṣanū'a to rethink his representations of the Sudanese, at least those still living and fighting in the Sudan. As the first cartoon illustrates, a dignified Mahdī extends his arms and his unsheathed sword over the heads of his followers, who gather excitedly around him before going into battle against the British (see fig. 2). The Mahdī does not look down at the men

3.   Caricature of the Sudanese Mahdī addressing his followers, from *Abū Nazzara Zarqa*, 1885.

circled around him, but at the reader, and the caption underneath describes the scene simply as a speech to his men. Facing an even greater challenge than that seen by Ṣanū'a and his servant, the Mahdī and his men show no fear, only heroism. Ṣanū'a drew the strength of this Mahdī in even larger strokes in the second cartoon, published in 1885, in which the figure of England, a feeble old lady, stands dwarfed between her two biggest foreign policy problems, Russia and the Sudan (see fig. 3). This time, the Sudan is personified as an obese man with a dagger hanging from his robe, about to gobble up tiny British soldiers. The Sudan figure here is exaggerated and oversized, but not infantilized. This warrior represented the external, foreign Sudanese for Ṣanū'a, not always understandable but ever worthy of respect, different from the domesticated brother who worked in the interior world of Egyptian society.[30]

How did Ṣanū'a come to sketch such drastically different images of Sudanese figures? From the early 1870 to 1872, when he was writing his short plays in colloquial Arabic and having them performed, through his first issues of *Abū Nazzara Zarqa*, published from 1875 to 1878, Ṣanū'a's writings incorporated a tradition of cultural stereotypes about Nubians and Sudanese that had long been found in Egyptian popular entertainment. Was he questioning these stereotypes by reflecting them so boldly in these early dramas? Or was he reinforcing them? Did the political turbulence of the Mahdīya truly cause him to reassess the situation in the Sudan and perhaps the awareness of the Sudanese around him, thus enabling him to cast these old caricatures in new roles?

After 1878, exile further changed Ṣanūʿa's vision and his perspective on Egypt. He missed the actual rebellion of Colonel ʿUrābī. Unable to see first-hand the effects of the failed rebellion and the British occupation—and under the influence of the increasingly dramatic news of the Sudanese uprising from within his homeland—his writings from overseas assumed a much more idealistic tone toward Egypt and the Sudan. Ṣanūʿa recognized the importance of the Mahdīya, but he misjudged how deep a blow the Mahdīya's success was to Egyptian nationalism. And though the Mahdī's rebellion shrank Egypt's borders (both imagined and physical), Ṣanūʿa saw the Mahdī as an ally in the Egyptian struggle against the increasing British presence, a presence he considered to be a direct challenge to Egyptian polit-ical aspirations. He wrote many articles about the Sudan and Egypt joining together to defeat their common enemy, misinterpreting the message of the Mahdī's revolution completely.

So who were the new Sudanese in Ṣanūʿa's work? For Ṣanūʿa in exile, Egypt became a dreamed-of place, always hovering between its new position as an occupied country and the desired status of a free nation. Imagined from afar, Egypt was populated by archetypes lifted from Ṣanūʿa's memory and nostalgia. True to these old stereotypes, the new Sudanese characters in Ṣanūʿa's writings never acted or spoke in their own interest; they answered to and for Egyptians. The Sudan may have seemed transformed from an Egyptian colony into a bulwark of anti-British imperialism, but the trans-formation never shed the imprint of the past; Muḥammad the Nubian's servitude to his Egyptian employer metamorphosed into the ferocious pro-tectiveness shown by the Mahdī for Egypt, against the British, the new men knocking at the door.

THE WRITER AND THE KHEDIVE: ECHOING THE LANGUAGE OF EXPANSIONISM AND NATIONALISM

Nationalist writers like Ṣanūʿa helped create Khedive Ismaʿīl's reputation for deceit and greed, and held him culpable for bankrupting Egypt and eventu-ally causing it to be occupied by the British. But it is important to under-stand that, without Ismaʿīl, there might not have been the schools to educate these writers, nor the opportunities for cultural renaissance like the opening of local theaters and newspapers. In many important ways, the autocratic and careless Ismaʿīl was himself the engine behind Egypt's *nahḍa* (renais-sance). He was also the first to manipulate the language of nationalism, to employ double meanings when referring to Egypt's position in the Middle East and Africa. This linguistic creativity emerged first when Ismaʿīl heralded his control of substantial parts of the Sudan and East Africa. He could not claim this as empire building, not with all the scrutiny by and objections of British members of Parliament and the Anti-Slavery Society, but he could continue to call it a civilizing mission. And, adding to the heteroglossic confusion about the word *empire*, a heated debate during and after the years of expansion focused on one particular question: in exactly whose name, Egypt's or the Ottoman Empire's, was Isma'il acting when he moved into eastern Africa? Furthermore, as he lost more and more control of Egypt's finances to the banks of western Europe, he defended "Egyptian" independence. Although he clearly meant his own independence and that of his ministers, the term quickly accumulated different meanings.[31]

The linguistic schizophrenia of Isma'il's imperialist policies in Africa coincided with an increased cultural sensitivity to political language that took place in Egyptian society during the *nahḍa*. In addition to pointing out the political uses of language, writers from across the intellectual and cultural spectrum of Egyptian society paid careful attention to Isma'il's activities in Africa and their contradictory results: the irresolute strategies of the Egyptian army in the Abyssinian campaigns; the fears of Egyptian soldiers stationed in the Sudan who had looked to the army as an opportunity for upward mobility and who were now threatened by the Dual Control's demand that the military be reduced; the extensive and much-publicized plans for the building of the railroad and telegraph system connecting Egypt to the Sudan;[32] and the 1877 treaty abolishing the slave trade in the Sudan. Although many of the frustrated officers, bureaucrats, and intelligentsia disagreed with Isma'il on his autocratic ideas about government in Egypt and disliked his exploitation of the country's resources and manpower for exploration of Sudanese territories, they ingested the basic idea of his ambitions for the Sudan with little question. No matter how distant it seemed culturally, nor how obscure its people, the Sudan belonged, by nature of geography and tradition, to Egypt.[33]

Many of the writers of the *nahḍa* saw the Sudan as wild territory that needed to be conquered according to Isma'il's wishes. The ideas of subjugation and control were intimately bound up with almost all aspects of the Sudan's relationship to Egypt. At times, the Sudan stood for exile, the terrible place to which one could be forcibly removed from life in Egypt, as al-Ṭahṭawī so vividly recounted. Egyptian rulers, beginning with Muḥammad 'Alī, had a long tradition of exiling rivals and enemies to the region of Tokar or the penal camp in Fazughlī. In the nineteenth century, it took a very long time to travel to the Sudan: twenty-seven days to go from Aswan in Upper Egypt to Khartoum in the north of the Sudan. Articles in newspapers like *al-Ahram* brought this point home to their readers in Cairo and Alexandria.[34] The use of the Sudan as a site of exile reinforces even further the almost schizophrenic constructions of the Sudan as both a natural part of Egypt and a place for the removal of Egyptians from Egypt. And even when such removal was not officially a prison sentence, as when bureaucrats were ordered there for service in the administration of the territory, it symbolized autochthonous bureaucrats' dispensability and their distance from the workings of government. Like al-Ṭahṭawī, many Egyptian civil employees who were sent to the Sudan grew deeply embittered. For them, the province was the farthest possible distance from Cairo, and a site at which there was little chance for advancement.[35]

The land itself was forbidding, its heat considered overwhelming even for Egyptians accustomed to the intense sun of the Sahara. From the first exploratory expedition led by Qapudan in 1840 to the famous Nile odyssey of Sir Samuel Baker in the 1860s, reports that floated back to Egypt told of the dense vegetation that physically blocked ships' passage up the White Nile in various parts of the Sudan.[36] The farther south into the Sudan explorers trekked, the farther away from the influence of Islam they wandered. There, they confronted tribes with unrecognizable costumes and customs that only intensified the wild image of the Sudan.

Yet, if the land itself seemed a frightening and foreign place, its immigrants to Egypt came across as tame. Throughout most of the century, the Sudanese in Egypt guarded houses and harems; cleaned and cooked as servants and slaves; traded camels, gum, and feathers; and drove carriages.[37] Their presence in the doorways and kitchens of Egyptian households made them familiar icons of the domestic scene, very much the caretakers of daily life. In most of their roles the Sudanese were in subservient positions, helping and supporting Egyptian family structures. But the majority of Egyptians do not seem to have seen the Sudanese or Nubians beyond this iconographic level, as the experiences of Nubian traders and guild members attested to in the late 1870s. Many of these men found that the Egyptian guilds discriminated against them, and they made their own appeals for independent guilds, so difficult was their integration.[38]

In their literature of the 1870s, Egyptians compressed these contradictory images of the Sudan and the Sudanese into stereotypes. These images go far in revealing Egypt's ambivalence about imperialism and where Egyptians saw their society fitting into a political world in which empire building had become so important. On one hand, Egyptian writers depicted subdued and dependent Sudanese servants as familiar characters in domestic Egyptian life. On the other hand, there was this savage and unknown territory from which these familiar people came. The idea emerged, powerfully, that the Sudanese benefited from crossing over into Egyptian culture, and that the civilizing hand of the Egyptian government would tame the awesome territory of the Sudan itself. After 1882, the failure of 'Urābī's forces and the British occupation occurred within the context of the European scramble for Africa, a context about which Egyptians were growing more aware thanks to the spread of newspapers and journals in their country. A third, disquieting element entered Egyptians' ideas of territorial conquest in Africa. This was the uncomfortable realization that, in the eyes of western European culture, Egypt stood somewhere closer to Africa than to Europe when measured on a scale that calibrated the achievements of each civilization, and that Egypt was just as vulnerable to conquest and colonization as the Sudan. Against this tense and conflicted background, Egyptian writers and politicians labored to assert Egypt's separateness from such vulnerability in their descriptions and characterizations of their own society.

Both the popularity of translated French, Italian, and English popular literature and increased travel to European cities reinforced this self-consciousness, as educated Egyptians saw themselves being molded into characters for European readers, and as Egyptian society was itself displayed in well-organized exhibitions across Europe.[39] As Egyptians' awareness of the Sudan increased, Europeans stepped more and more often into the African landscape, making Egyptians even more sensitive to their own vulnerability to European expansionism. Isma'īl contributed further to Egypt's confused identify as a would-be imperialist power when, in efforts to legitimize his ambitious plans for conquering East Africa, he hired Europeans like General Charles Gordon to take charge of the administration in the Sudan and of the exploration surveys up the White Nile. Other surveys were sponsored by their own governments, as the European powers began claiming territory in Africa. European encroachment in Africa became, for many nationalists, uncomfortably linked to Egyptian interests there, evoking a powerful proprietary feeling toward the Sudan. And this sense of European menace enshrined the important contradiction of Egyptian nationalism: the fight against European imperialism that marched hand-in-hand with the fight to regain imperial control of the Sudan.

Under these pressures, Egyptians tried to identify what they valued in their cultural and political lives, as well as what had to be reformed. This required naming Egyptian culture: what was indigenous and what was foreign, what was "national" and what was alien. As Benedict Anderson describes it, Egyptians in the 1870s were beginning the process of imagining their community, and they were using newspapers, short stories, and plays to do it.[40] These became tools with which to create identifiably Egyptian characters, whose accents, expressions, and circumstances—though usually rendered in symbolic, almost stereotypic, terms—became emblems of Egyptian social and cultural unity. But differing somewhat from writers of other cultures included in Anderson's brilliant presentation of the birth of literature among colonized peoples of the nineteenth century, Egyptian writers existed in a greater colonialist limbo: not yet independent from the Ottoman Empire, but not quite colonized by Great Britain. Furthermore, Anderson posits that this adoption of print media was an expression of cultural revolution and anti-imperialism among the colonized. In Egypt, however, the artists and writers who were helping to fashion this imagined community were themselves parading Egyptian society along a very traditional stage. Their characters were locked into a recognizable series of linguistic, stereotypical tics. Perhaps this made it easier for them to be imagined.

VOICES OF TRUE EGYPT

Despite the pride in his native tongue that his stay overseas instilled in him, Ṣanūʿa learned to view his native country with the perspective of an outsider. He turned a new eye on other Egyptians and their circumstances: the position of women, the plight of the *fallah,* the poverty of street beggars, the humor of entertainers, and the frustration of soldiers. Using criteria learned in Europe, he began to define "Egyptian-ness," beginning with language as the first and largest building block. In this sense, Ṣanūʿa was very much a man of his times. As Gendzier writes, men like him

> belonged to the second generation brought up in the Egyptian Kultur-kampf that had been based on the adaptation of western ideas. In a more personal way, they were also the products of Ismaʿil's ambition; to the extent that he believed a cultural renaissance indispensable to the achievement of his goals, he subsidized the labors of a group of hand-picked intellectuals. That they eventually turned against him was tragicomic proof of the success of his westernizing mission.[41]

Ṣanūʿa first expressed his sense of Egyptian identity in his plays. Though far from being the first to introduce drama to Egyptian audiences, he was the first to set his plays in Egyptian households, with characters speaking in the everyday rhythms of colloquial Arabic. In this way, Egypt, or more particularly, Cairo, becomes the backdrop against which Ṣanūʿa presented Egyptians with an image of themselves. The brevity of these plays precludes character-building of great depth, as does the satiric tone. Ṣanūʿa created characters out of recognizable characteristics, some that the audience would find endearingly familiar, others that symbolized foreigners. These types fit into a social niche, particularly the Sudanese; through the proverbs and jokes his characters make about them, Ṣanūʿa offers a glimpse into where the Sudanese fit in the domestic, everyday life of Cairene society.

Ṣanūʿa used his plays to criticize what he saw as the deterioration of values and respect for others in Egyptian life, and was especially bitter about the greed exhibited by the members of Cairo's ruling class, those who exploited the peasant and who imitated too well the avarice of European financiers. In *Būrṣat Miṣr* (The Stock Market of Egypt), Ṣanūʿa confronts the issues of arranged marriages and this new greed.[42] The play begins in front of the stock market building, where a wealthy young character has sent her servant, Faraj, to find her lover and warn him that she can no longer wait to inform her father of their intentions to get married. Faraj turns to the audience and describes his futile attempt to enter the market hall:

> I went into the stock market trying to see my master *[al-khawāja]*. This Nubian grabbed me at the door and said to me, "Servants don't come in here. Servants have no business here in the stock market. Leave, peasant. You have no business here. Go sweep your master's room, and [straighten up] the straw. Go!"[43] And he shoved me until there were only a few centimeters between me and the door. What could I say? Even the Nubians get their day. All that comes from the gentlemen who spoil them.[44]

The subtlety of this humor emerges in the fact that this is an Egyptian peasant imitating the accent of the Sudanese. In this instance, as so frequently happens in Ṣanūʿa's plays, the *fallaḥīn* represents one of the true voices of Egypt, albeit a humorous one, replete with a great deal of ignorance about the surrounding world. Faraj's words here perform two important functions: the first a reformist function illustrating how social change in Egypt had not been extended to the *fallaḥīn*, the second a corrective function, putting the Nubian in his appropriate social place by means of a verbal agreement between the character Faraj and his audience. The imitation of the Nubian accent cements that agreement. As Jacob Landau and others note in their analyses of early Egyptian drama, the strangeness of an accent, in Arabic, delineated the degree of foreignness of the speaking character.[45] Images of Turkish-speaking pashas were always good for a laugh, especially when they stumbled through the colloquial Arabic of Egypt as they tried to issue orders to the subject class of the *fallaḥīn*. This situation represented an ironic view of the unsuitability of the pashas as rulers that resulted from their linguistic distance from Egyptian culture. Accents provided a social map of all classes. The mistakes characters made, the vocabulary they used, all worked to distinguish them on a social, economic, national, ethnic, and racial scale.[46] This acute sensitivity to the social stratification of Egyptian society ran through plays like Ṣanūʿa's, with their characterization of British officials, whose butchery of the Egyptian dialect, and stubborn insistence on communicating in classical Arabic, revealed the hollowness of their claim to familiarity with the culture.

There is an interesting uneasiness about economic and political power within Ṣanūʿa's humorous linguistic depictions. Both the Ottoman elite and the British officials are cut down to size by their accents and grammatical mistakes when speaking in colloquial Arabic, and they are further humiliated by the witty asides of the Egyptian characters confronting them. These portraits, or dramatic cartoons, also reveal another side to the issue of authority, as they stress the rightfulness, or normalcy, of Egyptian authority. Egyptians may not have been at the source of economic and political power in their society, but Ṣanūʿa's assertion of linguistic dominance shows where cultural power lay. The Egyptian characters are thus able to undermine foreign domination of their society. Yet, in a fascinating exercise of linguistic anxiety, they undermine the dominance of others only by *imitating* and mocking the speech of authority.

Ṣanūʿa clearly defines who is an Egyptian by the way his characters speak, but he is not as clear when it comes to the Sudanese or Nubians. In plays and other representations of the time, the Sudanese were just as constant a source of laughter when they spoke. But with the Sudanese, many of whom spoke Arabic as their native tongue, the linguistic stereotyping assumes another dimension in assertions of Egyptian authority. The Sudanese and Nubian characters' problems in Arabic come not from having a poor grasp of grammar or a lack of vocabulary, as the Turks and British had, but from a seeming inability to pronounce key Arabic letters correctly, for instance, the ʿayn, the hard *h*, and the kaf. There emerges, then, a linguistic tutorial between Egyptian and Nubian in Ṣanūʿa's work, in which the Egyptian instructs the latter in how to speak his native tongue. The lessons are dictated by educated, middle- to upper-class Egyptians.[47] This tutorial reinforces the intimate ties between Egyptian and Sudanese cultures while also repeating the pattern and goals of domination established by both the khedive's foreign policy and the traditional employment of the Sudanese as servants in Egyptian homes. Given this, Faraj's complaint about the Nubian's presumption of authority over him takes on added resonance. Just as interesting is his attribution of the Nubian's arrogance to the gentlemen *(khawajāt)* who "spoil" people like him, elevating them to positions for which Faraj perhaps sees himself better suited, which calls to mind the mission of civilizing the Sudan assumed by the Egyptian government.

Even within the confines of conversation, Egyptians thus maintained the parameters of Sudanese roles in their society, and complained when these borders were crossed. The issue of Sudanese overstepping these social boundaries reappears, in much more detail, in the play *Abū Rida wa Kaʿb al-Khayr* (Abū Rida and Kaʿb al-Khayr). In this play, people from both the highest strata of society and the peasant class raise their eyebrows at what they perceive to be Sudanese presumptions of social airs. The play shows starkly how race and ethnicity competed with wealth and family name in Egyptians' construction of society. Here, the salon of a wealthy home becomes a battleground for questions of identity. Abū Rida is a Nubian servant in the home of Banbah, an unmarried, perhaps widowed, woman of substance (the play leaves her exact status unclear). He is in love with Kaʿb al-Khayr, who is also Nubian and who works as a domestic in the same household. Abū Rida tells his mistress of his passion for Kaʿb al-Khayr, and she swears to him that she will help him arrange a marriage to this woman, who was a slave and had been freed upon the death of Banbah's father. Unfortunately for Abū Rida, Kaʿb al-Khayr absolutely refuses to marry him. Meanwhile, a neighborhood matchmaker, Mabrūka, tells Banbah that the Khawaja Nakhla is in love with her and desires marriage. Banbah is interested but tied to her oath to Abū Rida, and she tells Mabrūka that she cannot be married until she settles the love problems of Abū Rida.

As in other Ṣanūʿa plays, the jokes often are contained within the accents of the protagonists; Abu Rida uses what seems to be a stereotypical pattern of Nubian speech, with no hard *h*, and no ʿayn. Kaʿb al-Khayr speaks with an even harder accent. The play opens with Abū Rida in the front parlor, sweeping and singing a rhymed poem about the beauty of his beloved and her cooking abilities. With his back to the door of the parlor, he does not see Banbah enter, so when she speaks to him, he responds as if she were Kaʿb al-Khayr. The following dialogue reveals the boundaries of their relationship, clearly defined by Banbah.

BANBAH: You still haven't finished cleaning the room? Time is flying.

ABŪ RIDA: Oh, it's getting cleaned, my darling.

BANBAH: Darling?! You call me darling?! What's wrong with your brain, have you gone mad? You are truly shameless. Get out, you pig. You don't actually think . . . you take me for one of those who believe whites and blacks to be equal? I am not like that. Go on, get out of my house. Go find yourself a woman from those who see you as an equal.

ABŪ RIDA: I implore you, my lady, forgive me. I thought you were Kaʿb al-Khayr and I was telling you of my love for you.

BANBAH: So you're flirting with the slave girl instead of attending to your
work.

ABŪ RIDA: No, my lady, on the life of the Prophet, I'm doing my work and
I'm not flirting. We love Ka'b al-Khayr from afar and we still
haven't told her, not one word. I swear by the prophets Hassan
and Hussein. Love, my lady, is killing your servant.

BANBAH [*to herself*]: Well, this is a strange affair. I believe it now when
people say the world is getting more civilized, to the point where
Nubians court each other. [*To Abū Rida:*] So what do you want
with Ka'b al-Khayr?

ABŪ RIDA: We, my lady, know that the forbidden is not the permissible.
We fear the forbidden.[48]

With even greater indignation than that displayed by Faraj, the peasant character from the play *Būrṣat Miṣr*, Banbah excoriates Abū Rida for daring to
mix love and race. And, as Ṣanū'a's lines make clear, her indignation is not
provoked by Abū Rida's status as a servant (in fact, Ṣanū'a repeatedly criticized the snobbery of rich Egyptians and the airs they took in relation to
their poorer neighbors), but by his color. Her other discovery, that Nubians
actually court each other, exemplifies an attitude prevalent in other contemporary sources as well, that Nubians and Sudanese were sexually uncon-
trolled and voracious, unconcerned with the amenities of legal marriage.

It is hard to know if Ṣanū'a is presenting a satiric portrait of a young
upper-class woman when he puts these words in Banbah's mouth, and thus
criticizing this kind of racial divide. I think Juan Cole's assessment of the
interplay between journalist and reader is applicable to the communication
between audience and playwright (in his discussion of journalists, Cole
addresses Ṣanū'a as well). As Cole states, "Their [the dissident journalists']
political essays constituted an open text with which the audience could
interact, teasing out their full semiotic implications. In this conception, audiences formed no helpless target of a fully elaborated, crystalline discourse,
but rather constituted partners in the enterprise of sign generation and
interpretation. Dissident journalism, especially given the circumlocution
and ambiguity forced on it by censorship, was a game it took two to play."[49]
This same intimate comprehension and exchange of meanings is responsible for the resonance of these Sudanese characters for both Ṣanū'a and his
audience. Abū Rida, however lovable, is replete with tics that identify him to
the audience as a familiar, but non-Egyptian, prop in Egyptian life. If Cole's
formulation about the communicative patterns between writer and audience
are correct, then perhaps Ṣanū'a was articulating native Egyptians' anger at
Ottoman Egyptians' assumptions of superiority, which would mean that,

on some level, they would sympathize with Abū Rida. On another level, Banbah would be speaking for them in her assertion of Egyptians' rights to be just as lordly as Circassians.

If some sympathy between Abū Rida and Ṣanū'a's audience was evoked, then Abū Rida is only a mouthpiece, but one who does not speak directly about the difficult social position of Nubians in late-nineteenth-century Egypt. In other ways, Nubians in Ṣanū'a's plays are not permitted to speak on their own terms. Nowhere does the author, a linguist, seem to have studied their dialect as carefully as he did that of Upper Egyptians and the Lebanese. His knowledge of Turkish, which he displays continuously as the rulers of Egypt mangle Arabic, reveals an impressive awareness of Turkish conjugations. The Nubians speak a bastardized Cairene dialect, and even their attempts at love and its poetry raise the eyebrows of Ṣanū'a's Egyptians.

When attempting poetic expression in a mangled form of classical Arabic, the Nubian and Sudanese characters surprise the Egyptian characters. When assuming greater social status than the Egyptian characters of Ṣanū'a believe they warrant, the black characters anger and provoke them. But when they act ignorant and respectful of the help provided by more educated Egyptians, they become lovable. Abū Rida, for example, goes out to the market for Banbah and, upon his return, tries to explain to her how much he spent per item. He adds it up incorrectly, and Banbah attempts to explain his mistake to him:

ABŪ RIDA: You're wrong, my lady, you're wrong. We added up the sums with our brother Driss four times yesterday. And if you don't believe me, go ahead and blame him. I swear, on your head, my lady, that Abū Rida is not wrong.

BANBAH *[laughing]:* The five cents, you donkey, were for the tomatoes, which we added up twice.

ABŪ RIDA: You're right, my lady, you're right. It's clear that love has not entered your heart nor made your head soar like Abū Rida's head.

BANBAH *[laughing to herself]:* I really like this Nubian. He makes me laugh and keeps my mind off my own troubles. *[To Abū Rida:]* OK, go back to the market, because I hear Ka'b al-Khayr coming in.[50]

If Abū Rida is adorably befuddled by his love for Ka'b al-Khayr, she is only ignorant, and unpleasantly so. The slave girl enters the room right after Abū Rida leaves, and the following exchange takes place:

BANBAH *[to herself]:* This one I don't like. *[To Ka'b al-Khayr:]* Abū Rida has just gone to the market for a bit and will be coming back soon.

KA'B AL-KHAYR *[looking around the room]*: My lady, my lady, don't you
see the trash in the basket? . . . That Abū Rida, may God curse
him, he didn't clean up this room at all. By God, my lady, that
Nubian, better for you to let him go and hire a real servant in his
place who works like the servant of the neighbors. He doesn't
sweep or dust or clean and everything falls on my head. Abū Rida
doesn't work, he just eats and drinks and keeps his eyes open for
money. Throw him out of your house.

BANBAH *[to herself]*: She really recommends him. *[To Ka'b al-Khayr:]*
What did he do to you that you hate him so much?

KA'B AL-KHAYR: My lady, a Nubian like that, what could he do to me? He
comes in with his little game, but I wouldn't let a Nubian like that
do anything to me, my lady. I don't like the Nubian race *[jins al-
barābira]*.

BANBAH *[to herself]*: From her talk it seems she prefers one of the
Mamlūks. *[To Ka'b al-Khayr:]* But Abū Rida loves you and wants
to marry you, and he's a good boy, and a proper one too.

KA'B AL-KHAYR: You say he's a good and proper boy? Believe me, he's a
scoundrel *[ibn haram]*. There's no worse fellow among all the
Nubians. You say he loves me? If he loved me he wouldn't try to
talk to Bakhīta, the slave girl next door, and tell her eyes are like
the evening and . . . her cheeks are like apples. He never said anything like that to me, so how can he love me and want to marry
me? He's a liar, my lady, he just wants to take my gold earrings
from my ears and my anklets off my legs, and my silver bracelets
from my hands and give them to Bakhīta as a gift and go to her
village, where both of them will laugh at Ka'b al-Khayr.[51]

Banbah discerns from Ka'b al-Khayr's long complaint that she is jealous, and
really is interested in Abū Rida. Her comment on Ka'b al-Khayr's dislike of
Nubians, that "she prefers one of the Mamlūks" employs a common nineteenth-century epithet for the ruling class of Ottoman Egyptians, descendants of the slave-soldiers taken, as children, from Anatolia, the Balkans, and
later the Circassian region, and who rose as military leaders and ruled Egypt
from the twelfth to the sixteenth centuries.[52] Banbah ironically contests any
desire of Ka'b al-Khayr either to perceive herself as a marriageable peer to
the white "Mamlūks" (who had real social power) or to distance herself as
a black slave from the social caste of other Nubians.

Far from distinguishing between Abū Rida and Ka'b al-Khayr, Mabrūka,
the matchmaker, finds the entire Nubian presence in the drama of love and
marriage irrelevant. It intrudes on her attempts to marry Banbah off to the
wealthy gentleman, Nakhla, and thus to earn her commission. She com-

plains about having to help the Nubian, saying, "OK, brother, let's now deal with this affair, and see what we can do with this son-of-a-bitch Nubian and Ka'b al-Khayr *al-zarbūna*."[53] With a historical emphasis that Ṣanū'a's audience would have immediately understood, the last word speaks volumes to the Nubians, with its implication of "once a slave, always a slave."[54]

Mabrūka uses Abū Rida to situate herself higher on the social scale. In the following scene, all the parties are sitting together, and Abū Rida begs Mabrūka to help him. His pronunciation of certain words launches the joke of the scene (pronunciation that is hard to see in the translation):

ABŪ RIDA: Get me married, my lady, marry me off quick or love will kill me.

MABRŪKA: What?! God forbid I should marry a Nubian. Bless my late husband's soul, now there was a man.

ABŪ RIDA: Not you marrying me, I have no taste for old women.

MABRŪKA: I'm an old woman? The hell you say, you Nubian. I have to be the go-between for this? Ka'b al-Khayr is wasted on this Nubian![55]

Ka'b al-Khayr continues to refuse marriage, denying Mabrūka the chance to profit from the match of Banbah and Nakhla and trying the matchmaker's patience, until finally Mabrūka erupts, exclaiming, "Oooh, this slave girl is being so coy *[tata'ziz]*, like she's the daughter of the prince. Even slaves have their day. May God damn her!"[56] Finally, after passionate protestations of love from Abū Rida, who threatens to kill himself if she refuses to marry him, Ka'b al-Khayr breaks down and agrees. In the very last line of the play, Abū Rida issues a statement of fact to his audience: "O sirs! You bring young Nubians here to serve as your groomsmen."[57] It is a curious ending for the play, implying how little of Nubian servants many Egyptians knew, as if all the romantic activity previously staged was a glimpse into a secret world. But the ending line also reasserts the rigidity of the reason for the presence of Nubians in Egyptian homes—to serve.

If there is any doubt as to the self-consciousness of Ṣanū'a's characterizations of Nubians, it is quickly dispelled by his play about his writing and his theater, *Moliere Misr wa ma yuqasīhi* (The Egyptian Molière and What He Suffered). In it, Ṣanū'a dramatizes the financial difficulties of his troupe, how half of his actors refused to perform any more until they were paid, and how the plays were, when possible, rehearsed. His instructions for how to make Nubian accents sound humorous are clear. In the following scene, he directs a rehearsal between Matilda, the actress portraying Banbah, and Habib, who portrays Abū Rida.

MATILDA: In the skit "Abū Rida the Nubian," I play Sitt Banbah and Abū
    Rida is my servant. So come on, Habib, play the Nubian and check
    my speech *[ward ʿala kalamī]*.

HABIB: I've memorized the role of the Nubian. Remember your voice,
    which is prettier than the cooing of pigeons.

MATILDA *[imitating Banbah]:* You still haven't finished cleaning the room,
    and time is flying.

HABIB *[imitating Abū Rida, with the corresponding accent]:* We've been
    cleaning and sweeping since morning, and by the Prophet, Abū
    Rida's word is true. O my sweetheart, O my beauty.

MATILDA: I'm your sweetheart, you slave *[zarbūn]?* I am your mistress,
    cursed one. I am a free woman, you Nubian, you rotten bum *[ya
    mafsūd]*, not like those who consider blacks and whites to be
    equal *[mish min illi ʿandahum ʿala ḥad sawa al-bayḍ wa al-sūd]*.

JAMES *[to Matilda]:* Brilliant, my girl, just right, tonight all the notables
    will be applauding you and tossing flowers to you.[58]

Banbah-Matilda's rebuke to Abū Rida is even harsher in this play-within-
the-play, with her calling him a *zarbūn* and insisting that she is a "free
woman" unlike those who believe blacks and whites to be socially equal.[59]
This is a fascinating presentation of the actual construction of a stereotype
and the importance, particularly for the actor Habib, of properly mimicking
the accent of a Nubian servant, perhaps not in the way Nubians actually
spoke, but according to the structure of Nubian dialect passed down from the
traditions of puppet shows and humorous skits from earlier generations.[60]

ABŪ NAẒẒARA IN REVOLT

Ismaʿil closed Ṣanūʿa's theater in 1872, either out of sensitivity to what he
perceived to be the social criticism inherent in Ṣanūʿa's work, or under direct
pressure from English officials angry with Ṣanūʿa's profoundly anti-British
stance.[61] But as mentioned earlier, Ṣanūʿa's political activism only increased:
he founded two secret societies in 1873 and 1874. When the secret societies
were closed by Ismaʿil, the journal *Abū Naẓẓara Zarqa* became Ṣanūʿa's loudest political instrument. Compared to his plays, Ṣanūʿa's political sketches in
Abū Naẓẓara Zarqa used even more radical and critical language against the
regime. In these, the Sudanese and the whole issue of color become instruments of satire against what Ṣanūʿa considered an arrogant and cruel regime.
In an illustrated sketch titled "Malʿab al-Ḥidiq" (The Clever Man's Trick), the
eunuch Khulkhāl Aga, a dark-skinned Sudanese (as drawn in the accompa-

ديوان خلخال آغا ناظر حريم أم عزيز أوغلو السنجق

4.   The Diwan of Khulkhāl Aga, illustrated in *Abū Naẓẓara Zarqa*, 1878.

nying pictures and as shown by his accent) guarding the khedive's harem suffers from the dual torment of being castrated and yet surrounded by the most beautiful women in Egypt. (See fig. 4.)[62] His friend, Shaykh Yasīn, tries to console him by complimenting him on his learning, but that offers no succor to the poor Khulkhāl Aga, who laments:

> I wish I had never read, never memorized, and never learnt the Qur'an, because if I had remained in my ignorance, it would have been better for me. I was God's bull in his clover, not knowing good from evil. Now I read Arabic and Turkish newspapers, and my friend Alexander Effendi translates the foreign gazettes only because I don't know those languages. Then, disaster befell me and I saw myself the most miserable of God's creatures, because night and day my eyes observe heaven and my heart burns with the fires of hell.[63]

Although Khulkhāl Aga is alleged by his friend to be a learned man, his spoken grammar betrays him. It is a strange mix of dialect and classical Arabic, with the characteristic mispronunciation of particular letters so familiar in Ṣanū'a's Sudanese characters. His speech also reinforces the debate over progress for black Sudanese, an issue Ṣanū'a had touched on in his earlier plays. Was ignorance not actually bliss for the Sudanese, as many of Ṣanū'a's Egyptian characters imply after learning that "even the Nubian has his day"? Khulkhāl Aga also makes an interesting parallel between his new, "civilized" life—indicated as such by the nature of what he reads—and the almost primordial existence he led before being brought to Egypt, when he was God's bull in his clover. He has become a sadly conscious noble savage.

Although Khulkhāl Aga represents one of the more formidable guardians of the khedive's rarified existence in his service as harem keeper, and although he is an instrument of the authority that bears so heavily on the lives of Egyptians, he himself bears witness to the scheming of the khedive's family and the ways in which, by keeping all military leadership within the hands of the Ottoman Egyptians, Isma'īl permitted the exploitation and degradation of Egyptian soldiers. What is clear in his speech, however, is Ṣanū'a's idea of the sense of dread that the Turkish-speaking officers inspired in the Egyptian soldiers, and how abusive they could be with the authority they claimed there. The rest of the sketch is about the peril into which a young officer's debts place his marriage to a beautiful white slave, and how his debtor wants to claim the bride and two African slave girls as repayment. The officer, 'Alī Effendi, claims to be broke because the government has overtaxed the land he inherited from his father. He also complains about the wars he and his fellow Egyptian soldiers have been sent to fight "against people who have never done anything to us while we go to deprive them of their freedom."[64] This is a direct reference to the disastrous Abyssinian campaigns of 1876, during which Circassian-led Egyptian troops were completely routed by a much less "modern" African army, and to the continual campaigns into the southern Sudan that occurred at the same time. Khulkhāl Aga is moved by the speech, and gives 'Alī Effendi the money to pay his debtor.

Khulkhāl Aga, who appears in several other sketches, is the supreme gatekeeper and guardian of that most intimate part of the khedive's life, just as Abū Rida performs the duties that keep Sitt Banbah's household running. But Khulkhāl Aga also offers Ṣanū'a's audience insights into the outer peripheries of Egypt's borders, because, with his amputation, he personifies the very act of conquest of the Sudan. It seems clearer here, though, that Khulkhāl Aga is as much a victim of the Ottoman ruling class as any Egyptian: he lost his manhood and is thus symbolic of Egyptians' own inability to gain autonomy in the government that ruled them.

Al-Quradātī (The Monkey Showman), first published in 1878, offers another example of Ṣanū'a's use of the Sudanese in the domain of intimate Egyptian life to criticize Egyptian politics. Sa'd, the street entertainer who performs with monkeys, confronts the abusive behavior of more Turkish officers (the story itself is set in "the days of the Ottomans" [*fī ayām al-ghuzz]*) and the khedive, here called Shaykh al-Ḥāra (chief of the quarter). Saʿd and the khedive's entourage bump into each other, and Baclava Agha, speaking mostly in Turkish, orders Saʿd to get away from them. But the khedive wants the tax money he insists the entertainer owes. Saʿd protests poverty and is threatened with imprisonment. He agrees to prison, if they will help find someone to look after his monkey, his donkey, his cat, and so on, but al-Ḥāra persists in his demands. In the following speech, Saʿd describes the difference color makes in Egyptian society, and the way one is treated as a consequence of dark color:

> Now where on earth am I supposed to go to raise these two thousand
> silver coins? He who said this would be the last service to the Turks was
> right. If only my wife had craved a Turkish soldier, and had then born
> me a handsome white son like my cousin Aḥmad, then I would have
> been able to sell him the way Aḥmad sold his son, to the Mamlūks, and
> thus paid his tax. But what can I do? She bears me black sons, since she
> craves nothing but Nubian men.[65]

His sex appeal aside, Saʿd attributes his limited resources and the color of his sons to his wife; in doing so, Saʿd provides a glimpse of the hierarchy of color that existed in the army and in the levels of authority. Historically, Circassian children, sold by their parents to the Ottomans in the system known as *devshirme,* were raised to become members of the ruling class; hence they were considered to be more valuable, and cost more than darker children, who would be groomed only as slaves or servants. His final comment alludes to the mystique of unbridled sexuality that hung over Nubians and Sudanese in Egypt. From Abū Rida to Khulkhāl Aga to Saʿad's fantasies, Ṣanūʿa left his audiences titillated with hints about the prowess (or even the genitalia) of his Nubian characters.

THE ʿURĀBĪ REBELLION AND THE IMMINENCE OF EMPIRE

Around the time that Ṣanūʿa wrote the previous sketches, he was exiled to France, where his criticism of Ismaʿīl grew even harsher. Smuggling his paper into Egypt with friends headed there by ship, he continued to reach Egyptian readers, who read the skits in his journal to each other in the coffeehouses and social clubs of Cairo and Alexandria.[66] In the case of Ṣanūʿa, exile proved to be a wrong step for the khedive. Once out of Egypt, Ṣanūʿa could write with even greater impunity about Egyptian politics. His journals gained notoriety. With the most famous and popular practitioner of the new political journalism now out of his control, the khedive found that his repressive acts and taxes became more transparent. Moreover, Egyptians became aware of his increasing loss of financial control of his country, the humiliation of the government's declaration of bankruptcy in 1875, and British and French officials' formal assumption of control of Egypt's treasury, with the creation of the Caisse de la Dette Publique in 1878.[67] The Egyptian officers in the army grew even more politicized by the consequences of these events and by the tutorials in nationalist feeling they were receiving at the hands of journalists like the exiled Ṣanū'a and his formidable counterpart who had remained in Egypt, the writer and orator 'Abdallah al-Nadīm.

'Abdallah al-Nadīm came of age very differently from Ṣanū'a, although he was only six years younger. Unlike Ṣanū'a, whose early promise in languages earned him an overseas education and entry into the circles of Cairo's elite, al-Nadīm began his education in an elementary Islamic school, or *kuttāb*, in Alexandria. In 1863, at the age of eighteen, he left Alexandria for Cairo to train at al-Azhar University. However, like 'Alī Mubārak years before, he saw little future in such an education, left the university, and went instead to work for the telegraph service. This work brought him into contact with the elite houses of Cairo, but more important, into the world of the lettered and poetic-minded.[68] For several years he worked as a tutor and as the manager of a lingerie boutique, a place where he and his friends could discuss literature and poetry and each other's writing. He returned home to Alexandria in 1878, where the political world had become much more charged, and talk against the khedive much more strident. He joined secret societies led by the activist Jamāl al-Dīn al-Afghānī and by the writers Adib Ishaq and Salim Naqqash, and soon began to try publicizing his own sense of pride in Egyptian culture and the Arabic language.[69] He also tried to establish his own school with the help of Tawfīq, the new khedive, in 1879. But by 1881, al-Nadīm had become thoroughly disenchanted with Khedive Tawfīq and threw his considerable talents into supporting the movement of Colonel Aḥmad 'Urābī and publishing his own newspaper, *al-Tankīt wa al-tabkīt* (Satire and Reproach).

Al-Nadīm captured the imaginations of many of his contemporaries, as well as a great deal of historical attention. His activities as a leader of the 'Urābī rebellion can be studied in the works of Delanoue, Cole, Scholch, Ramadan, and 'Asfur, to name a few. He shared with Ṣanū'a deep disdain for the British, but al-Nadīm's antagonism to European customs and politics went much further. Again and again he contradicted what were then prevalent notions of civilization *[tamaddun]* and the idea that lessons in progress and modernization could be learned from Europeans, particularly the British. In one essay, titled "Al-farq bayna al-tamaddun al-sharqī wa al-Ūrūbī" (The Difference between Eastern and European Civilization), al-Nadīm presents a dialogue between two men, one Egyptian and one British. After the Egyptian asks the Englishman what Great Britain wants with Egypt, the latter answers, "To abolish your barbarity" *(khalāṣak min al-tawaḥḥash)*. The Egyptian denies that in an old trading nation like Egypt there remains any barbarity. He then turns to a practice that he considers barbaric, which he noticed while on a trip to London—the integration of men and women working in close quarters in a factory. When the Englishman responds by saying that only poor people would be in that situation, and would never notice the offense, the Egyptian counters by saying that the Egyptian poor would never allow such intermingling to take place. "Leave us to civilize ourselves according to our own customs," he says to the Englishmen.[70]

If, as al-Nadīm posited often, there was a basic Eastern sense of civilization, built on the principles of Islam, then it was the duty of patriotic Egyptians to behave respectfully toward it. Those who blindly used European models as their guides betrayed their own heritage, and so did those of certain classes who mistreated the poor of Egypt, especially the rural farming classes of the *fallaḥīn*. Those lucky enough to be educated and to have servants and large households also bore a responsibility to be respectful toward the underclasses; he wrote in another essay, "You are not yourself and the one supposedly similar is not similar" *(la inta inta wa la al-mathīl mathilan)*. This echoes a famous poem by the ninth-century poet Abu Tamam, "Lā inta inta wa lā al-diyar diyar," about the discrepancies between appearance and reality.[71] In "Ayyuhā al-mutamaddun" (To the civilized), al-Nadīm asks this fictionalized reader to look at his fine clothes, beautiful house, scholarly books, and imported finery. He then demands that the reader look at his servant, with his torn clothes, crumbling hut, and illiteracy. Al-Nadīm accuses the reader of disregarding this loyal and kind servant so terribly, of not even looking him in the eyes when he "kisses your hand," of never considering his wife or his children, and, worst of all, of not helping him learn to see himself as an Egyptian. It is the responsibility of those with "civilization" to teach those whose share in life is deprivation and ignorance. Those who try to prove how civilized Egypt is, without trying to help the *fallaḥīn*, serve as no model for the troubled country.[72]

But other essays, written to exhort Egyptians to look hard at the roots and responsibilities of nationalism, did not always portray servants as innocent victims of foreigners or selfish upper-class Egyptians. The ignorance of black slaves, for example, could have insidious effects on society, both publicly and privately. As presented in a short parable, two Sudanese slaves named Nakhla and Oshama have brought a curse to their neighborhood, where they sell both hashish and their specially brewed beer to increasingly large crowds and have made quite a bit of money in the process.[73] But the damage that Nakhla and Oshama cause is nothing compared to the insidiousness of other slaves' ignorance, particularly the behavior and influence of slave women in Muslim households when left unchecked and undisciplined. In another essay, called "Ḥadīth khurāfa" (Silly Talk), al-Nadīm relates the experience of a fictional reader who witnesses a ceremony in which the several Sudanese slave women are invited by women of his house and some of their friends to perform a kind of séance where they sing and dance in a circle, with the slave women in the middle. At the most powerful point of the ceremony, the oldest of the slave women is visited by the spirit of a shaykh and, in this persona, speaks to the surrounding Egyptian women, trying to treat their different complaints. One woman says that her little boy is very ill and that her husband demands that a medical doctor be brought to the house to cure him. The "shaykh"-slave woman insists that this is the wrong treatment and that the wife should kill a "black hen and a black rooster, with no other marks on them," and then bring this to the "shaykh" along with a little piece of the boy's clothing. The "shaykh" says then she will spend the night with the boy, after which he will recover. When the mother of the boy reminds the slave woman that her husband wants the doctor, the "shaykh" replies, "What do you need of doctors?" and glares angrily at her. Frightened, the mother agrees. But the next day, the reader who witnessed all this goes directly to the boy's father to warn him of the ignorant mother's plans. Luckily, the story ends with the mother telling her husband, who scolds her for believing in such superstitions.[74]

Al-Nadīm presented this scene to show why Egyptian women needed more education in order to be able to protect not only themselves but their children from the even greater ignorance of the Sudanese in their own homes. The ceremony he describes in "Silly Talk" was known as a *zār*, a traditional ceremony of spirit visitation performed for medicinal purposes that was brought by Sudanese women into Egypt (and still practiced today).[75] Part of his discussion of the *zār* reflects contemporary debates about the value of Western medicine versus traditional medicine. But it also reflects al-Nadīm's investment in the Egyptian household as an idealized structure whose foundations can truly be undermined only by the negligence of the family's patriarch. The threats introduced by the slave women—drugs, alcohol, unorthodox ceremonies—can be abolished, but only when the men responsible for order are properly vigilant. These are men of substance, of education (as al-Nadīm's literary references make clear), who must not shirk the responsibility of sharing their knowledge charitably with the rest of Egyptian society. If they fail in this, then even the structure of the family is challenged, with a female black slave in the guise of a man of learning becoming the authoritative figure and deciding the fate of Egyptian children. Things fall apart if the center cannot hold.

PAN-ISLAMISM AND THE SUDAN

Cultural self-respect was one of the most important aspects of the new pan-Islamist movement that sprang up among members of Egypt's secular and religious intelligentsia around the time of the 'Urābīya. As Alexander Scholch notes, the movement's ideas—which took shape amid terrible financial pressure suffered by both the Ottoman state and the Egyptian government—were, above all, the beginning of resistance to economic exploitation by the European powers. Scholch helpfully lists the different, intermingling shapes that the concept of nationalism took in Egypt of the late 1870s: "Ismaʿīl's striving for independence, his imperial dreams, his attempt to resist European intervention with the help of a 'national party'; genuine Egyptian patriotism; the 'quasi-national' ideas of a pan-Arab sociocultural risorgimento; pan-Islamic thought based on the religious authority of the Sultan; secularist endeavors to strengthen the Ottoman Empire in the East as a whole against the European danger. These ideas often overlapped, and sometimes they were adopted at the same time by one and the same person."[76]

One of those who best captured the imaginations of Egyptians as they struggled through these different concepts of communal identity was the famous intellectual wanderer of the late nineteenth century, Jamāl al-Dīn al-Afghānī. Al-Afghānī had long before become an international figure and the most famous proponent of pan-Islamism. In the years between 1879 and 1881, however, pan-Islamic pride retreated from its global aims and then blossomed into a more Egyptian-centered struggle for the control of government by indigenous, reform-minded Islamic forces. Al-Afghānī brought his ideas to Egypt himself during his lectureship at al-Azhar. Through his lectures, his membership in numerous secret societies, and his growing connections to intellectuals concerned with Islamic reform and nationalism, he encouraged Egyptians to ameliorate their cultural and political circumstances by reforming their spiritual commitment to, and understanding of, Islam.[77] Drawing a new political confidence from al-Afghānī's teachings about Islam, many contemporaries believed that the khedive had failed in his role as a spiritual leader, and they looked elsewhere for a more spiritual leadership. This idea certainly motivated 'Urābī; it became one of the primary reasons he and his officers rebelled in 1881 against the Turco-Circassian cultural domination of the military.

The Mahdīya in the Sudan created new heroes for the pan-Islamic movement. By 1883, the forces of the Mahdī were imposing defeat after defeat on Egyptian troops, with some startling victories over regiments commanded by British officers. The Mahdīya's forces decried the rule of the "Turks," their word for the Circassian-led Egyptian army, for their religious laxness, for their economic exploitation of the Sudan, and for the disruption of the slave trade in the late 1870s. Although they cursed Egyptians, the Mahdī and his forces began to attract a great deal of favorable attention within Egypt itself. Ṣanū'a, for example, in *Abū Naẓẓara Zarqa*, paid great attention to the Sudanese Mahdī, as did many other writers and thinkers promoting the idea of Islamic reform, notably Jamāl al-Dīn al-Afghānī himself. The Mahdī became a completely different symbol, in what had previously been the narrow spectrum of figure allowed in literary and dramatic characterizations of the Sudanese and Nubians. Through the Mahdī's speeches, and through his military victories, the Sudanese seemed to have a new voice.

But voices of such magnitude are often changed in translation. Muḥammad Aḥmad (the Mahdī) was an important example of how to use Islam as a potent political weapon against the encroaching British empire. To al-Afghānī he was not a real *Mahdī*, or messiah, nor could his call for government to promote his Islamic principles elsewhere (notably by means of a Sudanese conquest of Egypt) be accepted by al-Afghānī, who had so closely allied himself with the most important figures of Egyptian nationalism. Yet a powerful ambivalence about the Mahdī runs throughout the many articles published by al-Afghānī in his journal *Al-'Urwa al-Wuthqa'* (The Indissoluble Link). Writing from exile in Paris with his brilliant student, the Egyptian scholar and thinker Muḥammad 'Abduh, and in constant contact with Ṣanū'a, al-Afghānī fashioned Muḥammad Aḥmad into a more controllable political force, until General Gordon's death in the overthrow of Khartoum was discovered and the Mahdī's image in Europe could no longer be whitewashed.

For a time, especially as the siege of Khartoum became a daily fixation for the readers of British newspapers, al-Afghānī characterized himself as a go-between for the British government and Muḥammad Aḥmad.[78] Muḥammad Aḥmad, al-Afghānī often argued, was fighting a nationalist cause against the British. In one article, al-Afghānī and 'Abduh relate how the *Daily Telegraph* and the *Standard* reported that the Mahdī had maneuvered two of his armies around Dongola. Doom for the British was immediate, but there was another message for Muslims as well: Muḥammad Aḥmad was setting an example, drawing from both Islamic law and the laws of nature, of how to defend one's country against the imperialism of the British:

> We have known that all Muslims and patriots regard among the duties
> of their conscience obstructing the path of the British, setting up all
> obstacles in their way to the best of their ability and power, bearing
> in mind all duties of religion and homeland *[waṭan]*, and none need,
> in the provocation of this holy work, an order from the sultan, for the
> divine shariʿa and the natural laws *[nawāmīs]* of every sect and every
> region of the corners of the earth demand this of every individual
> guarding his nation.[79]

Al-Afghānī thus bestows on Muḥammad Aḥmad the flexibility of conforming to the precepts of Islam as they merge with al-Afghānī's ideas of Islamic nationalism. Later in the same article, he addresses his Egyptian readers, reminding them that "your territory, your money, and your efforts and the creed of your religion and your morals and your shariʿa have all been seized by the enemy to spend."[80] Al-Afghānī admonishes Egyptians for having allowed the British to take over and infiltrate the Sudan and thus surround Egyptian territory. "Why," he asks, "do you act as if you aren't equal *[tuʾadduna anfusakum]* to the level of those who truly are your equals. Do you not resemble your enemy? Are you not more distinguished in your faith than they are?"[81]

Despite his urging Egyptians to learn from the Mahdists' example, he made frequent insinuations about Egypt's natural right to the territories of the Sudan and expressed many suspicions about Muḥammad Aḥmad's claims to being the Mahdī, fearing that such an approach to leadership disguised a more venal kind of fanaticism.[82] The zeal that Muḥammad Aḥmad, as al-Afghānī always referred to him, inspired in his followers was fine for confronting the British but painfully inappropriate when directed against fellow Muslims. Muḥammad Aḥmad inspired the religion-heated nationalism of Muslims from New Delhi to North Africa, for which al-Afghānī praised him over and over; but al-Afghānī believed that Aḥmad's continued call for the conquest of Egypt would destroy the filaments of pan-Islamic fraternity. This expansionism would be as serious a threat as British imperialism:

> I do not know what the result would be if the Sudan fell wholly into
> Muḥammad Aḥmad's possession and he set up government over those
> vast lands, with no way left to him but to continue on his path and
> propagate his message among all the Arab tribes, with all of his capabili-

ties. And he would not stop there but mobilize his dense armies up to the borders of Upper Egypt, perhaps; rather it is likely he will do this, as it has never happened that the flames of revolution did not hurry, by their very nature, along the tracks of their natural path.[83]

This menace looms even more darkly when al-Afghānī tells his readers that the dervishes, as they were popularly known at the time in both Europe and Egypt, had already cut the telegraph lines from Korosko to Aswan, the same distance, he reminds them, that lay between Aswan and Qena.[84]

Al-Afghānī's articles on the Mahdīya adhered closely to the religiously bordered, nationalistically resonant global map of Africa and the Middle East then the source of conflict between indigenous peoples and the European powers. Muslim territory belonged to Muslims, and it was their natural right to fight for and protect their *waṭan*. Although it was Islam that linked Muslims to their land, al-Afghānī's articles made it clear that they could not exist in a land without internal borders of its own, between territories within the same religion. It was his hope, or so he intimated to the spy hired by the British government, Professor Anthony Habib Salmone, to be an intermediary between the Mahdī, 'Urābī, and the British.[85] He also aspired to be the leader of a great "Arab empire" in Africa and Asia, with the Mahdī's military help, once negotiations were finalized.[86] Yet, he urged Egyptians to fight for the integrity of their own land, against the British and Sudanese attempts to nullify those borders. Although he proscribed Egyptians from fighting in the Sudan against their fellow Muslims, the Sudan was rightfully theirs.

Ya'qūb Ṣanū'a lived in exile in Paris at the same time as al-Afghānī and voiced very similar opinions about the Mahdī in his journal, *Abū Naẓẓara Zarqa*, although he was somewhat less critical of Muḥammad Aḥmad's claims to being the Mahdī. In his articles of this period (1883–1886), and especially in his sketches, the Mahdī is the Sudan, looming large over the chastened heads of the Egyptians, filling the void left by the British defeat of 'Urābī Pasha. Like al-Afghānī, Ṣanū'a viewed the Mahdī's victories less in religious terms than as successful political strategy.

Even more, Ṣanū'a's writings on the Mahdī brought the Sudan into the public domain. Ṣanū'a discussed him possessively, claiming him as a hero not only because he fought for the Sudanese nationalist cause but also because he upheld Egyptian independence. From his perspective, in Paris, the protagonists in the struggle in the Sudan were grouped quite simply: the invading armies were British, the brave warriors were Sudanese, and the grateful cousins were Egyptians. There is little mention of the fact that there remained, in 1885, many Egyptian soldiers still fighting in the Egyptian army against the Mahdī's forces and that, in fact, the khedive saw the Sudan as an appropriate place to send the disgruntled soldiers who had supported ʿUrābī.[87] Instead, Ṣanūʿa presents all confrontations between the Mahdist armies and the British generals as heroic tableaus of nationalism, from which the entire Nile Valley will emerge victorious.

Most important, to an exiled nationalist shocked at a perceived complacency among his countrymen at home after the defeat of the ʿUrābī revolt, the Sudanese tribesmen and warriors represented epic heroes. In this more classical vein, Ṣanūʿa departed from his practice of writing in colloquial Arabic when giving voice to his Sudanese characters, as demonstrated on 27 June 1885 in an article about the doomed efforts of a British campaign in the Sudan:

> Summer approached, and the land set out for bitter fighting, the sun-baked ground burning the hides, broiling the flesh, the brains rising to the top of the head, and in the far distance, the vast destination, the frightening road, the enemy hardened, the call to war a religious call, and those fighting would have exchanged their spirits without hardship, hopeful of meeting their lord and satisfied with his leaders, barricading the English from the road inch by inch, blocking the road step-by-step [*marḥalatan baʿd marḥalatan*].
>
> The English have fought only small bands, getting from them a taste of the pain of torment, and they know what incredible strength the Mahdī possesses; they know what terrible battles will occur between them and the Mahdists, battles that baffle the mind [*al-ʿuqul*], causing it to break into bitterness, the heart crumbling. For that reason, the English have seen fit to appeal to Italy, asking her humbly to come to the rescue with soldiers from the direction of the Red Sea, in this way hoping to save themselves from the casualties that will befall them when they try to get out of the dilemma into which they have fallen.[88]

In an article written several months later, Ṣanūʿa uses the Mahdī in a satiric attack on Khedive Tawfīq, in which the Sudanese leader stands with, and stands up for, the Egyptians who suffer under Tawfīq's rule. Ṣanūʿa drew Tawfīq as puffy and useless-looking, tied to a tree and surrounded by his enemies, who by this time included just about everyone in the world. The sketch is followed by a rather long caption, in which each of Tawfīq's symbolic enemies explain why they are throwing rocks at him. The *fallaḥ* stones him in the name of "the waters of the Nile that you have deprived me of, killing me and my land off with thirst, and not just for that but also for bringing the red demons here to destroy my property," "red demons" being a common Ṣanūʿa epithet for the British. The Egyptian soldier also throws a rock at him for the British occupation. The pious *ʿalīm* (religious instructor) stones him for contradicting the laws of the Prophet, for joining with the infidel British to destroy Egypt, and for betraying Islam. Then "al-Sayyid Muḥammad Aḥmad, hero of the Sudan" says to Tawfīq:

> I throw this rock at you, O enemy to the faith, first of all because of what you did to the poor *fallaḥ*, and the Egyptian soldier, and the *'ālim*, learned in the Qur'an, and second because you handed over the treasures of your country to the greed of the British, then you made their priests rulers of Islam. Third, for your sitting on the khedivial throne, which is itself a contradiction of the Islamic shari'a. You did not rightly inherit the throne.[89]

(See fig. 5.) These were very strong words for the time, that Ṣanū'a could afford to write only because of the luxury of distance his exile afforded him. This distance, however, also enabled him to conjure up an image of the Mahdī as protector of true Egyptian values, although it is extremely unlikely that the Mahdī would have supported any Egyptian soldier or any of the Egyptian *'ulamā'* who cast public doubts over his claims to the Mahdīya. In this satiric tableau, which included everyone in the contemporary political scene, from the *fallaḥ* to the British politician to the British banker to Isma'īl, the former khedive, Ṣanū'a uses the Mahdī to raise the most unimpeachable doubts about the very basis of Tawfīq's rule over Egypt.

In the same issue, Ṣanū'a celebrated, in stately classical Arabic, the miracle of someone like Muḥammad Aḥmad rising up and rescuing the Sudan. After a lengthy discussion of the mysteries of God's designs on earth, Ṣanū'a asks his readers,

> Who would have thought that al-Sayyid Aḥmad Muḥammad *[sic]*, a poor man from Dongola, would achieve the rescue of the Sudan from the clutches *[bi thamamihi min aydī al-zhulma]* of oppression, in spite of the British tyrants defeating armies and scattering populations. Who would have imagined him resisting, with his little dagger, the powerful cannon; cutting down with his knife British stallions with all their excellent weapons and their military training? Yes, this is the work of God, who supports His will with victory. God saw a violation of his will; the result is the miracle of worship. Isn't God He who created the rifts between Russia and England while the British prepared their troops, and made them come here to oppose the black leader of the blacks *[qa'id al-iswid al-sud]*, who claimed he was not of this humble world, and who then defeated someone like Gordon, in Khartoum?[90]

The Mahdī's humble origins thus enable him, in Ṣanū'a's construction, to be even more the embodiment of a divine miracle that revolutionizes the confining social constructions resulting from British imperialism. There are

5. The khedive attacked by the Mahdī and others, depicted in *Abū Naẓẓara Zarqa*, September 1885.

some echoes here of the *fallaḥ* Faraj and the matchmaker Mabrūka, who marveled at the behavior of Sudanese who tried to lift themselves from traditional roles. Even more important, Ṣanū'a, unlike the more skeptical al-Afghānī, accepts Muḥammad Aḥmad's efforts to change the Sudan spiritually. He refers to him as the Mahdī, which al-Afghānī never did, and he himself cloaks all descriptions of Muḥammad Aḥmad in religious terms, often in classical Arabic.

Like al-Afghānī, however, Ṣanū'a elected himself the Mahdī's spokesman in Europe, particularly to the French audience to whom he increasingly directed his work after the defeat of the 'Urābī revolt. For the benefit of the Europeans, to whom the Mahdī had come to symbolize a despotic, fanatical, and wildly popular Islam, Ṣanū'a tried to transform the Mahdīya into a branch of the more stately and refined Islamic intellectualism of al-Afghānī and Shaykh Muḥammad 'Abduh. The Mahdī's very identity became fertile ground for fiction. For instance, in a statement published in French in late 1885, Ṣanū'a declared that he had himself met the Mahdī at the home of one of his then colleagues, from the Polytechnic School (this alleged meeting, for which there is no basis in fact, would have taken place in the early 1870s). The Mahdī was traveling around Cairo on his way to Mecca. Ṣanū'a found him, he wrote, "un littérateur arabe fort érudit et un remarkable théologien."[91] Through this alleged personal contact, Ṣanū'a elected himself a spokesman for the Mahdī, manipulating the latter's voice to make it comprehensible to both Egyptians and Europeans, thus framing him within the context of religious and nationalist legitimacy, as if the roughness of the Mahdī's language made no sense without Ṣanū'a's translation and interpretation.

Ṣanū'a claimed to be sorting through the Mahdī's image as a fanatic. What complicated the Mahdīya, Ṣanū'a explained, was not the leader's fanaticism but the fanatical feelings the Mahdī inspired in people, which resulted from the fact that, since the times of the Fatimids, the Abbasids, the Muwahids, and the Murabits, political authority had been deeply entwined with the concept of a Mahdī. The result of this, said Ṣanū'a, was that "there are not yet, among Muslims, free thinkers. That is what has made the Sayyid Muḥammad Aḥmad successful, rendered even greater by his fighting the English, hated by Islam."[92] The Mahdīya was the personification of nationalism run slightly amok, among people not quite ready for the disciplined communal activity of self-government. The Sudanese thus provided an important model for their more civilized cousins, the Egyptians, of what nationalist fervor could accomplish; but they also demonstrated the dangers of untutored uprisings.

Ironically, into this realm of traditional and unquestioning adherence to religious authority stepped a number of Ṣanū'a's old colleagues and fellow 'Urabists, many of whom, he and other sources claim, joined the Mahdīya after their defeat at Tel al-Kabīr in 1883.[93] In the *Abū Naẓẓara Zarqa* of 7 February 1885, Ṣanū'a addresses "the chiefs of the Nationalist Party," in the French section of the paper (which was by then divided into two linguistic halves: one in Arabic, the other in French), saying:

> Observe that I don't blame at all those among you, former soldiers and officers of 'Arabī, who have joined the Mahdī, to fight the common enemy in the ranks of his army. If you are not of the same country, then you are of the same faith. Patriotism has its despairs, and the English have the bad grace to reproach you for it, they who, in Spain, united with the fanatics of the Inquisition in order to defeat the Napoleonic invasion.
>
> But allying with fanaticism has its limits. Do not ever cross them. Do not permit that in Egypt people follow the Russian nihilists, the "Fennians" of England, and the anarchists of France. No one has ever made their cause victorious, or liberated a nation, by cowardly murder and foolish destruction. May your hearts be strong.[94]

Five months later, however, Ṣanū'a found a different apology for his colleagues fighting in the Sudan. Discussing his extreme hatred of Khedive Tawfīq, he again raises the issue in the French section of his journal, saying,

"The former officers of 'Arabī who, in the Sudan, have passed into the ranks of the rebellion and have given, bit by bit, a regularized organization to the Mahdist bands, have done so out of hatred for the British, with no doubt, but they have also done it, principally, out of resentment against Tawfīq's betrayal of them."[95] Tawfīq's betrayal of the Egyptian nationalists to the British thus provided their excuse for defecting from Egypt to join the Mahdīya; yet the same nationalists continued to perform a civic duty by providing the "bands of the Mahdī" with some kind of organization, in a sense taming the fanaticism of the dervishes.

According to Ṣanū'a, Egyptian soldiers rarely found a fair fight in African wars. Either they were sent by the khedive to fight people who had never waged war against them, as 'Alī Effendi mentions in the sketch about Khulkhāl Aga, or they were used as cannon fodder in the front lines by their British commanders, as Ṣanū'a insisted was common practice.[96] If Egyptians fought in the Sudan under the British, an issue that Ṣanū'a increasingly wrote about in the 1890s while the British parliament debated the reconquest of Omdurman, then they were taking up arms against "brothers," a kinship that Ṣanū'a claimed originated in their common faith.[97] Ṣanū'a thus openly prayed that the Sudan would prove to be a sinkhole for the British, and that Africa on the whole would be as inhospitable to their expansionism as the continent was to Khedive Isma'īl's similar ambitions. He mocked these efforts in a fascinating scene in *Yalla Bina ila as-Sudan* (Let's Go to the Sudan), in which General Kitchener, the commander of the Anglo-Egyptian forces that have conquered Berber, decides to send the captured dervishes to London to present them to Her Majesty the Queen. He orders the translator to tell them where they are going, and the translator, in a subversive scrambling of his meaning, says to the prisoners, "O joy! We're going to the land of the pretty Englishwomen who are enchanted with our love. There we can drink the expensive brandy they'll give us, out of love for us. O what luck! Where's our stuff? Let's gather it together and travel to the land of the beauties."[98] How quickly the much vaunted religious zeal of the Mahdī's followers evaporates, in Ṣanū'a's imagination, when challenged by the world of libertine women that exist, in his imagination, in London. They seem to be echoing the prejudices of Ṣanū'a's other character, Banbah, with all her ideas about Sudanese licentiousness.

THE MAHDĪ, STILL A SERVANT

Although his journal continued to be read with enthusiasm in Egypt, Ṣanū'a's constructions of Egypt, particularly in regard to Egypt's relationship to the Sudan, grew more distanced and idealized as the years of his exile elapsed. The lively depictions of Sudanese and Nubian servants that he sketched during the 1870s from social circumstances witnessed in Cairo and Alexandria also changed with the dramatic events in the Sudan during the following decade. Whereas at first a private and domestic empire, Egypt's Sudan became the Mahdī's Sudan, ushering in a fiery and eloquent new character among the Sudanese that had previously peopled Ṣanū'a's literary repertoire. The Mahdī picked up the nationalist gauntlet dropped by the 'Urābī rebels, and, in Ṣanū'a's construction of events, used it to challenge and defeat the British.

As Ṣanū'a's sketches show, in some ways the Mahdī became more Egyptian than the Egyptians, personifying all the traits of courage and patriotic resistance Ṣanū'a wished for his fellow Egyptians. But in other ways, the Mahdī retained aspects of the traditional roles ascribed to the Sudanese in Ṣanū'a's Egypt. His bravery was garnered in defense of Egypt, his martial genius mobilized against the British. Yet he remained a gate-keeper, a guard defending the Egyptian household. Even though the Mahdī was portrayed as more admirable, virile, and eloquent, he stood as stead-fastly against the door, protecting Egyptians, as had Ṣanū'a's earlier character, Muḥammad the Nubian.

3 The Lived Experience
of Contradiction

Ibrahīm Fawzī's Narrative of the Sudan

> "Reverend sir, I am ignorant and you are learned. Tell me, shall I
> believe that this man is the Expected Mahdī?"
>
> "I know not what to say concerning him," he replied. "But, son of
> Bedri"—and here he fingered his beard to give force to his words—
> "at the end the English will rule you all."
>
> BABIKR BEDRI, *The Memoirs of Babikr Bedri*

Khedive Ismaʿīl's ambitious and optimistic project to reorder Egyptian society also extended to the Sudan, with consequences as profound as those that
so alarmed Yaʿqūb Ṣanūʿa and ʿAbdallah al-Nadīm. In the words of P. M.
Holt, the Egyptian administration of the Sudan made it "the first region in
the interior of Africa to experience (although at one remove) the tensions
characteristic of Western colonialism."[1] These tensions, which Holt characterizes as a "general incompatibility between Sudanese traditional society
and the new model derived ultimately from Europe" caused a social and
political upheaval that was eventually "resolved" in the Mahdīya.[2] But this
so-called resolution also brought out the contradictions that Egypt's colonial
relationship with the Sudan, and its new and forced dependency on Great
Britain, had engendered. Both the ʿUrābī rebellion and the Mahdīya brought
to light the fact that there were Sudanese, Nubian, and Egyptian individuals trapped between upheavals.

Although the Mahdī denounced the Turkīya as a tyrannical administration, many Sudanese traders and sometimes entire northern tribes benefited
from it. Notable among these were the Jaʿaliyūn, the Danāqla, and the
Shayqīya. There were Sudanese individuals who profited enormously from
the changes wrought by the administration, like the Jaʿali trader al-Zubayr
Raḥman Pasha Mansur, who eventually became governor of Dārfūr, and
Aḥmad Bey ʿAwad al-Karīm Abu Sinn, who served as governor of
Khartoum from 1860 to 1870.[3] Many Sudanese also took advantage of various opportunities for careers in a range of areas such as the government
bureaucracy, the official reorganization of Islamic education, and the admin-

istration of Islamic law as practiced in Egypt and the Ottoman Empire.[4] Others, like Ja'far Pasha Mazhar, were loyal officers in the Egyptian army. Ja'far Pasha's abilities led him to become governor-general of the Sudan from 1866 to 71, where he tried to promote cultural activities by sending Sudanese works of art and products to the Exposition Universelle de Paris of 1867 and by organizing a salon of Sudanese poets and writers in Khartoum.[5] Then there were men like Babikr Bedri, a devoted follower of the Mahdī who found himself imprisoned in Egypt after the disastrous effort of the Mahdists to conquer Egyptian territory. On his eventual return to the Sudan he became the founder of the country's first school for girls.

For many in Egypt before the Mahdīya, the Sudan had long been a remote place of exile, a natural prison for the disgraced. For Egyptian soldiers however, the Sudan often represented chances for promotion, rare enough in the military establishment run by Ottoman Egyptians during the reign of Khedive Isma'īl. After the defeat of the 'Urābī rebellion, many Egyptian soldiers who had been loyal to the colonel defected from the Egyptian army and joined the growing forces of the Mahdī. But few embodied the contradiction between colonizer and colonized as much as Ibrahīm Fawzī Pasha. Soldier, trader, police chief, 'Urabist, and the most famous Egyptian prisoner of the Mahdī, Ibrahīm Fawzī Pasha became a living monument to Egypt's attempts at empire in the Sudan, at a time when such monuments had become all too fragile.

ARTIFACTS OF EMPIRE

In the fall of 1875, Khedive Isma'īl opened the doors of the newly built halls of the Khedivial Geographic Society to the Cairo public. In the kind of grand and imitative gesture that characterized his governing style, Isma'īl had the Geographic Society constructed and organized on the model of European institutes similarly devoted to the study of other cultures. African artifacts such as tools and weapons were clustered in the display cases of the Society, taken from Sudanese and East African villages by intrepid explorer-soldiers who had also sent objects to the halls of geographic institutes in Berlin, Paris, and London. The very presence of these carved ivory tusks, pipes, spears, and shields in the gilt halls of the Society attested to Egypt's imperial stance in Africa: the bric-a-brac of empire suspended in a museum of conquest.

The building symbolized Isma'īl's imperial hopes for the Sudan and East Africa, and the very presence of the spears and shields was testimony to his optimism about the military campaigns he had waged for years in the lands south of Egypt.[6] But though the institute was built as a gesture to Egypt's empire in East Africa, when it was completed the Society invited only a few Egyptians to give lectures or participate directly in its operation. The directors were Europeans with long experience in the Sudan and the Nile Valley, and so were the majority of lecturers, who spoke in French or English to an audience in which Egyptians were a tiny minority.[7] Isma'il also maintained this distinction in the expeditions he sent into the uppermost regions of the Nile Valley, often hiring prominent European military men to lead campaigns of both exploration and colonization. In this way Isma'il tried to expand Egypt's borders, but it was an Egypt represented by either European or Turco-Circassian faces; he never utilized the experience of native-born Egyptians who had also served for years in the Sudan and shared religious beliefs and a language with the majority of the Sudanese. They remained, for the most part, foot soldiers in Isma'il's imperial army.

There were Egyptians, however, who responded to Isma'il's dreams of expansion and wished to overcome their lack of representation in the scramble for Africa, hoping to assert themselves in the arena of empire building. At the time of the founding of the Geographic Society, Ibrāhīm Fawzī was a twenty-six-year-old army officer serving his country as governor of the Equatorial Provinces in the southern Sudan. He had been appointed by the famous English general Charles Gordon, who had himself been hired by Isma'il to bring order and civilization to the territories along the White Nile and to put an end to the slave trade there. Ibrāhīm Fawzī took these goals personally. He dedicated almost his entire military career to reinforcing the khedivial administration in the Sudan and, more important, the Egyptian character of that control. Despite his intimacy with the Sudan at a crucial point in both Egyptian and Sudanese history, he was not a member, nor was he even invited to become a member, of the Geographic Society (situated, incidentally, only a block away from the offices of the War Ministry, where Ibrāhīm Fawzī's orders originated).

Many Egyptians fought or campaigned in the Sudan, but Fawzī's experiences in the army were unusual. Fawzī first fought in the Sudan under General Charles Gordon when Gordon served Isma'il in the southernmost regions of the Nile Valley. In this way, unlike the experience of men like 'Urābī, Fawzī was not directly answerable to a Circassian officer. Gordon promoted Fawzī to the governorship of the Equatorial Provinces in 1877, a relatively high rank for so young an officer, and an Egyptian officer at that.[8] But Fawzī was soon ousted from this position and sent back to Cairo, where he joined the ranks of disaffected officers rallying around 'Urābī. He returned to the Sudan, again under Gordon, when the 'Urābī rebellion had failed and British forces occupied Egypt. In Khartoum, Fawzī served as

Gordon's aide-de-camp and as the second in command during the evacuation of Egyptian troops as they retreated from the increasingly powerful Sudanese Mahdī. When the Mahdī's forces laid siege to Khartoum, Fawzī was there; after General Gordon was killed, Fawzī was captured. He spent fourteen years as a prisoner of the Mahdī. After his release, he wrote an account of his experiences, *Kitāb al-sūdān bayna aydī Gordon wa Kitchener* (The Sudan under Gordon and Kitchener), in which he related the tale of Egypt's empire in the Sudan, as well as his personal experiences as a senior officer in the army and the most famous Egyptian prisoner of the Mahdī.

Although he strongly protested the British occupation of Egypt, Fawzī believed fully in the idea of a hierarchy of civilizations in the world of the late nineteenth century, according to which schema the advanced cultures bore both the right and the responsibility to colonize and "civilize" societies considered less developed. In Fawzī's perception, the acts of empire united a culture and made it a nation; the agents of his empire were therefore Egyptians, native-born and nationalist-minded. His two-volume work waved the flag of Egypt with as much flourish as any official institute, and perhaps no other monument or text better represents the conflicts of identity that shaped Egyptian nationalists. Ibrahīm Fawzī was an enforcer of colonialism in the Sudan and a colonized subject at home in Cairo. His memoirs offer a unique glimpse into one patriot who could attempt to bridge the contradictions of early Egyptian nationalism.

THE SOLDIER'S LOSS

Egyptian soldiers, their loyalties to their homeland first stirred by 'Urābī and then dashed by the British, experienced with special sensitivity the loss of the Sudan to the Mahdī. Thousands of Egyptian soldiers had spent years in the Sudan and knew the region well.[9] The Mahdī's rebellion meant something more personal to them than it may have to other Egyptians reading about it in newspapers or hearing it discussed in Cairo's and Alexandria's coffee shops. The speed with which both the occupation of their country and the loss of Egypt's territory in the Sudan occurred made the events all the more painful. One particular moment sums up the personal sting of this simultaneous loss of sovereignty and colony. After the trials of the 'Urābī rebellion were over, 'Urābī and his six closest associates were sentenced to exile in Ceylon. The punishment for many of the soldiers of lesser rank who had participated in the rebellion was reassignment to the Sudan to fight the Mahdī (a fate considered by many to be equal to capital punishment). As the British lawyer who defended 'Urābī and his officers wrote:

> I myself saw the nucleus of the Soudan contingent leaving Cairo for
> Suez. It was a sorry and not easily-to-be-forgotten spectacle. The Egyp-
> tian soldiers were placed in vans and cattle-trucks like animals. They
> quitted the capital without arms, as prisoners, and with all the circum-
> stances of dishonour. Their native officers were selected from those who
> were most obnoxious to the new regime, and their very appointment
> was an avowed and undisguised measure of punishment and repression.
> On the 1st of Jan. 1883, two steamers were moored alongside the wharf
> at Suez. The deck of one was crowded by the disgraced and disbanded
> soldiers of the First Regiment (of which Arabi had been colonel); upon
> the deck of the other stood Arabi and his six companions. An hour
> or two later the disarmed Egyptian soldiers were forced to witness
> in sullen silence the Mareotis [Arabi's ship] steaming down the Red
> Sea, headed for Ceylon.[10]

But how to express this particular bitterness? These soldiers were rarely
men of letters. Unlike the beliefs of nationalist writers and publicists Ya'qūb
Sanū'a and 'Abdallah al-Nadīm, or the newspaper editor 'Alī Yusuf who
wrote pages and pages on the issue of the Sudan and its meaning for Egypt,
the soldiers' perspectives on the Egyptian experience in the Sudan remained
a subject for letters sent home.[11] The living military memory of the Sudan
circulated, but only privately, until Ibrahīm Fawzī published his memoirs.

As Ibrahīm Fawzī recounted it, his adult life reverberated in Cairo and
Khartoum. He offered few other details on his background, however, omitting details about where he was educated, by whom, from which part of
Egypt his family came, or why he first volunteered for service with then-
Colonel Gordon in the Sudan in 1874, when other young cadets were buying their way out of a Sudanese tour of duty.[12] As mentioned previously,
Fawzī was forced out of his command in the southern Sudan and "convicted
of irregularities" like slave trading.[13] Gordon replaced him immediately with
a German convert to Islam known as Emin Pasha, a man that Fawzī and
other officers, including Europeans, suspected of conspiring with another
German doctor in Gordon's favor to arrange Fawzī's dismissal.[14] This ouster
infuriated and humiliated Fawzī, who felt he had performed well as governor
and had intimate knowledge of the customs of the tribes of the Equatorial
Provinces. Even more humiliating, Gordon had not taken him at his word but
had instead been swayed by other Europeans.[15] Fawzī then returned to Cairo,
looking for reassignment. Unfortunately for Fawzī, Gordon had been very
angry with him when he left Khartoum, and had refused to give him the necessary documents to substantiate his claim to the rank of colonel and *bey*.
Fawzī could produce no such proof to his suspicious Ottoman Egyptian superiors at the War Ministry, and languished for some months with no assign-

ment.[16] This issue of rank for Fawzī arose at a particularly sensitive time in Egyptian politics: Egyptian officers like Ibrahīm Fawzī had grown more desperate and frustrated at the refusal of ethnic Circassian administrators to promote them. The military grades that were equated with the social ranks of *pasha* and *bey* were intended almost exclusively for Circassians, and Egyptians claiming these titles met with arrogance and condescension, as Fawzī related when he returned to the War Ministry in 1879:

> Two days after my return to Cairo I went to the Bureau of War wearing my uniform, and I met Shahin Pasha, the minister of military and naval affairs. He seemed friendly and easy with me, but after we drank coffee together, he asked me, with a surprised and astonished look on his face, "So you've achieved the rank of colonel?" I told him yes. He then asked me from where had I come, and I responded the Sudan.
>
> "What is your name?" he said, and I told him. Then he asked me if I had a letter from the governor of the Sudan, and when I told him that I didn't, he asked, "Then with what can we confirm your identity?" I related to him what had prevented the governor of the Sudan from giving me such a letter, and then Shahin Pasha inquired as to what that matter had been about. I said that I wasn't exactly sure, and then he asked me for which authorized rank that I had reached could I show the proper credentials. I responded that would be for the rank of second lieutenant up to the rank of colonel. Shahin Pasha said he wished to see those documents. At that point I could no longer conceal my anger, and I said, "What do you think, that I falsified these ranks? If that's what you think, then you have Lt. General ʿUthman Rifqī Pasha who used to be the general commander of the soldiers in the Sudan. Ask him about me and he can confirm this. And if you want, the Khedive's attendants can inform you about what he will do to you for leveling these questions at me!" And with that, I turned away from him, while he tried to reassure me and said that he hoped I'd return tomorrow.[17]

This matter took Fawzī all the way to Tawfīq Pasha, the khedive. Tawfīq also needed to see confirmation from Gordon, and it became clear to Fawzī that the khedive's ministers were annoyed with Gordon because he had granted promotions so haphazardly. Fawzī in fact tried to placate one of these Circassian commanders by saying he was sure that the Circassian had been much younger than he was when the former had reached the same rank. Their conversation revealed that Fawzī had actually been younger, a point that rankled the Circassian officer and which Fawzī explained by saying, "I deserved to achieve that rank because I underwent hardships and suffered great difficulties in the conquest of a new country." The conversation ended there. But these exchanges between Fawzī and the members of the

Circassian ruling class reveal how deeply sensitized to rank and promotion all these men were. Added to this was Fawzī's sharp watchfulness against Circassian discrimination, a wariness that he shared with ʿUrābī and the other officers beginning then to organize themselves. A complicating factor was Fawzī's need to rely on the British General Gordon to prove his military worth and rank.[18] The matter was not cleared up until Gordon returned from the Sudan to Cairo, where two British soldiers who had worked closely with Gordon and Fawzī interceded on the latter's behalf. Gordon wrote immediately to the Ministry of War, but the ministry was unable to find anything suitable for Fawzī. Not until late in the year 1879 was Fawzī appointed to the rank of commissioner of works and welfare in the provinces of Gharbīya and then Giza. Soon his superior was fired for corruption, and the Egyptian officers at last rebelled against the stultifying and discriminatory military infrastructure.

No wonder, then, that in 1881 Fawzī joined this movement. He served in high offices during the ʿUrābīya, and in early 1882, with new officers in charge of the army, Fawzī became the police chief of Cairo. Fawzī Bey, as he was known, was not one of the six closest companions of ʿUrābī, but as revealed by his book and his careful testimony to the Commission of Inquiry investigating the rebellion after its failure, he was certainly among the inner core of military leaders, well respected and depended on by ʿUrābī himself.[19] When the rebellion failed, Fawzī, still protesting his loyalty to the khedive, was arrested by the British General Wood and imprisoned along with the other leaders of the rebellion. Fawzī was called to testify at least five times before the Committee of Inquiry about his role in the demonstrations at ʿAbdin Palace and his alleged responsibility in the razing of Alexandria after the British bombardment. He was exonerated of the second accusation because he and other officers testified against one colleague who had run amok, encouraging mobs to loot and kill foreigners and Christians, and who had therefore flouted high standards of civility and respect for international law that ʿUrābī had tried hard to incorporate in his followers.[20] Fawzī and the other leaders were deeply afraid of Circassian officers exacting a terrible revenge and were able to obtain as defense counsel the British lawyer A. M. Broadley.

The irony of the situation was clear to all involved. Broadley himself quoted one of ʿUrābī's closest associates, Aḥmad Rifāt Bey, as saying, "The very Englishmen who have defeated us in battle now demand for us an impartial trial. We can entertain no possible illusion on the subject— England and the English people are our real judges."[21] The ʿUrābī rebellion had broken out as a protest against a tradition of Circassian abuse and discrimination against native-born Egyptians. It had expanded, with the support of Ṣanū'a and al-Nadīm and the participation of wealthy Egyptian landowners, into a protest against the loss of Egyptian political autonomy in the face of increasing British and French domination. However, all the officers in their hour of extreme need appealed to British lawyers, and perhaps more than any other of the rebel officers, Fawzī had depended on an English officer for his upward mobility through the hierarchy of the Egyptian army. A further irony in the situation was the way Fawzī justified his right to high rank through his actions as a colonizing officer of the Egyptian army. If anything clearly emerges from these parallels it is that the idea of colonialism was much more fluid, much less dependent on the European model. After all, Egyptians in 1882 were negotiators familiar with the Ottoman Empire and fearful of the threat of European colonization, and yet also eager to see themselves as a nation in a synonymous position of power.

It was difficult for the nationalists of the 'Urābī rebellion to be in this position, caught between Circassian anger and British censure. Fortunately, Fawzī and his colleagues were spared the death penalty that the khedive had at first hoped to impose, but they suffered months of imprisonment. Fawzī was stripped of the medals, honors, and rank that he had struggled for so long to achieve in the Sudan and then so zealously guarded for years. But unlike the soldiers Broadley saw stripped of their arms and herded ignominiously onto steamers, headed for almost certain defeat in the Sudan, Ibrahīm Fawzī actually gained a ray of professional hope from the momentum of the Mahdī's movement. As events in the Sudan continued to escalate, the khedive called upon General Gordon to return to the Sudan and take charge of the Egyptian troops still present. Gordon quickly sent telegrams to General Wodehouse, leader of the British troops in Egypt, and to Lord Cromer, who had become the British consul-general in Egypt, requesting the services of Ibrahīm Fawzī. These two men were the pillars of the British administration in Egypt, and without their consent Fawzī would never have been returned to service, an irony that was not lost on him as he strode with Gordon past the "army of occupation" *(jaysh al-iḥtilāl)* toward the steamers headed for the Sudan. Gordon also returned Fawzī's honor, bestowing on him the high rank of *liwā'* (general) of the army, and the title of pasha that this conveyed.[22] It was to be Fawzī's great frustration that he would have to fight for the legitimacy of this title for the rest of his life.

Fawzī shared this frustration with the rest of his colleagues in the 'Urābī movement, a frustration most notably articulated by Aḥmad 'Urābī himself. But unlike any other Egyptian officer in the army, Fawzī was the protégé of a high-ranking British officer who had made himself responsible for the promotion of this still young officer. Although Fawzī was able to summon up anger at the resentment of Turco-Circassian officers against him, he was not beholden to them for his professional mobility. With the exception of his two years as an upper-level officer in the nationalist movement's administration, Fawzī owed the distinctions of his career to General Gordon's recognition of his abilities. Without Gordon's signatures, Fawzī was a man bare of all rank and honor.

As is well-known, General Gordon and Ibrahīm Fawzī were unable to evacuate all the troops from the besieged city of Khartoum. The Egyptian government was powerless to send in more reinforcements, and neither Lord Cromer nor the British Parliament was inclined to bankroll a large-scale campaign into the Sudan against the Mahdī. After months of siege, in which the food supplies grew ever shorter and conditions ever more miserable, the soldiers of the Mahdī stormed the city in January 1885. Charles Gordon was killed near his bed chambers. Ibrahīm Fawzī was severely beaten and taken prisoner by the Mahdists. Yet, even in his death, Gordon conferred distinction upon Fawzī Pasha. There are many, many accounts of Gordon's final moments written by English and other European authors, but none challenged the eyewitness reliability or immediacy of Fawzī's description of Gordon bidding him good night and farewell before the final attack at dawn.[23]

DOCUMENTING IBRAHĪM FAWZĪ

People who had escaped the Mahdī's devastation of Khartoum, and the prisons created in Omdurman, publicized the idea in Egypt and abroad that Fawzī and Gordon had suffered and starved together during the ten-month siege of Khartoum. For years after the fall of the city, Gordon's martyrdom reflected on Fawzī Pasha, who gained both fame and notoriety as the highest-ranking Egyptian official lost to the prisons of the Mahdī. In the fourteen years between the defeat of ʿUrābī's forces and the reconquest of the Sudan in 1898, the aura of tragedy that hung over the images of Khartoum and Gordon turned Fawzī Pasha into an enigmatic hero in Egyptian newspapers and stories and created a legal dilemma for the Ministries of War and Finance. For about five years, no one in Cairo knew if Fawzī was dead or alive. This purgatory of official existence made life very difficult for the families of officers like Fawzī, because without proof of their loved ones' survival, the Ministry of Finance paid them lower pensions and benefits. In 1886, however, a group of officers emerged from the Sudan, and declared in their briefings that there were other officers being held prisoner by the

Mahdī. This information galvanized the families of such officers to demand from the Ministry of Finance pensions at a higher rate that had accrued to their husbands and fathers. The ministry rejected these pleas and continued to pay pensions at the lower rate.[24] Further threats to these pensions over the next couple of years created a great deal of anxiety for the families of soldiers and officers still held in the Sudan.

Then, in August of 1889, it came to the attention of the Ministry of Finance, indirectly by way of the chief officer of the governorate of Cairo [*muḥāfaẓat miṣr*], that Ibrahīm Fawzī had smuggled a large packet of letters and documents out of Omdurman, some of them addressed to different consuls, others to various individuals in Cairo and Alexandria. There was no postage on these letters, and they had been sent from postmaster to postmaster in provinces all the way from Aswan.[25] According to military law governing these regions, any mail out of the Sudan was to be forwarded immediately to the headquarters of the Egyptian army, as it was considered military intelligence.[26] This was lucky for Fawzī, because his letters attracted a lot of media attention. The existence of these letters, most of which were appeals for a larger pension based on his rank of *liwā'* as created by General Gordon, reinforced the constant appeals that his wife, 'Aisha, had been making to the Ministry of Finance for a larger stipend from the government.

In the large dossier of materials on the pensions of officers "lost" in the Sudan, one of 'Aisha's letters survives. It is not dated, but as the contents make clear, she was writing immediately after she had become aware of her husband's survival (so sometime after 1889 or 1890). In this letter she traces her numerous suits and appeals in support of her claims for a larger pension, all of which were denied because she had no proof of her husband's survival. But now, with his existence confirmed, 'Aisha points to the valor of his long service in the Sudan, the fact that he volunteered to go out of loyalty to his country, and the fact that he was then taken prisoner by force. "Is that not enough to ensure that his family would not be cut off from all government funds?" she asks.[27] Impressed by her appeal, and by Fawzī's resourcefulness in smuggling out his letters and thus verifying his existence, the Ministry of Finance proposed to the Council of Ministers the virtual tripling of the monthly stipend of Fawzī's wife. The letter from the president of the committee left it to further adjudication what Fawzī's final pension would be.[28] His very identity and existence had become intricately linked with the level of government pensions accorded to all Egyptian soldiers.

These were old complaints and issues, dating for men like Fawzī and his peers since before the 'Urābī rebellion. People sympathized with his efforts for these reasons, and also because Fawzī Pasha's name had become famous enough to evoke the personal humiliation many Egyptians felt about the loss of the Sudan. While still in Omdurman, Fawzī Pasha was characterized respectfully in Jurji Zaydan's historical novel *Asir al-mutamahdī* (Prisoner of the False Mahdī) first printed in 1892. The figure of Fawzī Pasha added historical weight to this fictional piece, self-consciously intended to represent "objective" truths about the Sudan problem. Zaydan had worked as an interpreter for British intelligence in the Sudan in 1884, and he claimed intimate "familiarity with the customs of the Sudanese people and the circumstances of the rising of their false Prophet." Zaydan said, in his introduction to *Asir*'s first edition, that he also relied heavily on the testimonies of those who had escaped the Mahdī, making the novel just as "reliable as any book of history."[29] In this novel in which any supporter of ʿUrābī appears foolishly naive if not treacherous to Egypt, and in which the British are romanticized, Fawzī Pasha is portrayed as sorrowfully describing the deprivations of the inhabitants of Khartoum and the lost hopes of the besieged for any sight of their delayed English rescuers. Zaydan has Gordon listening respectfully to Fawzī's speech, which is interrupted only by the attack of the dervishes! Although Zaydan had no sympathy for the ʿUrābī rebels, he accorded to Fawzī that crucial authenticity that proximity to Gordon bestowed, allowing Fawzī to be the last person talking with Gordon before the English hero's death.

But for some European explorers of the Sudan, especially rivals in the administration, Ibrahīm Fawzī embodied political evil, a particularly Egyptian type of despotism that had wrought havoc on the Sudanese. Branded a corrupt scoundrel by Giegler Pasha, another European that Ismaʿīl appointed to a Sudanese administrative service, Ibrahīm Fawzī was known to the British and Foreign Anti-Slavery Society as a violent slave dealer who had abused his position as governor of Equatoria to plunder the very tribes Gordon had employed him to protect.[30] His successor to that governorship, the German Emin Pasha, wasted little time in decrying Ibrahīm Fawzī's inclusion in the Sudan Ministry in Cairo, under the ʿUrābī government. "Under these conditions," Emin Pasha railed, "how is the government to be carried on? What about the slave question?"[31]

But other Europeans involved in service in the Sudan or in Egypt respected Fawzī immensely. In the fearful and anxious days after the British bombardment of Alexandria, when Egyptian soldiers following ʿUrābī were almost at fever pitch, Europeans unsympathetic to the rebellion were impressed by Fawzī's ability to keep Cairo secure and calm. As A. M. Broadley wrote in his account, Signor G. B. Messidaglia, a former subordinate governor in the Sudan, brought forth a petition signed by other Italians resident in Cairo testifying to the "praise-worthy conduct of Ibrahīm Bey Fouzy, Arabi's Prefect of Police."[32] And for Charles Neufeld, a German merchant who was himself imprisoned by the Mahdī's forces, Fawzī was a friend and a hero.

To Egyptian newspaper editors, especially those who espoused the Sudan's return to Egypt as a pillar of the nationalist movement, Ibrahīm Fawzī Pasha remained a steadfast hero, a defender of law and order. In September of 1898, the details of the battle of Omdurman splashed across *Miṣbaḥ al-sharq*'s front pages. These details grew more dramatic with the news that the commander *(sirdār)* of the Egyptian Army, General Herbert Kitchener, ignored the pillage of the city by former slaves of the Mahdīya. An eyewitness to the destruction, quoted at length, recounted how these slaves went after Ibrahīm Fawzī, who had just returned to his Omdurman hut after being released from the prison of the khalifa (the successor to the Mahdī), when he intervened in their attempts to steal a donkey. The pasha "scolded them personally, but they did not listen. They threatened to kill him, so the Pasha himself paid [the rightful owner] for the donkey, even giving them his saddle."[33] Only after the general heard of this insult to Fawzī Pasha did he regulate the behavior of the slaves and soldiers.

THE POLITICAL AND THE PERSONAL: WRITING MEMOIRS OF THE SUDAN

With all the political baggage he carried, and his considerably romanticized public image, Ibrahīm Fawzī Pasha could not have helped but be singularly conscious of what he represented to so many different people when he finally returned to his native Egypt in 1899. He waited longer to publish his memoirs than his European coprisoners did. Some of them had escaped before the reconquest, whereas others had been freed with him. When he finally did speak out about his experience, his calculated self-representation as an *Egyptian* eyewitness to such important events took on amplified significance, whether he wrote in Arabic or was interviewed in English.

In addition to political and cultural considerations, there were important material considerations behind the way Ibrahīm Fawzī framed his life for both the British and the Egyptian public. He was then awaiting the final verdict on his appeal for back pay and pension accrued over fourteen years at the rank of *liwā'* of the Egyptian army. He insisted that Gordon had promoted him to this rank, and many government officials, both Egyptian and British, believed him. Of course, these claims had been followed up by his wife in his absence, and his smuggled letters had attested to the same facts.

But the Council of Ministers had let final judgment on the issue hang in 1891, and nine years later it remained unresolved. Technicalities were raised, however, during investigations into the extent of Gordon's authority as governor-general of the Sudan, in the service of the khedive. Fawzī offered a précis of his entire career, documented with letters from Gordon, and orders from Tawfīq to Gordon, that he hoped would prove his status.[34] Fawzī then enlisted the help of the press, most interestingly the Anglo-Egyptian press, in support of his case. His plea was hampered, though, by a decided lack of sympathy from key British officials like Sir Reginald Wingate and other old Sudan hands who believed Fawzī Pasha to be nothing but a slave dealer.[35] His application dragged on for two years, until 1901, when he lost his appeal. This judgment capped a lifetime's worth of frustration and self-justification.

The act of writing memoirs for Fawzī was thus heavily laden with financial urgency, and not just a desire for wealth and fame. Frequently in his long career, he had to prove his rank and worth to different superiors—of different nationalities, but rarely Egyptian—under difficult political circumstances. The act of writing had always been for Fawzī a means of testifying: either to prove his innocence, as was the case after the ʿUrābī revolution; to prove his very existence, as smuggling his letters out of the Sudan under the Mahdīya demonstrated; or to prove his rank, as his précis and all the other important documents he authored in his professional life showed. The act of writing a political history like *Kitāb al-sūdān* was also the act of creating an autobiography, an intensely personal undertaking for Fawzī, in which he created a new kind of nationalist writing not easily fitted into pre-existing forms of Egyptian nationalist literature. In his memoirs, Fawzī allowed himself to become the personification of all Egypt's experiences with empire. Like Egypt undergoing the invasive supervision of Great Britain in East Africa, Fawzī was dogged and eventually disgraced by European officials accusing him of crimes and slave trading. As Egypt as a nation and a culture had to prove to the occupying administration that it was capable of self-government, Fawzī had to prove that he deserved the high rank of *liwāʾ* to British officials. Fawzī and other Egyptian officers also had to confront the arrogance of Circassian officials who felt more allegiance to the Ottoman sultan than they did to Egypt, or Egyptians. And most important, this son of Egypt, so angry with those who would colonize his country, expressed in his professional actions and in his writing how deeply he believed in the Egyptian civilizing mission in the Sudan. Fawzī understood the pain and power of colonialism from all sides.

The irony of the colonized colonizer's existence was as clear to Ibrahīm

Fawzī as it was to other contemporaries, and it prompted many interesting articles and discussions in both the Egyptian and the British press. But the subjects of such discussion, men like Fawzī or his onetime Sudanese rival al-Zubayr Raḥman Pasha Manṣūr, asserted that this irony was more an injustice, such as being purposely misunderstood by a European audiences, than a contradiction. Their qualities as "modern," "civilized" men had been honed in the generous acts of bring higher civilization to remote villages in the Sudan. The debate focused not on the validity of the civilizing mission but on who was qualified to lead it.

In many ways, Ibrahīm Fawzī Pasha and al-Zubayr came of political age almost simultaneously. Al-Zubayr was a trader from Khartoum, born ten years after the Egyptian government had first conquered the Sudan. In the 1850s and 1860s, he built up a vast, lucrative, and well-armed trade network in the Bahr al-Ghazal region of the Sudan, becoming governor of the region in 1873. A year later he had grown powerful enough to conquer the province of Dārfūr, which brought him into direct confrontation with the Egyptian government. In 1875, when General Gordon had become the governor of the Equatorial Provinces (with Ibrahīm Fawzī in his service), al-Zubayr grew frustrated with Gordon's attempts to restrict his power and tax his caravans. In what became a public drama, al-Zubayr appealed directly to Khedive Ismaʿīl, who invited him to Cairo to negotiate. Once al-Zubayr arrived in Cairo, the khedive made a palace available for him, and met with him, but refused to let him leave. Al-Zubayr became a prisoner in a gilded cage, the most famous Sudanese figure in Egypt, until the emergence of the Mahdī. His son, Sulayman, attempted to rescue his father's land from the Egyptian government but was killed by the army in 1879. Al-Zubayr was not able to return to the Sudan until 1884, when Gordon, once again governor-general of the Sudan, welcomed him as a potential alternative to the Mahdī.[36] But al-Zubayr's attempts to create an independent understanding with the Mahdī frightened Gordon again, and he was sent back to Cairo, to be put on a British ship and exiled to Gibraltar. This exile signaled the end of al-Zubayr's political life, although public fascination with him continued to be strong.

Flora Shaw, a British journalist, conducted a series of interviews with al-Zubayr in 1887 that were published in English in the journal *Contemporary Review*. Interestingly, Shaw was the wife of Lord Frederick Lugard, the British officer who helped establish colonial rule over Nigeria and much of central Africa (for example, Uganda, not far from al-Zubayr's Sudan). In these interviews, which took place over the course of four months, Shaw asked al-Zubayr for his side of the story. Surrounded by black servants from the regions over which he once had reigned supreme, and with the help of an interpreter, al-Zubayr tried to explain his motives for creating large slave-trading networks between remote areas of the Sudan. His interviewer was herself aware of the different filters through which al-Zubayr's case would be perceived by his audience, and she wrote in the first article of the series that "I had the powerful sense of strong differences and gaps between what *[sic]* the content of what he recounted and what I had heard about him." She thus tried to tell her readers that there were many elements in this narrative that they could not see: the translator, the differences in understandings of geographical and political entities that existed between her and al-Zubayr, his passionate way of speaking, and the scrutiny of the soldiers guarding him.[37]

But the interviews make surprising connections with European culture of the time. From al-Zubayr, Shaw understood that the spirit of exploration that had sparked the departure of so many young Britons for "unknown" territories in distant places had also lit the imaginations of men like himself:

> In those times, the provinces situated south of the White Nile held for the young men of Khartoum the same kind of attraction that enticed certain British youth and pushed them at different times to explore the unknown regions of America and savage Australia. The expeditions that the Sudanese launched to penetrate these areas were trading expeditions. But those who undertook them had to prepare completely for the plunge into personal, ongoing and difficult adventures. For many regions of the country were unknown and had not yet been discovered and the stories told about them inspired wonder and amazement, exactly as happened in Europe in the beginning about the wonders of the West and its legends.[38]

Clearly, as the interviewer tried to show, Rudyard Kipling would have sympathized with al-Zubayr Pasha. From this initial wonder at the legends of unknown people and places, much of al-Zubayr's story focused on his rise to economic power in the Sudan and how he was able to gain the confidence of so many different tribes. The customs of some of these tribes did not disappoint the expectations of wild adventure anticipated by the young al-Zubayr. As he related, the tribe he knew as the Nyam Nyam had no organized religion; one individual would worship a tree, another a chicken or a snake. Even worse, they were cannibals and traded the bodies of those they had killed in the markets, where the meat was sold like beef. As al-Zubayr learned to negotiate with these people, he claimed to have been guided by the necessity of bringing certain basics of civilization to them: "I had no desire to be king! All I desired was to trade and to work towards spreading civilization and culture." But civilization and modern culture could not be brought to these regions unless accompanied by a true understanding of the customs and beliefs of the inhabitants. The governor really had to understand those whom he governed. This was why, according to al-Zubayr, the Egyptian government (the Turks, as he and other Sudanese termed the government) was never able to hold on to the Sudan. They did not possess any understanding of the Sudanese "and treated them as if they were the inhabitants of Cairo, or Istanbul."[39]

The picture of this unusual man discussing the elements of which proper government consists is striking: a warrior-trader-governor exiled in what was theoretically his land (but which he was unable to leave) by the government to which he professed allegiance, but in whose ability to govern an empire he had no confidence—a man trapped for years in prison yet pontificating about control. This description also shows the parallels between al-Zubayr Pasha and Ibrahīm Fawzī, who was himself caught in a triangle of loyalties and allegiances, whose abilities were quite singular, and who also used a prison setting to discuss the nature of governmental power and the meaning of colonialism. This analogous position is obvious in a 1901 interview that Fawzī gave to the English language daily, the *Egyptian Gazette.* The interview preceded both the publication of his memoirs by a few weeks and the final decision on his appeal for back pay. In the article, he recounted the last days of Khartoum and the bravery of General Gordon. His intimate connection to the administration of the city emerged in the details he offers of steps that could have been taken to reinforce the stores of the besieged city.[40] The most striking aspect of Fawzī Pasha's story, however, is the photograph that introduced him to the reader. Over the headline "A Prisoner of the Khalifa," a phrase borrowed from the recently published memoirs of Fawzī Pasha's German friend, the merchant Charles Neufeld, several figures sit in a thatched room. To the extreme right is Ibrahīm Fawzī, across from Neufeld. Opposite him is Fawzī's son, born during the Mahdīya, staring sadly if not purposefully into the distance. All three wear heavy chains around their feet and the Mahdist *jubba* (uniform). (See fig. 6.)

Yet this portrait of imprisonment bristles with contradictions. The three are positioned sitting before a meal, which is being served to them by two black men. The caption identifies these two men as jailers, yet they are frozen in the moment of servile gesture, looking much more like slaves. Neufeld looks poignantly at one of them, but the intent of his gaze is unclear: perhaps it expresses fear, or perhaps he is conveying an order. Fawzī Pasha and Neufeld are sitting on the same level, equal in both the weight of their chains and their social status. Their pose reinforces their superiority

6. Ibrahīm Fawzī *(far right)* in prison, from the *Egyptian Gazette*, 1901.

over the two black jailers-slaves who hover near them, even though they recline in shackles and the black men move unhindered.

The *Gazette* reporter first attributed the taking of the photo to General Kitchener, at the very moment in which he liberated the Omdurman jail, but corrected this statement in response to several letters from readers, saying instead that the original was so faded that "it was decided to have it retaken in Cairo."[41] Neither Ibrahīm Fawzī nor Neufeld could remember who took the photo. Several letters had also claimed that the costumes had been rented, later, in Atbara, but the reporter asserted that the costumes and the arms were "exactly what the two prisoners wore on the day of the entry of the troops into the city and are at present still in their possession here."[42]

Fawzī's self-conscious self-display—clothing himself in what had been the dress of humiliation as an emblem of historical evidence and proof of position, and staging his imprisonment as if for an exhibition on the exotic Sudan in the Geographical Society halls—recurred, with even more spectacle, in *Kitāb al-sūdān bayna aydī Gordon wa Kitchener*. Proving his rank and worth motivated Fawzī Pasha's orchestration of the details of his career, but his experiences in the Sudan, with the Sudanese, shaped the greater part of his self-esteem and certainly his cultural pride. What makes Ibrahīm Fawzī's book an important historical source is that he shared, with two generations of Egyptians, a struggle for a certain kind of recognition, on a national and cultural level, that bound them closely to the Sudan. Fawzī

Pasha appropriated the role of explorer and conqueror, usually narrated by Europeans in the last decades of the nineteenth century, and carried back to Cairo his own specimens, artifacts, and anecdotes of the Sudan. His claim to intimate knowledge of the place was a claim to ownership, a protest against the Anglo-Egyptian Condominium, with its British domination of the Sudan. His book placed the Sudan, and the Sudanese, at the feet of Egyptian society.

THE HISTORY OF THE SUDAN BETWEEN
THE TIMES OF GORDON AND KITCHENER

The very title of the book frames the ambiguous route between British and Egyptian authority in the Sudan that Fawzī Pasha had to negotiate. Gordon introduced Fawzī to the Sudan, Kitchener freed him from it. Again, Fawzī Pasha's clever use of photographs offers an example of his conflicted stance. On the third page of *Kitāb al-sūdān,* right after the photo of Khedive 'Abbas Hilmī, there sits a large picture of Gordon, one page before Fawzī's own. A reprinted letter from Gordon's sister follows his photo, in which she thanked Fawzī for providing details of her brother's last moments. This demonstration of connection places Fawzī within the Gordon family circle and establishes his value as a historical eyewitness.[43]

But for whom did Fawzī Pasha intend this type of validation? Surely his readers were almost exclusively made up of educated Egyptians of the upper, or military, classes. Furthermore, his book was published by *al-Mu'ayid,* one of the most prominent and outspoken of the contemporary nationalist newspapers and, in fact, funded by Tawfīq's successor, the often vocally anti-British khedive Abbas Hilmī II. Why, then, did Fawzī Pasha frame his own story with two of the most important standard bearers of British imperialism?

Only an officer of high rank would have been near Gordon in his final moments, Fawzī's text implies, only someone indispensable to the Egyptian administration of the Sudan. As Fawzī knew, and as other Egyptians witnessed, when the news of Gordon's death finally reached England, the British public arose in anger and demanded vengeance against the Mahdi. Though momentum for reconquest moved slowly through the Foreign Office, Kitchener's mobilization was characterized as revenge for Gordon. This emotional jihad against the Sudanese completely precluded any Egyptian role in the fall of Khartoum, however.[44] The reconquest of the Sudan was not organized by Egyptian leaders but by British officials. Egyptian officers did not lead Egyptian troops back into the Sudan fourteen years after their predecessors had been evacuated from it; on the contrary, British officers led the Egyptian soldiers up the Nile toward Omdurman. Fawzī's reaffirmed presence at that violent moment penetrates this exclusion, reasserting an Egyptian role, three years after the declaration of the humiliating Anglo-Egyptian Condominium of the Sudan.

Fawzī declared himself the voice of true Egypt in his introduction to his book, when he stated, "I saw that it was my duty to my people and my nation [*min wājib qawmī wa ummatī*] and to myself to write this book, including all that happened to me, or connected me to the events of the Sudan during this period."[45] And Ibrahīm Fawzī reiterated his reliability by adding a communal sense of the Sudan: "I did not limit myself to narrating events that personally happened to me, but also referred to the group of high officials in the Sudanese government who were, before the dervishes, spread out across the different parts of the Sudan, in order for us to have all the events from every possible perspective."[46] All those foreigners who suffered the prison of the Mahdī and lived to write about it, whether career military men like the Austrian Rudolph Slatin Pasha, European merchants taking advantage of the chaos in trade like Charles Neufeld, or the German priest Father Ohrwalder, were therefore enlisted by Fawzī as co-eyewitnesses in this book, thus conferring legitimacy on his account of the Sudanese. The act of writing this history as shared history may have, in Fawzī's eyes, made it seem even truer to his audience. He suggested this somewhat defiantly when, even though apologizing for possible mistakes (he is, after all, just a soldier, he says), he posed a challenge to anyone else who had seen of Gordon what he saw, who had witnessed what he witnessed of the Mahdīya: "Then let him write for posterity the way I have done."[47] This was Fawzī's assertion of his voice and narrative as being equally, if not more intimately, connected to the Sudan than those of the Europeans.

Fawzī Pasha viewed his world with a dichotomized perspective that is evident throughout his writing. Aware of his multiple allegiances, Fawzī Pasha had to manipulate historical events of great political sensitivity to fit political circumstances that had changed greatly during the long period of his captivity. When *Kitāb al-sūdān* was published, the calls by once proud nationalists for the retaking of the Sudan (or as many contemporaries phrased it, the "return" of the Sudan to Egypt) had been muffled by outspoken regret over the Anglo-Egyptian Condominium, viewed by many in Egypt as another slice in the British carve-up of Africa and a seizure of Egyptian rights to the area.[48] This change in attitude rendered Fawzī Pasha's position much more delicate, as he owed his freedom to that same Anglo-

Egyptian force which other nationalists writers were now denouncing. He wore the nationalist credentials he had earned under 'Urābī proudly, but just as proudly he carried his medals and his rank, returned to him by none other than Gordon. And finally, he had been an important figure not only in Egyptian expansionism in the Sudan but also in the humiliating loss of Khartoum.

He saved his position through a deft maneuver that combined the arts of ventriloquism, camouflage, and disguise. In the following passage, he narrates how the army, under Gordon, established the rule of the Egyptian government in the southeastern regions of the Sudan, in the domain of King Mtesa (Mtesa ruled over what is now Uganda, and was an extremely important regional leader who managed for years to play Egypt and the European powers off each other):

> When we arrived at the first part of this mudīriya [district], in the territory of the king, we started building a post to make use of as our first way station, but the slaves [*abīd*] began skirmishing with us, trying to distract us from reinforcing the situation. We kept on like that for a long time, with them never mobilizing to attack us, nor leaving us to finish the post we were building in peace.
>
> Then Gordon began speaking to Mtesa, scolding him for the natives' having fled from us, leaving their land so that we couldn't employ them to fulfill the tasks of building. Then Gordon informed him that we had come in the name of the Egyptian government, forceful in power, strong in courage, a government that didn't want from that region any more than to spread civilization and justice throughout, and to open the lands to the benefits of trade, through which people exchanged their goods. If King Mtesa wished happiness for his land, he would then deal honestly with the Egyptian government, and would place himself under the protection of her extensive wisdom; that way, the government would not come to him with soldiers, over whom he would have no sway, to show him her might and her power that could flatten mountains and cliffs, that defied tyrants. "I am staying in Meruly," Gordon said, "waiting to hear your intentions."
>
> Four days had not passed before King Mtesa's messenger appeared, and he censured Gordon for threatening the king, since he did not know the extent of Mtesa's strength, and he was capable of bringing down great tribulations on Gordon, and everyone with him. He did not need the force of the Egyptian government, nor did he seek help from Egypt, no matter how strong it was. Then the messenger asked Gordon why he had come to Mtesa's land to dethrone the king, saying, in the king's own words, we are satisfied with our condition. We never sent you a complaint, nor a plea for help, and we can do without this civilization of yours that plunders our happiness and our present independence.[49]

As it turned out, Mtesa's forceful message was only a smokescreen; he permitted Gordon and the army to finish the way station, and he allowed the villagers to trade freely with the Egyptian soldiers. When the outpost was finished, the army hoisted the Egyptian flag over it, then shot off a twenty-one-gun salute "announcing the conquest of this district. With regard to all this, Mtesa displayed affection and friendship to Gordon, and said to us, 'We are one hand, and I derive my strength from the Egyptian government, which extends my authority over the governed, for their security and welfare.'"[50] Fawzī rewarded Mtesa for his capitulation by telling the reader that, after that point, the king became the strongest ruler in "unknown" Africa *[majāhil ifrīqīya],* and that his people developed to a degree that far outstripped natives of neighboring regions. Gordon's language and his capacity to threaten dominate this narrative of the setting up of empire. Using the classical forms of imperialism, Gordon stated the terms of the army's expansion: the government wanted nothing more than to spread civilization and justice throughout. But there existed much more within the partnership of "we" implied in the sentence, as remembered and reconstructed by Ibrahīm Fawzī, for it established Gordon as a tool, a carefully chosen figure through whom Egyptian hegemony in the Sudan was articulated.[51] In Fawzī's description of him, Gordon became the instrument for the ventriloquism of the khedive. Gordon spoke for Egyptian authority, for a government that coopted his identity as a European to legitimize its own goals in the Sudan. Gordon's presence, his words, and his uniform provided a disguise for Egyptian officials in the Sudan, such as Fawzī. Gordon spoke formally, as a colonizer and as a Briton, which cloaked the actions and goals of Egyptians in the Sudan at that time. In his shadow, however, lurked the real colonizers, the Egyptians Ibrahīm Fawzī mentioned frequently throughout the book who performed the actual building of infrastructure in the Sudan; even after the Mahdīya, Fawzī mentioned Egyptians who served as clerks and doctors to the khalifa. Gordon may have spoken the language of treaty and conquest, and in so doing may have represented the khedive, but it was ordinary Egyptians, those who looked at the Sudanese from a much less lofty perch, who truly instructed the Sudanese about government. Though many of these contributors remained anonymous, their actions accumulate in the book, testimony to Fawzī's pride in those whom he considered to be the real modernizers of "unknown Africa."[52]

But situating official legitimacy for Egypt's presence in the Sudan proved to be a difficult issue for Ibrahīm Fawzī. He insisted that Great Britain's true purpose in sending Gordon to Khartoum was to create chaos in the Sudan and to cut Egyptian influence over the territories. Tawfīq, on the other hand, fully intended to restore peace and order eventually, but the British modified his plans, forcing him to remove his "devoted subjects" from the dangers surrounding them in Khartoum and to evacuate all the Egyptians and "other settlers from civilized countries" from the Sudan.[53] Yet he knew that many Sudanese, whether following the Mahdī or protesting Egyptian settlements in their southern villages, called the Egyptian soldiers "Turks."[54] If, as Fawzī Pasha stated repeatedly, Egyptians intended to civilize the Sudan, then under what kind of flag should unity between the regions be forged? What ideals would fuel an ideology of expansionist nationalism for a man like Fawzī Pasha, in the troubled and tumultuous years between the ʿUrābī revolt and the Anglo-Egyptian Condominium? Clearly this confusion over what was "Egyptian" in the administration of the Sudan pricked at the loyalties of a committed soldier like Fawzī, especially when he and the other Egyptians in the Sudan were being labeled "Turks," the very group whose corrupt domination of the army and the country had provoked the ʿUrābī rebellion.

No clarification came from the Egyptian ruler. In Fawzī's narrative, Khedive Tawfīq inspired none but the sycophantic and the desperate. In order to be reinstated in the army, Fawzī had to distance himself publicly, in front of the khedive, from the ʿUrabists to whom he was once politically loyal. Gordon made an appointment for him, telling him to paint as black a picture as possible of ʿUrābī and to laud the memory of the khedive's father, Ismaʿīl. Armed with Gordon's words, in yet another demonstration of oral camouflage, Fawzī went off "to meet with shame" [*fi adhyāl al-khajal*].[55]

Although the circumstances required Fawzī to later label the ʿUrābī movement a *fiṭna* (disturbance), his narrative reveals an even greater uneasiness about Tawfīq's government. He admitted that he kowtowed with great flourish before the khedive, but he admitted this only after satirizing the khedive's entourage, among whom he was forced to wait before his appointment with Tawfīq. With the exception of one, these officers, all contemporaries of Fawzī's, either refused to return his greeting or rudely stared at him in disbelief at the boldness of this former ʿUrabist daring to face the khedive. The one officer who did greet him immediately warned him of the khedive's residual fury over the rebellion. But when Fawzī Pasha showed everyone the letter General Gordon had sent on his behalf, and when it was announced that the khedive would receive him, there was a sudden clamor of greetings from his formerly condescending peers. And Fawzī writes, "But I did not turn to them or respond to any one of their greetings, saying to myself, what goes around, comes around."[56]

Such dismissal of the people with whom the khedive surrounded himself speaks volumes about Fawzī Pasha's disdain and his recognition of the hollowness of the Egyptian government's authority. Several pages later, Fawzī relates the ceremony that sent him and General Gordon off to the Sudan, in which British soldiers stood around the khedive on the dais. Fawzī refers to them as the "occupying army" *[(jaysh al-iḥtilāl]*. This term further distances Fawzī from a government in which he had no faith and to which he felt little loyalty. Clearly, without Gordon's interceding letter, the khedive would never have reinstated Fawzī Pasha in the army, and without Gordon, Fawzī Pasha would have had no status. On the other hand, Fawzī resented the British army as an occupying force even as he traveled with one of the highest ranking British officers in Egypt. His text thus shows that Fawzī Pasha lived these years on the brink, his loyalties and allegiances so divided and confused that he could spend months in jail, unrepentant over his protest against Tawfīq's capitulations to the British administrators in the occupying government, yet sail off to the Sudan with Gordon, grateful to return to a land that, in his firm opinion, required civilizing.

Officially, this hollowness of authority made Egypt's presence in the Sudan futile. If servants of empire were unable to rely on the long, protective arm of the motherland while they were in overseas territories, the motherland itself lost meaning and cohesion. True to form, Fawzī never said this directly but presented it as a lesson learned from Gordon. In the final days of the siege of Khartoum, Gordon lost hope that British forces would rescue him and his men in time, and, as conditions deteriorated, he looked for ways to evacuate others. He asked Fawzī to escape with the remaining foreign consuls to Metemmeh. Gordon authorized Fawzī to save himself from the disaster about to fall on the city because, according to Gordon, "If I become a prisoner in the hands of those scoundrels, the government of the Queen will not abandon me, and will send tremendous amounts of gold for my ransom, and I wish, from the bottom of my heart, my dear Fawzī, to save you, because if you become a prisoner in their hands, your government will not send even one dirham for your ransom."[57] Fawzī's quotation from Gordon infused irony into the writing of his own narrative, since he remembered these words, publicly, after fourteen years of not being ransomed by the Egyptian government. When the long-awaited rescuers finally came, they carried the ambiguous flag of the "Anglo-Egyptian" forces led by General Kitchener (it should also be remembered, however, that political hesitation in London prevented the forces of his majesty's government from arriving on time to rescue Gordon from the Mahdī's armies).

But if Fawzī could not help but be outspoken in his ambivalence about the Egyptian government, he remained unwavering in his conviction that the Sudanese required cultural and social development, and that Egyptians were the leaders of this progress. In his many descriptions of the Sudanese tribes, he articulated his ideas about what elements constitute a nation and what he perceived as a lax sense of honor among the Sudanese, who in his eyes did little to protect their own, to sanctify the ties that bind members of a tribe or of one family. Over and over, he reprimanded the Sudanese for their unbridled sexuality. He relates, for instance, that the Baqqara tribe were renowned for their bravery, but says they were equally famous for drinking alcohol, and that incest was rampant among them. Moreover, they paid no attention to morality. Among their women, "it is a terrible shame to marry before they have borne three male children." Fawzī Pasha says the Mahdī forbade these unlawful practices, and the Baqqara only continued their illicit activities "fearfully." In another chapter, Fawzī says that among the worst of Sudanese customs was the practice of fathers giving their daughters or other female dependents as presents to the Mahdī, and that there was absolutely no shame in doing so, as if, Fawzī writes, "what was forbidden was for them permissible *[ka'anna kul harām hallalahu hallalan 'indahum]*."[58] Fawzī translated Sudanese gestures of sharing to mean that the Sudanese had no cultural unity, nothing that bound them together as a cohesive, protective community. In his writings, all that linked the numerous tribes of the Sudan were his description of these un-Islamic customs, making the Muslim northerners as ignorant of religion as the pagan southern tribes, rendering the entire Sudan as needful of Egyptian control. If fathers do not protect their daughters, if family honor bears no significance, then, according to Fawzī, Sudanese women amount to little more than prostitutes or slaves. Thus, the Sudanese would never know exactly who they were without Egyptian cultural intervention. Here, Fawzī reveals his profound sympathy to British definitions of a nation and to the prevailing arguments for the cohesion that imperialism could offer weaker societies.

Fawzī's idea of cultural intervention for the resolution of Sudanese identity was based exclusively on external factors; despite his claims of intimate knowledge of the Sudan, the inhabitants' means of defining each other is never consulted or represented. For instance, Fawzī generalizes the term *Sudanese* to mean all the people native to the Sudan; but for men like al-Zubayr Pasha and Babikr Bedri, the term signified the tribes of the southern Sudan. Al-Zubayr Pasha or Bedri would have referred to northerners by tribal designation or by the term *arab*.[59] These men would have bristled at the term *Sudanese*, an epithet they would have reserved for slaves or the descendants of slaves. To mingle or intermarry with Sudanese (by which they meant Negroes) would have been a great disgrace.[60]

Obviously, Fawzī's relationship with the people of the Sudan was extremely complicated (he did marry a Sudanese woman and father a son by her). Those closest to him in Omdurman, and then in prison, were Europeans. But although he turned to the memoirs of other European prisoners of the Mahdī to provide, as he wrote, a more complete spectrum of historical truth to his own narrative, his accounts of the Sudan during the Mahdīya differed from theirs in significant ways. Two narratives, those of Rudolph Slatin Pasha and Charles Neufeld, best exemplify these differences. Slatin Pasha was an Austrian officer employed by Ismaʿīl as the governor of Dara province, and he surrendered to the Mahdī before the fall of Khartoum. Slatin Pasha spoke fluent Arabic, converted to Islam, and was eventually able to escape to Egypt three years before the battle of Omdurman. Several years later, he wrote an account of his experience titled *Fire and Sword in the Sudan*, which became very popular in Great Britain. Neufeld, another chronicler of the Mahdīya, was a German merchant with little of Slatin's experience in the Sudan who found himself in prison in Omdurman not long after Slatin had fled. He was freed with Ibrahīm Fawzī, and quickly wrote a book, *A Prisoner of the Khaleefa*, that offered his perspective on the Mahdīya. As both narratives show, neither Slatin Pasha nor Neufeld was troubled by the contradiction of identifying with both the colonizers and the colonized. Even when in chains in Omdurman, they viewed themselves much more assertively, and wrote their accounts with much greater cultural assurance, than Fawzī did.

Unlike many other European eyewitnesses to the Mahdīya, Slatin Pasha included a great deal of dialogue in his memoirs, allowing the Sudanese their own voices in his narrative. He always, however, colored their words with a patina of doubt because he believed the Sudanese, to a man, were either liars or idiots. Some of his disdain came from his virulent distrust of the Mahdī's sense of Islam, and some emanated from his profound prejudice against blacks. Another element of disingenuousness came, however, from Slatin's refusal to see himself in the role that the Mahdī, and his successor the khalifa, created for him.

The khalifa usually kept Slatin close to him, as one of his *mulazimīn*, or personal bodyguards, and as a translator of documents the Mahdists found in Khartoum after the siege. But before the city was taken, Slatin Pasha was put in prison, in chains, and released only to identify the decapitated head of General Gordon when it was presented to the Mahdī. He was then summoned before the khalifa, and this scene followed:

> I was now alone with the Khalifa. "And you," said he, "where do you
> wish to go; have you anyone to take care of you?" And I felt him gazing
> at me, whilst I cast my eyes to the ground, knowing that was what he

wished me to do. "Besides God and yourself," I replied, "I have no one, sire; deal with me as you think best for my future."

"I had hoped [for] and expected this answer from you," said the Khalifa, "[and] from this day you may consider yourself a member of my household. I shall care for you and shall never allow you to want for anything; and you will have the benefit of being brought up under my eye, on condition that, from this day forth, you absolutely sever your connection with all your former friends and acquaintances, and associate only with my relatives and servants; you must, moreover, obey implicitly every order you receive from me. During the day, your duty will be to stay with the mulazameen employed in my personal service at the door of my house; and at night, when I return, you will be permitted to go out to the house which I shall assign to you. When I go out, you must always accompany me: if I ride, you must walk beside, until the time comes when, should I see fit, I will provide you with an animal to ride. Do you agree to these conditions, and do you promise to put them into full effect?"

"Master," I replied, "I agree with pleasure to your conditions. In me, you will find a willing and obedient servant; and I hope I may have strength to enter upon my new duties."[61]

These lines were translated from the German by Sir Reginald Wingate, a persistent advocate of Britain's formal colonization of the Sudan who became governor-general of the Sudan after 1900. With the translator's political persuasion in mind, one sees how the words *master* and *sire*, uttered by a European to a Sudanese, hang in the air, always ironic apostrophes, particularly in the last paragraph of the passage. Slatin, with Wingate's support, represents himself as if he were a character in a play. Not only did he have the new, Mahdist name 'Abd al-Qadr, but he also followed a script, shown when, for example, he says he cast his eyes downward, knowing this was what the khalifa wanted, or used words he knows the khalifa wanted to hear, as in his cynical use of the word *sire*. In the litany of steps narrated by what he assumed to be the khalifa's preference, Slatin knew what his humbled status meant for the khalifa's own position. He continues, "Probably it flattered his vanity to know he could point to me, his slave, once a high official of the Government, who had commanded his [the khalifa's] own tribe, which was now the foundation on which his power rested, and show them and the other western tribes that I was now his humble servant."[62] Slatin admits his servile role, but his certainty about the khalifa's wishes and expectations projects a degree of superiority over the khalifa, who is always presented in the position of asking, of questioning Slatin. Slatin offers a neatly reversed example of the philosopher Hegel's portrayal of master and slave in this memoir, in which the master depends more on the slave than vice versa. In this way, Slatin restored order to his world, setting himself up as naturally dominating the African who rules him.

Charles Neufeld, Fawzī Pasha's friend and biographer, was unable to achieve that same sense of distance and hauteur during his imprisonment in Omdurman, refusing to follow the script, even when urged to do so by his coprisoner Slatin Pasha himself. Neufeld did not have Slatin's or Fawzī's experience in the Sudan, nor did he speak much Arabic; he was a German soldier turned merchant trader in Suakin who ventured too close to the Mahdīya and was captured, suspected of spying for the Egyptian government. Unlike Fawzī and Slatin, Neufeld had no interest in civilizing or colonizing the Sudanese—he was there for profit alone. The stunning strangeness of blacks having the upper hand over him almost cost Neufeld his sanity, as he repeats throughout his account. The following excerpt reveals the powerful aversion he had to this inversion of social status, when he was flogged for an infraction committed by another prisoner:

> There was I, a European, a Prussian, a man who had fought with the British troops in what transpired to be the "too late" expedition for the rescue of Gordon, now in the clutches of the tyrant and his myrmidons, whom we had hoped to rescue Gordon from; a white and a Christian— the only professing Christian—chained and helpless, being flogged by a black, as much a captive and a slave as I was, and yet my superior and master. It is impossible for any one not having undergone a similar experience to appreciate the mental agonies I endured.[63]

Neufeld asserted his European-ness as loudly as possible, in front of Sudanese guards who either ignored his assertions or punished them. Ibrahīm Fawzī, however much he borrowed from the narratives of Slatin Pasha and Neufeld, never adopted so aloof, or so combative, a stance with respect to the Sudanese. No matter how much he scorned and ridiculed the Sudanese, he included, in his text, moments in which the Sudanese deeply insulted him too. There were strong connections between Ibrahīm Fawzī and the Sudanese: Arabic was the native tongue and Islam the religion of both. His Sudanese contemporaries in Omdurman were as aware as he was of the traditional hierarchy of status long played out in the relationship between Egyptians and Sudanese. When the khalifa relegated him to the status of a servant, even a slave, it deeply bruised Fawzī's acute sensitivity to rank and self-esteem. One example of the social injuries Fawzī endured occurs in the story he relates of a certain 'Abd al-Mawla, an army leader and, as Fawzī describes him, a dark-skinned former slave. Fawzī writes:

> Two years after the fall of Khartoum, a slave of mine escaped and joined
> the jihādīyya [regiments of black soldiers, often slaves], led by this same
> ʿAbd al-Mawla. I went to him and asked him to give me that slave, or
> compensate me for him. The first thing he said to me was, "Why are
> you so fat, *ya walad al-rīf* [you Egyptian]; do you have money stashed
> away to waste on yourself?" This talk angered me and I responded, "No,
> master, I am a poor man, living off the benevolence of my masters, com-
> manders like yourself."
>
> "Has the benevolence of the commanders fattened you up this
> much?" he asked.
>
> "Yes," I said, "and my master, the Khalifa of the Mahdī, peace be
> upon him, often extends his generosity to me." That blunted his rage,
> and he asked me what I wanted from him now.
>
> "I would like my slave," I said.
>
> "You are his slave," he said.
>
> "Yes, I am his slave," I said, "because he has your slave." Then one of
> the people present spoke up on my behalf.
>
> ʿAbd al-Mawla said, "I permit you to take this slave for the sake of he
> who spoke up for you, but I warn you, if you ever come back to me with
> a similar request, I will cut your head off from that fat neck of yours, on
> the spot!"[64]

Like Slatin Pasha, Ibrahīm Fawzī was familiar with the role-playing of master and slave, and this scene shows how horribly, for him, the roles had
become reversed. Despite his insistence to the contrary, Fawzī Pasha became
a slave, socially lower than those over whom he had recently been master.
The Mahdists overturned the very structure on which Fawzī based his social
and cultural identity. He lost his social autonomy with the loss of authority
over his slave, a slave who linked him to his previous status and rank. Even
worse, his own words and protests meant nothing. He followed the pre-
scribed script, offering the answers he imagined the Mahdist leaders wanted
to hear, but only the intercession of another Sudanese leader, who remains
unnamed, saved him.

In the act of writing about it, however, Fawzī Pasha responded inge-
niously to this indignity. With his customary habit of ventriloquism, Fawzī
affirmed his cultural identity with greater subtlety; his assertion of himself
as an Egyptian of high rank comes from the mouths of the Sudanese. In
Fawzī's frame of reference, black skin is closely associated with slavery. By
making the black Sudanese paint him as foreign, linked with the white
Europeans, he preserved his natural rank as master, for him and his readers.
His connection to empire and imperial representatives, was, like Slatin
Pasha's and Neufeld's, also maintained. The next passage, which takes place
after Slatin escaped from Omdurman, illustrates this point:

> [The khalifa] summoned the leaders and many of his advisors together
> to meet with him, and he enumerated the many generosities he had
> extended to Slatin Pasha, how abundant had his benevolence been, yet
> how, even after that, Slatin Pasha had cursed his kindness, had only pre-
> tended to embrace Islam and had fled to the land of unbelievers. They
> responded to him with surprise, and one of them said to the khalifa that
> he didn't trust anyone with a white face, especially those who had been
> employed by the government. Another said to him that Slatin had
> maintained his loyalty to unbelievers although outwardly he professed
> Islam, and the proof of this was his intimate relationship with Ibrahīm
> Fawzī. The two of them met together in their houses, drinking wine and
> smoking tobacco.[65]

The khalifa then had Fawzī beaten and thrown into the dungeon cell where
he encountered Charles Neufeld. Neufeld came over to help the wounded
Fawzī,[66] until the prison guards reentered the cell and began whipping and
cursing both of them, yelling, "Why are you *awlād al-rīf* [Sudanese epithet
for Egyptians], you infidels, all sitting together?"[67] They then separated
Neufeld and Fawzī, but not before Fawzī made his point. Describing it this
way, he allowed the Sudanese to combine the elements of unbelief, culture,
and most important, race, to elevate him to his desired status. It is a masterly
manipulation of insult. By having the Sudanese themselves color him white
and group him with the Europeans (though significantly they label Neufeld
and Fawzī as *awlād al-rīf*, Fawzī turns the indignities and insults heaped on
him into legitimization of his social superiority. Race, for Fawzī, was the
ultimate, irrefutable badge of cultural identity and social status. Nothing
erases this, no matter how the traditional roles are reversed. Fawzī describes
the various services that Egyptians, many of them former ranking officers,
performed for the Mahdīya, including clerical work and help in the manu-
facture of gunpowder and weapons; some even opened small restaurants
and bakeries in Omdurman. Despite their industriousness, these Egyptians
lived under oppressive conditions and were hated by the Sudanese because
of their white skin, which revealed *jinsīyatuhum* (their nationality).[68] He
makes clear that blackness belonged to slaves, most starkly when he relates
how he was moved from the cell he shared with Neufeld into another. He
found himself sitting next to a "black slave" [*ʿabd aswad*] who looked rather
unhealthy. Fawzī asked him what crime he committed to be in prison, and
the man answers,

> "But you know me."
> "No, I don't," I said.
> "I am Jesus, son of Mary, prophet of God and His messenger."
> I thought he was joking, so I said, "Really? You don't say!"

He turned to me, saying, "You'll see proof, soon."

"Jesus, may God's blessing be upon him, was white in color," I said, "and you are a black slave."

He answered me firmly, and heatedly. "All colors are in my hands; if I wanted to I could change my color to white, but I have chosen black out of modesty to God."

Fawzī turned to the prisoner on his other side, to ask him if anyone could possibly believe such lies, but this man refused to respond. Fawzī then noticed two other men in the corner laughing, who told him this second man also considered himself to be Jesus Christ.[69]

This anecdote testifies to the absurdity of Omdurman society, in Fawzī Pasha's mind, and the unreality and insanity of the social structure that had been imposed by the Mahdīya. But it also underscores his position as a white, which the Sudanese characters help him to reaffirm, and therefore his position in a real, civilized, society. Thus, his text reorders the world into what is tolerable, for Fawzī, and transforms the alienation of fourteen years' captivity into a medal of honor.

And so, like the Sudan in the title of his memoirs, Fawzī is himself balanced carefully against the British. Though his gratitude to them was monumentalized in the names of Gordon and Kitchener, his dependence on the Sudanese, who entrenched and supported his identity as conqueror and colonizer, remains muted, unless one realizes how metaphorically the word *Sudan* sits in the title of Fawzī Pasha's autobiography. *Kitāb al-sūdān* is *Kitāb Ibrahīm Fawzī;* he was, as his memoirs show, completely and essentially linked to the Sudan. As a true and proud Egyptian, he embodied all by himself the entire Nile Valley and could, therefore, in the crowning title of his work, allow the Sudan to subsume his own name.

4 The Tools of the Master

Slavery, Family, and the Unity of the Nile Valley

The master's tools will never
dismantle the master's house.
AUDRE LORDE, *Sister Outsider:
Essays and Speeches*

We have seen in the writings of Yaʿqūb Ṣanūʿa and ʿAbdallah al-Nadīm how
the representation of the Sudanese as slaves came to be part of a public discussion of cultural reform and early nationalism in Egypt during the 1870s
and 1880s. We have also witnessed the impact of slavery on Ibrāhīm Fawzī's
life, how suspicions of his slave-trading past troubled his relationship with
General Gordon, how he maintained a sense of personal status by owning at
least one slave while a prisoner of the Mahdīya in Omdurman, and finally,
how similar accusations led British officials of the occupying government to
deny him the pension he and his wife had sought for years. But the experience and existence of actual Sudanese slaves had an even greater impact on
Egyptian history in the late nineteenth century. Their presence in Egypt
exacerbated the ongoing debate between the English and Egyptians over the
future of Egyptian society, and, as the British settled into their occupation of
Egypt, over the potential for Egyptian independence. The debate in turn
produced legal and historical arguments about the history and experience of
black slaves in Egypt, which revealed how differently their lives and the
institution of slavery were interpreted by British and Egyptian observers. As
one highly politicized trial over slave trading demonstrated, the significance
of slave trading and abolition in Egypt had become an issue of British imperialist control versus Egyptian cultural sovereignty.

The debate about the experience of African slaves also aggravated an
increasingly bitter controversy over the relationship between Egypt and its
former colony, the Sudan. This controversy arose as the Mahdist state itself
weakened and then fell to the British-led Egyptian armies in 1898. Not long
after General Herbert Kitchener liberated hundreds of prisoners of the
Mahdī, including Fawzī Pasha, the Sudan was named the Anglo-Egyptian
Condominium, a unique designation under which a British administrator

would govern the Sudan and the Egyptian treasury would finance the territory. The British and Egyptian flags flew side-by-side over administrative buildings in Khartoum, but it was clear to most that the so-called condominium paid only sanctimonious attention to Egyptian claims to the Sudan. Many nationalists were left wondering what the next step should be, and how to free Egypt and the Sudan together from the grips of Great Britain's powerful empire.

INVASIVE ABOLITIONISM

> That moral flagship of Britain's civilizing mission sailed with all its zeal toward the Ottoman horizon proudly flying all its glorious colors. Curiously enough, however, the two "fleets" never really met.
>
> EHUD TOLEDANO, *Slavery and Abolition in the Ottoman Middle East*

British attention to slavery in the Ottoman Empire began in the middle of the nineteenth century, decades after the antislavery movement succeeded in abolishing the slave trade in 1807 and slavery in 1833 within territories governed by the British empire. Much of the success of the abolitionist movement was due to its religion-based indignation over the enslavement of blacks, in which abolitionist leaders were able to define slavery as a violation of universal human rights. But as difficult a struggle as that had been within the British empire, exposure to Ottoman slavery presented British observers with a different and more complicated version of a trade and an institution that was multiracial, multiethnic, and generally domestic. For many in Great Britain, these differences made little sense, or even little difference, and the cruel circumstances of Caribbean and American plantation slavery that informed British commentators' definitions of slavery framed their perspective on domestic slavery, concubinage, and military slavery in the Ottoman Empire. As Ehud Toledano has noted, this narrow definition was met with an equally oversimplified response from Ottoman statesmen and writers.[1] These elites countered that "kul/harem," or domestic slavery, was a considerably milder forms of the institution; in so doing, they ignored the more difficult circumstances of domestic slavery in which the majority of slaves were African.[2] Nor did they account for the violent uprooting and harrowing migrations of these slaves' middle passage from Africa to the Ottoman provinces or to Istanbul.

A similar lack of communication about the nature of slavery occurred between British officials and the Egyptian government in the late nineteenth century. Here, too, Egyptian elites emphasized the differences between Islamic slavery and Western slavery, and personalized the definition of domestic slavery. Many took pride in direct descent from slaves, a claim that became easier to make as more and more Egyptians entered the ranks of the elite and thus were able to marry (or were given in marriage) the freed slave-women of the Ottoman-Egyptian ruling classes, who were considered to be members of the nobility. There was thus honor and social mobility inherent in the intermarriage between women of the Ottoman-Egyptian households and ambitious Egyptians, demonstrating that a certain kind of slavery led to social mobility.[3] This also created a level of society whose members were half Egyptian and half Circassian, like the lawyer and statesman Aḥmad Shafik. These people took pride in their mothers' descent and in their ability to marry wives whose slave past ensured them access to nobility.[4] The enslavement of black Africans in North Africa was described (often erroneously so) as being synonymous with this type of intimate slavery.

But increasing foreign pressure and changed sensibilities about cultural and political reform created a deep internal conflict over the question of slavery for many in the Ottoman Empire. Toledano writes that, by the 1870s, "patriotic, Westernized Ottomans were torn between a growing rejection of slavery and a deep attachment to their sociocultural heritage, of which they remained proud. They tried hard to reconcile the conflict between a system in which they were born and raised—often by mothers, wet nurses, nannies, and female relatives of slave origins—and the demands and principles of a foreign culture they grew to respect, wanted to acquire, and wished to be recognized by as equals."[5] Many Egyptians felt this conflict, which was exacerbated by the British occupation and the deepening of Egyptian nationalism. The particular geographical and cultural position of Egypt was threatened by being categorically collapsed into one of the worst examples of African slavery in the West. Looking at the presence of slaves within their own homes or in the households of friends and relatives, "they could pretend that this was where slavery actually began and that what had happened before belonged to another world—uncivilized, unruly, beyond their control."[6] Toledano is describing in this sentence the feelings of Ottomans, but the question of whether that other African "world," from which many slaves came, was beyond control was problematic in the wake of Egyptian claims to the Sudan and its painful loss to the Mahdīya. And this African "world" could easily be blamed for the existence of slavery, for creating a cultureless vulnerability and lack of family structure, and even, it seemed, for going to war in order to defend the right to slavery.[7]

British, Ottoman, and Egyptian officials all agreed that there was no hope in pursuing the issue of trade in Circassian and Caucasian slaves with the Ottoman sultan or the Egyptian khedive, so deeply connected to the entire infrastructure of the military and the royal families had this system become.[8] It was also clear that, by the middle of the nineteenth century, increased Russian hegemony over the Caucasus Mountains and ensuing struggles with Circassian populations had cut off most of the potential supply of those slaves, so that the remaining few came from within Anatolia itself.[9] But African slavery was treated as an entirely different matter in Egypt. Ismāʿīl's efforts to expand Egyptian authority beyond the source of the Nile into East Africa coincided with the close attention that British abolitionists were paying to the trade in African slaves. Imperialism, nationalism, and abolitionism found yet another location to fight for: the Nile Valley.

In Great Britain, the abolitionists were aided by a tight network of information about Africa that was fed through cooperation between the Royal Geographic Society, the British and Foreign Anti-Slavery Society, and the Church Missionary Society. Explorers like Dr. David Livingstone, John H. Speke, James Grant, Charles Gordon, and Samuel Baker became celebrated experts of the Royal Geographic Society for the firsthand information they brought or sent home from the Nile Valley or Lake Victoria. Their stories about the victimization of innocents that slavery wrought inspired both Protestant and Catholic missionaries to set up stations in different parts of the African heartland. Sketches they sent home of enslaved Africans encouraged the urgent appeals of the Anti-Slavery Society and were reprinted in newspapers, giving readers opportunities to view the human face of slavery.

It was a tremendous and evocative human rights campaign that shaped the view of Africa for much of the British public. Many people gained what little they knew about Africans from the writings of Livingstone, the explorer and missionary who so carefully and passionately related his experience of the slave trade and thus contributed profoundly to the Anti-Slavery Society's campaign in East Africa.[10] Livingstone was deeply outraged by the slave trade and wrote down example after example of the suffering the trade caused to Africans. In his last diaries, he illustrated how African slaves often affected him, as in this passage he wrote in Zanzibar: "On visiting the slave-market, I found about three hundred slaves exposed for sale, the greater part of whom came from the Lake Nyassa and the Shire River; I am so familiar with the peculiar faces and markings or tattooings, that I expect them to recognize me."[11] Using his position as a foreigner, Livingstone often did try to intercede on slaves' behalf and rescue or buy the freedom of as many slaves as he could. This happened so many times that they became an archetype of victimization for him, and, as the above quote shows, he considered himself an archetype of salvation for them. Until that point, he implied, no one else had tried to help them or free them. And in the terrifying world in which the slaves lived, Arabs and Muslims alternatively become the personification of evil, the barbaric slave-raiding villains.

Livingstone was unimpressed with arguments that Islam had brought education, morality, and civilization to eastern and central Africa. He was struck by what he considered an absence of Muslim missionary activity among the pagan Africans, and wondered at the missed opportunity this lack of proselytizing created. He wrote in his diary, "As they [the Arabs] never translate the Koran, they neglect the best means of influencing the Africans, who invariably wish to understand what they are about."[12] Livingstone reasoned that Islam had only attained a superficial influence among the natives of Africa, whose religious practices in mosques were pantomime, or as he put it, "a dumb show."

These ideas gained widespread currency in England, particularly at a time when few traveled to Africa itself. For the newspaper-reading public in both Europe and Egypt, for visitors to the free lectures at geographic societies, or for strollers through the exotic panoramas of international world exhibitions, central and East African territories unofficially bore the imprint of Livingstone's illustrious name and reputation.[13] The name of Sir Samuel Baker clung to the upper regions of the Blue Nile, even while he ceremoniously affixed that of his monarch to Lake Albert Nyanza. But Egyptian or Muslim figures whose names were connected to sub-Saharan Africa were not similarly monumentalized as explorers and liberators of Africa, and were almost always implicated as agents in the slave trade. A national hero to many Egyptians, Fawzī could never shake off the stigma of his having traded in slaves when governor of Equatoria; this fact made him as reprehensible to British authorities as his participation in the 'Urābī rebellion and kept him from gaining the back pay he had accrued while a prisoner in the Sudan. And even Fawzī, with his Egypt-centric vision of the Sudan, could not separate the names of Gordon and Kitchener from his narrative of Sudanese and Egyptian history. Fawzī was not the only Egyptian to vacillate between claiming the Sudan as his own and honoring the exploration of men like Livingstone. In many ways, the discoveries of the Europeans, with their addition of detail to public knowledge of the sub-Saharan landscape, gave contemporary Egyptians their most comprehensive picture of the Sudan. And the context of rooting out slavery, in which these explorations were made, meant that by the last quarter of the nineteenth century Egyptians had to answer somehow the myriad accusations about slavery that informed international perceptions of their relationship with Africa.

The primary accuser was the aggressive British and Foreign Anti-Slavery Society in London, which took full advantage of its political clout to lobby for particular British policies in Egypt and East Africa.[14] The Society's influence eventually reached so far that it felt itself able to pressure and petition Khedive Ismāʿīl directly when it learned of his plans to expand Egyptian influence along the Nile. In one petition, the members of the Society praised the khedive for statements he had made against the slave trade in 1867, but questioned the lack of movement toward abolition of the institution since that time. The members of the Society chose their words carefully in addressing a ruler whose goal of raising Egypt to the level of Europe were well-known. In crushing the trade in slaves, they informed him, "Your Highness would thus become the pioneer of liberty, and Egypt[,] being a land of freedom[,] would take rank among the most civilized nations of the world."[15]

The members of the Society were also well aware that they had public opinion on their side. The pressure they exerted, which often had the support of members of Parliament, resulted in the Anglo-Egyptian Convention of 1877, which abolished the trade in African slaves in all territory held by the Egyptian government, although it did not outlaw the institution of slavery itself. The Anti-Slavery Convention was posted by decree throughout Egypt's cities and the Sudan, and allowed for the creation of slave trade bureaus in Cairo, Alexandria, the Delta, and Upper Egypt. These bureaus were intended not only to record the manumission of individual slaves but also to find suitable employment for freed slaves and possible education for their children. The authorities of these bureaus were also responsible for the punishment of "any person depriving a freed slave of his freedom or taking from him his manumission certificate"; such a person was to be handled as a slave dealer.[16]

The Anti-Slavery Convention may have provided a clear date from which the trade in slaves was no longer permissible, but it left open wide-ranging and important questions about the nature of the trade in Egypt. It also created a very thick wall: on one side stood the British officials of the occupation, who were quickly coming to believe that a proslavery solidarity existed among the Muslims of Egypt, and that any Egyptian who supported the officials of the slave trade bureaus would be considered a traitor by other Egyptians. On the other side of the wall stood the majority of Egyptians, who saw slaves as closely connected to their households and often treated them as part of their families, and who believed that the more gentle domestic bondage of Egypt actually benefited the slaves themselves. Then there were those who were deeply ambivalent about slavery yet who considered the officials of the slave trade bureaus to be trespassers broaching the privacy of the Egyptian family and revealing its secrets to the outside world.[17]

This sense of invaded privacy put on the defensive those nationalists who called for the reconquest of the Sudan, because the British authorities in Egypt and participants in the antislavery movement in England heard with suspicion the nationalists' rhetoric that linked the Sudan corporeally to Egypt and interpreted such calls as defenses of slavery. And the issue of slavery and its intrinsic connectedness to the Sudan raised difficult questions for the nationalists about their own society and their own sense of communal unity. The expression of the corporeal connection between Egypt and the Sudan also reflected then-current debates and anxieties about more intimate customs, like marriage, and social notions about gender and race. With so much of the political and physical geography in question, literary constructions of the Sudan were often all that kept intact politically minded Egyptians' sense of the borders of their own land and culture.

WIFE, SLAVE, OR MATRIARCH?

The nature of the slavery lived by black men and women in Egypt in the nineteenth century is rarely if ever discussed without being compared to the searing experiences of African slaves in the United States and the Caribbean. From all accounts, it is clear that African slaves in Egypt did not suffer the brutality that so characterized the treatment of blacks in the American South. There was no similar plantation culture in which nuclear families were torn apart or in which slaves were subjected to horrifying physical abuse. Although the experience of being captured and the treks of slave caravans on the Forty Days' Road (*darb al-arba'īn*) were notoriously difficult for recently enslaved Sudanese, once in Egypt their experiences did tend to be milder than those of American slaves.

There is no agreement on the exact number of black slaves in Egypt during the latter half of the nineteenth century, when the trade in slaves from the Sudan reached its peak. Gabriel Baer writes that it was impossible to establish the exact number of slaves in Egypt at any time in that century, but basing his estimation on contemporary British accounts, the census of 1850, and the records of the slave trade bureaus established after the Anglo-Egyptian Convention in 1877, he figured that throughout the century the number of slaves remained between twenty and thirty thousand.[18] Judith Tucker never arrived at a total figure of slaves, although she posits that, between 1877 and 1905, twenty-five thousand slaves were manumitted in

Egypt.[19] The majority of African slaves in Egypt were women who served as domestic workers in private homes, although in upper Egypt there were documented examples of agricultural slavery, and many slaves were recruited for military service early in the century.[20]

There was a well-established hierarchy of labor that constructed the work and world of the slave in Egypt in the nineteenth century and was itself a construction of stereotyping about the qualities of different races and ethnicities. Circassian women were at the top of this ladder and were welcomed into the harems of the wealthiest and most prestigious households. Ethiopian women came next, bought often as concubines for the middle class. They were prized for their beauty, not for their ability to do household work, as were other African women, who stood much lower in this hierarchy.[21] There is surprisingly much less information about the nature of black male slaves' domestic work in Egypt in the late nineteenth century. After the end of the American Civil War, Egypt's cotton industry faced intense competition. The large-scale plantation projects that Khedive Ismāʿīl had encouraged and on which black slaves were employed shrank, but there is little surviving record of later work for those slaves.

The historical record makes clear, however, that, once purchased, most African slaves in Egypt worked in the homes of the middle and the upper classes. Baer cites examples of slaves working for "beduins, village notables, fellahs, millers, butchers, shopkeepers, a bookseller, all kinds of merchants, a banker, clerks, all grades of officials and government employees, all ranks of army officers, religious functionaries, some muftis, a judge, a physician and others" during the 1860s and 1870s. Some of the households the slaves served in would have been large, with many slaves and servants, but the majority would have been small, with only one slave, who became a member of an intimate group, privy to all the family life and dependent on its other members for his or her health, well-being, food, and clothing. She or he would perhaps help raise the children, and in some cases, female slaves would have children with the head of the household. From both Egyptian and British accounts, black slaves definitely formed part of the family.[22]

The intimacy of this relationship and the extension of family ties to slaves provoked a mixture of titillation and disgust from British observers, reactions similar to those elicited by the exoticism of the harem, which, for European observers, was closely connected to slavery. By the last decade of the nineteenth century, the idea of the Egyptian family's structure had become politicized within Egypt and sharply scrutinized from without, particularly by Great Britain and France. European scholars like Ernest Renan debated the concept of marriage within Islam, with its recognition of the legality of polygamy, often drawing the conclusion that these marriages were examples of a reflexive tendency toward Islamic despotism, that the inferior position of women in Muslim societies proved Islam's incompatibility with social reform and progress. The debate over marriage was conducted just as strongly in Egypt, especially after the publication of Qāsim Amīn's *Taḥrīr al-Mar'a* (The Liberation of Women), in 1897, which pleaded for the social emancipation of Egyptian women. The custom of arranged marriage was also widely debated, beginning with the plays of Ya'qūb Ṣanū'a.[23] Romantic novels circulated in which heroines fell in love and chose their husbands, a revolutionary prospect for many of the more traditional members of Egyptian society.[24]

But as intellectuals in Egyptian society were beginning to consider the possibilities of new and different roles for women, as Egyptian women began to insert themselves more and more into the discussion, most of the British administrators in Egypt had difficulty believing in the viability of any of these changes as long as slavery existed. Many in fact felt that Egyptians were constitutionally unable to oppose slavery or even to manage without it. As one highly placed and experienced administrator phrased it in a letter to the president of the Anti-Slavery Society, "I need scarcely remark to you that no Turk and no Egyptian[,] whether Moslem or Christian in his religion[,] can be trusted to desire or carry out effective measures for preventing the introduction of slaves into the country, because [he] neither has any conscientious feeling or opposition to the system itself as existing in the Turkish Empire. No native Egyptian official has any heart in anti-slavery movements."[25]

From its very inception, the nationalist movement was forced to respond to this question, and the leaders of the Nationalist Party delegated Sir Wilfred Blunt, one of their staunchest British supporters, to address the Anti-Slavery Society directly on their behalf. In a letter to the Society, Blunt explained the party's views: "The liberal views in politics and religion which now for the first time are finding their free expression in the movement known as National, have it for a first principle that slavery is a *qabīḥa*, an abomination, one to be utterly abolished in all its forms and branches in the modern world." Explaining that the shaykhs of al-Azhār supported this view, Blunt continued that slavery was permitted by the Qur'an "only when Islam was in a state of war with idolaters." The first act of the party's Minister of the Interior was "to appoint a new Governor General of the Soudan and the Red Sea coast, with the most positive orders to suppress the trade; and in Lower Egypt a secret system is being organised . . . for the discovery and liberation of all persons still held in bondage there."[26]

But even rebels against the system were distrusted by both current and former British officials. Few believed in the existence of the public opinion that 'Urābī and his associates claimed to be spokesmen for, and even fewer thought that any Egyptian could oppose so old and intrinsic an institution. Samuel Baker, the famous explorer who had earlier been hired by Khedive Ismā'īl to abolish slavery in the regions of the southern Sudan, responded publicly to the appeal that Blunt had sent to the Anti-Slavery Society, asserting that 'Urābī and the other nationalists were as involved as any Turco-Circassian in their hypocrisy over eliminating slavery in Egyptian society.[27]

While the 'Urābī rebellion leaders claimed to be stamping out the slave trade in the Sudan, the government was receiving news that the Mahdī was gaining control of more and more territories. There was little they could actually do in the face of increasing British military pressure and the political atmosphere of intense suspicion and fear being fomented by Khedive Tawfīq. Months later, their stated efforts to wipe out both slavery and the slave trade were completely laid to rest by the British occupation of Egypt. This made the British more directly responsible for the issue of slavery, and changed the terms of the debate. Now the British linked the issue of slavery to Egyptian independence, and nationalists had to prove their capacity for self-government within the context of Egypt's long history of enslaving Sudanese and Nubians.

THE BRANCHES OF SLAVERY

The slave trade bureaus sanctioned by the Anglo-Egyptian Anti-Slavery Convention of 1877 now answered directly to the British Agent and consul-general of Egypt, Sir Evelyn Baring, soon to be named Lord Cromer, who funded them amply and supported their director, Colonel Charles Schaefer, enthusiastically. Cromer was not easily persuaded by the Anti-Slavery Society, which he in fact considered dangerously unacquainted with the political realities of Egypt and the Sudan.[28] Part of his impatience with the Society stemmed from his sense that slavery was practically respectable in Egyptian society. Schaefer helped convince him of this, as shown in a letter that Cromer later forwarded to London because of its valuable insights:

> It must not be forgotten that, in this country[,] the selling of slaves
> from a Musulman point of view is considered legal, that amongst the
> natives, the custom of employing paid female servants is far from gen-
> eral: so that the possession of slaves or even the selling of them, does
> not offend public morality as it would in a civilized country[,] so that

the public has no interest in helping us as they would in cases affecting the general security.[29]

Egyptians heard these ideas and accusations in a variety of ways: through the press, in speeches, and in meetings with British officials. Many chose the same venues to argue publicly with European interlocutors about the legality of slavery itself. In 1888, Aḥmad Shafīk, while still a law student in Paris, listened uncomfortably in the Cathedrale de Saint Sulpice to a sermon by the renowned Cardinal Lavigerie against the Islamic slave trade in Africa. This was the same cardinal who, with the help of the Association for the Propagation of the Faith, launched the mission of the White Fathers in equatorial Africa in 1878. Before then, he began his missionary work in Algeria, fighting French authorities for the right to proselytize among Muslims; eventually, he would continue to work in what became known as the Belgian Congo.[30] His authority substantiated by his fame as a missionary strategist, the cardinal used example after example to single out Islam as being inhumane for its supposed support of slavery. In response, Shafīk (who had been educated in France under sponsorship by Khedive Tawfīq and who, after such careful grooming, would eventually become an eminent political official in his own right) prepared an eloquent history of slavery through the ages, in defense of the practice in Egypt. It is interesting to see how carefully he researched his facts, consulting not only Schaefer Bey for manumission statistics but also records from both the British Consul office and the British Parliament. Once finished, he sent his article to the khedive, who added his own notes and comments, which Shafīk dutifully incorporated.[31] He clearly intended this to be an official response to European and Christian condemnations of Islamic slavery. He presented it to the Khedivial Geographic Society in Cairo in two parts, one in November, followed by another lecture two weeks later in December of 1890.[32] Speaking before an audience whose members included Ya'qub Pasha Artin, Muḥammad Pasha Falaki, Qāsim Amīn, and many foreign consuls, Shafīk discussed how European abolitionists who condemned the trade in the Islamic world had forgotten that in the past the Christian Church had long sanctioned slavery.[33] In his account, these crusaders for the antislavery cause were projecting the harshness of the trade and enslavement practiced by the British in the West Indies, or the Americans in the southern United States, onto Middle Eastern societies, where in comparison, domestic slavery was very mild. In his view, the abolitionists of England and France were right to condemn the horrid institution with which they were familiar; Shafīk carefully detailed the "revolting severity" of Western slavery—that is, the stigmatizing of black skin, the passive existence of the black slave as "thing," and the torture of whippings and beatings.[34]

Shafik stipulated that, while Islam "did not directly condemn slavery," it did not accept it in the form in which the prophet Muḥammad found it, and thus the Prophet had tried to "attenuate its effects." Because of this, slavery within Islam was inherently different and intrinsically gentler than that practiced in Christian lands. Islamic law actually protected the rights of slaves, and European abolitionists needed to erase from their eyes the clichéd images of slavery and look anew at its different aspects under Islam. Muslims, for example, did not enslave other Muslims, and as soon as the "fetishists" of Africa converted to Islam, the practice would die out altogether.[35]

Interestingly, despite his erudite defense of Islamic slavery within Egypt, Shafik concluded his discussion with the point that prominent contemporary Muslim scholars and judges condemned slavery within the Islamic world.[36] And even though Shafik in his later memoirs claimed that the publication of his lectures in the *Egyptian Gazette* was used by an Ottoman diplomat to convince the Portuguese government about the necessity of abolition (without the intervention of the British), his arguments seemed to have done little to assuage the doubts of British and French observers.[37] The intimacy with which Shafik claimed slaves were integrated into the family structure in Egyptian homes sounded to the members of the Anti-Slavery Society too much like the secretive and remote relationships of Islamic marriage.[38] It also seemed an affront to holy relationships sanctioned by the Church. A member of the Geographic Society, the Russian Count Zalowski, erupted with anger over Shafik's points about slavery and Christianity. If the length of the meeting's published minutes offers any indication, he pontificated for at least twenty minutes about the consolation the Christian Church offered to slaves. Excerpts of Aḥmad Shafik's study were quickly published in the English-language *Egyptian Gazette*, where it gained its author even greater notoriety among Europeans. The pressure grew until Shafik issued a statement through the Geographic Society and asserted that his intention had never been to slander the doctrine of the Christian Church, but simply to correct "the false idea prevalent in the European world that the Muslim religion sanctions the horrors committed in central Africa."[39]

Clearly, slavery was a terrible conundrum for Egyptian Muslims. Shafik's articles focused primarily on the experience of African slaves, as if the sanctity of marriage to Circassian slaves was too private an issue to be discussed. In doing this, he relegated African slaves to the same status as Circassian slaves, gentrifying their experience in Egypt while identifying the harshness of their severance from their own families in the Sudan with the institution of Western slavery. And clearly, his belief in the legality of Islamic slavery was made even more complicated by the nationalist struggle against the British. The very fact that the British abolitionists were right, that the Qur'an did not forbid slavery and the shari'a made provision for it, touched a nerve that had existed deep in the core of Egyptian nationalism since its inception.[40] One of the most complicated and interesting responses to this uncomfortable situation was written by 'Abdallah al-Nadīm, who had returned to Egypt from a decade-long exile after the defeat of the 'Urābī rebellion and had begun, almost immediately, a new newspaper called *al-Ustādh* (The Teacher). Actually, the British authorities had given al-Nadīm's brother permission to launch the paper, and had warned that current politics could not be directly addressed. Al-Nadīm thus had to approach the issue of slavery from a nuanced perspective. He created a dialogue, in Egyptian colloquial Arabic, between two recently freed slaves, Sa'id and Bakhīta, in which the two try to figure out what to do with the rest of their lives.

The dialogue begins when Sa'id meets Bakhīta and asks her where she is now working, and she answers that she has no work, and that she wishes they were still slaves, still being cared for and fed by their masters. Sa'id reminds her that they were also regularly beaten by these same masters, and Bakhīta concedes that she finds pleasure in freedom. But still she laments, "We came from our country like beasts *[zay al-bahā'im]*, and it was our masters who taught us about Islam *[al-kalām wa al-hadīth]* and taught us about cleanliness, food, drink, how to dress and how to speak properly, since we spoke in a way that no one could understand." Continuing to praise the kindness of her masters, Bakhīta recounts how she was like a daughter to her mistress—"If my master tried to beat me, she would argue and yell at him."[41]

Sa'id, however, remembers the terrible journey with the slave dealers more vividly than he does any kindnesses from his former masters. But Bakhīta makes one point on which they both agree, that it is confusing and difficult to parcel themselves out to different households, to work for one household one month and another the next. Slavery is not better than freedom, she admits, but the uncertainty of independent living is intolerable. Sa'id agrees that the employment situation of former slaves is dire, and he tells Bakhīta that he thinks the government should take responsibility for them and give every manumitted slave a plot of land from royal estates and the necessary machinery and tools. After all, he says, the government used them to cultivate a lot of land, year after year, and also conscripted many soldiers out of the Sudan. Sa'id says he has even heard that the Ottoman sultan offered such a gesture to the Sudanese, from whose agricultural effort the empire profited.

This was a daring and singular suggestion on al-Nadīm's part, asking the Egyptian government to take responsibility for the futures of the men and women formerly enslaved by Egyptians. He also recognized, in this dialogue, how difficult it was for freed slaves, especially women, to find places for themselves in society. Much to Sa'id's annoyance, Bakhīta cannot stop referring to her previous "masters," even as her friend tries to get her to see them as simply the wealthy class *(jamā'a al-aghniyā)*, who could create new entrepreneurs out of their former slaves.[42] Sa'id envisions the freed slaves as storekeepers and contractors with their own teams of workers. He imagines Sudanese working in a wide range of occupations, not only as the servants many had been for so long. Bakhīta balks at the impossibility of Sa'id's dreams, but he ends the dialogue with a challenge and a hope: "We'll publish this conversation in *al-Ustādh*, and we'll see what progressive people will do with us."[43]

Al-Nadīm knew that many of his pieces were read out loud, and thus he forced his readers to articulate this challenge to themselves as well as to illiterate listeners. The reader would therefore become both subject and object for a brief moment, before he and his listeners began to discuss the merits of al-Nadīm's points.[44] Unlike the dialogues of Ya'qūb Ṣanū'a, in which Sudanese characters regularly mispronounce Egyptian dialect, al-Nadīm offers no indication of accent in this discussion. Would people reading this dialogue out loud have mimicked Sudanese or Nubian accents? Would that last sentence have felt like a rebuke of such mimicry, or would it have been an effective means of driving home the point about Sa'id's humanity?

It is also interesting how the dialogue treated gender roles. Sa'id states several times that, if only the government would provide them with the plots of land they deserve, then the Sudanese could marry each other and create the sort of family life he feels they deserve.[45] The idea of marriage accompanies the suggestion of the Sudanese getting the chance to create their own community. While it would depend the investments of previous employers, this would be a community of individuals liberated from the homes of wealthy Egyptians and able to create their own. Several sentences later, Sa'id repeats the idea about the respectability of the Sudanese being able to marry and create homes with their women, "our sisters."[46] But Bakhīta has more trouble envisioning this kind of family setting, so rooted does her loyalty remain to her former mistress, to whom she was like a daughter.[47] Bakhīta's heart is intimately connected to her Egyptian "family." She is not ready to become the matriarch of her own family. She is paralyzed in a kind of perpetual childhood, not able to take up her position as a mature Muslim woman. Al-Nadīm thus held up proper marriage within Islam as an ideal and, with Bakhīta's incapacity to even imagine herself as an active part of this ideal, demonstrates one sad consequence of long years of servitude. In revealing a woman stunted by her "education," he contradicts the traditional assertion that slavery had taught the Sudanese how to be civilized.

THE MASTER'S HOUSE

One point drawn from al-Nadīm's dialogue was that slavery was an internal matter for Egyptians to settle. It presented a painful and troubling history to Egyptians, the ramifications of which they had not even begun to cope with. But nowhere in al-Nadīm's poignant dialogue, or earlier articles on similar subjects, do the British appear. For al-Nadīm, slavery was part and parcel of Egypt's historic relation with the Sudan; the British did not, and should not, figure in the debate. This crisis over internal slavery was further fueled by the unfolding events in the Sudan: by the mid-1890s, reports of escaped prisoners had made it clear to both the Egyptian and British public that the Mahdist state in the Sudan, then being run by the Mahdī's successor, the khalifa 'Abdullah al-Ta'ishī, was overwhelmed with famine and war. British officials waged a propaganda campaign to garner public support for the reconquest of the Sudan, brandishing the memory of General Charles Gordon like a sword. General Reginald Wingate, chief of intelligence in Egypt, spearheaded his own literary campaign for colonizing the Sudan, by translating and popularizing works by the Mahdī's escaped prisoners, contemporaries of Ibrāhīm Fawzī, such as Rudolph Slatin Pasha.[48] His propaganda campaign horrified Egyptian nationalists, who wanted the Sudan returned to Egypt but not to an Egypt subdued and occupied by the British.

But the perceived chaos in the Sudan was not the same, many felt, as the situation in Egypt. In Egypt there was no war, and many nationalist thinkers believed the British to be conflating the two. Their focus on slavery asserted the primacy of Egyptian voices—it had to be left to Egyptians to decide. Others felt the British abolitionists, with little sense of or feeling for the differences between local custom in Egypt or the Sudan, were crossing into interiors where they had no business. One of the most outspoken of these objectors was 'Alī Pasha Sharīf, the president of the Legislative Assembly, an advisory board to the government with no legislative independence of its own. But some of the Legislative Assembly's members were elected, and this small sample of elected representation fueled the popularity of its members, who were seen as guardians of some of the few opportunities available for

Egyptian participation in the government. In 1894, 'Alī Pasha Sharīf repeatedly called for the dismissal of Schaefer, the head of the Slave Trade Bureau, and the dissolution of all its branches around the country. He protested the inflated salaries of its officials and what he claimed was a lack of need for such internal policing, as slavery was no longer an issue in Egypt.[49] So it was with great irony and fanfare that 'Alī Pasha Sharīf himself was arrested and, along with three other prominent members of the pasha class, charged with illegally buying six Sudanese slave women from a caravan that had crossed the Libyan desert in August of 1894.

The court case that ensued revealed, more than any other event up to this point, how intricately connected the issue of slavery was to the question of controlling the Sudan, in the views of contemporary Egyptian nationalists and British officials. In this case, a woman named Zanūba, in the company of five other young Sudanese women and three Egyptian traders, had walked barefoot across the desert in the August heat to be sold as a slave in the profitable underground slave market of Cairo. There, the dealers hoped to find wealthy buyers who would place the women in their households, clothe them, and rename them. Working clandestinely, they did find several buyers: a prominent doctor; a former director of the Waqf (Religious Endowment), Husayn Wassif; Shawarbī Pasha, another wealthy member of the Legislative Assembly; and of course the controversial figure, 'Alī Pasha Sharīf himself. The occupation government ordered the trial to take place within the framework of a military court-martial,[50] and the tribunal dramatically pitted the government against the Egyptian nationalists. While the British ostensibly defended the slave women's right to freedom, the nationalists defended the pashas' right to buy them. In between sat Zanūba, who would testify against these pillars of the Egyptian community. Zanūba and the question of her guardianship served as a metaphor for the Sudan question of the time. Each side fought over these tired women in ragged clothing with the same ideologies and slogans with which they fought over the Sudan itself. All participants in the trial, from the British officials to the reporters and editors of the nationalist press, seemed aware that only the proper custodian of these women could fly his flag over the reconquered Sudan.

Ironically, 'Alī Pasha Sharīf's case had been separated from the others, as he had almost immediately claimed to be an Italian citizen and thus exempt from the jurisdiction of the Egyptian government for whom he worked in the Legislative Assembly. His case was handed over to the Italian consul, and he was not forced to appear before the court-martial. British officials noted with great smugness that "this supposed Egyptian President of what is looked on as the most exclusively national institution, who had always ostensibly availed himself of Egyptian nationality and used the Native Tribunals, should, when detected in breaking the Egyptian law, endeavor to shield himself by announcing that he was an Italian subject."[51] British observers considered 'Alī Pasha Sharīf to have conceded his guilt once he applied to the Italian consul for protection. Although the Italian government turned down his request, it was considered appropriate to grant him a separate trial because of missed deadlines.[52]

The press of Cairo and Alexandria covered the trial with attention to minute detail, as did the foreign language papers of Egypt and the European press, particularly the British papers. With some exceptions, notably two Egyptian editors and the editor of the English-language *Egyptian Gazette*, all the newspapers proved proud defenders of Egyptian nationalism and the wealthy defendants. Every day from 3 to 15 September 1894, reporters from the various newspapers elbowed each other for room in the packed courtroom to record the day's proceedings. No matter what the individual newspaper's political perspective, all the articles expressed profound shock at the sight of such prominent pashas sitting next to the Bedouin slave traders in the dock. The accounts also reflect an equal degree of surprise at the spectacle of three of the six black slave women testifying against the pashas. While slaves frequently petitioned the shari'a courts of Egypt on domestic matters, their presence, not to mention their testimony, in a case of such *national* ramifications was rare, if not completely unprecedented.[53] Although Zanūba's testimony was crucial to the prosecutor's case, had she sat there silently her presence would have been just as dramatic. It was the bodies of these women, with the question of who clothed, named, and fed them—who owned them—around which the metaphor for guardianship of the Sudan lay and on which the whole issue centered. (See fig. 7.)

Zanūba answered very clearly the questions about her actual position in this whole affair. In his own defense, one of the traders had claimed Zanūba was not his slave but his wife. Zanūba countered, in her own testimony, "I am not his wife, and I am not his freed slave. I am a slave he brought here to be sold for money." All the papers quoted verbatim this startling declaration of identity, this clear assertion by a slave of being a slave, but one accompanied by no claim of connection, or belonging, to any master.[54] She had refused to go along with the subterfuge of his claim of marriage. She thus indicted the traders, but her assertion still kept her strangely unsituated.

The two other traders offered the same defense, that they were married to these women, an excuse that provoked a strong reaction from the one British officer sitting on the court as president, Frith Bey. In his summation

7.   Drawing of the Sudanese slave women made famous in the Cairo trial of 1894, from the *Anti-Slavery Record*, July 1894.

of the trial's proceedings, he scoffed at this claim of marriage. If the six women were truly their wives, he asked, why did they need to be hidden when brought to Egypt? When Slave Trade Bureau agents searched the house in which the women had been hidden, why did the traders deny their presence? Why, if they were married, could the women be brought into Cairo only by night?[55]

Frith Bey's questions regarding the traders' claims of marriage reflect the venal connection between slavery and Islamic wedlock that contemporary British officials saw in Egyptian society. In the years of the occupation, this bias against Islamic practices became increasingly institutionalized as English officeholders gained greater administrative power and greater experience in Egypt. These administrators were hotly pursued by the British and Foreign Anti-Slavery Society for detailed information on slaves and slave raids. Through this network that disseminated information about the qualities of Egyptian government and culture, the idea spread that Muslim slaveholders used the cloak of Islamic tradition to veil the presence of the slave trade, and that this same subterfuge was employed to justify Egypt's presence in the Sudan. Egypt's attempts at empire were thus dismissed, and Britain's empire in Egypt and the Sudan justified.

These interpretations gathered momentum over the years, influencing the arrangement of institutions under the occupying government, which concretized the interpretations. For example, in 1887, the Slavery Trade Bureau had been incorporated into the Ministry of the Interior, giving

Colonel Schaefer (by then an Anti-Slavery Society hero) broad jurisdiction over antislavery policy and greater access to Lord Cromer and the Foreign Office back home. Schaefer filled his reports with information about raiding the slave dealers of the Sudan and Egypt, and his numerous documents were canonized by the Anti-Slavery Society.[56] Cromer forwarded the following details to London, verbatim, from a report by Schaefer about claims of marriage used by Egyptians to disguise their transport of slaves into their country after performing the hajj.

> When these people have slaves with them, before boarding the ship, they obtain from the Court of Mecca certificates stating that the slave was liberated by her master, or better yet, though less often, they obtain deeds from the aforesaid Court stating that they are legally married to the slave. These documents may have been granted in good faith by the religious authorities[,] but in general these authorities are aware of the abusive ends to which these documents are put, and only dispense them after being compensated. As for the slaves, they are thoroughly instructed in what they are to say, and they are made to believe that the Egyptian authorities have no other goal in coming to see them except to seize and torture them.
>
> Naturally, these slaves, who are very ignorant and under the impression they will be harmed, even if they wanted to desert their masters, are so afraid of the Egyptian authorities that all repeat the learned lesson,[57] and say they are free and are accompanying their masters of their own free will. Faced with such declarations, the Egyptian authorities have to retreat. However, 90 per cent of these slaves, if not under so great a fear, and if one released them from the grips of their masters, would say they had been brought there to be sold, or to be offered as a bribe.[58]

These pictographic ideas circulated unabated in 1894, particularly during the pashas' trial, when Herbert Kitchener, the *sirdār* (commander) of Egypt, suggested that ʿAlī Pasha Sharīf's harem be searched for three other slaves, "white women being identified by their hands and allowed to pass without being examined."[59] In the eyes of these British officials, the black hands and black skin of any woman living in an Egyptian household automatically signified a slave: thus black women in Egyptian homes could only have been brought there illegally, in a state of criminally imposed bondage. Zanūba identified herself as a slave, uncoached and unencumbered by fear, unlike so many other slave women encountered. With her testimony being in itself an iconoclasm, she made perfect sense to a man like Frith Bey.

So heightened had racial sensitivity become for the British that even the unauthorized presence of unmarried black women on the streets of cities like Cairo sounded alarms. Foreign Office officials registered their fears that, once freed from slavery, black Sudanese women with few skills and fewer familial connections would fall back into the clutches of Muslim households, prey once more either to slavery, concubinage, or prostitution. To circumvent this, the Home for Freed Black Slave Women (also known as the Cairo Home for Freed Slaves) was founded in Cairo in 1886 to place Sudanese and Ethiopian women in appropriate domestic employment.[60]

The confusion over the legitimacy of the work of slave women was joined with legalistic wrangling over the nature of the pashas' actions. The pashas' defense lawyers insisted that there was a gaping inconsistency in the 1877 treaty itself. While the treaty clearly delineated the punishment for the slave trader and his accomplices, it said nothing at all about the buyer.

All the Egyptian newspaper editors were deeply sympathetic to the pashas for the indignity the tribunal inflicted on them, but only the editor of the Coptic paper *al-Fayūm* condemned both buyer and seller and the entire institution of slavery. Anybody, buyer or seller, involved in slavery, he writes, is a barbarian. The editor, Ibrahīm Ramzi, also chided 'Alī Pasha Sharīf and his codefendant, Shawarbi Pasha, both members of the Legislative Assembly and, therefore, representatives of the nation, men in whom an entire community had placed its faith. They must be among the most diligent observers of these basic truths. If they were corrupt, Ramzi worried, then so was the entire nation![61]

The editor of *al-Fayūm* touched on a highly charged subject when he mentioned barbarity, for in the debate about slavery then being argued throughout Egyptian society, the question of slavery's abolition was always intermingled with the idea of being civilized. The measurements and proofs of civilization were vague, yet Egyptian independence rested on Egyptians' ability to prove social and moral compatibility with western Europe. Shawarbi Pasha's lawyer exploited the sensitivity of this issue when he asked, in his summary argument before the court, "What guilt is there for the man who takes the kidnapped from misery to happiness, from hunger to ease of life, replacing their ragged clothes with beautiful robes, supporting them with money, treating them with the kindness that both his religion and his sense of humanity dictate to him? He does not buy them for trade, or for profit."[62]

Buying slaves was thus a benevolent mission of rescue, and buyers were civilizing agents for the wretched of the Sudan. The English editor of the *Egyptian Gazette*, a paper heavily subsidized by Lord Cromer, predictably rejected the claims of inherent mercy in the purchase of slaves and amplified the relationship of this argument to the larger issue on trial: which culture, British or Egyptian, was better equipped to control the Sudan itself? For the *Gazette* editor, Egyptian society was irrevocably tainted by Islamic despotism both publicly and privately, a factor that made Egyptians as incapable of governing others as they were of managing their own political independence: "Surely it would not be safe to entrust persons with so slight a sense of moral and political responsibility with more power than they now have. They are clearly not yet educated up to the positions which they hold. These incidents, though ludicrous at first sight, warn us how unwise it would be to remove the authority which exposes and checks practices like these."[63]

The slave trial ended with the conviction of the one pasha who had actually confessed to buying one of the slaves. The Bedouin traders were also found guilty and sentenced to five years' hard labor. The court acquitted the other pashas of all charges, a verdict that the majority of Egyptian newspapers heralded as a national victory. Not all the slaves had been as clear as Zanūba about the identity of the men who had bought them, and not one had recognized Shawarbi Pasha at all in court. This weakened the prosecution's charges against him. The khedive ordered 'Alī Pasha Sharīf to resign from his position as president of the Legislative Assembly, and it was widely believed that he had lost all popular support. But, after making a confession, he was soon acquitted on the grounds of his age and poor health.[64] Zanūba and the other five women walked out of the courtroom free. The Slave Trade Bureau gave them their manumission papers, and they rejoined each other for a time in the Cairo Home for Freed Slaves, where their stay was subsidized by the British and Foreign Anti-Slavery Society.[65] When they left the home, either for employment as domestics or for marriage, they walked out into historical oblivion.

For several weeks, however, these women had appeared like mirrors before the Egyptian and British public, reflecting how deeply both cultures had invested in the image of the civilizing savior of African peoples. The figures of these women also reflected the fears of both societies: British anxieties about black women as agents of sexual licentiousness and crime; Egyptian fears of being identified with these women, of being uncivilized, of being made slaves to the British. Though these apprehensions became clear in the way the slave women were represented in both newspaper and official accounts of the trial, the verdict left the question of actual ownership—of these women and of the Sudan—wide open. The perimeters of Egyptian geography, its form and its limits, the full extent of the body politic, were still to be mapped.

THE BODY POLITIC OF THE NILE VALLEY

At the time of the pashas' trial in Cairo, Muṣṭafa Kāmil led the nationalism movement; he was the founder of the *Ḥizb al-waṭanī*, or the Nationalist Party, whose ideas about the Egyptian nation (and the Islamic nation, a concept that incorporated loyalty to both religion and the Ottoman Empire) would be extremely influential for decades to come.[66] Both at home and while traveling in Europe, he campaigned for French and German support for Egyptians in their struggle with Great Britain. In his eloquent pleas for the recognition of his country's difficulties, Kāmil created an image of a wounded Sudan, a spectacle of victimization that evoked the figure of Zanūba, sitting alone before foreign judges. Just as Zanūba had testified she was a slave, a masterless slave, Kāmil presented the Sudan as stuck in a netherworld: neither an outright colony of Great Britain nor the natural dependent of Egypt. Egypt too was off-kilter. The British occupation had overpowered Ottoman authority over Egypt, had estranged Egyptian Muslims from the sultan of the Ottoman Empire, the amir al-Mu'minīn, and had cost Egypt the Sudan. As a body politic, Kāmil's Egypt suffered amputation; as a people, Egyptians were orphaned.[67]

Kāmil mourned the amorphousness of Egypt's political geography, particularly with regard to the Sudan, in corporeal terms that soon gained great currency in the nationalist movement. In a speech he gave in Toulouse, in July of 1895, Kāmil presented an almost medical depiction of the violence committed against the Egyptian government by the British occupation government in 1884, when, during the Mahdīya, the British forced the Egyptians to evacuate the Sudan, "the Sudan which we consider the spirit of our dear land, on which hangs the life of our country, and its death."[68] The loss of this spirit had depleted the force of the khedive and had deprived Egyptians of any sense of direction in the most important workings of the country's infrastructure. Egyptians were not even allowed to police themselves in their own cities. Even worse, for Kāmil, the vitality of the army, an institution crucial to any viable nation, had been completely sapped. In the few Sudanese territories still held by Egypt after 1885, army command was monopolized by British officers, which cost Egyptian soldiers their sense of patriotism, forcing them to fight like automatons for the very people against whom they should have been rebelling. As Kāmil put it, in Paris in late 1895, "The spirit which pervades every army in the world, the spirit of love for the motherland [al-waṭan], does not exist in our army. If any sense of nationalism appears in any one Egyptian officer, it is enough for his dismissal. Uniformed soldiers in the army, who cannot leave, consider their military service forced labor. The presence of one lone English officer as the head of the army is sufficient to kill any nationalist sentiment within it."

In the same speech, Kāmil praised the memory of Colonel Sèves, the French officer who had reorganized the Egyptian army during Muḥammad 'Alī's reign, not only for helping to instill a sense of patriotism among Egyptians but also for repatriating himself and converting to Islam, thus proving his personal commitment to Egypt. The present circumstances provided a terrible contrast:

> Now there are seventy-five British officers who control the Egyptian army, who confer among themselves about military secrets. Not one Egyptian officer knows why he is in Suakin instead of Tokar, or why he is in Wadi Halfa and not in Cairo. There is not one Egyptian in the Intelligence Bureau who does not disguise his attachment to the Sudan [*'alāqātahu ma' al-Sūdān*] and the dervishes. How many orders arrive here, how many reports are sent from the tribal chiefs to the government and even the Khedive himself and his ministers do not know a thing about them?[69]

Kāmil also saw British disdain for the Egyptian nationalist spirit in the ignominious services required of Egyptian soldiers. He claimed that British officers forced Egyptian servicemen to work as servants, an insult that "unmanned" Egypt when compared to the respect accorded to soldiers of other nations. While other soldiers learned how to dig ditches and build forts, along with the finer points of military arts, Egyptians serving in the Sudan carried food packages when they were not building rails for the railroad, or worse, toting the bundles of British officers. "Is this the enslavement of the people in the name of civilization?" Kāmil wrote.[70]

Kāmil's outraged protest at this indignity leaves out an important element. As Fawzī's memoirs show, the menial work required of Egyptian soldiers had previously been performed by Sudanese slaves—either slave soldiers or slaves belonging personally to Egyptian soldiers and officers, as in Fawzī Pasha's case.[71] In the Sudan during the Turkīya, slaves were often conscripted as soldiers in the army regiments known as the *jihādīya*. By the 1890s they actually outnumbered the contracted Egyptian soldiers by a ratio of two to one.[72] These slave soldiers were absolutely essential to the maintenance of the military camps, work that presumably included the tasks Kāmil so dreaded for Egyptian soldiers.[73] His indignation also echoed with resentment over Egyptians' loss of authority over the Sudanese themselves, and the consequent shame at occupying the low status once belonging to the Sudanese.

The plaintive description of Egyptians victimized by the British reversal of Egyptian-Sudanese social roles in the army was juxtaposed in Kāmil's speeches with the naturalness and intimacy of Egyptian domination of the Sudan. He repeated in many articles that the Sudan was part of the Egyptian body, but there are particular passages that treat this metaphor with singular aggression. In an article he wrote for *al-Ahrām* in 1893, Kāmil describes how the Egyptians had earned the Sudan:

> The Sudan would never have been interjoined with this land *[lam tultahim bi hādhā al-qatr]* were it not for the blood of its men [Egyptians], would never have been subdued under the Ottoman flag if not for the resolution of its heroes, and the flow of its money. She is the maiden territory *[al-aqtar ash-shābah]* in which the blood of martyrs has spilled, not so she would become easy prey *[ghanīma barda]* for the British, but rather to be the treasure *[mudakhiran]* of Egyptians, a wide sanctuary for the comfort of the two peoples, the source of all riches and the stop for all trade.[74]

The Sudan was a testing ground for Egyptian virility, for the individuals who had shed their blood there (fighting the Sudanese), and for the entire national project of independence at a time when the dominant worldview insisted that independent, self-reliant nations were by definition also regional, if not global, conquerors.[75]

By 1898, as it became clearer that the British were about to reconquer the Sudan, Kāmil mourned the impending castration of his nation. Almost like a eunuch, Egypt was to suffer in its most sensitive part. He mourns this in vivid language in an article in the French newspaper *Le Clair*, after the retaking of Atbara in the Sudan: "There is no doubt that the blood and money of Egyptians were sacrificed in order to conquer the Sudan *[fath al-sūdān]*, which gave Egyptians the first right in its administration and in mastering its resources."[76]

But the British, in their eternal greed for the Sudan, were seizing the harvest sown by Egyptians and would leave the Egyptians nothing; worse, they would make the Egyptians as helpless and "feminine" as the Sudanese. Egyptian soldiers had trekked through the killing heat of the Sudan, toiling and fighting and proving victorious, only to hear it said that "the Egyptian is not humane enough, not worthy enough, of governing."[77] Now the British had wielded their most damaging weapon:

> The Sudan, as is clear to the reader, is a piece of Egypt and has been stripped from her with no legal right, because the Egyptian khedivial government has not the least right to give up even a foot of her land or allow someone else to possess it. With this to be considered, the Sudan is still Egyptian property, and the British do not have the right

to any claims to it. It returned to khedivial authority after almost twenty years of the dervishes' upheaval, and even if British soldiers participated with us in the reconquest, we did not need their help. Our army, even less than our whole army, would have been enough to accomplish this result.[78]

Kāmil's words—territories or sections *(quṭiʿāt)* "stripped" and "detached" *(sulikha)* from the mainland by the British, Egyptian "possession" and "ownership" *(mulk)* of the Sudan—stirred powerful images for his public. His sense of his audience, whether French or Egyptian, and the emotions they shared against the British, enabled him to deconstruct the words used to describe imperialism, and to delineate two meanings for the same word, one a natural linkage between the Sudan and Egypt, the other a cold, calculated strategy of greed on the part of Great Britain. This linguistic dualism fortified the image he created of the orphaned amputee, Egypt, against the cold authority of the English officials of the occupation. The Egyptian David fighting the British Goliath is self-consciously reenacted in a dialogue between Kāmil and Admiral Baring, the brother of Lord Cromer, that Kāmil prepared for *al-Ahrām*, in which they wrangle over the word *mulk*, or ownership:

BARING: Even if I agreed with you and said that Europe will help you to victory and force us to withdraw, that will happen only after your fallaḥ sells all his land and his condition deteriorates, after we fill our pockets with money thanks to our possession of the Sudan, which, as you of course know, is the soul of your country.

KĀMIL: How can you own the Sudan while the Sudan still belongs to us?

BARING *[laughing]:* If it was your possession, then why did you not retake it, why did you lose Wadlay and Kassala?

KĀMIL: That was due to your machinations and your opposition to its return to us, but once you leave, it will be easy for us to retake it.

BARING: Your possession has for a long time not returned to you. In fact, it is now the goods *[matāʿ]* of whomever seizes it. May God grant Nubar Pasha blessings, for it was easy in the past to detach it from you, and it will be easy for us to own it forever.[79]

Baring's steely and glinting lust for the Sudan seems scandalous; his laughing at Kāmil is like the mockery of a cuckolded rival. Putting these words in his mouth, Kāmil vilifies Baring and the unlawful seizure of what was rightfully, legally Egypt's. For Kāmil, Egypt and the Sudan were irrevocably linked by the bonds of Islam. Only coreligionists could communicate or understand each other. Given both Egypt's physical proximity to the Sudan and the shared culture and spiritual background of the two regions, only Egyptians could in truth *know* the Sudanese and, on the strength of this knowledge, be their lawful and benevolent guardians.

But Admiral Baring's question still rang: if the Sudan was really Egypt's possession, how did the Egyptians lose it? Kāmil placed responsibility for this first on the British when he spoke in Alexandria in 1896: "Why did the Sudanese keep on determinedly rebelling against Egypt? Why would they not accept any agreement with us? No one can deny that the British presence in Egypt made the Sudanese behave that way."[80] But another quality in the Sudanese propelled them into the Mahdīya against the Egyptians (and Kāmil never denies that the Mahdists rebelled against an Egyptian, and not Ottoman, authority)—a native fanaticism:

> In reality, the Muslims of the Sudan are very rigid and fanatical; they would never and will never accept that any but Muslims rule them. In order to win them over, it is not necessary to use force; rather, we will call to them in the name of Islam. We will send to them in the name of the khedive and the sultan a religious embassy consisting of several *'ulamā'*. It would be enough, in stanching the fire of the revolution between them and bringing them to our side, for us to enter their territory carrying the Holy Qur'an in one hand and the flag of the Prophet in the other.[81]

Here, Kāmil echoes claims about native Sudanese excess (either religious or sexual) that Muḥammad al-Tunisī and Shaykh Rifaʿah Rafiʿ al-Ṭahṭawī had discussed two generations before. As a culture, Kāmil continues, Egypt was uniquely imbued with the capacity to bridge this untamed religious energy and western European society. He asks, "Is there any other country in the world as suited by religious liberalism *[al-muḥidd]* and absolute moderation to be the medium between civilized Europe and fanatical Africa if not Egypt?" And this unique though combustible blend of qualities should have properly distanced Egypt and the Sudan from the rest of the continent's vulnerability to the scramble for Africa. He adds, "Egypt does not resemble other African countries, which can be seized simply by treaties between the Powers. Egypt is a different place. Behind the Egyptian question is actually a very dangerous and important issue. Behind the Egyptian question there is the White Nile question and the African question and the Christian question and the Muslim question."[82]

But two years after this speech, through what was, for Kāmil, its shameful and shaming seizure of Omdurman in 1898, Great Britain opened the Pandora's box that was Africa. In doing so, British military officials had revealed a degree of their own savagery and fanaticism when they revenged Gordon's death by ripping apart the tomb of the Mahdī. Kāmil mourned the desecration, but even more, he resented that it had been committed in the name of General Gordon. With this act of disrespect, the British had stamped their name onto the Sudan:

> [They] pulverized the Mahdī's tomb completely, then took out his head in the most repulsive manner, then all gathered and made speeches, saluting and honoring the spirit of the martyr [Gordon's spirit]. They raised flags in victory for having recaptured his remains. The Egyptians look at this spectacle and ask themselves: Is there no price for the blood of those of us who died? Is there no value for our men? Is not the Egyptian, in the law of the Merciful, a human being like any other? Did not our heroic soldiers die before the recovery *[istirdād]* of the Sudan, for its recovery, and no one mentions a thing about them? Instead, there are those among us who congratulate the British for reclaiming Gordon's remains. Is the blood of one Englishman of higher price, while the blood of thousands of Egyptians has no price and gets nothing but oblivion?[83]

In Kāmil's representation, the British wiped away the names and memory of the Egyptian dead in the Sudan as they engraved their own mark on the region with the letters of Gordon's name. With the collusion of the Egyptian public, this action succeeded in rendering anonymous Egypt's role in the reclamation of the Sudan or, as Kāmil suggests, in rendering Egypt flagless there. British officials used their power to distort the name and reputation of the Egyptian people by asserting that it was Egyptians, especially nationalists, who were fanatical and beyond the pale of self-control. This projected an image of Egyptian savagery: "Egypt's enemies would like to represent us in front of Europe as a collective of barbarians *[qawm mutawaḥishīn]* ready to annihilate every European living in our country as soon as the British soldiers leave us. They wanted to disguise you and ridicule your peaceful intentions by repeating these lies in front of you in the newspapers and in every possible place." In a speech on the same theme given one year later, Kāmil directly equated fanaticism with barbarism, as he resisted this image that the occupying authorities propagated about Egypt.[84]

Kāmil's equation of fanaticism with barbarism also bore racial ramifications. These were made more explicit in a book inspired by Kāmil's work that was published anonymously in 1898 by "one of Egypt's men of letters." The author actually blamed the British for sowing seeds of racial discord between the black Sudanese and the white Egyptians, yet he was careful to name those tribes who had good Muslim customs and those with whom no contact was possible due to their uncivilized, un-Islamic behavior. His descriptions of Egyptian colonial life in Khartoum and Berber portray Egyptians as aloof from Sudanese culture, living in an exclusive enclave and behaving very much like British colonialists: "In Berber, thousands of Egyptians reside in a village reserved for them. Most of them are from the *mudirīyas* of Qena, Girga, and Assiout, and they have maintained their customs and their Egyptian way of life with little change worth mentioning. Most of them spend summers in the Egyptian countryside and winters in Berber."[85]

Keeping contact minimal between Egyptians and Sudanese in his accounts of the Sudan, the author also set up a racial scale by which he measured Sudanese tribes, which depended on how savage their customs were. People of Sennār, for example, practiced a frightening magic, in which they could turn themselves into wolves. Though such devilish practices were not appropriate for discussion, the author wrote coyly, presenting them in his book made certain his readers knew that people from Sennār were not at all like Egyptians. The blackest of all tribes, the Dinka and the Shilluk, lived way beyond the pale, worshiping pagan idols and wearing hardly any clothes.[86] And yet, page after page, the author asserted that indissoluble links existed between Egypt and the Sudan based on Islam.

Kāmil originated this particular dualism in the definitions of fanatical [*mutʿaṣib*] and barbarian [*mutawaḥish*] and asserted it as a basis for Egyptian domination. As he described them, the Sudanese were fanatic and savage, particularly in terms of religion. Only Egyptian Muslims knew how to translate this wild energy into a viable society. "We know them," Kāmil seemed to be saying of the Sudanese, "but we are not them." His representation of the Sudanese, however, distorted their image with the same force that British invectives against savagery visited on the image of Egyptians. The identification with both colonizer and colonized within the Egyptian nationalist movement presents itself vividly here. The speeches and writings of Kāmil and his imitators shows an effort to twist through the narrow parameters by which civilization was gauged in the 1890s. But by using the measurements and instruments of the master, Kāmil in important ways offered his submission to British hegemony. Kāmil castigated contemporaries like Muḥammad Sultan Pasha for caving into the British when it proved advantageous,[87] calling for total opposition to the occupying government. Under closer scrutiny, however, his opposition was replete with the same prejudices and hierarchies.

TOOLS OF THE MASTER

On 7 January 1899, Egyptians first heard from the newspapers the new name that Lord Cromer had invented for the Sudan: the Anglo-Egyptian Condominium. *Al-Muʾayid* published the entire speech that Cromer had delivered to the inhabitants of Khartoum the previous day, in which he spelled out the new arrangement for the government of the Sudan. The condominium meant sharing: a British governor-general of the Sudan, appointed by the khedive on the "recommendation" of the British government, would govern the country, whereas the Egyptian Treasury would pay for the enterprise. More than anyone, its inventor knew it to be an enigmatic name, almost literary.[88]

Nationalists reacted strongly to the condominium's implication that Egypt and England were equal partners in governing the Sudan. Made second-rate citizens in their own capital and now also in the Sudan, Egyptians had lost the meaning of their flag, which now stood for nothing, wrote Shaykh 'Alī Yusuf.[89] He printed full translations of the proclamation and, in a very public close reading, analyzed the language of the condominium's proclamation term by term.[90] He offered a long description of the geographic boundaries of Egypt and the Sudan, then painstakingly mapped out the razor lines of the new borders decreed by the British,[91] which pushed the Sudan all the way into Aswan, far enough, he worried, to erase the public's memory of Egyptian rule in the south.

In the years that followed the condominium's establishment, a literature emerged in Egypt in which every aspect of British society and culture was dissected and explored for clues to the success of Great Britain's empire. Some of these works were filled with admiration for a culture like England's that could rule almost the entire world. Aḥmad Fatḥī Zaghlūl, brother of the Wafd Party leader and future prime minister Sa'd Zaghlūl, published *Sirr al-taqaddum al-Anglo-Saxīyīn?*, a translation of the book *À quoi tient la supériorité des anglo-saxons?* (What Is the Secret of Anglo-Saxon Superiority?), written in 1898 by Edmond Demolins. This book explored the successes of the British empire, looking for formulas for other societies to emulate, and became popular throughout Europe.[92] Aḥmad Zaghlūl prefaced his translation with an admonition to his Egyptian reader to "compare their customs to our customs, their knowledge to our knowledge, their concerns to our concerns, their abilities to our abilities" for the formula of success.[93] Another well-publicized work that compared Egypt to England was Muḥammad 'Umar's *Ḥāḍir al-miṣrīyīn aw sirr ta'akhurihim* (The Present State of the Egyptians, or the Cause of Their Retrogression), published in 1902. The secret, as Muḥammad 'Umar saw it, was colonialism. With this word very much in mind, Salaḥ Hamdī Ḥamad published another study of British ascendancy in 1906, with the simple title *Naḥnu wa al-Rūqī* (Our Progress). This too presented a mirror of England in an effort to teach Egyptians the art of national self-determination, but it went further toward explaining how to recreate the Egyptian empire. It was important for Egyptians to understand that true imperialism *[istiʿmār]* benefited everyone. Through one community's settlement in another's land, for the purpose of making a living, the exchange of expertise about trade, crafts, and agricultural development was spread to the host country.[94]

All the great civilizations were imperial, Salaḥ Ḥamad wrote, although many, like Spain in America or Britain in Australia, had butchered and committed genocide; but England and the rest of Europe had developed a more sympathetic and humane colonization, exemplified in the abolitionists' care for African blacks. Egyptians could also trace historical precedents for imperialism in their own history, and Ḥamad turned to the links with the Sudan:

> There is no doubt that the Egyptian Sudan is part of our beloved Egypt like the soul to the body; from it comes the blessed Nile, the life of the country and the source of Egypt's resources and welfare. Everyone who rules the Sudan realizes these truths. From ancient times, their care had been to keep the Sudan together with Egypt. The pharaohs conquered the Sudan, then the Arabs, then Muḥammad ʿAlī Pasha, who had it explored and excavated by teams of specialists, searching for its hidden minerals, which companies there now refine. All this is to say that the remains of Egypt's imperialism in the Sudan show she has long been a part of the country, whose benefits come thanks to such endeavors.[95]

But how could modern Egyptians live up to this illustrious past? They could move to the Sudan en masse, Ḥamad wrote; only fear and hesitation kept Egyptian society from realizing this goal. This would homogenize agricultural and husbandry techniques all along the Nile Valley, link the peoples, language, and customs of both cultures. The Egyptians, with their native industry and intellect, would teach their neighbors how better to develop their country. And most important of all, colonizing Africa, as Europe's example showed, was one of the profoundest expressions of patriotism: "Groups of Frenchmen have grown famous for their love of France because they emigrated to their colonies, especially in Africa, with all its difficulties, to gain enough livelihood." The British did the same, displaying great national courage in toiling through adversity to bring prosperity to themselves and Africa. "So why can't Egyptians demonstrate the same vigor and life, and harvest the fruits of the Sudan for our country?"[96] Ḥamad asks.

The science of empire, as modeled by Europe, appealed to many subsequent writers, a notable representative being Aḥmad Luṭfī al-Sayyid, who, along with Muṣṭafa Kāmil, became a leading voice of Egyptian nationalism, as well as founded his own party, *Ḥizb al-umma*, or Party of the Nation.[97] He established the party's newspaper, *al-Jarīda*, and was a major proponent of greater educational opportunities for Egyptians. After Kāmil's death in 1908, Luṭfī al-Sayyid would become one of the most respected nationalist thinkers of Egypt. Like Kāmil's, he supported Egypt's claim to the Sudan as a colony. He writes:

> The Sudan is Egypt's by right of conquest. She is a part of Egypt, and her not being separated is vital to Egypt's life, due to her holding the source of the Nile and being her neighbor. We loathed giving her up, then she was reconquered, this time with the participation of the English. During all of that we were submissive to the contract of the Condominium and the triumphant power [England]. That administration is void before public opinion and the law. The arrangement of the Condominium alters nothing of the correct concept that all Egyptians hold dear, and that is that colonizing *[istiʿmār]* the Sudan is the right of Egyptians, and no one else, just as the subsidizing of the Sudan is the duty of Egyptians, and no one else. Egyptians look at the Sudanese as brothers, as a part of their community, so it's their responsibility to look out for their brothers' welfare.[98]

Luṭfī al-Sayyid's newspaper, *al-Jarīda*, regularly set aside front-page space for the issue of colonizing the Sudan. So tight were the bonds between the two countries that even the name *Sudan* made no sense, wrote 'Abd al-Qadir Hamza, a frequent contributor. In language that removes a separate identity from the Sudanese, he states, "I do not know why the Sudan is named anything other than Egypt, and it amazes me that we accepted this appellation during eras of oppression."[99] The Sudan was not a separate nation, no matter what its name, but the name had the deleterious effect of making people think it was separate. The connections between Egypt and the Sudan defied political language;

> We are the first among all peoples to colonize the Sudan, which as I said is an organ of Egypt's. She is closer to us than any other country, her history linked to our history, her people the closest to ever have mixed with us. In fact, you can hardly tell the difference between us, our Nile is the Sudan's Nile, and our blood has flowed there in ancient and in modern times, our money spent there in the tens of millions.[100]

Hamza wrote in a unique style about the importance of geographical names in public conceptions of the political map, but the rest of the imagery he used to illustrate the Sudan's links with Egypt had become clichéd by the time of his writing. The Sudan as Egypt's soul was a standard formula in the nationalist lexicon, until Luṭfī al-Sayyid deepened the discussion with his ideas about shared culture creating family ties. The Egyptians had experienced everything the Sudanese had experienced, and this past bound their culture. By linking the two peoples culturally, Luṭfī al-Sayyid again changed the definition of the word *imperialism* for Egyptian society, because only foreigners could colonize.

> It is a mistake to consider the Sudan an Egyptian colony. The Sudan is rather a part of what makes up Egypt; she completes Egypt. There is Lower Egypt, and the Sudan is Upper Egypt. Every Sudanese bears the same responsibilities to the nation of Egypt as every native Egyptian. When Sudanese people mention the tyranny of some Egyptian rulers, Egyptians can also relate the despotism of their own rulers. Egypt at times suffered autocrats the entire length of the nation. If it was within a governor's power in the Sudan to hang a Sudanese, it was also within the power of the *mudīr* of Daqhiliyya or Sharqiyya [Egyptian provinces] to hang an Egyptian.

Luṭfī al-Sayyid "bitterly disapproved" of the class distinctions that Egyptians recognized among themselves. The sharing of such close historical and political experiences should make any right-minded Egyptian forget the artificial prejudice that so many harbored against the Sudanese. After all, there are those "among the sons of Lower Egypt who continue to view the Saʿīdī [villager from southern Egypt] with a prejudiced eye *[bi naẓratī al-makhṣūṣa]*, but that viewpoint cannot remove the Saʿīdī from his equality with the British. Likewise, those who view the Sudanese with short-sightedness do not remove the Sudanese from their equality with Egyptians in all rights and duties."[101]

These were new concepts in the development of Egyptian nationalist thought and the issue of the Sudan. Luṭfī al-Sayyid's vision elevated the Sudanese from the stereotypical wild fanatics or sorcerers to cocitizens. He defied the traditional Egyptian belief in the backwardness of Sudanese Islam by not linking Egyptians and Sudanese under the rubric of Islam or the leadership of the Ottoman amir al-Muʾminīn. A more conscious awareness of history and the path of politics united the Egyptians and the Sudan, and Luṭfī al-Sayyid asked both to recreate mentally their sense of community and their place in the world.

Such social sensitivity redefined the image of the Sudanese; ironically, Luṭfī al-Sayyid's rupture with the stereotypes allowed no room for dissenting Sudanese voices. Both the figure of the Mahdī, who represented by far the loudest Sudanese voice Egyptians had ever heard, and the state he created, which had lasted almost fifteen years, were diminished to mere dots on the historical record for the sake of family peace. Luṭfī al-Sayyid notes that

> some Sudanese did revolt against the Egyptian community, but the rebels were disciplined and the discord ended *[w-intahit al-fitna]*. It was

> necessary after that to return conditions to what they had been before
> the Mahdī's rebellion.
>
> That is why every Egyptian, on one hand, and every Sudanese, on
> the other, must consider each other as immediate brothers or as cousins
> [*ibn 'amm*], all from one mother, within the borders of one country.[102]

After the thoughtfulness of his earlier comments about the Sudanese, these paragraphs registered a startling obliviousness to the recent and cataclysmic events of the Mahdīya. Luṭfī al-Sayyid claimed that "it was necessary after that to return conditions" to their antebellum status, but no such return ever occurred. The Mahdī had caused the Sudan to be lost to Egypt, and in the twenty-five years that had elapsed between the fall of Khartoum and Luṭfī al-Sayyid's writing, Egypt remained a partner only nominally in the administration of the Anglo-Egyptian Condominium. And when he encouraged both Egyptians and Sudanese to regard each other as brothers and not to respect the borders that separated the two countries, Luṭfī al-Sayyid asked his readers to conjure a new geography and imagine an alternative reality with the sheer force of hope and rhetoric. He invited his readers to rethink their cultural and political map from within. And as the resilience of his ideas shows, many accepted the invitation.

Notwithstanding the originality of Luṭfī al-Sayyid's viewpoint, several themes embedded in Egyptian nationalistic constructions of the Sudan over the sixteen years between 1894 and 1910 still framed the Sudan's image. Islam's adhesiveness no longer glued the two territories together, yet the people in them were still family, still sharing blood and experience, sharing all privileges—but they shared all these only as dictated by Egyptians, in keeping with Egyptians' sense of themselves. As long as the Sudanese respected that sense, their participation was welcome; but if they registered any protest against Egyptian views on the Nile Valley, as the Mahdists clearly did, they were rendered invisible. To writers in the paper *al-Jarīda*, even the name *Sudan*, with its implication of geographical, cultural, and political distinction from Egypt, made the place and its people too separate and autonomous. The idea of Egyptian domination of the Sudan loomed vibrantly; the belief in empire was still stoked by Egyptian nationalists. But the true masters of empire building, the British, gave up nothing. Though the nationalists in this chapter analyzed and adopted the instruments of cultural and political hegemony so well used in the British empire, they were still nowhere near to regaining their authority over the Sudan, or their own country.

5 Egyptians in Blackface

Revolution and Popular Culture, World War I to 1925

In 1910 Aḥmad Luṭfī al-Sayyid had argued with great force that the unity of the Nile Valley was sacred, but this projected unity often missed, or dismissed, some of the core issues that more painfully united the cultures along the Nile. It was neither the experience of British occupation nor World War I that integrated Egypt with the Sudan. In fact, the two experienced the political and economic circumstances of 1910 through 1919 very differently. Whereas Egypt had by then a well-established tradition of nationalism, the Sudan had only recently been conquered by Great Britain, and any national voice there remained muted. Whereas the Sudan faced the challenges of recovering from years of famine and the great losses of life suffered by the Mahdist forces in 1899, Egypt's relative prosperity was overshadowed by the continued and deepening entrenchment of British control over the political system. While Egyptian nationalists lamented the loss of Egypt's participation in the governing of the Sudan under the terms of the Anglo-Egyptian Condominium, British officials in the Sudan were implementing an educational and political system in which the Muslim communities of the north were separated from non-Muslim tribes in the south. Contemporaries of these events and later historians have explored how these experiences affected each country: how the economics of occupation affected the Egyptian nationalist movements; how the British response to the challenges presented by missionaries, slavery, and the local economy in the Sudan brought about an enduring and problematic duality to the country; and how politicized the issue of the Nile Valley became after the end of World War I and the breakup of the Ottoman Empire.[1]

I see a more enduring unity in how communities in both Egypt and the Sudan struggled, in different ways, to incorporate African slaves, former slaves, and their immediate descendants into nationalist visions of each

168

country's identity. There is also a similarity in how these slaves and their relatives were ignored or stereotyped and how what were considered to be "African" traces in Egyptian and Sudanese cultural heritage were problematized. This again underlines how the ongoing and controversial issue of the Sudan, so volatile for elements of Egyptian nationalism, affected people's constructions of race and identity all along the Nile Valley. The carefully crafted speeches of speakers like Luṭfī al-Sayyid included all Nile Valley inhabitants in the nationalist movement yet excluded those people who had been born and raised in Egypt but enjoyed little political or cultural status because their parents had been Sudanese slaves—people for whom identification as an "Egyptian" or as a "Sudanese" raised more questions than answers. Many who considered themselves part of a majority— nationalists in Egypt, *tarīqa* (Sufi lodges) leaders in the Sudan, and British administrators—were unable to consider manumitted slaves or their descendants as legitimate nationalist spokesmen for Egypt or for the Sudan. It took decades before those whose lives really did represent a heritage shared in Nile Valley culture—the legatees of the African slave trade— could be seen and heard in anything but stereotyped caricatures created by someone else.

MUḤAMMAD IMĀM AL-ʿABD AND THE POETRY OF RACE

Muḥammad Imām al-ʿAbd grew up in roughly the same generation as Aḥmad Luṭfī al-Sayyid. Born in either 1860 or 1861, he came of age in the house of an Ottoman-Egyptian pasha in the wealthy Cairo neighborhood of Garden City, not far from the British barracks.[2] This area was also a short distance from the ʿAzbakīya Gardens, the part of the city that, by the late nineteenth century, had become a vibrant cultural center studded with theaters and music halls and coffeehouses frequented by young musicians, poets, writers, and journalists. Like his artistic contemporaries, Imām al-ʿAbd began his education in a *kuttab* and then entered one of the elementary schools created by Khedive Ismaʿīl; like them, as he grew up he wanted to write poetry. As an adult, he spent many hours at the same coffeehouses with budding young poets like Ḥafiẓ Ibrāhīm, the musician Sayyid Darwīsh, and the comedic playwright Badiʿ Khayrī. But unlike them, Imām al-ʿAbd was the child of two Sudanese slaves. He had grown up watching his parents perform domestic work in that beautiful villa in Garden City, perhaps helping out with their duties when he was a child.[3] Similar to the majority of the figures discussed in this book, Imām al-ʿAbd had intimate memories of slavery. But whereas Ibrāhīm Fawzī Pasha lived the experience of owning slaves, and Aḥmad Shafīk remembered that his mother had been a Circassian slave, Imām al-ʿAbd's parents were Sudanese, taken in childhood as slaves, raising their child while working as domestic slaves.[4] And of course Zanūba and the five slave women who came with her from the Sudan knew such work as well, but they did not have a place in which to relate their feelings about their enslavement. Imām al-ʿAbd, however, became a poet and, before he died in 1911, expressed through his *qaṣīdas* and his *zajal* poetry what it was like living in Cairo as a dark-skinned man who, because of his parents, had inherited the stigma of black slave ancestry.

Imām al-ʿAbd's parents came from the group of people so easily caricatured as cartoons and humorous characters in Egyptian sketches and plays. It is with some irony, then, that the critic ʿAbd al-ʿAzīz al-Bishrī framed the talents of his old and long-deceased friend Imām al-ʿAbd for Egyptian society in an essay first broadcast on the radio, called "Fun and Humor: The Egyptian Joke in the Modern Period."[5] Again and again in the essay, al-Bishrī recounts how witty and lighthearted this poet was and what he looked like:

> Imām (may God have mercy upon him) was a Negro in every sense of the word *[kāna zanjiyan bi manʿat al-kalima]*, as they say, if not for the fluency of his language and the fact that he had been born and raised in Egypt. The morals of its people were native to him; he followed their customs and their livelihoods. He had thick nostrils, a flat nose, red pupils, and flexible muscles, peppery hair. As for the color of his skin, it was as black as the darkest gloom.[6]

The passage is revealing—Imām al-ʿAbd was as Egyptian as any other native resident of Cairo, but his physique, for al-Bishrī, contradicts that indigenousness. All the features that made Imām al-ʿAbd black detracted from his identity as an Egyptian. His physical features belied, at least for the Egyptian audience envisioned by al-Bishrī, his real fluency in Arabic, both classical and colloquial. And historically, language did mark a difference between slaves and Egyptians. As ʿUmad Ahmad Hilāl has written, slaves in all their forms in Egypt had no knowledge of classical Arabic. Even after Circassian-Ottoman slaves were manumitted, the majority remained affiliated with the Turkish-speaking social classes and were fairly isolated from Arabic-speaking groups. Sudanese slaves, the majority of whom came from the non-Muslim territories of the Sudan, communicated with each other in the colloquial dialect. This may well be why Imām al-ʿAbd presented so stark a linguistic enigma to al-Bishrī and others.[7]

Yet sensitivity about color fills al-Bishrī's article with sympathy too. He recounts how a group of young students came up to him and Ḥafiẓ Ibrahīm (who became known in the 1920s as the "poet of the Nile") in a café, after hearing Imām al-ʿAbd recite several poems at a special university gathering, and praised the speaker's eloquence and genius. But later that same day, Ḥafiẓ Ibrahīm ran into Imām al-ʿAbd himself and told him of the favorable reports. Imām al-ʿAbd responded sarcastically, saying, "By God, people don't applaud Imām's eloquence or the beauty of his poetry, but the fact that he is a slave, as they'd say if he lit a lamp skillfully, 'Bravo ya Imām!'"[8] And he addressed this issue in his poetry, too, as in this verse:

> People linked me to the slave figuratively,
>> Despite my refinement: they cited my blackness.
> My value eroded and I began to lament my fate,
>> Because my blackness I wear like an iron robe.[9]

Imām al-ʿAbd also composed poetry about how the "iron robe" he wore prevented him from finding a wife among Egyptian women.

> I wanted to be together and she said, perplexed,
>> O poet, what is this passionate love?
> You are a slave, and love tells me
>> That to fall in love with a slave is forbidden.
> I said, What madness, I am a slave of love,
>> And love judges what is between dreamers.
> And even if I am a black slave,
>> Please know I am also a young man, free of speech.[10]

Despite such passion, this woman rejected him. A little later, he wrote a *qaṣīda* called "Al-zanjiya al-ḥusna" (The Beautiful Negro), in which he turned the alienation people felt about the color of his skin into a celebration of Sudanese women. Instead of using the word *ʿabd* here to mean *slaves*, he uses common names for black slaves to situate this love:

> People have their own school, preferring whites,
>> But my school is the love of blacks.
> Murjan is enthralled by his Bakhīta
>> And Bakhīta is crazy for Murjan.
> Who said that love is a reproof?
>> O people of love, guide me.
> Who said that absence is torture?
>> O people of love, give me a *fatwa* [order].
> The night and my beloved are friends,
>> How can my ill-wishers see me?
> The sun hates my beloved
>> Like the sparrows' hatred of the crows.[11]

Hilāl sees the poet's clever play on stereotypes and language as part of his importance as a historical resource, which offers a glimpse into the condition of slaves in Egyptian society, especially after they obtained manumission documents from the slave trade bureaus. But the personal is more political for the critic Hilāl, who also sees in Imām al-'Abd's oeuvre a revolt against the society that attached slavery to his name and never granted him full rights, either as a person or as a poet.[12]

It is important to add to those insights, however, that although Imām al-'Abd wrote about how alone he felt in Egyptian society, he also clearly expressed how much a part of it he considered himself politically. In fact, Imām al-'Abd added his own words to the nationalist literature so popular in his lifetime. He wrote a nationalistic *qaṣīda* of praise for and pride in the pyramids, "'Ala qimat al-ahrām" (On the Summit of the Pyramids), in which he scolded his generation of Egyptians for their lack of political motivation:

> Woe to a people whose buildings have collapsed
>   and still their hearts have not been alarmed, their mouths have not
>   been opened.
> They sleep while time brings forth new catastrophes.
>   I wonder, does glory look at those who sleep?
> It is sorrow enough that the East is dark in the morning
>   while in the West the stars come out on the horizon?
> If a nation does not race against the West,
>   then write on the grave of the one who perished
> that he passed away in pain.
>   So do not honor me after my death,
>   for I see that the one who returns glory to the East
> is the one more worthy of being honored.
>   If I do not please my country with my energy and determination,
> then may my hand not move the well-carved reed.[13]

In these words, it is easy to sense the responsibility in belonging to Egypt, a duty that the poet takes very seriously. His poetry, then, was an important instrument in his participation in a vibrant literary movement, as a master of Arabic in its written and spoken forms. It is striking, though, that his memory, described by Ḥafiẓ Ibrāhīm and al-Bishrī to the historian 'Amr al-'Aqad, evokes the same doubling of exclusion and inclusion that he himself lived. While none ignore the sensitivity of his racial identity, his greatest gift to Egyptian society, they stated, was his humor and the jokes he was famous for playing on others and on himself. It was this humor that ultimately humanized him in the eyes of many of his contemporaries, even more than his gift for poetry. But for the historian 'Umad Ahmad Hilāl, who was looking for the actual voices of slaves and their immediate descendants in the late nineteenth century, Imām al-ʿAbd signified a great sadness and social loneliness, a man whose eloquence was, for others, belied by the color of his skin.

THE 1919 REVOLUTION

Egyptians' nationalistic feeling suffered during World War I, when London declared Egypt a protectorate of the British empire. With the dissolution of the Ottoman Empire, Egyptian nationalists lost the nominal alternative of allegiance to the sultan; although it took longer to abolish the caliphate, the Islamic empire that had united them with other Muslims around the world was terribly weakened and a bulwark against European imperialism was lost. But there seemed to be ideological support from outside Egypt's borders that, if mobilized, could fill the political vacuum left by this loss, demonstrated most dramatically when President Woodrow Wilson delivered a powerful speech to the League of Nations declaring that all nations had the right to self-determination.[14] Saʿd Zaghlūl, an accomplished lawyer in Cairo, seized on this statement of Wilson's. It had seemed to many nationalists that the British government's declaration of the protectorate over Egypt had been a wartime necessity, but once the war ended and there was no indication given of lifting the protectorate. Zaghlūl and his associates hoped that, as representatives of Egypt, they could travel to Paris for the postwar peace conference to present their country's case for independence from the British empire.[15] Zaghlūl and the other members of the delegation, or Wafd as their party came to be known, asked in late 1918 for permission from the British Resident, Sir Reginald Wingate, to leave for Europe for the conference. Wingate refused to allow them even passports. Zaghlūl continued to insist on his suitability as a political representative of Egypt's interests and met frequently and publicly with prominent politicians and nationalists. Members of the Wafd published thousands of copies of a pamphlet stating its purpose and distributed these throughout the country. On 8 March 1919, Zaghlūl and three other members of the Wafd were arrested and deported to Malta.[16]

News of their arrest provoked demonstrations first in Cairo, Alexandria, and other major cities, then in the countryside. The demonstrators ranged from lawyers and pashas to students and peasants. In a new kind of political gesture, upper-class women joined the demonstrations, and their participation was welcomed. As Huda Shaʿrawī, the wife of the Wafd delegate ʿAlī Shaʿrawī, described in her memoirs, well-connected women organized demonstrations quickly and efficiently and created a network that became crucial to the nationalist movement.[17] Religious leaders added their voices as well, and Coptic bishops joined al-Azhār shaykhs to proclaim their allegiance to the revolution. For the first time, Egyptian society, in all its shapes, classes, and perspectives, seemed to stand shoulder to shoulder in support of Zaghlūl. To one eyewitness, the news of the arrests was like an explosion in every Egyptian's ears, and all, to the last individual, rose in protest.[18] This newly cohesive crowd reveled in the act of joining together, of transforming itself into a collective instead of being transformed by the unilateral actions of Great Britain into just another British colony. On one level, the demonstrations allowed Egyptians to see each other in positions of power and protest, as they wanted to be seen, and not as subjugated, colonized people. This protest against being the debased "Other" reinforced collective identity. As the contemporary observer and historian Muḥammad Sabry puts it, "Egypt suffered at seeing herself treated with disdain and cruelty, like 'damn niggers' and gypsies (bohemians) by the innumerable and ignorant functionaries, filled with arrogance, that England had been sending to Egypt since the declaration of the protectorate, and by the Tommies who believed that 'Egypt was English and that the natives were people of colour imported to the country.'"[19] Sabry's choice of words reveals how powerful the stigma of race had become under these semicolonial circumstances: not only did the British treat Egyptians like blacks and possess all the expectations of subservience inherent in that concept, they denied them the right of being native in their own land. In imposing a color stigma on Egyptians and making them black, Sabry believed that the British had deracinated them in their own homeland, as if they were servants imported from Africa for the pleasure of the British occupiers, or, to put it more ironically, as if the Egyptians were like the Sudanese.

After a confrontational and sometimes violent month of demonstrations, the British authorities conceded their tactical mistake, released Zaghlūl and his companions, and granted them permission to travel to Paris. Sir Reginald Wingate was relieved of his duties, replaced by Field Marshal Edmund H. Allenby, and a four-year-long process of negotiations between Egypt and Great Britain began. Although many points of contention were not fully resolved in these negotiations, the uprisings of 1919 succeeded in surprising the British government and changing the terms that even officials long familiar with Egypt had to use to define the country.[20] The British abolished the protectorate and granted Egypt nominal independence. Sultan Husayn Kamil was retired, succeeded by his son Fu'ad, who now bore the title of king, although his claims of being "king of Egypt and the Sudan" were resisted by the British. Another important institution to emerge from the negotiations was the new Egyptian Parliament, which met for the first time in 1924.

But loopholes in Egyptian political autonomy remained. The British government reserved the right to station soldiers at the Suez Canal and elsewhere in Egypt and to negotiate on behalf of Egypt in several areas of foreign policy. Even though British officials in Cairo had conceded there were legal loopholes in Egypt's status as a protectorate, loopholes which Sa'd Zaghlūl derided in his speeches, the British continued to deny the territorial integrity of the Nile Valley so important to Egyptian politicians.[21] The Foreign Office and Field Marshal Allenby insisted that Great Britain continue the administration of the Sudan separately from the new arrangement with Egypt. Egypt was no longer a colony, but the issue of the Sudan, left unresolved in the eyes of many, heightened nationalists' sensitivities to political semantics and colored the debates between nationalists and British officials in racial terms. Lord Milner, the minister of colonization, as Huda Sha'rawī called him, represented the British government on a fact-finding mission that met with the Wafd and discussed their demands in late spring of 1919. After the meetings, he saw this sensitivity clearly, as he notes in his report: "The word 'Protectorate' had become a symbol of servitude in the minds of Egyptians, and they insisted that it must mean what they said it meant."[22] Allenby, the new Resident, also confronted the nationalists' sharp awareness of race, political terminology, and legal realities. From Cairo, he forwarded to Lord Curzon at the Foreign Office in London a letter he had received from an anonymous "young Egyptian" in which such keen sensibilities were directly expressed over the issue of Egyptian progress and self-determination. The letter states:

> They say the country has improved, and that [the city of] Ṭanṭa is now better than it was before, and they think that this is a sufficient reason for your enslaving us more and more from a temporary occupation to a permanent one to a protectorate to a total annexation. Now, Sir, this is a sort of reasoning for the central Africans to accept but not for the Egyptians, who look now on every improvement made by the English as a source of servitude and a burden which will always keep us down.[23]

As the letter writer makes clear, Africa haunted politicized Egyptians. Echoing the fears mentioned by the historian Muḥammad Sabry, the idea of colonization that threatened Egyptians was a also a racial construction in which they were deemed unequals. Nationalists fended off any identification with those who were more "properly" the objects of European imperialism, and who were, in their minds, Africans.

The territorial integrity of the Nile Valley and the struggle for control of the Sudan brought this frightening specter even closer to home. The Egyptian Wafd Party continually raised the issue of the Sudan's political status and promoted the concept of the geographic and political unity of the Nile Valley; but the British officials refused to concede any ground on the extent of their authority in the Sudan. For twenty years, since 1899 and the reclamation of the Sudan from the Mahdīya, the British government had insisted on the sanctity of the Anglo-Egyptian Condominium, through which Britain ruled the Sudan while the Egyptian treasury paid the bills. The British claimed that, since the establishment of the condominium, projects organized and administered by the Sudan government had actually reformed the chaos wrought on the Sudan during the Turkīya and the Mahdīya. Although Egyptian soldiers and bureaucrats were still needed to run the political and financial infrastructure of the Sudan, British administrators in Khartoum favored growth in rudimentary education, particularly instruction in agricultural development, which, it was thought, would bring peace and prosperity. Education that could bring about the level of sophistication necessary for the Sudanese to govern themselves was not part of their immediate plan.[24]

Nor was that kind of educational reform part of the nationalists' platform where the Sudan was concerned. Nationalistic assertions over the political map of the Nile Valley had changed little during the same twenty-year period: the Sudan was Egypt's, geographically, politically, and culturally. The Wafd delegation argued that Egypt, even more than Great Britain, had gained the right of conquest in the Sudan during 1899 by the sheer numbers of Egyptian soldiers who had fought under General Kitchener. In addition to suffering casualties in the war, Egypt had spent millions of pounds on the Sudan since the reconquest. Despite that support, Egyptian interests were now threatened by the economic schemes being adopted by the Sudan government, such as the irrigation development project for the Gezira district, and the cotton plantations encouraged in the Sudan by the British.[25] These schemes were considered divisive, having added unnecessary borders between Egypt and the Sudan and thereby compounding the urgency with which the Wafd pushed for Nile Valley unity.[26]

An important reason why these negotiations remained frozen was that it was difficult to air the debates over sovereignty diplomatically. Whenever possible, British officials tried to remove the Sudan from the realm of discussion. In his report on the agreement between his mission and Egyptian officials, Lord Milner insisted that the Sudan was not to be brought into negotiations, as it was "a country entirely distinct from Egypt in its character and constitution, the status of which is not, like that of Egypt, still inde-terminate."[27] Milner continued to differentiate the Sudan from Egypt in racial terms:

> While the majority of the people of Egypt are comparatively homoge-neous, the Sudan is divided between Arabs and Negroes, and within each of these two great racial groups there are a number of races and tribes differing widely from one another and often mutually antagonis-tic. The Arabs of the Sudan speak dialects of the same language as the people of Egypt and are united to them by the bond of religion. Islam, moreover, is spreading even among the non-Arab races of the Sudan. These influences mitigate in various degrees, but they do not overcome the antagonism of the two countries, which rankling memories of Egyptian misgovernment in the past have done much to intensify.
>
> The political bonds which have at intervals in the past united Egypt with the Sudan have always been fragile. Egyptian conquerors have at various times overrun parts and even the whole of the Sudan. But it has never been really subdued by, or in any sense amalgamated with, Egypt.[28]

Intelligence officers worked hard to prove Milner's words and watched the Sudanese very carefully for any signs of "Zaghlūlist" agitation. The Wafd did make forays into the Sudan, feeling out public opinion among the Sudanese as well as reaching out to the Egyptian community working in Khartoum, and such contacts were closely scrutinized. One intelligence report claimed that two prominent Egyptians, "volunteers of the Wafd," had met with the "Grand Qadi" and other notables (presumably Egyptian, given that they bore the title *bey*) to learn which Sudanese parties could be approached for support of the Wafd movement. The report continued, mim-icking the language of nationalism: "The Egyptian notables were advised not to try to interview or utter a word to any Soudan personality; the reli-gious leaders being traitors to their religion, who have sold their conscience during the war for British money, and other Soudanese are animals who know nothing except their women and food. The Soudanese nation is still in an ignorant condition, does not comprehend higher things, and requires fanatical leaders to move it."[29] The report also stated that the Egyptian vol-unteers did not leave Khartoum without hope, however, as they were opti-mistically counseled that a new generation of merchants who had "just begun to understand the British method of enslaving people" would be coming of political age in about nine or ten years, and would be of even more trouble to the English than the Egyptian nationalists themselves.[30] British attitudes about the potential for Sudanese nationalism seemed to say that what bound the Sudanese to each other was different from what shaped Egyptian nationalism, and therefore, Sudanese nationalism would have to be shaped out of British-made material. Sir Reginald Wingate, before his dismissal as British Resident in Cairo, had had his own observations on the political development of the Sudanese, views based on years of experience as *sirdār* (commander) of the Sudan, which were shared by Sir Lee Stack, his successor in Khartoum. Any progress the Sudanese made toward expressing political autonomy could have sprung only from their English training, According to Wingate:

> There is to my mind no doubt that we are face to face with the early beginnings of a Sudanese nation, and it is our business to decide in good time what we are to do with it. I do not speak in any alarmist sense, nor threaten the creation of a "Soudan for the Soudanese" party of Europeanised natives. I mean rather that we have got to recognize that decent government is producing what it ought to produce—a sense of national self-respect—and it is our duty to decide how to turn it to the best account.[31]

Wingate's tone was unwavering: he knew the Sudan and he knew its government, with a surety that he felt enabled him to predict the Sudan's political future. This type of outcome was not to be left to fate, however; the British officials in the Sudanese government, many of them dabblers in anthropology, set out to make their idea of Sudanese political potential a certainty. These administrators had easy access to the many tribes and regions of the Sudan. Not only did they share their knowledge with London by means of confidential intelligence reports, but they also published their findings and research in ethnographies and other works. Right after World War I, a group of academic-minded administrators founded a journal in which to publish their increasing data on the Sudanese. In the first issue of this journal, *Sudan Notes and Records,* H. A. MacMichael published an article in which he asserted the racial differences between the Nuba of Nubia and the Nuba of South Kordofan, the former being Arabs and the latter Negroes.[32] Four years later, his most famous work, *A History of the Arabs in the Sudan,* appeared, and it has since become a classic in the field of Sudanese anthropology and history.[33]

Works such as these, and there were many, could well have gathered dust on the shelves of the administrators' own libraries were it not for the fact that their jobs turned such explorations of Sudanese identity into political realities. For example, when his influential works were published, MacMichael was the district commissioner of Kordofan and responsible for settling tribal land claims, distributing government funds, and supervising the secular education of young Sudanese within his jurisdiction. His conclusions about the identities of the Sudanese played a large role in how they were included by his government. Fortunately, as the scholar Abdullahi Ali Ibrahim claims, MacMichael actually paid attention to local genealogies and what historical and cultural identities Sudanese tribes ascribed to themselves; but other officials were not always so thoughtful.[34]

With less of a grasp on the instruments of power, Egyptian officials in the Sudan had a more difficult time trying to shape Sudanese political identities. In addition to nationalist volunteers previously mentioned in British intelligence reports, several local committees, made up of Egyptian army officers and bureaucrats, tried by means of a pamphlet campaign to inspire the Sudanese to support Saʿd Zaghlūl and join them in destabilizing the British-led government.[35] This met with some success, but pamphlets took time to spread through the population, and then reached only a small fraction of Sudanese.[36] There were also Egyptian efforts to participate in the burgeoning press of the northern Sudan, such as the weekly *Rāʾid al-sūdān*, which began publication in 1913. This Arabic journal sponsored poetry competitions and asked readers to elaborate on works by well-known Egyptian nationalist poets like Ḥafiẓ Ibrāhīm, Aḥmad Shawqī, and Maḥmūd Samī al-Barūdī. As Heather Sharkey points out, this journal offered a platform on which northern Sudanese contributors could argue that "pagan, superstitious, or otherwise 'un-Islamic' customs were thwarting hopes for new Arab glory in Sudan."[37] Thus, cultural links with Egypt apparently were prized as a way of reinforcing those elements of Sudanese culture that were not "African."

It is important to remember that many groups in the Sudan detested the condominium and had risen against the British even before 1919. The British had repeatedly sent troops to combat the defiant Dinka in the southern Sudan almost from the time the condominium was established, in 1899, until 1917, when they were finally able to suppress the rebellions. Revolts in the Nuba Mountains had begun as early as 1903, and the Nyam Nyam continued to fight the British until 1916. But these struggles garnered little attention in Egypt, where they were not considered representative of any kind of "nationalist" movement. In the perspective of the time, these were tribal actions, eruptions of black tribes considered beyond the pale of organized political movements.[38] No wonder then that, in 1919, the most visible and dramatic Sudanese action came from a distinguished group of religious dignitaries and *tarīqa* leaders, headed by Sayyid ʿAlī al-Mirghānī, spiritual leader of the Sufi Khatimīya order, and Sayyid ʿAbd al-Raḥmān al-Mahdī, the oldest living son of the legendary Mahdī. In an elaborate gesture of support for Great Britain, they traveled to London, some time after Zaghlūl's own Wafd Party had arrived in Paris, and, with breathtaking irony, Sayyid al-Mahdī offered the sword of his revolutionary father to the Prince of Wales. The prince refused it, but the point had been made.[39] The men of this Sudanese delegation were older, all survivors of the Mahdīya, and whether or not they had supported the Mahdī, they all had bitter memories of Egyptian rule in the Sudan.[40] At about the same time as their trip to London, the men of this delegation had become the principal owners of another newspaper, *Ḥaḍārat al-sūdān*, which was founded in 1919, two years after the closing of *Rā'id al-sūdān*. The slogan promoted by *Ḥaḍārat al-sūdān* was "Sudan for the Sudanese"—an idea of "eventual Sudanese independence" that "rejected ideals of political or cultural unity with Egypt."[41]

The Egyptian nationalist press did not like the message of *Ḥaḍārat al-sūdān* and responded angrily to the London trip made by the famous Sudanese sayyids, but their protest was irrelevant: the members of this delegation were old enemies and were not expected to be reliable participants in an Egyptian-Sudanese nationalist movement. The Wafd leaders looked for loyalty from other segments of the Sudanese population.[42] But the Egyptian nationalist movement's influence in the Sudan was limited by the narrow scope of Egyptian political power within the Sudanese government. Egyptian nationalists were also thwarted by a difficulty in conceptualizing new groups within the Sudan, like the British-termed "negroid but detribalized" former slaves and children of slaves from the southern Sudan who had converted to Islam and were being educated in the north of the country, but who had little if any contact with the cultural past of their childhoods. This was an ignorance they shared with the British and with the neo-Mahdists of the northern Sudan, who had few coherent policies for how to deal politically with these former slaves.[43]

HUDA SHAʿRAWĪ: FROM SUDANESE IN THE HAREM
TO THE SUDAN OVER THE HORIZON

Egyptian officials of the Wafd may have shared with the policy makers in Khartoum a lack of knowledge about Sudanese history, but they certainly felt they had an inimitable, irrevocable, and intimate connection with Sudanese people and, if one reads between the lines of certain narratives, particularly such a connection with Sudanese slaves and servants. Egyptian nationalist activists who grew up in large households in the upper echelons of society came of age under the care of domestic slaves and servants, the majority of whom were Sudanese.[44] Slaves would have thus been part of nationalists' pronounced sense of home, and not only the physical household but also the traditions of family structure that bound these Sudanese servants to them. What did this signify for their sense of how the Sudanese and the Sudan in general were bound to Egyptians and to Egypt?

Sha'rawi's memoirs reveal her struggle against the constraints of her childhood and upbringing and her unique way of questioning the premises upon which Egyptian upper-class households were both structured and idealized in the late nineteenth century. Her relationship to the slaves of the household, whom she remembered with tenderness, exemplifies the close personal ties and intimacy with which many political activists of her generation viewed the Sudanese. Sha'rawi was, of course, not an official of the Wafd Party itself but the wife of one of its founding members. But her activism overshadowed her husband's in a variety of ways, including her capacity to organize Egyptian women into demonstrations against the British in 1919, her founding of the Egyptian Feminist Union in 1923, and her own public unveiling, also in 1923. She became a more visible public figure during the years of the Wafd's rise to political power and, once Zaghlūl became prime minister of Egypt in 1921, she openly criticized what she considered his increasing willingness to negotiate with the British over the Sudan. Many sections of her memoirs discuss this issue and her desire to play a leading role in the struggle to achieve the unity of the Nile Valley. But why did she propagate this issue so strongly, to the point where, as she herself wrote, the issue of the Sudan began to appear synonymous with the issue of women's rights in Egypt?[45] How did she translate the personal into the political?

As is well-known, Sha'rawi was the daughter of Muḥammad Sulṭan Pasha, an advisor to Khedive Isma'īl and then to his successor, Tawfīq. Sulṭan Pasha was also an extremely wealthy landowner whose nationalist loyalties were called into question after what seemed to be his lack of support for the 'Urābī rebellion of 1881. This shadow over the family's past was a sad circumstance for Sha'rawi, who insisted that her father had not betrayed Egypt or sought protection from Great Britain. But there were other aspects of the way her father ran his household about which Sha'rawi was much more ambivalent, if not highly critical. This was a large household, with several wives and many servants who helped raise Sha'rawi and her brother, as well as their cousins. Her sense of commitment to this large family was strong, but she later described the enforced ignorance of children as one of the worst parts of her childhood: "The family used to hide from the children all events and circumstances that occurred around them. If someone in the family died, for example, the children were told that he had gone on a journey. If the child wanted to ask a question about the facts of life, he was told that it wasn't polite to intrude in matters that did not concern him."[46]

This insistence on shrouding the truth was intended to keep women and children in their place in a hierarchy of authority within the household. But another hierarchy also had to be invoked—that which separated slaves from the rest of the family. Sha'rawi respected one tradition begun by her grandfather and continued by her father, which was to make sure that one was loved by one's slaves and servants.[47] But this love was more complicated for the children of the household, whom the slaves had to discipline in the name of the children's father and the slaves' master. The embodiment of this was the obedient yet authoritative black eunuch of Sulṭan Pasha's household, Lala Sa'īd Agha, guardian of the children, the last word among the other servants, and the overseer of the children's education. Sa'īd Agha was suspicious of Sha'rawi's interest in Arabic grammar and refused her wish to be tutored further in it, saying, "There's no reason for grammar . . . because she is not going to be a lawyer ever!"[48] In her memoirs, he personified her frustrations with the differences in the way she and her brother were educated as children.

Sa'īd Agha's authority over Sha'rawi made him a confusing and frightening figure. The children of the house could go out only under his supervision and had to be vigilant not to commit some faux pas, for which they could be struck on the palms with a branch. When they cried, though, he wiped their tears with his handkerchief. And after that, he would play with them as if he were a child himself, allowing Sha'rawi to forget his severity. Her beloved little brother, however, complained bitterly to their mother about such treatment, crying, "That slave struck me!" Their mother would then talk to Sa'īd Agha, and come back to the boy to tell him, "He is your guardian and only strikes you for your own good." Sha'rawi also had learned to recognize this, remembering as well that if the children were ever in danger, he would grab them to his chest and, ignoring his own safety, murmur, "O children of my master!" Sa'īd Agha was proud of belonging to so elite a household. Sha'rawi's mother was very kind to him because he had been purchased when just a child, and Sulṭan Pasha had taken great care with his upbringing and his education. As Sha'rawi remembered, Sa'īd Agha "loved my father to the point of worship."[49] Yet what immediately follows her remembrance of this harsh yet kindly slave is a lament for those customs, so prized by her family, that kept children from understanding frankness and honesty. Slaves were integral to these traditions, enacting them not only through obedience to them but by the slaves' very presence in the household.

Both African and Circassian slaves worked in the house. They were industrious, "completing their duties with sincerity," and "respectful of their employers." They loved the children of their employers, whom they brought up in their hands, "and we returned that love and that sincerity." The governesses, maids, and wet nurses who took care of them had been with the family since well before the children's birth and knew the history of all the household's members. Interestingly, the children knew a great deal about the slaves too, but the pasts of the slaves became nursery tales, told to soothe the children: "Our nurses used to tell us stories about how they had been captured, and about what their own countries had been like and the customs of their people, until we grew exhausted and they would tuck us in our beds."[50]

Sha'rawī and her brother thus knew that these slaves were not indigenous to Egypt, but they had been there so long, and had been in the household so long, that the pain of their separation from their own families and the memories of their own childhoods were candlelight stories, told and remembered like lullaby folktales. It is hard to tell from the memoirs how Sha'rawī incorporated this knowledge of the slaves' pasts, but it may explain why the only person who could give her comfort when she was engaged to her much older cousin was Sa'īd Agha, who whispered into her ear not to cry, not to dishonor her father's memory or make her mother sick. Who else, she implies, could understand as well the meaning of passage into captivity?

Sha'rawī was eighteen years old when the fury over Qāsim Amīn's *Taḥrīr al-Mar'a* (The Liberation of Women) blew through Egypt in 1899. In her memoirs she defended the book, seeing it as a door through which she and other women were able to pass into public life later, but she was surprised, at the time of its publication, that many of her contemporaries, all women of her class, disliked the book intensely: "How many times did we hear then women denying the issues and principles about which Qāsim Amīn wrote, despite the fact that these principles were for their betterment, because to recognize that would have meant recognizing their own powerlessness and this would have injured their arrogance. They reminded me of slave women who, when presented with their manumission papers, would cry for their past lives of obedience and imprisonment."[51] This is the only statement in her memoirs in which Sha'rawī indirectly criticizes the institution of slavery for the pathos of forced obedience it engendered not only in slaves but also in the children of elite households, particularly women. She does not summon up a protest when remembering Sa'īd Agha or the nursemaids' oral histories of their own childhoods; perhaps this was too deeply embedded in her conflict with the much loved household in which she grew up and against which she had to struggle to become a different kind of woman.

As an adult, Sha'rawī shared with other nationalists the duality about colonialism in the Sudan and the imperialism of Great Britain. An intimate of the Wafdist leaders and one of the most prominent women to join the nationalist cause during the 1919 revolution, Sha'rawī repeated all the Wafd's ideas about the Sudan, saying, "We must hold on to our rights with respect to the issue of the Sudan, considering the Sudan an inseparable part of Egypt, and not a colony." But by 1921, Sha'rawī had become one of the most vociferous activists in the Sudan issue, and she used her role as the leader of the Central Wafd Committee for Women to publicize her views and criticize Sa'd Zaghlūl for what she considered his increasing laxity in pressuring the British on this point. She tirelessly sent letters to the press and to Zaghlūl himself during the years 1921 to 1926, in which she criticized him for not using his position as prime minister to persuade the British to concede control of the Sudan. In one such letter, sent to the press on 24 March 1924 she berates Zaghlūl, "who knows as every one else knows that Egypt cannot tolerate her soldiers being forced out of the Sudan."[52]

So much had Sha'rawī come to personify the demands about the Sudan that a parliament member from the Nationalist Party, Fikri Abaza, sent a letter to the women's newspaper *al-Jins al-latīfa* (The Gentle Sex) in the fall of 1924 in which he publicly remembered the times when "women thought of nothing but about new clothes," while now they had begun to support the Sudan more than men did. He accused men of failing on this issue. Women followed every detail of the Sudan, worrying about the evils perpetrated in the Sudan, the prisons of the Sudan, leaving to men the "arrangements of the house." Onto the men had fallen the tasks of laundry, cooking, and nursing the children. When the women came home, should the men ululate with joy?[53]

Abaza continued, now directly addressing Sha'rawī, saying that the male politicians were preoccupied not only with the circumstances of Sir Lee Stack's assassination and the party rivalries in Parliament itself but also huge domestic and international issues. Could she not understand if they delayed a bit on the issue of the Sudan, when so much else was going on? Could she and the other women worry about "the world of women" and leave him and his colleagues to worry about "the world of men?" But Sha'rawī, impervious to such sarcasm, pursued the matter for as long as she could. When the British government published a white paper on the Sudan in November of 1924, soon after Fikrī Abaza sent his missive to the press, she protested the recommended separation of the Sudan from Egypt, again publicly, and alerted her audience: "Have you learned what has happened to our brothers in the Sudan, imprisoned, subjected to torture and to exile? And their only guilt is the expression of their feelings toward Egypt, and their attachment to her?"[54]

Let us return to the primary question about why Sha'rawī was so committed to the issue of the Sudan and to the possible connection of this commitment to her past relationship with Sudanese members of her childhood household. In her memoirs, she shared many pieces of her childhood life spent growing up in her father's house that was filled with slaves, a house in which severity and tenderness were contradictory but intimate companions. Part of her struggle with how she had been raised, and how those who raised her looked at childhood itself, was the enforcement of blind obedience to rules that children, women, and slaves were not allowed to question, yet which left all with confusing memories of violence and kindness. As her life unfolds over the pages of the memoirs, the restrictiveness of the household fades and is replaced by the image of an eloquent and defiant woman determined to keep the issue of the Sudan alive in the minds of fellow nationalists. From the personal aspect of her past to the broader questions of politics, Sha'rawī defended the Sudanese from abandonment by Egyptians while denying in her pleas that the circumstances that tethered the Sudan to Egypt might have had any relation to the historic colonial relationship. Perhaps her attempt to address the symbolic relationship between Egypt and the Sudan gave Sha'rawī a chance to create a more independent role for herself than she had experienced as a child in her father's house. Her activism went only so far, however, in creating a new kind of family. One can only wonder, when Huda and 'Alī Sha'rawī finally created their own household, what roles Sudanese domestics may have played in its upkeep.

SINGING AND DANCING WITH THE SUDANESE

Political strategies also motivated the stance of Sha'rawī and her male colleagues toward the unity of the Nile Valley. The Sha'rawī's and the Zaghlūl's, to name two important families, were large landowners with interests in the territorial integrity of the Nile River, an integrity they feared would be damaged by the British-organized Gezira irrigation scheme in the Sudan itself, intended to promote cotton farming. It was not just the emotive power of relationships between slaves and wealthy families that provoked these individuals into action. Still, these interests often made it difficult for them to understand the economic conditions of the Sudan in 1919, and few had any opportunities to explore the circumstances of the

Sudanese under the British administration. Deprived of the opportunities that British officials in the Sudan had to study Sudanese culture and society, Egyptian nationalists still employed their own inventiveness in trying to shape the Sudan. Unable to describe (or invent, as some have suggested) Sudanese tribal culture as H. A. MacMichael could, they invented other roles for the Sudanese to play, as characters in their propaganda. In the growing sphere of Egyptian popular culture, artists with strong nationalist perspectives continued to create the "true" voice of the Sudan, hear what they wanted to hear, and exercise a kind of ventriloquism, putting words in the mouths of Sudanese characters when they could not find real Sudanese to fit the role. In the absence of the "right" kind of Sudanese political allies—that is, those who would proclaim a desire for the unity of the Nile Valley—the Egyptian artists and writers deeply involved in the promulgation of the nationalist message made up their own Sudanese. These icons were never presented within the context of their own culture, which seemed to have remained somewhat of a mystery to most Egyptians of this period, but were instead almost uniformly portrayed as friendly servants and *bawābīn* (doormen), grateful and proud to be installed in Egyptian households or to be in Egypt itself.

One of the most popular venues for the presentation of these Sudanese characters was the concerts performed during the 1919 rebellion. In these concerts, contests were held for the best composition of a national anthem, and local songs with verses in dialect were performed.[55] These concerts contributed to two of the revolution's greatest successes: the expansion of contemporary Egyptians' sense of community and the broadening of the audience for local art, drama, and music. Many of Egypt's musicians and songwriters first achieved fame at these popular celebrations, the most famous being the composer Sayyid Darwīsh.

The revolution of 1919 inspired some of Darwīsh's best music, but the piece for which he is best remembered was actually composed before the revolution, in 1916. The song was titled "Maṣr w-al-Sūdān" (Egypt and the Sudan), but was popularly known as "Dinga Dinga Dinga."[56] Badiʿ Khayrī, a lyricist and comedic playwright who, like Darwīsh, was to earn his great renown in 1919, had written the verses for "Dinga" in an imagined Nubian dialect. They were published in the newspaper *Alf ṣinf* in Alexandria in 1916 as part of the play (the title of which was meant to be pronounced with a Nubian accent) *They Stole the Box, Muḥammad (Ṣaraqu al-ṣunduq, ya Muḥammad).*[57] Interestingly, this play was an Arabic translation of Molière's *The Miser,* versions of which had become very popular in Egypt and were performed every three to four years.[58] In this version, the Nubian servant sings the song, and, as Mahmud Aḥmad al-Hafna writes in his biography of Darwīsh, no other song was performed as often or expressed as clearly Egyptians' sentiments about the Sudan.[59] Here are excerpts from the song as it appeared after Khayrī and Darwīsh met and reworked the original lyrics:

> There is nothing named Egypt, and nothing named the Sudan.
> The head of the Nile is at one end, its feet at the other. . . .
>
> Black and white, O Benevolent God, living together . . .
> The Sudanese is generous, the Egyptian's life full of praise.
> The two are neighbors of one country, side by side.[60]

The original song, as published in *Alf ṣinf,* included many verses al-Hafna did not mention in his study, some of which give greater detail about what the Sudanese were traditionally imagined to be doing in Egypt:

> We are children of Wadi Halfa, come to Egypt to be raised.
> We drink beer and get happy, we are never afraid, and we never run away.
> . . . .
>
> We work here in the houses of the pashas.
> One day we eat *faṣulīyā,* one day baklava, one day *mulukhīya,* and one
>   day *bukasha.*
>
> The bey and his wife, I love them like a son.
> Even without a contract, I wouldn't leave them nor would they leave me.
> . . . .
>
> Hey, Egyptians! Take our hands. Here, we put them in your hands.
> We swear in faith to your religion
> there is no foreigner who can act as go-between for us.
> Our house is your house, we are like brothers and friends.[61]

As mentioned earlier, these verses were intended to mimic the way the Sudanese pronounced Egyptian colloquial Arabic. Certain letters are fudged, like the ʿayn, the ghayn, and the hard *h,* an accent that had been transcribed in this manner since the dialogues of Yaʿqūb Ṣanūʿa, written over forty years before. However, composition is the most interesting aspect of these verses. They are written entirely in the first person yet, ironically, seem intended to be sung by Egyptians, not Sudanese; hence the guidelines for pronunciation in this obvious effort at making the lyrics recognizable and pronounceable for all Egyptians. Sayyid Darwīsh's son wrote of the long hours Darwīsh spent in local coffeehouses all over Cairo, where he could note and record with accuracy the different accents of people on Cairene streets.[62] But such attention to a "realistic" depiction of Sudanese speech patterns would have been unnecessary if the singers were themselves Sudanese. Even more striking, the actions that take place in the song, the work that the Sudanese character performs and the food he eats, all exist within a familiar Egyptian environment. In a creative gesture of ventriloquism, this Sudanese character speaks the language of the Wafd Party. He welcomes this homey atmosphere and makes clear his sentiment that there is no difference, politically or geographically, between the Sudan and Egypt. There is no difference, however, because there is no real Sudan in this song—it is a place the Sudanese emigrate from quickly in order to stay and work in Egypt; as such, it is simply part of the Egyptian backyard. Would it have made Muḥammad Imām al-ʿAbd laugh?

In the theaters of Cairo, with which both Darwīsh and Khayrī were intimately involved, another Sudanese character with an Egyptian voice emerged who also gained widespread popularity. This character was the creation of ʿAlī al-Kassār, a popular comedian who had worked with the biggest names in Egyptian folk theater and who, by 1919, had a troupe of his own. Al-Kassār was a performer of reviews: raucous, often bawdy, and always musical variety shows in which only colloquial Arabic was used. While not considered to be among the elite of Egyptian dramatic arts, troupes like those of ʿAlī al-Kassār and his rival Najīb al-Riḥanī were hugely popular because, in an age when literacy was still the privilege of a minority, any Egyptian could understand the language of their skits.[63] Al-Kassār perfected a character known as Osman ʿAbd al-Basit, a servant whose affability and humor won al-Kassār the honorific Barbarī Maṣr al-Waḥīd (the one and only Nubian of Egypt). Al-Kassār performed in blackface at the Majestic Theater on ʿImad al-Dīn Street in downtown Cairo, in the heart of the theater district that grew so lively in World War I (see fig. 8).[64]

ʿAlī al-Kassār's Nubian was always the central character in each of the comedies, always having to defend his color and lack of education to more sophisticated characters. In *Al-Qadiya nimra 14* (Court Case Number 14), first performed on 6 January 1919, Osman takes on the British officials of the occupation, serving as a defender of three Nubian friends who had been arrested. In one scene, Osman's musters his dignity and patriotism against racial stereotyping by the English constable:

OSMAN *[entering]:* Peace be upon you.

CONSTABLE: And upon you. What are you? *[Spoken in grammatically incorrect Arabic.]*

OSMAN: What am I? I am the devil. You mean, why did I come here? I came to ingratiate myself with you. I am a witness in the affair of these boys here.

8.   ʿAlī al-Kassār in blackface, performing at the Du Barry Theater, Cairo, 1917, from Ministry of Culture and National Center for Drama, Music, and Folkloric Arts, "Raʾid al-masraḥ al-kūmīdī ʿAlī al-Kassār."

CONSTABLE: You saw something with your own eye?

OSMAN: How could I not see, being right there with them?

CONSTABLE: At the time you were all arguing?

OSMAN: At that time like any other time.

CONSTABLE: What is that supposed to mean, you Nubian?

OSMAN *[still being ingratiating but defending himself as well]:* Oh my! Peace be upon you and on your words as well. Every one of you says "you Nubian." Do you mean a Nubian isn't one of God's creations just like you?[65]

The scene continues with the constable preparing to arrest Osman himself, but Osman's self-deprecating and dignified humor enables him finally to wriggle out of the increasingly contentious situation. As ʿAlī al-Kassār's son wrote in the biography of his father, *Al-Qadiya nimra 14*, this play offered audiences an example of patriotic defiance against the British authorities and of the tendency of those authorities to label and insult the population over which they ruled.[66] In this sense, particularly within the context of the mounting nationalistic anger in Egypt right before the uprising of 1919, Osman's Nubian identity becomes a conduit through which Egyptians could express anger at British racism.

Yet al-Kassār always came onstage in blackface to play Osman, a deliberately darker figure than the other characters of the plays, who made many jokes and comments about his skin color and the question of his actual nationality. For example, in the play "Al-Barbarī f-il-Jaysh" (The Nubian in the Army), first performed at the Majestic Theater on 28 March 1920, Osman's entire body and political identity is subjected to intense scrutiny before his induction into the army. The play opens with a meeting of the council of the armed forces in Aswan and Halfa, with the shaykhs and *'umdas* of each village claiming that all the men eligible for conscription in their respective towns are dead or otherwise incapacitated for service in the army. But the *'umda* from Aswan answers truthfully that he has two conscripts, one insane and the other a Nubian named Osman 'abd al-Basit.

THE CHIEF: Nubian. Nubian. How can you be the *'umda*, son of the *'umda*, and not know that Nubians are eligible for military service?

THE 'UMDA: No, well, this Osman, he is a mixed Nubian.

THE CHIEF: Mixed, how?

THE 'UMDA: That's right, I'll explain to you how. That boy's mother is Nubian and his father is Sudanese. With us, that means he's mixed.[67]

This question of parentage determines who is considered draftable into the army: had Osman's origins been completely Sudanese he might not have been eligible. The scene also expresses a surprising lack of clarity about where Nubians and Sudanese actually fit into the national community on the whole. These points are raised again and again, after soldiers bring Osman to the council, which he mistakenly thinks is a police station, and force him to submit to a physical. The doctor looks at Osman and asks the *'umda* once more if he is sure of the nationality of the man.

THE 'UMDA: What does nationality *[jinsīya]* mean?

THE CHIEF: It means that his mother is Nubian and his father is Sudanese, like I told you.

THE 'UMDA: That's right, *effendim* [sir]. His father is a Sudanese son of a Sudanese. *[The next word in the text is illegible.]*

THE DOCTOR: Interesting. Well, then, we have the right to conscript him.

OSMAN: And I have the right to exemption.[68]

Osman's body is then weighed and inspected, much to his horror. Once clothed in a uniform, though, his identity within the Egyptian army still appears strange to the other characters, as one officer says after watching Osman try to figure out how to use military parlance and the canteen.

FODA: You appear to be very new.

OSMAN: Very. I'm ultra new.

FODA: Strange that you're a Nubian.

OSMAN: Nubian on my mother's side, Sudanese on my father's.

FODA: Ah! I'm also astonished because your language is completely Nubian.[69]

Osman never seems able to fit in as a soldier, as if everyone looking at him cannot quite place him as an Egyptian who would naturally have to serve in the military. All this confusion occurs as the other village headmen try—and fail—to come up with one live Egyptian conscript. Yet Osman has entry into the secrets of the Egyptian characters that they do not even share with each other. He gained access to those secrets through the intimacy he had as a servant to Egyptians. For Osman, this means persisting in his hope that Egyptians will treat him as a regular fellow, not merely as a black-skinned Nubian. But for characters like Foda, who are struggling with morality, treating Osman as an equal is difficult given his skin color. For example, the plot thickens when Officer Foda's attraction to the sister of the doctor who examined Osman (whose life Osman had saved from peril in the Sudan) is revealed. It turns out that Foda and Osman had met earlier, on the "night of the 14th" in Foda's own house. Foda wonders how it was possible not to realize that Osman's face was black. Osman answers, "No, you didn't know I was Nubian. You know Osman 'Abd al-Basit, and that's that."[70]

The doctor's sister has promised to kiss the man who saved her brother's life (a point that the playwright, Amīn Sidqī, layered over with racial innuendo), and when Foda discovers this he arranges to swap identities with Osman and gets that kiss. Meanwhile, Foda is on the run from his own wife, 'Azīza, while Osman's wife, Umm Aḥmad, has been trying to find her recently conscripted mate. As the conditions of this vaudeville would have it, Umm Aḥmad becomes the maid of Durīya (the doctor's sister) and tries to find her husband through this labyrinth of mistaken identities. In one scene, all the reversals sum up to the strangest of all: a black man being the superior to a white man. The very idea brings out the sarcasm in Foda:

FODA: We all know that your face is the face of an officer. . . . By God, that's the face of a first lieutenant.

OSMAN: Hey! Do you mean now I'm a first lieutenant?

FODA: That's right, O sir, O idiot. O Nubian sir *[Ya ḥaḍrit al-ghābī. Ya
ḥaḍrit al-barbarī]*.

OSMAN: Shut up, ugly!

FODA: What did you say?

OSMAN: You are here now in your capacity as the orderly of Osman 'abd
al-Basit, and you must serve your first lieutenant, so beware
[zinhār]!

FODA: Oh God, Oh God, have you gone absolutely nuts or what? What is
your point?[71]

As comic as it was supposed to be, "Al-Barbarī f-il-Jaysh" uses its central
character, Osman, to defy abusive authority and the immorality of foreign
cultural practices. In many ways, the play raises some of the same points that
were integral to the 1919 revolution's protest against the abuses of the
British protectorate and the mistreatment of Egyptians under its administration. The British in fact recognized the potential for political agitation that
popular theaters of the Ezbekiya section of Cairo presented (the same neighborhood in which al-Kassār performed); shortly after demonstrations led by
stage actors in 1919, the administration closed all theaters until the uprising
ended.[72] Conceived in this environment of confrontation, the politicization
of "Al-Barbarī f-il-Jaysh" was all the more dramatic in light of the fact that
audiences of the Majestic Theater were made up of many foreigners, including, it has been claimed, English officers and civil bureaucrats.[73]

This point both adds and subtracts from the message of the play and others like it. Osman must constantly stand up for his own dignity against the
continued racial differentiations that other Egyptian characters lob at him,
just as Sa'd Zaghlūl resisted the authority of the British. But neither Osman
nor the politicians of 1919 questioned the actual social hierarchies that the
British had used to their advantage to solidify control. In fact, in none of the
plays I examined did Osman 'abd al-Basit ever question the higher social
rank of Egyptians or insist on his right to greater upward social mobility.
His simple pleas for respect are significant, but the actor's identity as an
Egyptian, in Nubian disguise, presumes and appropriates an understanding
of Nubian and Sudanese sentiment.

This "Nubian" instrument is not only a servant to Egyptians but also a
gauge of true nationalistic feeling among Egyptians, as the play "Al-Hilāl"
(The Crescent) demonstrates. First performed in 1923, "Al-Hilāl" is a spy
story, with the beautiful young woman Oshaka trying to infiltrate the military intelligence of a country like Egypt. Osman serves in this army and has
actually won a medal for his bravery and the number of enemy soldiers he

killed. He is late for the awards ceremony and, when he finally shows up, he is drunk. The general awarding the medals is as surprised by his color as by his stupor, and remarks on how very brown Osman is, to which Osman replies, "It's my right to be so brown."[74] Every character calls him *ya iswid al-wihsh* (blackface), forcing him to repeatedly defend his right to be the color he is.

Like the other vehicles for al-Kassār, this play also derives great humor from mistaken identities. Oshaka thinks she is a foreigner, and so spies patriotically for her country, aided by the malevolent Shinshaw, who is keen on revenging the death of his soldier nephews killed in battle by Osman. Meanwhile, Oshaka is in love with Petrov, the patriotic officer of the other side. As the fast-paced events unfold, Oshaka and Shinshaw succeed in implicating Osman when important military records are stolen from under Petrov. As it happens, Oshaka is the long-lost daughter of the female doctor who tends the soldiers of Petrov's army, and who, long before, had tattooed her daughter's arm with her initials, her daughter's initials, and her husband's initials.

The play thus revolves on the genetics of nationalism. Nationalism is a blood matter, as shown by Oshaka when she realizes that she is the daughter of parents from a country she had long considered to be enemy territory. It is hard for her to answer for her misdeeds, as she tells the sympathetic Osman, who is the first to figure out where she is really from:

OSHAKA: I worked against my own nationality [*jinsīyatī*, followed in the manuscript by *waṭanī*, which is crossed out].

OSMAN: Don't think that that could be considered guilt.

OSHAKA: Why not?

OSMAN: Because now you can serve your true nationality in the same way that you served your false one.[75]

He returns her to her real parents and faces the military tribunal with her. At the tribunal, Oshaka demonstrates her new understanding of nationalism, revealing insights that Osman taught her:

OSHAKA: Your honor, everything that I did I did in total sincerity in defense of the nation that I thought was my nation. It was my duty to serve the nation. I thought I was a foreigner to this country. But now, here are documents in which you'll find all the information that I took from you. I will also brief you on all the secrets of the enemy that I possess. Here you are.

THE GENERAL: Your defense is your serving the country you thought was your own. And now you demonstrate the honorable love that runs through your veins. And here are your parents. Reunite

> with them, lost daughter. And as for you *[pointing to Osman]*,
> we judge that you are innocent, and that all the accused are inno-
> cent, God willing.[76]

This love of country is in the blood. Although Osman the Nubian is always answering for his blackness, he is the one who shows the other characters and the audience the truth about nationalism. He is once more the Nubian defender of the Egyptian heartland, speaking and singing in a language that all Egyptians could understand, about the meaning, duties, and responsibilities of being an Egyptian.

Osman ʿabd al-Basit was and remains a contested figure. Many critics contemporary to the times detested the rawness of the character's language and the bawdiness of the dialogues, particularly those between Osman and his wife, Umm Aḥmad, or between Osman and the foreign women he attempts to chat up. One critic attacked the nationalistic sincerity of audiences who laughed at the antics of the blackfaced al-Kassār and his chief stage rival, Najīb al-Riḥanī, when the nation was facing the Milner mission and the antipathy of Field Marshal Allenby, and went further to condemn the legendary Sayyid Darwīsh for his participation in the theater of these vaudeville comedians.[77] Darwīsh defended his musical compositions for these two comedians in a number of ways. His music was not limited to the dramatic theater but was intended to serve the entire Egyptian community. His efforts were intended to raise the level of popular theater and, he stated, to that end "I am the working hand, with Amīn Effendi Sidqī and ʿAlī Effendi al-Kassār."[78]

Part of the issue stemmed from ʿAlī al-Kassār's performing as a black character from the lower if not lowest rungs of Egyptian society and the question of whether such a character could possibly educate audiences about the goals of Egyptian nationalism. Recent criticism has defended al-Kassār's choice of character as a figure representative of many Nubians who had come to Egypt to seek their fortunes, and who tried to maintain their dignity in the face of British imperialism as well. In this sense, Osman ʿabd al-Basit was an interesting emblem of the Nile Valley's unity, and proof that Nubians and Sudanese alike had the same nationalistic feelings and were staunch supporters of the call for cohesion made by the Egyptians in 1919. From this the argument could be drawn that Osman taught his audiences an important geographic lesson, in which the Sudan and Nubia must always be considered part and parcel of the Egyptian nation.[79]

Al-Kassār continued to play Osman well into the 1930s and was, in that decade, also heard regularly on the radio, which underscores how easily blackface makeup translated into jokes about accents and foreign behavior that could be appreciated even on the airwaves.[80] But the fact of an Egyptian acting out the words of a Nubian who was in turn imitating Egyptians and foreigners adds yet another level of self-conscious irony to this portrayal: the character of the Nubian becomes a mouthpiece through which a native son could reflect on his own country. Through this manipulated and sanitized figure of the Sudan, the closeness and unity of the Nile Valley could be left unchallenged while the attention of the audience was turned toward their own society, and themselves.

NUBIANS AND SUDANESE IN THE FINER DRAMATIC ARTS

Now, returning, he saw through traveled eyes.

SALMAN RUSHDIE

After World War I, cultural activity in Egypt's big cities intensified, inspiring contemporaries to exclaim that Egyptian society was undergoing another *nahḍa,* or renaissance.[81] As popular as the diversions offered by Najīb al-Rihanī and ʿAlī al-Kassār were, audiences in Cairo and Alexandria crowded into many other theaters too, where a diverse array of high drama, musical comedy, and opera were performed. Quite a few of these works were translated European classics, but many more of them were written by and for Egyptians. As the push for political independence grew, a search began among certain artists for realistic ways to portray their own society. As the criticism of Darwīsh and al-Kassār made clear, determining the audience presented the biggest challenge for playwrights, songwriters, and poets in this period. To whom would they direct their works? For those smitten with the idea of offering a mirror to their audiences and presenting a panorama of true Egyptian life, the issue had a political burden as well, for if Egypt was no longer to be ruled by foreigners, then Egyptians had to grasp with their own hands not only the reins of power but also the instruments of social reform. Newspapers of the period reveal a public debate over the shape and form of these presentations of Egypt. Critics questioned whether the accuracy of the accents in some of Darwīsh's songs, or the folk [*baladī*] expressions exchanged in al-Rihanī's reviews, reflected a cheapened image of Egypt, one far from that presented by dignified and learned men like Saʿd Zaghlūl and the other members of the Wafd Party.[82] It was a debate between disguise and disclosure.

Many artists had to grapple with another issue as well, that of their own dual cultural identities. Those educated in Europe had to wrestle with their idealization of Egypt when abroad, and with their loyalty to the European classics and authors they felt had guided their artistic sensibilities. Muḥam-mad Taymūr, a young aristocrat who spent three years studying law in Paris, summarized this sense of doubled vision and feeling in the words of the narrator of his short story "Ḥaflat al-ṭarab" (Music Concert):

> I was obsessed with musical concerts during my days in Paris, never missing a night in which moving melodies and entertaining verses blended together with the clear faces, swaying bodies, and sharply vulnerable eyes. There my eyes feasted on the beauty that the Creator had shaped in those handsome faces, and my heart was filled with a pleasure combined with innocence; my ears filled with beautiful lyrics that expanded the bosom.
>
> Those days passed the way sweet dreams do. Now I am in Cairo, deprived of those rosy cheeks and smooth faces, sparkling dangers and spirited, moving lyrics. How badly I stand in need of seeing something like those delights, unequaled in beauty. At the very least, something that would spark the memory and stir up in my heart what forgetfulness has almost stamped out.[83]

Like his narrator, Taymūr looked back at France with a mournful nostalgia, to his stay prematurely cut off by the beginning of World War I. His vacation in Egypt in the summer of 1914 unforeseeably lengthened, Taymūr looked to fill the cultural gaps he experienced in what had once been the familiar setting of Cairo. He augmented his prolific writing with attempts to become a professional actor, but Sultan Husayn Kamil forbade him, as a young pasha, to continue an acting career, which many Egyptians considered suitable only for those of the lower classes.[84] Taymūr then focused on his writing. His short stories, essays, and plays are at once gracefully written and authoritarian, with his sense of Egypt's potential directing his representation of then current realities in the years right after World War I. Each piece ends with a moral directive for his audience, sometimes implicit in the choices his characters make for themselves, often explicit in the harsh ways in which they judge their own surroundings. Taymūr always kept one eye on French culture; the eye he turned to Egyptian literature and drama searched for authenticity. Taymūr felt strongly a need for "Egyptianizing" the literature of his country and creating a school of writing that was uniquely Egyptian.[85] In this quest for realism, Taymūr developed a dialogue with his readers in which he encouraged them to nod knowingly with him about the social "types" he presented in his stories while, at the same time, he challenged them to see themselves in much of the pettiness and snobbery his narrator recounted.

In this way, Taymūr's writing offers an important alternative representation of Egypt in the post–World War I period, when the powerful political need for a unified national image and a popular voice demanded that Egyptians present to the outside world all the elements of their society as functioning in unison. Along with many other artists and writers, Taymūr was strongly influenced by this political movement, and his characters symbolize a panoply of Egyptians from all walks of life. But as his harsh criticism of more populist artists reveals, Taymūr's sense of political unity conflicted with his deeper sense of, and belief in, hierarchies of class. Beneath the challenging questions Taymūr put to his audience about changing social morals, particularly about drug use and adultery, Taymūr's true question asked which class of Egyptians would lead Egypt into modernity.

The characters presented in the collection of short stories *Ma tarāhu al-'uyūn* (What the Eyes Saw) are not timeless archetypes of Egyptian society but are presented as being well aware of their own temporal elasticity. With social and cultural circumstances changing so quickly in Egypt as a result of the end of both the Ottoman Empire and World War I, and the growth of the nationalist movement, these characters struggle with a sense of their own mortality. The circumstances that created them were being effaced, creating new social habits and, in effect, new Egyptians.

Taymūr believed strongly that the entertainment provided by short stories and the theater had to offer moral instruction and realistic reflections of current events, rather than an escape from the troubles of daily life. Egyptian audiences were unable to find anything of their lives or themselves in the translated Italian and French plays and musicals that filled Egyptian theaters and opera houses.[86] In a work collectively called *Muḥakima mu'alifī al-riwaya al-tamthīlīya* (translated by M. M. Badawi as *Dialogue of the Dead*), Taymūr expressed the cultural ambivalence of Egyptian writers, adding another element to the debate about cultural self-representation. These pieces take place as a dream of the narrator, in which artists both dead and alive gather in the hall of Dar al-Opera al-Sultaniyya. The occasion is a trial in which the artistic ability of contemporary and well-known playwrights is to be judged by classical, canonical writers, all members of Muḥammad Taymūr's personal pantheon: Shakespeare, Molière, Corneille, Racine, Edmond Roustand, and Goethe. The audience also consists of Taymūr's favorites, among them Shaykh Salama al-Ḥijazī (a pioneer in the popularization of colloquial theater), the actress Rose al-Yūsuf, and Sayyid Darwīsh. Many of Taymūr's least favorite actors and directors are also present, like Najīb al-Riḥanī, 'Alī al-Kassār (here presented as al-Riḥanī's desperate and idiotic sidekick), and George Abyad, portrayed as falling asleep during the trial and snoring loudly. Taymūr presents himself as well, as one of the lesser artists being charged, lamenting his humiliation and that of the other artists to be tried.[87]

Shakespeare and company then begin the trial. Farah Antun, a Syrian actor who came to Egypt and ran one of the largest and most popular theater companies, stands accused of adapting too many European plays and importing the hideous American habit of advertising. Ibrahīm Ramzi, a poet, playwright, and contributor to the newspaper *al-Liwā'*, is accused of self-promotion and writing his pieces too hastily, while Luṭfī Juma', another well-known playwright, is accused of writing too slowly. The most interesting accusation is leveled against Khalil Bey Matran, at that time one of Egypt's most famous poets, for not adapting more of Shakespeare's plays into Arabic. Matran defends himself by saying the three plays he did adapt were performed so poorly by George Abyad, or were implanted with Egyptian music and dances when performed by Shaykh al-Ḥijazī and were in such poor taste, that he resolved never again to subject Shakespeare to Egyptian directors. The judges acquit Matran and thank him for his sensitivity to Hamlet.[88]

Muḥakima mu'alifī is a strange and funny glimpse into the Egyptian cultural scene of 1919–1920. It also offers insights into the powerful self-consciousness experienced by Egyptian writers when comparing themselves to European culture, a self-consciousness paralleled by the needs of nationalist politicians to prove their country's integrity overseas. The judges of Taymūr's articles seemed concerned with the improper importation of foreign dramatic customs (like American-style advertising) and poor translations, issues about which Taymūr had previously voiced his concern. Yet the issue of realism that so strongly concerned Taymūr in other writings is put aside here. As foreigners the judges are in no position to question the realism of the accused's work, but have full authority over artistic standards. What is most important in these articles, then, is the question of where Egypt stands as a culture with respect to Europe. When compared with such august luminaries as Molière and Corneille, Taymūr seems to say, we Egyptians are only comical imitators.

As interesting as his self-conscious discussion of art in Egypt was, when it came to the Sudanese Taymūr himself remained caught in representational clichés that defied his own pleas for realism. If Egyptians, at that point in their cultural history, were amusing imitators of Europe, then the Sudanese remained, for Taymūr, humorous diversions for Egyptians. Sudanese characters almost always appear as servants in Taymūr's written work.[89] In the first play he wrote in colloquial Arabic, *Al-'usfūr fi al-qafaṣ* (The Sparrow in the Cage), the Sudanese eunuch Fayrūz Agha injects an element of comedy in this otherwise tragic story of a wealthy Egyptian family.

Realism ends at the border between Fayrūz Agha and the other characters of the play, all of whom show depth and development. But Fayrūz Agha comes straight from older, stereotypical traditions of Sudanese characters, so much so that he evokes, for M. M. Badawi, the Sudanese servants of Yaʿqūb Ṣanūʿa's sketches, written in the 1870s.[90]

Intended to be both amusing and a true reflection of daily life, *Al-ʿusfūr* portrays a family of characters whose lives are completely shaped by the miserliness of the father, Muḥammad Pasha ʿAlī Ziftawi. Eager to be re-elected to the new Majlis al-Nuwāb (the recently created Egyptian House of Representatives), Muḥammad Pasha spends thousands of pounds to impress his peers but little to feed or clothe his family. His son, Hassan Bey, suffers greatly from this, and even though he manages to perform well in high school, his father is proud only if Hassan Bey saves him money. Hassan Bey has two cousins who love him dearly and who try to guide him through his troubles with his father, while his mother, ʿAzīza Hanim, remains completely cowed by Muḥammad Pasha.

So upset is Hassan Bey at his father's miserly behavior that he falls into the open arms of the household's Syrian maid, Marguerite. For a short while, they maintain a secret relationship, although Fayrūz Agha is suspicious from the beginning of the play. Muḥammad Pasha eventually discovers the affair and banishes Marguerite from the house. She reappears several months later, however, after informing Hassan Bey of her pregnancy. At first the cousins cast doubts on the morals of this foreign, Christian maid and question whether the baby is Hassan's, but he leaves the house to marry her. Disinherited by his father, Hassan Bey finds a job as a clerk.

Although, Muḥammad Pasha formally disowns Hassan and forbids the rest of his household to visit the rebellious son, ʿAzīza Hanim and Fayrūz Agha go regularly, in secret, to visit the baby. Hassan Bey then fortuitously saves the life of the same Pasha that his father is trying to impress in order to be reelected. Dangling the Majlis al-Nuwāb as a carrot, this pasha induces Muḥammad Pasha to meet his first grandchild and grant his son an allowance. Muḥammad Pasha agrees out of political ambition; however, the sight of his grandson moves him to tears and he raises the allowance.

Al-ʿusfūr fi al-qafaṣ ends on an interesting note, with the pasha warning Hassan's cousins not to view this reunion, or the increased allowance, as a reward for behavior that threatened to disrupt the family's social fabric. He admonishes them instead to keep clear in their minds that the relationship between a son of the *bāshawāt* and a servant is a terribly destabilizing social crime, and that this sort of breach of boundaries should not, in the future, be condoned.

Social position is, in fact, the kernel of the play, as the characters wrestle with what kind of relations are appropriate and inappropriate in Egyptian society. In this sense, the idea of the Sudanese as servants fits a long tradition in the representation of social borders. The Sudanese servant is part of an old and idealized image of the proper Ottoman–ruling class household and of the social boundaries upheld and enforced by Egypt's elites. Following this tradition, Fayrūz is lascivious, with hungry eyes for Marguerite, eager to cross social lines he does not clearly understand. As a eunuch, of course, he can have none of it. As a Sudanese servant, his crossing of boundaries into equal social status is equally as unthinkable.

The play begins in the salon of the household. Marguerite cleans house, following the orders of ʿAzīza Hanim, who then leaves the stage. Fayrūz Agha enters, asking Marguerite what she is doing. His entry startles her and she admonishes him for this. He shouts at her and she says she was only speaking slowly, so as calm him down:

MARGUERITE: I was speaking slowly.

FAYRŪZ: Speak slowly? No. No, impossible. I have to shout.

MARGUERITE: Why?

FAYRŪZ: That's the way it is for us Nubians.[91]

Fayrūz is looking for Muḥammad Pasha's bookkeeping ledger, which is nearby on the table, but he cannot seem to find it. Marguerite locates it quickly. They then begin to discuss Hassan Bey, for whom Marguerite feels very sorry. Fayrūz Agha starts to laugh inexplicably and, when questioned, says only that something funny occurred to him. Marguerite presses him, and then he answers her:

FAYRŪZ: I see that your heart is very tender for Hassan Bey.

MARGUERITE: What do you mean?

FAYRŪZ: Why do you ask me? Why don't you ask *[imitating her]* "poor Hassan Bey"?

MARGUERITE: You are overstepping your boundaries, O Bash Agha.

FAYRŪZ: Me and not you?[92]

There is something of a prophecy for the upcoming drama in Marguerite's life, but it also reaffirms how unseemly Fayrūz Agha's intrusion into the intimate appears to be. Marguerite then goes on to explain to Fayrūz Agha why Hassan Bey's plight is so pathetic, and why Muḥammad Pasha is only interested in false appearances. Still, Fayrūz tells her that she still sounds like somebody deeply in love.

MARGUERITE *[startled]:* And whom do I love?

FAYRŪZ: *[laughing a "Sudanese laugh"—ḍaḥka sūdāniya]:* Heh, heh, you love the eyes of *[imitating her]* "poor Hassan."

MARGUERITE: My God, Fayrūz! I love him? I am a poor, wretched servant.

FAYRŪZ: As if love knows rich and poor? You don't know what you're talking about!

MARGUERITE: Are you flirting with me or what?

FAYRŪZ: Does that mean it's forbidden, if I am flirting with you?

MARGUERITE: You're making eyes at me? Do you love me? *[She says that while starting to laugh.]*

FAYRŪZ *[surprised]:* What's so funny?

MARGUERITE: You love me? You love . . . *[bursts into laughter].*

FAYRŪZ: What's happened to you?

MARGUERITE: Are you flirting with me? *[Laughs hard.]*

FAYRŪZ *[screaming]:* What is so funny?

MARGUERITE: Nothing . . . I mean . . . no offense, ya Fayrūz *[still laughing].* Excuse me if I leave you and go out. I just can't stop laughing. *[Laughing, she walks off.]*

FAYRŪZ *[screaming]:* Stay here!

MARGUERITE: One more time *[she goes out, laughing hard].*[93]

Marguerite leaves, and the audience is privy to Fayrūz's fantasies of competitive rivalry with Hassan, at once made to seem ridiculous:

FAYRŪZ *[alone]:* The girl leaves . . . should I go crazy? Okay, but what did I say? I don't know, as God can attest. If he is handsome . . . well, I'm also not ugly. If his heart is tender [at this same moment Hassan and Mahmud enter and stand behind Fayrūz; he doesn't see them and keeps on talking] so is my heart gentle. If he knows love, I also know love. If love is confusing his mind, it's confusing mine also. If he's . . . *[he turns around and sees Hassan and Mahmud, so he lifts up the accounting ledger and reads].* God's blessings on our master Muḥammad and his family and his friends and his shelter and his comrades and all those in his house.[94]

Although the action that made Fayrūz a eunuch would have taken place somewhere else, his castration is reenacted verbally for the theater audience when his amorous feelings for Marguerite are made humorous. He is a character out of control, incapable of disciplining his libido, his grammar, his laughter, and the loudness of his voice. When questioned, Fayrūz Agha can only respond that the cause of his behavior is his Sudanese identity, as if this were a psychological complex that Egyptians would immediately have understood. As the play unfolds and grows more serious, Fayrūz Agha remains subservient and silent, controlled by others and then left in the background.

Fayrūz's status as a servant differs dramatically from that of Khalīfa, the Egyptian servant in *'Abd al-sitār effendi,* another Taymūr play, first staged in 1918. Khalīfa participates much more actively in this drama, in which the kindly but cowardly 'Abd al-Sitār Effendi tries to, and then does, thwart the efforts of his greedy wife, Nafūsa, and his spoiled and selfish son, Afifi, to marry his virtuous daughter off to a wealthy but dishonorable cad. Afifi has arranged this marriage with his treacherous friend, Farḥat, who will, in return, guarantee Afifi's own marriage to the daughter of a wealthy landowner. Unlike Fayrūz, who, no matter how many of the intimate details of the household he witnesses, is always addressed by the other characters as "Ya bash Agha" (a formal term reserved for eunuchs of Ottoman households and for other highly placed civil servants), Khalīfa is known as Uncle Khalīfa, and he is treated very much like a member of the family. Sometimes this means being dismissed with the utmost disrespect, as when his mistress, Nafūsa, berates him for not answering a knock at the door or doing any household chores, telling him, "You never were worth anything," followed by the query "You consider yourself to be the master of this house?"[95] But again unlike Fayrūz Agha, Khalīfa is never isolated in his humiliation, since Nafūsa treats her husband with the same abusive language.

And Khalīfa never answers his betters with the subservient expressions used by Fayrūz Agha. When Nafūsa or Afifi call for him, he responds, after three or four calls, with an abrupt "Eh?" In one scene, he contradicts Afifi's presumptions of achievement in the theater and mocks Afifīthe's claims to having a career as a dramatist. Even though Afifi is furious, the two reconcile, with Afifi kissing Uncle Khalīfa and admitting he is like a father to him, and both promising not to use the same hurtful terms with each other in the future.[96]

Like Fayrūz Agha, Khalīfa also has an innuendo-filled encounter with a female servant, and this scene too reveals important differences between their positions within their respective households. Both he and Hanim, the servant girl and Afifi's lover, are responsible for the care of Afifi's dog, Fox. In this scene, Fox becomes very sick. Hanim voices to Khalīfa her fears of the rage she is sure Afifi will fall into when he finds out, but Khalīfa puffs up his chest and feigns indifference to Afifi's moods. Hanim decides to play with this older man's vanity and begins teasing him. After telling him she thinks he's sexy when he prays, she begins to compliment him:

HANIM: I swear, Uncle Khalīfa, you are so handsome. I think I've fallen in love with you. My heart beats just for you, Uncle Khalīfa; it beats and beats.

KHALĪFA: You've fallen in love with me?

HANIM: Who could look at you and not fall for you, Uncle Khalīfa? You are like the full moon.

KHALĪFA *[getting closer to her]:* Really?

HANIM: Tell me, Uncle Khalīfa. Many women must have fallen for you.

KHALĪFA: Oh yes, many *[trying to remember]*.

HANIM *[lifting his (Khalīfa's) hand]:* Tell me a story about yourself.

KHALĪFA: When I was young, I swear by my eyes I had rosy cheeks, cheeks so red they looked like they were bleeding. I was skinny and I loved cleanliness. A charming boy.

HANIM: That's obvious, Uncle Khalīfa, very obvious. But then how did your beard grow?

KHALĪFA *[touching her neck again]:* Do you seriously find my beard attractive?

HANIM: Oh, very attractive. Bring it here and let me kiss it.

KHALĪFA: Take it, my girl, take it and kiss it. *[Instead of kissing it, Hanim passes wind and then laughs]:* You shameless girl, get out of here.[97]

As startlingly rude as Hanim is to Khalīfa, her act of leading him on does not mock the very idea of his sexual passion, as Marguerite does when she realizes Fayrūz Agha is attracted to her. Hanim takes advantage of Khalīfa's vanity in the same way that she teases and flirts with 'Abd al-Sitār Effendi. But the play carries the sense that any man would react similarly to this girl. And Jamila, the daughter of the household, rushes to Khalīfa's defense when she enters the room after Hanim has just made such a fool of him, telling the servant girl to leave him alone: "He's been with the family a long time, and he raised us children!"[98]

Khalīfa is never isolated socially like Fayrūz Agha. He is, in fact, the barometer of morality in this household. The immoral and greedy family members, Nafūsa and Afifī, treat him abusively, while the good-hearted 'Abd al-Sitār Effendi and Jamila love him and respect him insistently. And Khalīfa defends the vacillating 'Abd al-Sitār Effendi's authority, again and again warning Nafūsa and Afifī that their behavior toward the master and patriarch of the house is inappropriate. Although Khalīfa serves a family in which authority and morals have sunk to tragicomic levels, he maintains and upholds the ideal of the father-centered family that was so dear to Muḥammad Taymūr. Where Fayrūz Agha's character functions as an icon of servitude in a traditional family, Khalīfa's character actually articulates and explains the tradition. Khalīfa is the true son of Egypt, connected to his people in a way undreamed of by the wretched servant Fayrūz Agha.

In this period of Egyptians' efforts to explore their culture within the new context of political independence, journalism and theater served as mirrors in which Egyptians could look at themselves both critically and hopefully. Taymūr and his contemporaries tried to perfect an image of the people of their country that other Egyptians could recognize and relate to, while at the same time they questioned the direction in which Egyptian society was headed. But these investigators of new roles for Egyptians drew a sharp boundary when they reached the Nubians and Sudanese in Egypt, who remained stereotyped in much the same manner as they had been in the plays and articles of dramatists and journalists writing fifty years earlier. Most of these black characters remained gullible, manipulable, ugly, asexual, undisciplined, and above all, humorous. They were lovable characters but blank, at a time when Egyptian writers characterized their own culture with greater complexity and insights. It is ironic that 'Alī al-Kassār, considered by many to be the most simplistic and ribald figure in the Egyptian theater, created the most complicated Nubian figure, one who was at least allowed to stand up for himself against many of the racial attitudes common among Egyptians in this period. But his Osman 'abd al-Basit did not break the mold completely. However, while 'Alī al-Kassār was gaining notoriety portraying this honest, brave, and buffoonish character, people in the Sudan were growing more politicized themselves, and much of the impetus for the burgeoning Sudanese nationalist movement came from those blacks in the Sudan long considered, and called, slaves. Shortly, their voices would emerge on the political scene and show the Egyptians and British a completely different aspect of their own changing society and culture.

NOT SERVANTS BUT NATIONALISTS: 'ALĪ 'ABD AL-LAṬĪF AND THE WHITE FLAG LEAGUE

Many of the anecdotes related by Babikr Bedri in his memoirs show how surprising it was, after years in which Sudanese perspectives were excluded from the debate, for Egyptians to discover that many Sudanese accorded them a more complicated and arrogant image than their own nationalist projections created. Some, like Bedri, a former soldier in the Mahdī's army who had become an educational reformer, equated the Egyptians with the

British, considering them coimperialists. Other younger men, educated in secular schools, saw them more as guides in a nationalist struggle with the British. But all educated Sudanese wrestled with the idea of the "unity of the Nile Valley" because of its implied Egyptian hegemony over the Sudan. Thus they also recognized the liminal role of the colonizer-colonized acted out by Egyptian nationalists.

This spectrum of political perspectives within the Sudan was rarely if ever mentioned in the Egyptian media. Egyptians new to the Sudan were constantly surprised by the complexity of feeling toward Egypt that they found. As Bedri opened more schools in the northern Sudan, he came into greater contact with British and Egyptian figures and conducted many discussions with them about the nature of leadership and empire. One of the most interesting of these encounters occurred in 1916, between Bedri and an Egyptian administrator *(ma'mūr)* who had been impressed by Bedri when the latter had confronted the British governor. Feeling he was in the presence of a kindred, nationalist spirit, the Egyptian, Muḥammad Effendi Hilmi, decided to draw him out further over lunch:

MH: I'm going to take the chance of our being on our own together to ask you why it is that the Sudanese hate the Egyptians.

BB: Every subject hates his ruler. Do you not hate the British presence in your country? But now it is my turn to ask you why it is that the Egyptians hate the Sudanese.

MH: They don't hate them; they only despise them.

BB: And is there some good reason why they should despise the Sudanese?

MH: How do you mean?

BB: How dare a despised person despise others?

MH: Is an Egyptian to be despised?

BB: I saw Aḥmad Pasha al-Mitaynī, and he a Lewa [major], saluting an English Bimbashi, junior to him in rank, in public and at the station.[99]

The British officials who ran the Sudan government during World War I were sensitive to Sudanese reactions to Egyptian nationalism. They were aware that culture, religion, and language bound the Sudanese of the north to Egyptians, and that these ties were strengthened by the close contact between Egyptian soldiers stationed in the Sudan and their Sudanese colleagues. Sir Reginald Wingate, the head of the Sudan government during the war, faced the additional pressures of, on the one hand, Sudanese sympathy for the Ottoman Empire and, on the other, undermanned British regiments, stretched thin as a result of the external demands of mobilization. To counter these pressures, Wingate retreated from the strong, anti-Mahdist stance he had maintained for decades and sought a rapprochement with the Mahdī's leading supporters, the Ansar, and the Sufi religious orders that continued to attract young Sudanese.[100] He focused his attention on the Mahdī's posthumous son, Sayyid ʿAbd al-Raḥmān al-Mahdī, and on his rival, Sir ʿAlī al-Mirghānī.

Wingate and the officials of the Sudan government thus exploited the deep anti-Egyptian feeling among many of the Sudanese when they turned their support to the Mahdī's highly politicized son after they had fought for the Mahdīya. The British officials found other ways to mine the depths of alienation between Egyptians and Sudanese, particularly in the negotiations that began between the Wafd Party and Lord Milner's delegation after the revolution of 1919. They stressed racial and cultural differences in the official delineation of the boundaries between Egypt and the Sudan. The decision to emphasize such differences was reached during the 1919 revolt, and was reported to Lord Milner even before he had published his official report on the revolt. His report, it was suggested,

> would recommend such measure of internal self-government for Egypt as might be considered right, but would point out the absurdity of claims made by Egypt to Egyptian Nationalism for the Sudan, stating at the same time how the Sudan differs in race, tradition and sympathy from Egypt, and showing that Egypt's only legitimate interests in the Sudan are the safe-guarding of her water supply and the protection of her frontiers from external aggression. For these, H.M. Government would assume full responsibility, and, at the same time, take full charge of the Sudan, which would develop on lines of Sudanese Nationalism under British guidance, training and cultivating her institutions and watching over the interests of her people.[101]

British attempts to shape Sudanese nationalism and differentiate such a movement from Egyptian nationalism met with great success among older tribal shaykhs, the leaders of the Sufi *tarīqas,* and old supporters of the Mahdī. These groups blamed the Egyptians for bringing the British into the Sudan and destroying the Mahdīya, and felt strongly that Egyptian nationalists sought only to reestablish Egyptian authority over the Sudan. For these groups, the British were indeed colonizers and non-Muslims, but their homeland was far away; one day they inevitably would leave. Egyptians had proven themselves harder to evict. So the Mahdists accepted the status quo under the British temporarily, as a "tactical alliance."[102]

Babikr Bedri provided another example of this alliance when he accused the Egyptians of bad imperialism during a discussion with the future prime minister of Egypt, Husayn Bey Sirrī. Bedri was angry with the Egyptians for their continued protest against British-run irrigation projects for the Sudan and felt this protest showed the superficiality of their sense of unity. In indignation, he raised this point to the Egyptian politician: "But what your Ministers actually said was 'Irrigation in the Sudan will adversely affect the irrigation of Egypt at the present time.' Now does that really square with the picture which the Egyptian likes to paint of himself as the older brother caring for his younger, orphaned brother?"[103]

Given his position as an educator, Bedri was well aware of how thoroughly the British administration of the Sudan had alienated the younger generation of Sudanese. These younger students, clerks, and junior officials in the administration, and the military cadets of Gordon College, all used the model of Egyptian nationalism in much the same way that Egyptian writers had themselves been awakened to national pride by the literature of French and English liberalism. Bedri himself recognized the importance of their politicization, although it worried him. The instruments of nationalism that Benedict Anderson stresses as cultural unifiers during colonialism—newspapers, plays, and cartoons—trickled into the Sudan from Egypt and found an appreciative audience among the new intelligentsia there. Paradoxically, these students, cadets, and clerks refused to accept the idea of the "Sudan for the Sudanese," considering it a slogan engineered by the British. For them, nationalism meant an alliance with Egypt. In making this connection, they felt less isolated in their subjugation to imperialism, since Egyptians, like them, suffered political domination by the British. These groups believed that, once the British had been expelled, they could easily persuade the Egyptians to leave the Sudan truly to the Sudanese.[104]

As these currents of thought reveal, after 1919 the Sudanese had a stronger idea of whose hegemony they preferred than they had of what their own national identity was or who best represented it. But events quickly spiraled, leading to more concrete manifestations of Sudanese nationalism. Inspired by the 1919 demonstrations in Egypt and angered by the enforced separation between Egypt and the Sudan as delineated in the Milner report, a small group of clerks and minor government officials formed the League of Sudanese Union, one of whose members was a Muslim Dinka military cadet named 'Alī 'abd al-Laṭīf. An article he wrote in 1922, called "Self-Determination for the Sudanese," so angered the British authorities who governed the Sudan that they had him imprisoned.[105] When 'Alī 'abd al-Laṭīf first became known to the Egyptian Wafd Party, it was because of his arrest by the British for trying to publish this political manifesto in a Sudanese newspaper that seemed supportive of the Wafd's conception of the unity of the Nile Valley.[106] Then 'Alī 'abd al-Laṭīf's associate 'Ubayd Ḥajj al-Amīn sent a letter to the Egyptian prince Umar Tusun in 1922 in which he declared that Sudanese nationalists were in total support of the Egyptian people and against the separation of Egypt and the Sudan under any circumstances. The letter was promptly published in the newspaper *al-Ahram*.[107] Here was another black man demonstrating the same kind of pride and cultural assertion seen in Osman 'abd al-Basit, a man writing articles and sending telegraphs of support for the Egyptian king to Parliament in the name of a new Sudanese political party.[108] It seemed that the long-awaited Sudanese counterparts to Egyptian nationalism had at last arrived. While these Sudanese activists were first making themselves heard, the Egyptian Parliament created a Committee on Sudanese Affairs and, with Sa'd Zaghlūl's encouragement, tried with some success to reach out to Sudanese members of local parties.[109] These attempts were echoed by Sudanese efforts to approach Parliament and other Egyptian organizations, but the British authorities in Khartoum either refused to grant individuals the necessary travel papers or arrested the petitioners.[110]

The issue for many Sudanese was the British refusal to allow them a political voice. In 1924, 'Alī 'abd al-Laṭīf formed a political party with other Sudanese officers and lower-level civil servants called the White Flag League, named after the emblem they chose for their representation, a white flag with the map of the Nile Valley emblazoned on it. Their stated goals were to unite the Sudan with Egypt and to force the British to leave the Sudan eventually, although they claimed not to be hostile to the "present government which legitimately exists in the Sudan in accordance with the Anglo-Egyptian Conventions of 1899."[111] These somewhat nebulous and contradictory goals were to be achieved through protests that would be engineered to help Egypt in its negotiations with the Labor Government of Ramsey MacDonald. The league also declared its opposition to discrimination against the many tribes that composed the southern Sudan. Although they proclaimed strong support for unity with Egypt, this was a league that granted membership only to Sudanese. No Egyptians were allowed to join. Still, British officials considered 'Alī 'abd al-Laṭīf and his colleagues puppets, "half-civilized dupes of Egyptian politicians."[112]

Although there remains a great diversity of opinion about the apparent ambiguities of the White Flag League's manifesto, it was clearly an organization built on the idea of Sudanese political self-expression and on unifying the Sudan itself. This was significant at a time when the very word *Sudanese* signified the black tribes of the south from whom slaves had been taken for generations and sold to the north and to Egypt.[113] As a political entity, the descendants of these slaves—'Alī 'Abd al-Laṭīf being one important example—were a recent phenomenon. These former slaves and their children, known to the British as "negroid but detribalized" had met the demand for unskilled labor in the larger cities of the Sudan shortly after the establishment of the condominium. Employed in the building trades and other works promoted by the British-run government, these black workers remained in the cities, much to the concern of British officials, who saw in them a threat to the Sudan's traditional groupings and thus to social stability on the whole.[114] Many of them took advantage of opportunities in the military academies, one of the few means of upward social mobility available to them.

In addition to the effects of their "detribalization," these former southerners had to struggle with the ambitions and cultural expectations of other Sudanese tribes and classes. The traditional leaders so respected by the British administration—the "three Sayyids": 'Alī al-Mirghānī, al-Sharif Yusuf al-Hindī, and the Mahdī's son, Sayyid 'Abd al-Raḥman al-Mahdī—represented the two northern Arab tribes, the Barabra and the Dongolowi, tribes who for generations had bought and sold the ancestors of the soldiers and southerners that rallied around 'Alī 'abd al-Laṭīf. Al-Mahdī and the Ansar problematized the very term *Sudanese,* which in 1924 connoted "detribalized," signifying a person of slave origins, a group that included 'Alī 'abd al-Laṭīf.[115] Such individuals could lay no claim to a tribal name and, therefore, according to general opinion, spoke for no one. One newspaper account put the problem more pointedly: "Low is the nation if it can be led by 'Alī 'abd al-Laṭīf."[116]

Al-Laṭīf needed an organization that would accept his presence and assume his issues about race as well. His first political exercise was to join the League of Sudanese Union, formed in the early 1920s to counter the conservatism of the Mahdist and Sufi notables and in protest against the government's policies of taxation and its sugar and cotton monopolies, which were raising the prices of staples and forcing Sudanese economic development to focus on massive agricultural enterprises like the Gezira irrigation plan. The Sudanese Union also protested the exclusion of Sudanese and Egyptians from high official positions, an exclusion that was reinforced by the paucity of decent schools available to the Sudanese.[117] The union also stated its support for the unity of the Nile Valley, an issue strongly opposed by the sayyids of the Ansar group. But this concept of unity was ambiguous because it left open the question of who would actually speak for the Sudanese in such a union.

It is important to remember that there were still thousands of Egyptians working in the Sudan at the time, as soldiers and as bureaucrats, whose purported influence on their Sudanese colleagues also complicated the clarity of Sudanese articulations of nationalism. These Egyptians were sensitive to the fluctuations in political negotiations between Egypt and the Sudan after 1919; after the British commissioner Lord Milner published a report in which increased isolation of the Sudan from Egypt was suggested, Egyptians voiced their growing alarm to their Sudanese friends in Khartoum.[118] But the influence of Egyptians seems to have been both exaggerated and obfuscating. As mentioned earlier, the White Flag League was most eager to promote the unity of the Nile Valley but was inflexible on the rule that Egyptians could not be members of the league. Many Sudanese in the League of Sudanese Union, before it fell apart in 1924, also voiced their concerns about the Egyptians speaking for the Sudanese.[119] But most British officials in the Sudan expressed strong suspicions about the Egyptian presence there and often identified any sign of Sudanese rebellion against their government as yet another example of Egyptians intruding into Sudanese politics.[120] It was this controversial question of who spoke for the Sudanese that compelled 'Alī 'abd al-Laṭīf to form the White Flag League and that, soon after, ignited the revolution of 1924.

The conflict in 1924 came to a head quickly. In January of that year, Sa'd Zaghlūl became prime minister of Egypt, and his Wafd Party won the parliamentary elections on a platform of liberation for both Egypt and the Sudan. In September, negotiations resumed between the Wafd government and the British about the future status of the Sudan. Sir Lee Stack, the governor-general of the Sudan and commander *(sirdār)* of the Egyptian army, played a prominent role in these negotiations as he tried to lessen Egyptian involvement in the Sudan.[121] Meanwhile, the Wafd Party and the Parliamentary Committee on Sudanese Affairs stepped up their efforts to contact Sudanese politicians and, when frustrated by the British, used the press to amplify their support.[122] In June, British soldiers detained a Sudanese activist, Muḥammad al-Mahdī, for trying to reach Cairo and visit Parliament. His forced return on a train to Khartoum prompted anti-British demonstrations. These were soon followed by a funeral for a high-ranking and popular Egyptian official, in which speeches about the unity of the Nile Valley provoked yet another demonstration.[123]

The demonstrations continued and spread to Omdurman and other Sudanese towns. It is unclear which demonstrations were organized by the White Flag League, but the British attributed many violent schemes to them and, in July, arrested 'Alī 'abd al-Laṭīf. He was quickly sentenced to three years in prison. Other leaders of the White Flag League soon were arrested and imprisoned, but the demonstrations continued, as did the force with which they were met by the British. In November, Stack was murdered in Cairo. In angry response, Lord Allenby, then British consul in Egypt, quickly ordered the evacuation of all Egyptian troops from the Sudan. Zaghlūl refused to issue the order, and Egyptian troops stationed in the Sudan refused to evacuate. In a gesture of loyalty to Egypt, Sudanese troops in the Eleventh Battalion rebelled and tried to reach their Egyptian colleagues to the north of Khartoum. Under heavy British fire, the Sudanese troops were finally defeated after retreating to a military hospital. The troops were disappointed that no similar gesture of loyalty had come from the Egyptian soldiers, who did not fire against the British.[124] Then, the evacuation of Egyptian soldiers was accomplished quickly and completely, and by the end of November, the revolution in the Sudan had died down.

Historians of the modern Sudanese note that the revolution left several legacies, among them the dramatic cessation of Egyptian influence over the Sudan and a bitterness among the Sudanese, who resented Cairo's remaining inactive while scores of Sudanese were shot at or imprisoned during the demonstrations.[125] The Egyptian lack of response to events in the Sudan, so abhorrent to Huda Shaʿrawī, also provoked deep disillusionment among both Sudanese soldiers and participants in the White Flag League. This disappointment was as effective as British efforts in the smashing of the league. The 1924 revolt also stiffened the pro-British position of ʿAbd al-Raḥman al-Mahdī and the other sayyids. ʿAlī ʿAbd al-Laṭīf's efforts continued to carry some currency, certainly to the extent that Sudanese continued to look outside the Sudan for cultural models. Following an established trajectory of the sort described by Anderson, younger Sudanese emigrated to Egypt and the rest of the Arab world for their secular education. They hoped to acquire the tools to study their society more closely and to figure out ways to establish links between their class and the uneducated majority of Sudanese, who remained beholden to tribal shaykhs or Mahdists.[126] The question of a united Sudanese voice was not to be resolved for decades, either in the Sudan itself or in Egypt. The Sudanese continued under British rule, as did the Egyptians, although the latter gained more and more say in their government. As a symbol, the Sudan continued to be batted around between Egypt and England; the Sudanese themselves continued to compare the imperial techniques of the Egyptians and the British.

But if the revolt forced certain politicized members of Sudanese society to rethink their ties to Egypt, it also directed their attention to the question of who in the Sudan best spoke for the Sudanese. The events and slogans of the revolution itself reveal that, for many Sudanese activists, the idea of Nile Valley unity was both attractive and complicated. The songs and poems recited at the demonstrations offer glimpses into how this ambivalence expressed itself. One songwriter, Khalīl Farah, composed the following verses, which were popular during the revolution:

> We are, we are the proud east
>   The great snake, the peoples of the Nile
> We all alone defend our home with zeal
>   We loathe our enemies, long live the Nile
> There's no one else, Egyptian, Sudanese
>   We together are the people of the Nile.[127]

Another poet, Ibrahīm al-ʿAbadī, composed another *qaṣīḍa*, part of which says:

> Nile of Egypt and the Sudan together
>   We are related to each other under the same banner
> O Saʿd [Zaghlūl], let MacDonald know
>   The Sudan is Arab, not Indian.[128]

These and other examples of popular expression during the 1924 demonstrations show how interlinked many Sudanese considered the cultures of Egypt and the Sudan to be. They sang songs and chanted slogans and poetry in a mixture of classical Arabic and Sudanese dialect. The examples also reveal how much the constructions of Egyptian nationalism had influenced the struggle for autonomy between Egypt, Great Britain, and the Sudan. It is easy to understand how the British could believe that Egyptians were behind the White Flag League and other activist groups, so much did the songs, slogans, and poems of the revolution sound like those heard in Cairo in 1919.

The intensity of the pro-Egyptian feeling during the Sudanese revolution surprised and pleased many Egyptian politicians and nationalists, and the violence of the demonstrations inspired huge headlines in the Egyptian press. Yet the spectacle of Sudanese activists did not create in Egypt a greater awareness of Sudanese interests or issues. Newspaper writers emphasized instead the impact of the rebellion on Egypt and the Egyptians present in Khartoum and Omdurman. In one example of this, the newspaper *al-Laṭāʾif al-Muṣawwara* ran a banner headline across its front page announcing the arrest of the leaders of the "Sudanese renaissance" *(al-nahḍa al-sūdānīya)*. Underneath this was a large picture of ʿAlī ʿabd al-Laṭīf, ʿUbayd Ḥajj al-Amīn, and other leaders of the White Flag League, followed by another picture of First Lieutenant al-ʿAbdin ʿAbd al-Tam, whose imprison-

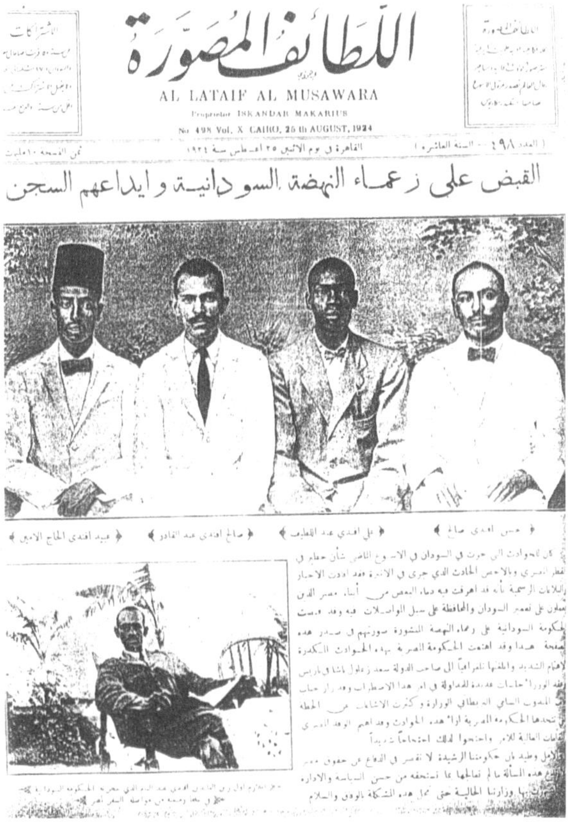
اللطائف المصورة

AL LATAIF AL MUSAWARA

Proprietor ISKANDAR MAKARIUS

No 498 Vol. X CAIRO, 25 th AUGUST, 1924

القبض على زعماء النهضة السودانية وايداعهم السجن

9. Front-page photographs of the White Flag League and the man whose attempt to speak to Parliament sparked the 1924 demonstrations, from *al-Latā'if al-Muṣawwara,* August 1924.

ment for trying to get to Cairo in order to speak to Parliament had sparked the 1924 demonstrations. The photos prominently display the leaders of the movement, but they frame a text in which these men hardly appear (see fig. 9):

> The events that took place within the Sudan last week were a serious matter for the Egyptian nation, especially the events at Atbara station, where news sources and official communiques relate that the blood of several Egyptian sons was spilled, men who worked for the civilizing of the Sudan and in the defense of its communications. The leaders of the *nahḍa,* pictured here, were also arrested. This is of great concern to the Egyptian government, which sent a telegraph to Prime Minister Sa'd

10.   Cartoon of the British John Bull trying to stop Sudan from running to her sister, Egypt, from *al-Laṭāʾif al-Muṣawwara*, September 1924.

> Zaghlūl in Paris, and ministers held a number of meetings for the deliberation of the strikes and demonstrations. The delegate of the British High Commissioner visited the Ministry to discuss the steps that the Egyptian government may take with regard to these events. The Egyptian delegates registered their high disapproval and protested against this strongly.
>
> There is widespread hope that our reasonable government will not hesitate to defend Egypt's rights and will not ignore this affair, which cannot be healed by proper politics alone, and that the administration concerned with this will find a way to resolve it peacefully.[129]

Clearly the events deserved press attention, but the attention paid to the interests of Egypt, and the lack of attention to the Sudanese casualties, is striking. One week later, *al-Laṭāʾif al-Muṣawwara* ran a cartoon in which more traditional views of the Sudan and the Sudanese were combined with some awareness of the plight of the Sudanese. In this cartoon (see fig. 10), John Bull in topcoat and high boots restrains a ragged and diminutive dark-skinned girl who represents the Sudan. John Bull hides a stick behind his back with one hand, the other grabbing the girl's rags as she tries to scale a fence and reach her graceful, light-skinned, and veiled big sister, Egypt. John Bull says angrily to the Sudan, "I cannot leave you until I have completed

11. Servant depicted in an advertisement for tea, from *al-Laṭā'if al-Muṣawwara*, September 1924.

your upbringing and education." But the Sudan answers, "Leave me alone! I'm going to my sister because I cannot live like this!" And Egypt, looking concerned over the fence, says to John Bull, "What have you to do with her? I'm her sister; I'm responsible for her." The caption goes on to explain to the readers that John Bull wants to separate the two siblings, but that nature is stronger and emotions are too powerful for this link to be broken. These emotions push the Sudan to forge a path over the obstacles put in her path to Egypt.[130] The cartoon indicates that the Sudan's actions are considered her own, but that she is so much smaller than the other two figures, and ragged and young, that one of the two, Egypt or Great Britain, has to be the caretaker. Ironically, a few pages farther on in the same issue, the message of this cartoon is complemented by an advertisement for tea, in which two Egyptian ladies talk at a table while being served by a Sudanese servant woman wearing popular *khulkhāl* anklets (see fig. 11). Despite the coverage of the intense and violent demonstrations in Khartoum, these images keep the Sudanese bent over in peaceful submission. Little wonder then that the idea of Nile Valley unity was loaded and troubling for so many Sudanese.

POSTSCRIPT: THE IRONIC END OF ʿALĪ ʿABD AL-LAṬĪF

The 1924 revolution put the Sudan firmly in British control, with no Egyptians left to serve in either the bureaucracy or the army. Egyptians were excluded until 1938, when the imminence of war altered the balance of negotiations between the British and Egyptian governments. Egypt never did return to the Sudan. Another legacy of this revolution was the developing awareness of a need for a new kind of movement in the Sudan, one that embraced the concept of "the Sudan for the Sudanese" and defined *Sudanese* as all who lived in this vast country.

If one life sums up the tragic irony of the historical situation concerning Egypt, Great Britain, and the Sudan, it is that of ʿAlī ʿabd al-Laṭīf. Although he had been sentenced to three years in prison after the 1924 uprising, the British would not release him when his sentence was up. Rumors spread throughout the Sudan and Egypt that he had lost his sanity. But Kurita writes that recent interviews with his wife and other members of his family have proven that it was not his mind that was the problem but the refusal of the British authorities to release him to any part of the Sudan. As a "detribalized negroid," ʿAlī ʿabd al-Laṭīf seemed to have no native home or district, yet his demonstrated political popularity determined that the British would not let him anywhere near Omdurman or Khartoum.[131]

ʿAlī ʿabd al-Laṭīf remained in different prisons in the south of the Sudan, far from his family and under harsh conditions, for over twelve years, until the prime minister of Egypt, Nahhas Pasha, appealed to the British to free him and let him live in Egypt. The British administration agreed to send him to Egypt, but under very strict conditions: the prisoner was removed in secret from the Sudan and had to be received with great discretion in Cairo. Once in Egypt, he was not free but instead had to be housed in a military hospital, where he could be observed at all times. He was soon placed in the ʿAbbasīya Hospital for Mental Diseases, where the many Egyptian and Sudanese dignitaries who came to visit him left impressed with his mental faculties. The long years in prison took their toll, however. According to his wife's description, toward the end of his life he become somewhat extreme in his suspicion of being spied on. He never regained his freedom, and he died in Cairo of natural causes in 1948. The man whose presence more than anyone else's had raised questions about Sudanese identity was rendered as mute and invisible as the dark-skinned servants who for fifty years had served as caricatures of the Sudanese in Egyptian popular and political culture.

Conclusion

A cartoon titled "British Delusions of Grandeur" appeared on the front page of the newspaper *al-Kashkūl* (The Scrapbook) in January 1926 (see fig. 12). It depicts two female figures representing Egypt and the Sudan as being rather intimately connected to a boastful Lord Lloyd. According to the caption, the Egyptian figure wonders who will tell him he is deluding himself, while the Sudanese figure wonders who will tell him that he is wasting his time in the Sudan. And yet, the poses of the female characters belie their vocal defiance. Egypt turns demurely toward Lord Lloyd and, though protected from his advances by a thin veil and modest clothing, stands quite close, part of her body obscured by his arrogant posture. The Sudan, however, assertively hangs onto the arm of Lord Lloyd, her right arm set provocatively on her hip. She too turns toward the Englishman but not at all demurely: there is active movement toward him in the swing of her necklace, and her naked left breast grazes his arm. Bare though she is, she seems not to need the same protection that Egypt requires, or to have the same propriety. She is muscled and brazen. So kinetic is this caricatured figure that one can almost hear the rustle of her skirt as she moves her hips.

The nudity of this "Sudan" is striking, but there are also considerable complexities covered up in the cartoon. This stereotyped triptych of Egypt, Great Britain, and the Sudan was constructed over the decades that their complex colonial relationship endured. While the figures of Britain and Egypt had changed between 1881 and 1925, stereotypes of the Sudan—oversexed, underclothed, and beyond the structures of either British or Egyptian morality—remained powerful and surprisingly unchanged. As I show in this study, such stereotypes had existed even before Muḥammad ʿAlī's armies conquered the Sudan in 1821, and they obviously continued to resonate with Egyptian readers and audiences through the 1920s.

12.   Front-page caricature of the threesome Sudan,
Lord Lloyd, and Egypt, from *al-Kashkūl*, January
1926.

But such fixed images do not disguise the important changes in the relationship between Egypt and the Sudan after World War I; in fact, the images defended against the feared impact of change. This picture, for example, appeared less than a year after the imprisonment of ʿAlī ʿabd al-Laṭīf and the assassination of Sir Lee Stack. Although from Cairo or Alexandria they may have been difficult to hear, the voices of more and more Sudanese entered the debate over the political shape of the Nile Valley. The persistent rendering of the Sudan as this type of feminized figure shows that it was "a privileged site for a larger ideological project." In this case, the project was one in which Egyptian nationalists not only packaged the Sudan in ways that continued to bind it to Egypt but also reconstructed a political relationship with Sudan's people while Egypt itself seemed to slip away into complete British control.[1] Mary Louise Roberts describes postwar French society's attempts to comprehend dramatic social and political change, noting that people "focused on a set of images, issues and power relationships that were both familiar and compelling."[2] In Egypt during the 1920s, nationalists were forced to do the same to keep the issue of the Sudan alive.

Unfortunately, though, these powerful stereotypes of the colonial relationships between Egypt, Great Britain, and the Sudan muted the much more sensitive issue of the influence of slavery and its legacy for Egyptian and Sudanese societies. One crucial theme of this study is the underlying centrality of slavery in the historical relationship between Egypt and the Sudan. None of the many figures discussed in this book lived untouched by slavery. It was intimately connected to their personal and cultural identities, often as a profound part of their childhoods and their families. As I have tried to show, such histories colored the symbol, even the name, of the Sudan itself. While nationalist thinkers and writers discussed the integration of the Sudan with Egypt, they in some way spoke about the many cultural traditions inherited from generations of trade in Sudanese slaves.

This book began with the experience of Zanūba and five other Sudanese slave women, central figures in a trial of Egyptian nationalists whose purchase of the women was considered a crime by British authorities. There was also an important British or European judge, in the guise of translator, mentor, editor, or official, reading over the shoulders of earlier Egyptian notables in the Sudan—such as Muḥammad al-Tunisī and Rifaʿah Rafiʿ al-Ṭahṭawī—who viewed the Sudanese, women in particular, with eyes trained to see unregulated sexuality and barbarity. Yaʿqūb Ṣanūʿa and ʿAbdallah al-Nadīm fought energetically against European judgments on Egyptian culture in many of their works, but they too could not remove the stereotyped image of the Sudanese slave woman. Ibrahīm Fawzī may have been the most honest in his acceptance of the contradiction inherent in the colonized colonizer, but nothing offended him as deeply as being identified as the slave of a Sudanese. Aḥmad Luṭfī al-Sayyid was the most candid in his discussion of racial prejudice in Egypt, but for him as well, the Sudan and the Sudanese had no past independent of Egypt. Even the beautiful voice of Muḥammad Imām al-ʿAbd could not be heard without the interfering fact of his parents' enslavement.

But I prefer not to end this book with the image of the Sudan as a slave or with the graphic caricature of a Sudanese woman. Nor do I wish to let the word *ʿabīd,* or slave, remain a stinging, timeless insult to people of Sudanese descent. Such a word goes only so far in describing the complicated and intimate historical connection between Egyptians and Sudanese. There are perhaps a million Sudanese in Cairo today, representing a community of great diversity racially, culturally, economically, and spiritually, all of whom found a second home in Egypt when forced to leave the Sudan.

Many of these are women—exiles or refugees from the devastation of war in the southern Sudan—and an increasingly vocal group among them have reclaimed the word *'abid* in a singular manner. They belong to a growing movement in the Catholic Church in both Egypt and in the Sudan that pays special attention to, and reveres, the memory of a religious black woman, Sister Josephine Bakhīta. The Blessed Bakhīta was sold into slavery in 1869 and spent years passing from master to master, until she was bought by the Italian consul in the Sudan, who took her with him to Italy in 1881.[3] She was sold again to a family and, as caretaker of their small daughter, went to the convent school with the girl. Bakhīta never left the convent. With the Pope interceding on her behalf, she became a novice, then a nun, and was canonized in 1982.

Bakhīta's martyrdom was her experience as a slave and, as the pamphlets about her printed by the Canossian Daughters of Charity emphasize, the loss of her childhood and her identity caused by her enslavement. But now, a century after she was seized by raiders and carried away from her family forever, displaced southern Sudanese communities are reclaiming her and instituting her in their sense of family. As a member of the Blessed Josephine Bakhīta Women's Association has said, Bakhīta's experience shows that one can be a slave in many different ways, and that Bakhīta's life offers an example and a guide for how to lead a difficult life.[4] There is a transforming power in this identification with Bakhīta's alienation and suffering, a statement about the honor that can come from having been a slave.

These women claim descent from Bakhīta and, in so doing, redefine an insult and make it a badge of courage. They remake their identity with the same kind of ingenuity—experienced under difficulties perhaps as powerful—shown by their ancestors, the Blessed Bakhīta and Zanūba. It is both striking and sad that Egyptian nationalists like Ya'qūb Ṣanū'a, Ibrahīm Fawzī Pasha, and even Huda Sha'rawī recognized these women and others like them as part of the Egyptian family but never seemed to have really known them.

Notes

INTRODUCTION

1. My summary of the slave trial follows closely the account in ʿIssa, *Hikayāt min Daftār al-Waṭan*, pp. 217–45. A more detailed account, including the newspaper and the British Foreign Office reports, follows in chapter 4.

2. Fahmy, *All the Pasha's Men*, pp. 88–90.

3. Kāmil, *Al-Maqalāt*, p. 298; excerpted from *Le Clair*, 19 April 1898.

4. For an interesting debate on the nationalist dimensions of Muḥammad ʿAlī's (or Mehmet ʿAlī's) ethnicity, see Fahmy, *All the Pasha's Men*.

5. Quoted from Said, *Orientalism*, p. 33.

6. Ibid., p. 44.

7. A. Ahmad, *In Theory*, p. 159.

8. Ibid., p. 174.

9. Young, *Colonial Desire*, pp. 4–5.

10. Loomba, *Colonialism/Postcolonialism*, p. 12.

11. Hobsbawm, *The Age of Empire*, p. 77.

12. Hourani, *The History of the Arab Peoples*, pp. 302–4.

13. Mitchell, *Colonising Egypt*, p. ix.

14. Ibid., pp. 1, 27.

15. Ibid., p. x.

16. Hobsbawm, *Nations and Nationalism since 1789*, p. 11.

17. Lockman, "Imagining the Working Class," p. 178.

18. Beinin, "Writing Class," pp. 192–93.

19. Ibid., pp. 194–95.

20. Hobsbawm, *Nations and Nationalism since 1789*, p. 63.

21. Anderson, *Imagined Communities*, pp. 12–15, 24–26.

22. Ibid., pp. 65, 81, 84, 116.

23. Ibid., pp. 141, 150.

24. Balibar, "Racism and Nationalism," p. 40.

25. Ibid., p. 44.

26. Bjorkelo, *Prelude to the Mahdiyya*, p. 34.

27. Woodward, *Sudan*, p. 47.
28. Bakhtin, *The Dialogic Imagination*, pp. xxi, 259, 428.
29. Ibid., pp. 262, 276.
30. Ibid., pp. 324, 326, 342, 365.
31. De Moraes Farias, "Models of the World and Categorical Models," p. 30.
32. Walz, *Trade between Egypt and Bilad as-Sudan*, pp. 228–29.
33. Tucker, *Women in Nineteenth-Century Egypt*, p. 125.
34. Amin, *The Liberation of Women*, p. 6.
35. Baron, *The Women's Awakening in Egypt*, pp. 66–67.
36. McClintock, *Imperial Leather*, p. 44.
37. Ibid., p. 45.
38. Walz, "Black Slavery in Nineteenth Century Egypt," p. 151.

CHAPTER 1. JOURNEYS FROM THE FANTASTIC
TO THE COLONIAL

EPIGRAPHS. Page 000: Walcott, *Omeros*, 167; Montesquieu, *Persian Letters*, p. 39. Page 000: Smollett, trans., *The Adventures of Telemachus*, p. 216; this is Smollett's translation of the original *Télémaque* by Fenelon. Page 000: ibid., p. 7. Page 000: ibid., p. 146. Page 000: Walcott, *Omeros*, p. 170. Page 000: Montesquieu, *Persian Letters*, p. ?

1. Paule, trans. and ed., *Voyageurs Arabes*, p. xxx.
2. De Moraes Farias, "Models of the World and Categorical Models," 28.
3. Harley, "Maps, Knowledge, and Power," p. 279.
4. The following collections are only the tip of the iceberg of the interesting work now being done on imperialism and geography: Godlewska and Smith, eds., *The Geography of Empire*; Driver, "Geography's Empire," pp. 23–40; Cosgrove and Daniels, eds., *The Iconography of Landscape*.
5. Al-Qadi, "East and West in 'Ali Mubarak's '*Alam al-Din*," pp. 23, 34.
6. For more details about the widespread reforms of Muḥammad Alī, see Marsot, *Egypt in the Reign of Muhammad Ali*; for their effect on the intelligentsia of Egypt, see Mitchell, *Colonising Egypt*.
7. Walz, *Trade between Egypt and Bilad as-Sudan*, pp. 29–64.
8. Holt and Daly, *A History of the Sudan*, p. 15.
9. De Moraes Farias, "Models of the World and Categorical Models," pp. 28–29.
10. Holt and Daly, *A History of the Sudan*, p. 15.
11. O'Fahey, *State and Society in Dar Fur*, p. 6.
12. Ibid., p. 11.
13. Helms, *Ulysses' Sail*, pp. 100–101.
14. Al-Tunisī, *Tashhīdh al-adhhān bi-sirat bilād al-'arab wal-sūdān*, p. 18.
15. Ibid., pp. 34–35.
16. Ibid., pp. 35–37.

17. Al-Tunisī, *Tashḥīdh al-adhhān bi-sirat bilād al-ʿarab wal-sūdān*, pp. 41–42, 45.

18. Ibid., p. 149.

19. Ibid., pp. 154, 155.

20. Ibid., pp. 256, 257.

21. Ibid., pp. 265–67.

22. Nachtigal, *Sahara and Sudan*, 136n.

23. Marsot, *Egypt in the Reign of Muhammad Ali*, p. 196.

24. Warburg, *Historical Discord in the Nile Valley*, pp. 1–2.

25. Holt and Daly, *History of the Sudan*, p. 48.

26. "The Egyptian Empire is, from henceforth, created." Sabry, *L'Empire égyptien sous Mohamed-Ali et la question d'Orient*, p. 74.

27. "He was moved as if by an ideal, even though the immediate goal of his Sudanese expedition was to bring back gold and slaves." Ibid.

28. Lawson, *The Social Origins of Egyptian Expansionism during the Muhammad ʿAli Period*, p. 2.

29. Ibid., p. 49.

30. Marsot, *Egypt in the Reign of Muhammad Ali*, p. 196.

31. Ibid., p. 197.

32. Holt and Daly, *History of the Sudan*, pp. 48–49.

33. Collins, "The Nilotic Slave Trade," p. 140.

34. Ramadan, *ʿUkdhubat al-Istaʾamar al-Miṣrī lil-Sudan*, pp. 24, 26, 28.

35. Ibid., p. 63.

36. Bonola Bey, *Sommaire historique des travaux geographiques*, p. 6.

37. Ibid., p. 22.

38. Santi and Hill, eds., *The Europeans in the Sudan*, p. 35.

39. Ibid., pp. 52–53.

40. Maqqar, *Al-Bekbashī al-miṣri Selim Qapudan wa-al-kashf ʿan manābiʿ al-nīl*, pp. 29–30.

41. Ibid., p. 33.

42. Ibid., p. 6.

43. Qapudan, *Al-riḥla al-ūla lil-baḥth ʿan yanābī al-baḥr al-abyaḍ*, p. 13.

44. Ibid., pp. 47–49.

45. Ibid., p. 50.

46. Ibid., p. 62.

47. Ibid., pp. 74, 86–87.

48. Ibid., p. 90.

49. Morag Bell, Robin A. Butlin, and Michael Heffernan, "Geography and Imperialism, 1820–1940," in *Geography and Imperialism*, ed. Morag Bell, Robin A. Butlin, and Michael Heffernan (Manchester: Manchester University Press, 1995), p. 3.

50. Ibid., p. 4.

51. Bonola Bey, *Sommaire historique des travaux geographiques*, p. 13.

52. Hourani, *Arabic Thought in the Liberal Age*, p. 81.

53. Ibid., p. 71.

54. Altman, "The Political Thought of Rifaʿah Rafiʿ al-Ṭahṭawī," p. 88.

55. Hourani, *Arabic Thought in the Liberal Age*, p. 72.

56. Ibid., pp. 69–70.

57. Moosa, *The Origins of Modern Arabic Fiction*, p. 6.

58. Berque, *Egypt*, p. 16.

59. Wendell, *The Evolution of the Egyptian National Image*, p. 6.

60. Hafez, *The Genesis of Arabic Narrative Discourse*, pp. 97–98.

61. Holt and Daly, *A History of the Sudan*, pp. 65–66.

62. Ibid., p. 67.

63. Ibid., p. 68.

64. Toledano, *State and Society in Mid–Nineteenth Century Egypt*, p. 92.

65. Ibid., p. 92.

66. Ibid.

67. Taylor, *Journey to Central Africa*, p. 285.

68. Ibid., p. 291.

69. Ibid., pp. 292–93.

70. Moosa, *The Origins of Modern Arabic Fiction*, p. 6.

71. Leslie Chilton, introduction to *The Adventures of Telemachus, the Son of Ulysses*, trans. Tobias Smollett (Athens: University of Georgia Press, 1997), pp. xx, xxi–ii.

72. Al-Ṭahṭawī, *Mawāqiʿ al-aflak fī waqāʾiʿ Telemaque*, p. 4.

73. Ibid., p. 5.

74. Ibid., p. 6.

75. Hourani, *Arabic Thought in the Liberal Age*, p. 72.

76. Ibid., p. 78.

77. Ibid., p. 79.

78. Altman, "The Political Thought of Rifaʿah Rafiʿ al-Ṭahṭawī," pp. 96–97.

79. Wendell, *Evolution of the Egyptian National Image*, p. 121.

80. Ibid., p. 130.

81. Al-Ṭahṭawī, *Manāhij al-albāb al-miṣriya fī mabāhij al-ʿadāb al-ʿasriya*, pp. 237, 244.

82. Ibid., p. 251.

83. Ibid., p. 263.

84. Ibid., pp. 267, 268.

85. Ibid., p. 279.

86. A. S. Ahmad, *Rifaʿah Rafiʿ al-Ṭahṭawī fī-l-Ṣūdān*, p. 124.

87. Ibid., p. 125.

88. Mubārak, *Ḥayatī*, p. 5. This edition, edited by ʿAbd al-Rahim Yusuf al-Jamal, contains the autobiographical passages of *Al-Khiṭaṭ*.

89. Delanoue, *Moralistes et politiques Musulmans dans l'Égypte du XIXe siècle*, p. 492.

90. Mubārak, *Ḥayatī*, pp. 8–9.

91. Ibid., p. 9.

92. Delanoue, *Moralistes et politiques Musulmans dans l'Égypte du XIXe siècle,* p. 493.

93. Ibid., p. 495.

94. Mubārak, *'Alam al-Dīn,* 1:72–73.

95. Al-Qadi, "East and West in 'Ali Mubarak's *'Alam al-Dīn,*" p. 30.

96. Ibid., pp. 23–25.

97. Mubārak, *'Alam al-Dīn,* 1:309–10.

98. Van Roosbeck, *Persian Letters before Montesquieu,* p. 38.

99. Ibid., p. 13.

100. Mubārak, *'Alam al-Dīn,* 2:643, 652, 670.

101. Ibid., 2:678.

102. Ibid., 2:680, 681.

103. Ibid., 2:690.

104. Ibid., 2:713–14.

105. Ibid., 2:734, 776.

106. Al-Qadi, "East and West in 'Ali Mubarak's *'Alam al-Dīn,*" p. 34, n. 10.

107. Nachtigal, *Sahara and Sudan.* This reliance on al-Tunisī's text is clearly shown by the abundance of notes Nachtigal's editor uses that refer to *Voyage au Darfour,* and by Nachtigal's own quest to correct many of al-Tunisī's observations.

108. Girard, *Memoire sur l'agriculture,* quoted from Anna Godlewska, "Napoleon's Geographers," in *The Geography of Empire,* ed. Anna Godlewska and Neil Smith (Oxford: Blackwell, 1994), p. 50.

CHAPTER 2. BLACK SERVANTS AND SAVIORS

EPIGRAPH. Page 000: Hourani, *A History of the Arab Peoples,* pp. 300–301.

1. Mitchell, *Colonising Egypt,* p. 63.

2. Ibid.

3. Ibid., pp. 64–67.

4. The term *Ottoman Egyptians,* first coined by Toledano in *State and Society in Mid–Nineteenth Century Egypt,* has come to replace the term *Turco-Circassians,* used by Hourani and many others to describe the ruling classes of Egypt in the mid– to late nineteenth century. *Ottoman Egyptian* attributes a greater sense of Egyptian roots to this elite group, many of whom had Circassian ancestry but were comfortable in both Turkish and Arabic and considered themselves native to Egypt. Within the context of the Sudan, however, even Arabic-speaking Egyptians were considered Turks, and the term *Ottoman Egyptians* may seem more problematic.

5. Scholch, *Egypt for the Egyptians!* p. 21.

6. Shukry, *Equatoria under Egyptian Rule,* pp. 29, 69–71; PRO, FO 141/100 Stanton to Derby, Cairo, 9 January 1876 and 7 April 1876.

7. A. I. M. Ali, *The British, the Slave Trade, and Slavery in the Sudan,* pp. 79–83.

8. Ibid., pp. 94–95.

9. BFASSP, Box G25, copy of memorial to Khedive Isma'il by Lord Clarence Paget, 1873.

10. Hourani, *A History of the Arab Peoples,* p. 283.

11. Mansfield, *A History of the Middle East,* p. 87.

12. Ibid., pp. 88–89.

13. Holt, *The Mahdist State in the Sudan,* p. 40.

14. Scholch, *Egypt for the Egyptians!,* p. 136.

15. 'Urābī Pasha, *Mudhākirāt 'Urābī,* 1:18.

16. Scholch, *Egypt for the Egyptians!* pp. 158–60. These demands now included the dismissal of the prime minister Riad Pasha's government, the convocation of a Chamber of Delegates, and an increase in the army, to eighteen thousand men.

17. Warburg, *Egypt and the Sudan,* pp. 48–49. See also Cromer, *Modern Egypt,* 1:386–90.

18. Cole, *Colonialism and Revolution in the Middle East,* p. 77; Gendzier, *The Practical Visions of Ya'qub Sanu'a,* p. 20.

19. Walz, *Trade Between Egypt and Bilad as-Sudan,* pp. 3, 12.

20. Ibid., p. 246.

21. Cole, *Colonialism and Revolution in the Middle East,* pp. 33–34. See also 'Urābī Pasha, *Mudhākirāt 'Urābī,* 1:45, 129.

22. I thank Dr. John Voll of Georgetown University for these insights.

23. Gendzier, *The Practical Visions of Ya'qub Sanu'a,* pp. 20–23.

24. Badawi, *Early Arabic Drama,* p. 32.

25. Ibid., p. 33.

26. Moosa, "Ya'qub Sanu' and the Rise of Arab Drama in Egypt," p. 408.

27. Ibid., p. 410.

28. ENA, Dar al-Watha'iq al-qawmiyya al-miṣrīya, watha'iq al-thawra al-'urābīya, Muhafizah 26, Milaf 1 [telegraph from His Highness the Khedive to the Sublime Porte, 18 Shawwal 1298 (11 September 1881)]. In this telegraph, Tawfīq informs the Ottoman sultan that much of the political movement of 'Urābī can be attributed to the newspaper *Abū Naẓẓara Zarqa.*

29. Baignières, *L'Égypte satirique,* p. 27.

30. Ibid., p. 34.

31. Scholch, *Egypt for the Egyptians!* pp. 50, 92.

32. On Dual Control's demand, see Ramadan, *Al-jaysh al-miṣrī fi-l-siyāsa,* pp. 13–14; on plans for the railroad and telegraph system, see Douin, "L'Empire africain," chap. 12.

33. Ibid., pp. 324, 346.

34. Rizq, "Al-Ahram."

35. Cole, *Colonialism and Revolution in the Middle East,* p. 77.

36. Qapudan, *Al-riḥla al-ūla lil-baḥth 'an yanābī al-baḥr al-abyaḍ,* pp. 36, 44; Baker, *Ismailia,* pp. 28, 53, 82, 93.

37. Cole, *Colonialism and Revolution in the Middle East,* p. 199. On pages 184–87, Cole also discusses a case of Nubian and Sudanese wagon drivers peti-

tioning the police chief in Cairo for a separate guild. They complained that the old guild master discriminated against men of their race *(jins)*. Cole sees this as an example of widespread ethnic redefinition occurring during the ʿUrābī revolt.

38. Ibid., pp. 184–85.

39. Mitchell, *Colonising Egypt,* pp. 1–5. See also Mackenzie, *Propaganda and Empire,* pp. 55–62.

40. Anderson, *Imagined Communities,* p. 6.

41. Gendzier, *The Practical Visions of Yaʿqub Sanuʿa,* pp. 25–26. In her discussion of Egyptian intellectual life in the 1860s and 1870s, Gendzier says these young men, who "wielded power out of proportion to [their] numbers[,] . . . were instrumental in creating an ambiance favorable to reforms."

42. Sanuʿaʾs theater was closed in 1872. All plays were written sometime before that, yet very few records exists that date plays to a specific year of publication or performance. Please see Moosa, "Yaʿqub Sanuʿ and the Rise of Arab Drama in Egypt," p. 424.

43. This speech is delivered in a thick accent, with certain Arabic letters left unpronounced. Regarding the character's identification as a Nubian, some contemporary critics of nineteenth-century Arabic literature translate the widely used word *barbarī* as *berber,* but my study of contemporary dictionaries (i.e., Socrates, *A Dictionary of the Colloquial Arabic of Modern Egypt*), as well as proverbs and the patterns of trade and migration between Egypt and the Sudan, make *Nubian* seem a more accurate translation. Berber is located just north of Atbara, which was a major trade center in the nineteenth century. There were also instances in the 1800s of the term *Barabra* being used inaccurately to refer to people in the Nuba mountains of the western Sudan, which was then an area of frequent slave-trading with Egypt.

44. Najm, *Al-masrah al-ʿarabī,* p. 5.

45. See Landau, *Studies in Arab Theatre and Cinema.* See also al-Khozai, *The Development of Early Arab Drama;* and Moosa, "Yaʿqub Sanuʿ and the Rise of Arab Drama in Egypt," pp. 401–33.

46. Anūs, *Al-Laʿbāt al-tiyatrīya taʿlīf Yaʿqūb Sanūʿa,* pp. 6, 12.

47. Cole, *Colonialism and Revolution in the Middle East,* pp. 131–32.

48. Najm, *Al-masrah al-ʿarabī,* pp. 82–83.

49. Cole, *Colonialism and Revolution in the Middle East,* p. 134.

50. Najm, *Al-masrah al-ʿarabī,* p. 85.

51. Ibid., p. 86.

52. See, for example, the many references to the different *jīnsīyat* (ethnicities)of Egypt that ʿUrābī Pasha referred to in volume 1 of *Mudhākirāt ʿUrābī.*

53. Najm, *Al-masrah al-ʿarabī,* p. 87.

54. Badawi and Hinds, *A Dictionary of Egyptian Arabic,* p. 367. Dr. Badawi defines *zarbuna* as an obsolete epithet for slave. I am also indebted to Dr. Devin Stewart for drawing my attention to the historical precedents of this word and its relating blackness to slavery.

55. Najm, *Al-masrah al-ʿarabī,* p. 102.

56. Ibid., p. 105.

57. Ibid., p. 106.

58. Ibid., pp. 213–14.

59. Given the repeated, and now even stronger, references to race that Sanu'a's characters make in both these plays, it is startling that so many analysts of these texts ignore the allusions completely. While I accept the thesis of Jacob Landau, who traced in *Studies in Arab Theater and Cinema* the tradition of caricaturing the accents of the Sudanese in Arabic, I notice that little if anything has been said about Sanu'a's political uses of this tradition and the identification of racial or ethnic difference among his characters. For some examples of this negligence, see al-Khozai, *The Development of Early Arab Drama;* Moosa, "Ya'qub Sanu' and the Rise of Arab Drama in Egypt," pp. 401–33.

60. Landau, *Studies in the Arab Theater and Cinema,* pp. 30–31; Badawi, *Early Arabic Drama,* p. 26.

61. Gendzier, *The Practical Visions of Ya'qub Sanu'a,* pp. 32–33.

62. First published in *Riḥlat Abī Naẓẓara,* 30 Tishrīn al-thānī, No. 2, 1878.

63. Anūs, *Al-La'bāt al-tiyatrīya ta'līf Ya'qūb Sanū'a,* p. 41.

64. Ibid., p. 46.

65. *Al-Quradātī,* in *Al-La'bāt al-tiyatrīya ta'līf Ya'qūb Sanū'a, 1839–1912,* by Najwa Anūs (Cairo: al-Hi'ya al-miṣrīya al-'amma l-il-kitāb, 1987), p. 18.

66. Gendzier, *The Practical Visions of Ya'qub Sanu'a,* p. 74.

67. Scholch, *Egypt for the Egyptians!*

68. Delanoue, "'Abd Allah Nadim," pp. 77–78.

69. Ibid., p. 83.

70. 'Abdallah al-Nadīm, "Al-Farq bayna al-tamaddun al-sharqi wal-urubi," *al-Tankīt wa al-tabkīt ,* al-'adad 8, 31 July 1881.

71. I am indebted to Magda al-Nowaihi for her insights into the literary antecedents of 'Abdallah al-Nadīm's writings here.

72. 'Abdallah al-Nadīm, "La inta inta wa la al-mathīl mathīl," *al-Tankīt wa al-tabkīt,* al-'adad 12, 4 September 1881.

73. 'Abdallah al-Nadīm, "Nakhla wa Oshama," *al-Tankīt wa al-tabkīt,* al-'adad 3, 24 November 1881.

74. 'Abdallah al-Nadīm, "Hadith Khurafa," *al-Tankīt wa al-tabkīt,* al-'adad 5, 10 July 1881.

75. For an excellent discussion of *zār* in the Sudan, please see Boddy, *Wombs and Alien Spirits.*

76. Scholch, *Egypt for the Egyptians!* p. 6.

77. On al-Afghānī's membership in secret societies, see Jacob M. Landau "Prolegomena to a Study of Secret Societies in Modern Egypt," p. 142.

78. PRO, HD 3/67, Habib Anthony Salmone, Confidential Report, 11 February 1885.

79. Al-Afghānī, *Al-'Urwa al-Wuthqa',* pp. 246–47.

80. Ibid., p. 248.

81. Ibid., p. 252.

82. PRO, HD 3/67, Salmone, Confidential Report, 5 March 1885.

83. Al-Afghānī, *Al-'Urwa al-Wuthqa',* p. 326.

84. Ibid., p. 326.

85. PRO, HD 3/67, Salmone, Private Report, 11 February 1885.

86. PRO, HD 3/67, Salmone, Result of Second Journey to Paris, 14 April 1885.

87. Ramadan, *Al-jaysh al-miṣrī fi-l-siyāsa*, pp. 49–50.

88. The "appeal to Italy" refers to the efforts of the British to coordinate armies with the Italians—after the fall of Khartoum in order to evacuate the remaining troops of the Egyptian army—and Emin Pasha. Ya'qub Sanu'a, "Al-Inkliiz w-al-Mahdi," *Abū Naẓẓara Zarqa*, 7 February 1885.

89. Ya'qub Sanu'a, *Abū Naẓẓara Zarqa*, 27 June 1885.

90. Ibid.

91. Baignieres, *L'Égypte satirique*, p. 111.

92. Ibid., p. 112.

93. Hassan, *Miṣr wa al-Sudan wa wajh al-thawra fi naṣīḥat Aḥmad al-'Awam*, p. 31.

94. Ya'qub Sanu'a, "Abou Naddara aux chefs du Parti National Égyptien," *Abū Naẓẓara Zarqa*, 7 February 1885.

95. Ya'qub Sanu'a, *Abū Naẓẓara Zarqa*, 27 June 1885.

96. From "Fath Berber" [The conquest of Berber], in *Miṣr lil-Miṣrīyīn* (Paris: n.p., Jumady al-Awil, A.H. 1315), reprinted in full in *Al-La'bāt al-tiyatrīya ta'līf Ya'qūb Sanū'a, 1839–1912*, by Najwa Anūs (Cairo: al-Hi'ya al-miṣrīya al-'amma l-il-kitāb, 1987), pp. 134–35.

97. *Yalla Bina ila as-Sudan*, first printed in *Miṣr lil-miṣrīyīn*, Paris, 29 June 1890, reprinted in Anūs, *La'bat al-Tiyatrīya*, p. 140.

98. "Fath Berber," p. 136.

CHAPTER 3. THE LIVED EXPERIENCE OF CONTRADICTION

EPIGRAPH. Page 000: Bedri, *The Memoirs of Babikr Bedri*, p. 14.

1. P. M. Holt, introduction to *The Memoirs of Babikr Bedri*, by Babikr Bedri, vol. 1, trans. Yusuf Bedri and George Scott (London: Oxford University Press, 1969), p. xi.

2. Ibid.

3. Ibid., p. x. See also Hill, *A Biographical Dictionary of the Sudan*, pp. 30, 390–91.

4. Holt, introduction to *The Memoirs of Babikr Bedri*, pp. x, xiii.

5. Hill, *A Biographical Dictionary of the Sudan*, pp. 189–90.

6. Reid, "The Egyptian Geographical Society," pp. 539–40.

7. Ibid., p. 548–49.

8. Fawzī Pasha, *Kitāb al-sūdān bayna aydī Gordon wa Kitchener*, 1:46.

9. Ramadan, *Al-jaysh al-miṣrī fi-l-siyāsa*, pp. 41–42.

10. Broadley, *How We Defended Arabi and His Friends*, pp. 496–97.

11. Salih, *Al-shaykh 'Alī Yusuf wa jarīdat al-Mu'ayid*, p. 33. For more on Shaykh 'Alī Yusuf, see Abbas Kelidar, "Shaykh 'Ali Yusuf: Political Journalist and Islamic Nationalist," in *Intellectual Life in the Arab East, 1890–1939*, ed.

Marwan al-Buheiry (Beirut: American University in Beirut Press, 1981), pp. 10–20.

12. Neufeld, *A Prisoner of the Khaleefa*, pp. 340–41.

13. Hill, *A Biographical History of the Sudan*, p. 172.

14. Fawzī Pasha, *Kitāb al-sūdān bayna aydī Gordon wa Kitchener*, 1:40–41; Sabry, *Le Soudan égyptien*, p. 60.

15. Fawzī Pasha, *Kitāb al-sūdān bayna aydī Gordon wa Kitchener*, 1:41.

16. Ibid., 1:44.

17. Ibid., 1:45.

18. ʿUrābī Pasha, *Mudhākirāt ʿUrābī*, p. 45. ʿUrābī makes quite clear in these pages how angry he was over continually being passed over by his superiors in favor of younger Circassian officers, many of whom he himself had trained. And his sensitivity to the ethnic divisions between Egyptians and Circassians stands out with equal starkness, especially in an article he sent to the *Times* of London, titled "The Circassians" (p. 129).

19. ENA, Wathaʾiq al-thawra al-ʿurābīya, Muhafizah 7, Milaf 7, hearing of Ibrahīm Fawzī Bey, former police chief, 1 October 1882; hearing of Ibrahīm Fawzī Bey, 7 October 1882; questioning of Ibrahīm Fawzī Bey, 23 October 1882.

20. Ibid., hearing of Ibrahīm Fawzī Bey on 7 October, 1882. See also Fawzī Pasha, *Kitāb al-sūdān bayna aydī Gordon wa Kitchener*, 1:54–55.

21. Broadley, *How We Defended Arabi and His Friends*, p. 204.

22. SAD, 630/8/1–33, Précis of Ibrahīm Pasha Fawzī: papers concerning the case of Ibrahīm Pasha Fawzī v. Egyptian Government (Minister of Finance) claiming a pension as Lewa from 1885; transcript of Fawzī's case, p. 5.

23. Fawzī Pasha, *Kitāb al-sūdān bayna aydī Gordon wa Kitchener*, 1:400–402.

24. ENA, Majlis al-Wuzaraʾ/al-Sudan/al-thawra al-mahdīya/"z"/1/9: letter from the Ministry of Finance to the Council of Ministers, Cairo, 24 April 1886.

25. Ibid., handwritten letter dated 22 August 1889.

26. Ibid., letter from the Council of Ministers to Selib Agladious, Postmaster of Assouan, dated 13 November 1885.

27. Ibid., undated letter signed by Aisha, the wife of Ibrahīm Bey Fawzī.

28. Ibid., note to the Council of Ministers from the Ministry of Finance, 11 January 1893.

29. Zaydan, *Asir al-Mutamahdi*, p. 2.

30. BFASSP, Box G-29 A.

31. BFASSP, Box G-30.

32. Broadley, *How We Defended Arabi and His Friends*, p. 185.

33. *Miṣbaḥ al-sharq*, September 29, 1898.

34. SAD, 630/8/1–33: Précis of Ibrahīm Pasha Fawzī for the case of Ibrahīm Pasha Fawzī v. Egyptian Government (Minister of Finance), 1901.

35. SAD, 630/8/49–51: Fawzī Pasha to J. K. Watson; Watson to Sir Reginald Wingate.

36. Al-Zubayr Pasha's saga is a long and extremely interesting one in the history shared by Egypt and the Sudan. During the Crimean War and his years

of forced imprisonment in Cairo, he was allowed to lead a regiment of Sudanese troops of the Egyptian army into the Balkans. Al-Zubayr associated with the wealthiest Egyptians and was a close friend to the family of Sultan Pasha, remembered by the latter's daughter as a loving but sometimes intimidating man with a fearsome reputation (Sha'rawī, *Harem Years,* pp. 15, 49, 64–66). His capabilities as a military leader were very clear to the British public, but he was covered by a cloud of suspicion as a result of slave raids and slave trading in the regions of the Sudan that he had controlled. His son's assassination by Gessi Pasha, one of the governors appointed by Gordon, was a sad act that made al-Zubayr's loyalties even harder to ascertain. Finally, in 1900, Lord Cromer allowed al-Zubayr Pasha to return to the Sudan. He remained there for several years until his return to Egypt in 1909, where he settled in Helwan to write his memoirs. He made one more trip to the Sudan, in 1912, and he died there a year later at the age of eighty-two. Al-'Abid, trans., *Al-zubayr basha,* pp. 99–112.

37. Al-'Abid, trans., *Al-zubayr basha,* pp. 15–16.

38. Ibid., pp. 17–18.

39. Ibid., pp. 22, 38, 42–43.

40. *Egyptian Gazette,* 22 and 23 March 1901.

41. *Egyptian Gazette,* 3 April 1901.

42. Ibid.

43. Fawzī Pasha, *Kitāb al-sūdān bayna aydī Gordon wa Kitchener,* 1:3–5.

44. Cromer, *Modern Egypt,* 2:80.

45. Fawzī Pasha, *Kitāb al-sūdān bayna aydī Gordon wa Kitchener,* 1:4–5.

46. Ibid.

47. Ibid., pp. 8–9.

48. See *al-Mu'ayīd,* March-June 1896; 7, 9, 21, and 25 January 1899. See also al-Messady, "The Relations between 'Abbas Hilmī II and Lord Cromer," p. 283.

49. Fawzī Pasha, *Kitāb al-sūdān bayna aydī Gordon wa Kitchener,* 1:23–24.

50. Ibid., 1:25.

51. It is important to note that Fawzī Pasha always uses the word *miṣrīyyūn* (Egyptians) when speaking of the administration in the Sudan. His text shows, however, that the Sudanese, particularly those from *abīd* tribes (non-Muslim tribes), also refer to all people in government uniforms or with military authority as Atrak (Turks).

52. Cf. Fawzī Pasha, *Kitāb al-sūdān bayna aydī Gordon wa Kitchener,* 2:61, 142, 260.

53. Ibid., 1:95.

54. Bedri, *The Memoirs of Babikr Bedri,* p. 24, n. 1. The note explains that in the Mahdist Sudan the term *Turk* had no "precise ethnic significance" and was later transferred to the Anglo-Egyptian elite.

55. Fawzī Pasha, *Kitāb al-sūdān bayna aydī Gordon wa Kitchener,* 1:262–63.

56. Ibid., 1:263, 394–95.

57. Ibid., 1:103–4.

58. Ibid., 1:103, 234–35.

59. Bedri, *The Memoirs of Babikr Bedri*, p. 77, n. 1.

60. Ibid., p. 117.

61. Slatin Pasha, *Fire and Sword in the Sudan*, p. 177.

62. Ibid., p. 178.

63. Neufeld, *A Prisoner of the Khaleefa*, p. 132.

64. Fawzī Pasha, *Kitāb al-sūdān bayna aydī Gordon wa Kitchener*, 2:284.

65. Ibid., 2:323.

66. It is interesting that, when introducing the other to their respective readers, both Fawzī and Neufeld present themselves as rescuer of the other. Fawzī recounts being chained to Neufeld, who had dysentery at the time, making everyone, particularly Fawzī, suffer also, whereas Neufeld describes telling Fawzī to act like a man and stop whining when the Mahdist guards were clamping on his chains.

67. Fawzī Pasha, *Kitāb al-sūdān bayna aydī Gordon wa Kitchener*, 2:325.

68. Ibid., 2:260.

69. Ibid., 2:325.

CHAPTER 4. THE TOOLS OF THE MASTER

EPIGRAPHS. Page 000: Lorde, *Sister Outsider*, p. 112. Page 000: Toledano, *Slavery and Abolition in the Ottoman Middle East*, p. 116.

1. Toledano, *Slavery and Abolition in the Ottoman Middle East*, p. 113.

2. Ibid.

3. Hilāl, *Al-raqīq fī miṣr fi-l-qarn al-tāsiʿ ʿashr*, pp. 236, 239–40.

4. Shafik, *Mudhakira fī niṣf qarn*, p. 90.

5. Toledano, *Slavery and Abolition in the Ottoman Middle East*, p. 123.

6. Ibid., p. 127.

7. Shafik, *Mudhakira fī niṣf qarn*, p. 265.

8. Toledano, *The Ottoman Slave Trade and Its Suppression*, pp. 169–71.

9. Gabriel Baer, "Slavery and Its Abolition," in *Studies in the Social History of Modern Egypt* (Chicago: University of Chicago Press, 1969), p. 167.

10. For insights into the influence of Dr. David Livingstone on western European understandings of the African slave trade, see Davidson, *The African Slave Trade*, pp. 200–201; Miers and Roberts, eds., *The End of Slavery in Africa*, p. 17; and Robinson and Gallagher, *Africa and the Victorians*, pp. 24–25.

11. Waller, ed. *The Last Journals of David Livingstone in Central Africa*, p. 21.

12. Ibid., p. 224.

13. Mitchell, *Colonising Egypt*, pp. 10–13.

14. Hargay, "The Suppression of Slavery in the Sudan," pp. 26–27.

15. BFASSP, "Petition to His Highness Ismaʿil Pasha, Viceroy of Egypt," Box G-26, probably 1869 or 1870.

16. Baer, "Slavery and Its Abolition," p. 179.

17. Ibid., p. 184.

18. Ibid., p. 167.

19. Tucker, *Women in Nineteenth-Century Egypt,* p. 166.

20. Ibid., p. 167; Baer, "Slavery and Its Abolition," p. 165; Hunwick, "Black Slaves in the Mediterranean World," p. 21.

21. Hunwick, "Black Slaves in the Mediterranean World," p. 15.

22. Baer quotes one typical observation from British officials sent back to the Foreign Office: "Since most of the slaves were an integral part of the families in which they lived, their manumission involved a breach in the secretiveness of the Arab family, so dear a value to the Egyptians" ("Slavery and Its Abolition," p. 184). But similar quotes can be found in the treatise on slavery by Aḥmad Shafīk, "L'Esclavage au point de vue musulman," p. 460.

23. For instance, *Al-ḍara* (1874), in which Ṣanū'a dramatized the difficulties of multiple marriage for the first wife. Ṣanū'a was the best known, but certainly not the only, playwright for whom this issue was important. Other playwrights also focused on the issue of arranged marriages, reevaluating the rights of fathers over daughters. Two of these playwrights were Mahmud Wassif (*'Ajā'ib al-aqḍar,* [Cairo: n.p., 1894]); and Khalil Kāmil, *Zalim al-'aba'* [Cairo: n.p., 1897]).

24. Baron, "The Making and Breaking of Marital Bonds in Modern Egypt."

25. BFASSP, Box G-29, Vivian to Allen, Cairo, 18 July 1881.

26. BFASSP, Box G-26, Sir Wilfred Scawen Blunt to Charles Allen (Secretary General of the Anti-Slavery Association), 17 March 1882.

27. *Anti-Slavery Reporter,* 28 March 1882.

28. Hargay, "The Suppression of Slavery in the Sudan," p. 80.

29. PRO, FO 84/1770, from Lord Cromer to the Earl of Rosebery, 19 April 1886, with an enclosed extract from Schaefer to Cromer, 18 April 1886.

30. Gray, "The Origins and Organisation of the Nineteenth-Century Missionary Movement," pp. 19–21.

31. Shafīk, *Mudhakira fī niṣf qarn,* p. 510.

32. Shafīk, "L'Esclavage au point de vue musulman," p. 409.

33. Ibid., p. 438; for accounts of the audience, see Shafīk, *Mudhakira fī niṣf qarn,* p. 510–11.

34. Shafīk, "L'Esclavage au point de vue musulman," pp. 429–33.

35. Ibid., pp. 438, 443–51, 439.

36. Ibid., p. 465.

37. Shafīk, *Mudhakira fī niṣf qarn,* p. 514.

38. BFASSP, Box G-25, "Report on Slaves Belonging to Pilgrims to Mecca," G. H. Portal, Cairo, 22 July 1886.

39. Aḥmad Shafīk, *Bulletin de la Société Khediviale,* Seance du 28 novembre 1890, p. 472.

40. Brunschvig, "Abd," pp. 26–31.

41. 'Abdallah al-Nadīm, "Sa'id wa Bakhīta," *al-Ustādh,* 13 September 1892, reprinted in al-Nadīm, *'Abdallah al-Nadīm,* 1:91.

42. Ibid., 1:92.

43. Ibid., 1:93.

44. Hafez, *The Genesis of Arabic Narrative Discourse,* 84.

45. Al-Nadīm, "Sa'id wa Bakhīta," 1:92.

46. Ibid., 1:93.

47. Daws, "Al-'ammiya al-miṣrīya 'inda 'Abdallah al-Nadīm," p. 295. Dr. Daws makes an interesting point about the different styles of dialect used by men and women in the work of al-Nadīm.

48. Warburg, *Historical Discord on the Nile Valley*, pp. 15–16.

49. 'Issa, *Hikayāt min Daftār al-Waṭan*, p. 224.

50. PRO, FO, 84/1770, Cromer to Earl of Rosebery, 19 April 1886. In the spring of 1886, the jurisdiction of all slave trade trials was officially granted by the occupying government to native military tribunals. Cromer remarks in this letter that members of the Legislative Assembly would protest the removal of these controversial cases from the jurisdiction of the *qadī* (Islamic judge).

51. PRO, FO, 407/127, no. 124, Rodd to Kimberly, Cairo, 31 August 1894.

52. Ibid., no. 125, Rodd to Kimberly, Cairo, 24 September 1894; no. 127, Kimberly to Rodd, 24 September 1894.

53. Tucker, *Women in Nineteenth-Century Egypt*, pp. 177–79.

54. See, for example, *al-Muqaṭṭam*, 5 September 1894.

55. *Egyptian Gazette*, 14 September 1894.

56. See *Anti-Slavery Reporter*, vol. 14, July-August 1894. This is the journal of the Anti-Slavery Society.

57. By "Egyptian authorities," Schaefer refers to the Slave Trade Bureau, which was funded and organized in the name of the Egyptian government.

58. PRO, FO, 84/1877, report of Schaefer's extracted in Cromer to Salisbury, 6 February 1887.

59. PRO, FO, 407/127, Rodd to Kimberly, 17 September 1894.

60. PRO, FO, 84/1770, report by C. G. Scott Moncrieff, May 1886.

61. *Al-Fayūm*, 6 September 1894.

62. This translation is quoted from *al-Muqaṭṭam*, 10 September 1894, but all the papers, except the *Gazette*, gave this portion of Khalil Bey Ibrahim's speech great prominence.

63. *Egyptian Gazette*, 31 August 1894.

64. PRO, FO, 407/127, nos. 125 and 126, Rodd to Kimberly, Cairo, 24 September 1894.

65. *Anti-Slavery Reporter*, vol. 14, July-August 1894, p. 246.

66. Gershoni and Jankowski, *Egypt, Islam, and the Arabs*, pp. 6–7.

67. Kāmil, *Al-khutub*, p. 201.

68. Ibid., p. 61.

69. Ibid., pp. 87–88. From a speech given at the Geographic Society of Paris, 11 December 1895. It should be taken into account that Kāmil's brother, 'Alī Fahmy Kāmil, was a military officer in the Sudan and was penalized by the British for his brother's nationalist activities. When he tried to resign from army service, he was imprisoned. See p. 108, n. 8.

70. Kāmil, *Al-Maqalāt*, pp. 275–76.

71. Fawzī Pasha, *Kitāb al-sūdān bayna aydī Gordon wa Kitchener*, 2:284.

72. Johnson, "Recruitment and Entrapment in Private Slave Armies," p. 168.

73. Ibid., pp. 168–69. See also Gerard Prunier, "Military Slavery in the

Sudan during the Turkiyya, 1820–1885," in the same issue of *Slavery and Abolition* (13, no. 1 [April 1992]: 129–139).

74. Kāmil, *Al-Maqalaat,* p. 92.

75. Hobsbawm, *The Age of Empire,* pp. 57–60, 70.

76. Kāmil, *Al-Maqalaat,* p. 298, excerpted from *Le Clair,* 19 April 1898.

77. Ibid., p. 299.

78. Ibid.

79. Kāmil, *Al-Maqalaat,* p. 141, excerpted from *al-Ahrām,* 28 January 1895.

80. Kāmil, *Al-khutub,* p. 115, from speech given 3 March 1896 at the High Chamber of the Abbas Theater, Alexandria; also published in *al-Mu'ayīd,* 4 March 1896.

81. Kāmil, *Al-khutub,* p. 115.

82. Ibid., pp. 116, 118.

83. Ibid., p. 181, from a speech given in Cairo, 23 December 1898.

84. Ibid., p. 123, from a speech given in Alexandria at the High Chamber of the Abbas Theater, 3 March 1896; p. 139, from a speech given on 3 June 1897.

85. *Al-Sūdān al-miṣrī wa al-inklīz,* pp. 1, 64, 426.

86. Ibid., pp. 97–99, 113, 129.

87. Kāmil, *Al-khutub,* p. 42.

88. Cromer, *Modern Egypt,* 2:118.

89. *Al-Mu'ayīd,* 22 January 1899.

90. *Al-Mu'ayīd,* 28 January 1899.

91. *Al-Mu'ayīd,* 25 January 1899.

92. Demolins, *A quoi tient la supériorité des anglo-saxons?*

93. Zaghlūl, *Sirr al-taqaddum al-Anglo-Saxīyīn?*

94. Ḥamad, *Naḥnu wa al-Ruqīy,* p. 63.

95. Ibid., pp. 65–66.

96. Ibid., pp. 68, 69, 70.

97. Gershoni and Jankowski, *Egypt, Islam, and the Arabs,* p. 18.

98. *Al-Jarīda,* 24 July 1910.

99. *Al-Jarīda,* 25 July 1910.

100. Ibid.

101. *Al-Jarīda,* 22 October 1910.

102. Ibid.

CHAPTER 5. EGYPTIANS IN BLACK FACE

EPIGRAPH. Page 000: Rushdie, *Midnight's Children,* p. 12.

1. On economics and nationalism, see Beinin and Lockman, *Workers on the Nile;* Tignor, *Modernization and British Colonial Rule in Egypt;* and Roger Owen, *The Middle East in the World Economy.* On the issue of the British in the Sudan and the struggle over the slave trade, see Sikainga, *Slaves into Workers;* and Collins, *Shadows in the Grass.* On the development of the 1919 revolution in Egypt, see Sabry, *La Revolution égyptienne;* and al-Rafi'i, *Thawra al-sana 1919.*

2. Al-ʿAqad, "Muḥammad Imām al-ʿAbd," p. 110.

3. Hilāl, *Al-raqīq fī miṣr fi-l-qarn al-tāsiʿ ʿashr*, p. 298.

4. Al-ʿAqad, "Muḥammad Imām al-ʿAbd," p. 110.

5. Al-Bishrī, "Al-mudaʿabāt wa al-afakakiya," p. 123. This essay was first broadcast on 30 January 1934 and published in the newspaper *al-Jihād* on 31 January 1934, twenty-three years after Imām al-ʿAbd's death.

6. Ibid., p. 127.

7. Hilāl, *Al-raqīq fī miṣr fi-l-qarn al-tāsiʿ ʿashr*, p. 278.

8. Ibid., p. 128.

9. Al-ʿAqad, "Muḥammad Imām al-ʿAbd," p. 111.

10. Hilāl, *Al-raqīq fī miṣr fi-l-qarn al-tāsiʿ ʿashr*, p. 281.

11. Al-ʿAqad, "Muḥammad Imām al-ʿAbd," p. 111.

12. Hilāl, *Al-raqīq fī miṣr fi-l-qarn al-tāsiʿ ʿashr*, p. 280.

13. Ibid., p. 112.

14. Al-Rafiʿi, *Thawra al-sana 1919*, pp. 73–75.

15. Ibid., p. 76.

16. Berque, *Egypt*, pp. 306–7.

17. Shaʿrawī, *Harem Years*, pp. 113–20.

18. Shafīk, *Ḥawliyāt Miṣr al-siyāsiya, Tamhid*, pp. 247–49.

19. Sabry, *La Revolution égyptienne*, p. 23.

20. Since the first, deeply enthusiastic, accounts of the 1919 revolution written by the historian and eyewitness Muḥammad Sabry in its immediate aftermath, the uprising has undergone many different interpretations within Egyptian historiography. ʿAbd al-Rahman al-Rafiʿi's *Thawra al-sana 1919*, a classic and detailed account, was first published during the twilight of King Farouq's reign; its second printing followed Gamal Abd al-Nasr's establishment of an independent government by three years. Al-Rafiʿi's book went far in keeping the legend of Saʿd Zaghlūl untarnished (and unexplored). While a strong belief in the nationalist movement continues among Egyptian historians, the idea of the events of 1919 having formed a "revolution" is currently in question, as evidenced by the 1992 conference on 1919, held at the American University in Cairo and sponsored jointly by that school and Cairo University.

21. Berque, *Egypt*, p. 305; Gershoni and Jankowski, *Egypt, Islam, and the Arabs*, p. 53.

22. Milner, *Report of the Special Mission to Egypt*, p. 37.

23. PRO, FO 407/84, Confidential Prints—Egypt and the Sudan, Allenby to Curzon, 30 April 1919.

24. Rizq, *Al-Sūdān fī ʿahd al-hukm al-thanāʾī al-Awwal*, pp. 399–413.

25. Ibid., pp. 397–99.

26. Ibid., p. 403.

27. Milner, *Report of the Special Mission to Egypt*, p. 32.

28. Ibid., p. 33.

29. PRO, FO 407/84, Allenby to Curzon, 13 April 1919; enclosure of report from Assistant Director of Intelligence in Khartoum. The language of the report is at times confusing. It is unclear exactly what position the "Grand

qadī" held. It is also uncertain whether the advice given to the Wafdists was reported in Allenby's own words or Intelligence officials were putting words in his mouth.

30. Ibid.

31. PRO, FO 407/84, Wingate to Curzon, 26 March 1919.

32. MacMichael, "Nubian Elements in Dar Fur" p. 35.

33. For an interesting discussion of these works and their relation to how Sudanese tribes traditionally identify themselves, see Ibrahim, "Breaking the Pen of Harold MacMichael," pp. 220, 228–29.

34. Ibid., p. 231.

35. Rizq, *Al-Sūdān fī 'ahd al-hukm al-thanā'ī al-Awwal*, pp. 435–37.

36. Bedri, *The Memoirs of Babikr Bedri* 2:292–94.

37. Sharkey, "A Century in Print," pp. 533–34.

38. Bashir, *Tārīkh al-harakāt al-wataniyya f-il-sūdān*, pp. 68–71.

39. PRO, FO 407/84, Wingate to Curzon, 26 March 1919. See the enclosed letter from Sir Lee Stack describing the religious shaykhs' request to travel to London and to spread pro-British propaganda among their own followers. For more on the trip to London, see Rizq, *Al-Sūdān fī 'ahd al-hukm al-thanā'ī al-Awwal*, p. 437. Babikr Bedri also includes an account of this visit that shocked many of the Sudanese as much as it horrified the Egyptians.

40. G. N. Sanderson, introduction to *The Memoirs of Babikr Bedri*, by Babikr Bedri, trans. Yusuf Bedri and George Scott (London: Oxford University Press, 1969), 1:61, 63.

41. Sharkey, "A Century in Print," p. 535.

42. Rizq, *Al-Sūdān fī 'ahd al-hukm al-thanā'ī al-Awwal*, p. 438.

43. Kurita, "The Role of the 'Negroid but Detribalized' People in Sudanese Society," p. 115.

44. Toledano, *Slavery and Abolition in the Ottoman Middle East*, p. 127.

45. Huda Sha'rawī, *Mudhākirātī*, p. 309.

46. Ibid., pp. 10, 16–17.

47. Ibid., p. 16.

48. Ibid., p. 43.

49. Ibid., pp. 51–52.

50. Ibid., pp. 56–57, 60.

51. Ibid., p. 103.

52. Ibid., pp. 226, 299–300.

53. Ibid., pp. 311–12.

54. Ibid., p. 313, 314.

55. Darwīsh, *Min Ajlī Abī Sayyid Darwīsh*, p. 109.

56. *Dinga Dinga* may have been a term for the Sudanese used by Egyptian soldiers serving in the Sudan and taken from the name of the Mahdist fighter Osman Digna or from the Dinka tribe, as suggested by Richard Hill.

57. Al-Hafna, *Sayyid Darwish*, pp. 113–14.

58. 'Alī, *Saraqu al-sunduq ya Muhammad*, p. 25.

59. Ibid., p. 114.

60. Ibid., pp. 115–16.

61. Darwīsh, *Min Ajlī Abī Sayyid Darwīsh*, p. 107.

62. Ibid., pp. 281, 287.

63. Taymūr, *Mu'alifāt Muhammad Taymūr: Hayatunah al-tamthīlīya* 2:26. Taymūr saw this linguistic accessibility as a problem, because it gave Egyptian audiences the jokes they wanted to hear but never offered a challenging, more nuanced picture of their society.

64. Landau, *Studies in Arab Theater and Cinema*, pp. 90–91.

65. Al-Kassār, *'Alī al-Kassār*, pp. 22–23.

66. Ibid., p. 25.

67. AENT, Amīn Sidqī, handwritten manuscript of "Al-Barbarī f-il-Jaysh," 1920, p. 4.

68. Ibid., p. 6.

69. Ibid., p. 11.

70. Ibid., p. 19.

71. Ibid., p. 33.

72. Al-Kassār, *'Alī al-Kassār*, p. 27.

73. 'Alī, *Saraqu al-sunduq ya Muhammad*, p. 19.

74. AENT, 'Abd al-Hamid Kamil, handwritten manuscript of "Al-Hilāl," 1923, p. 31.

75. Ibid., p. 94.

76. Ibid., p. 109.

77. Darwīsh, *Min Ajlī Abī Sayyid Darwīsh*, p. 187, quoted from "Al-Tamthil al-Hazli" [The comedic theater], *al-Shabab*, 6 March 1920.

78. Ibid., p. 188, quoted from "Fi Sabil al-Fann" [For the cause of art], *al-Munir*, 12 July 1920.

79. 'Alī, *Saraqu al-sunduq ya Muhammad*, p. 13.

80. Ibid., pp. 90–91.

81. Sabry, *La Revolution égyptienne*, p. 8.

82. Darwīsh, *Min Ajlī Abī Sayyid Darwīsh*, pp. 113–14.

83. Muhammad Taymūr, "Haflat al-tarab," in *Ma tarāhu al-'uyūn* (Cairo: Dar al-Salafiyya, 1927).

84. Taymūr, *Mu'alifāt Muhammad Taymūr: Wamīd al-Ruh*, 1:30, 35.

85. M. M. Badawi, *Early Arabic Drama*, p. 102.

86. Ibid., p. 104.

87. Taymūr, *Mu'alifāt Muhammad Taymūr: Hayatunah al-tamthīlīya*, 2:53, 56–57, 71.

88. Ibid., 2:75–84, 85–93, 94–103, 104–12.

89. For instance, the grim servant of *Lil-Fuqara Majanan* [Free services for the poor], Taymūr, *Mu'alifāt Muhammad Taymūr: Wamīd al-Ruh*, 1:104.

90. M. M. Badawi, *Early Arabic Drama*, p. 107.

91. Taymūr, *Mu'alifāt Muhammad Taymūr: al-Masrah al-Misrīya*, 3:26.

92. Ibid., 3:27.

93. Ibid., 3:28.

94. Ibid., 3:28–29.

95. Ibid., 3:112.

96. Ibid., 3:117–18.

97. Ibid., 3:147–48.

98. Ibid., 3:149.

99. Bedri, *The Memoirs of Babikr Bedri*, 2:191–92.

100. Holt and Daly, *A History of the Sudan*, pp. 129–30.

101. Rahim, *Imperialism and Nationalism in the Sudan*, p. 61. The quote comes from Keon-Boyd to the High Commissioner, 14 March 1920, Milner Papers, St. Anthony's College.

102. Ibid., p. 96.

103. Bedri, *The Memoirs of Babikr Bedri*, 2:276–77.

104. Ibid., 2:92–94, 102.

105. Woodward, *Sudan*, p. 42.

106. Kurita, "The Concept of Nationalism in the White Flag League," p. 10.

107. Bashir, *Tārīkh al-ḥarakāt al-waṭanīya f-il-sūdān*, p. 97.

108. Marqus, *Al-sūdān fī al-barlamān al-miṣrī*, p. 50.

109. Kurita, "The Concept of Nationalism in the White Flag League," p. 17; Marqus, *Al-sūdān fī al-barlamān al-miṣrī*, p. 41.

110. Marqus, *Al-sūdān fī al-barlamān al-miṣrī*, p. 44.

111. Kurita, "The Concept of Nationalism in the White Flag League," p. 18.

112. Holt and Daly, *A History of the Sudan*, pp. 131–32.

113. Woodward, *Sudan*, p. 47.

114. Kurita, "The Role of the 'Negroid but Detribalized' People in Sudanese Society," p. 113.

115. Woodward, *Sudan*, pp. 45, 47.

116. Ibid., p. 56.

117. Kurita, "The Concept of Nationalism in the White Flag League," p. 8.

118. Woodward, *Sudan*, p. 42.

119. Kurita, "Concept of Nationalism in the White Flag League," pp. 9–10.

120. PRO, FO 407/184, no. 111, Sir Lee Stack to Earl Curzon, Khartoum, 21 March 1919.

121. Holt and Daly, *A History of the Sudan*, pp. 133–34.

122. Bashir, *Tārīkh al-ḥarakāt al-waṭanīya f-il-sūdān*, p. 123.

123. Ibid., p. 125.

124. Woodward, *Sudan*, p. 42; Rahim, *Imperialism and Nationalism in the Sudan*, pp. 107–8.

125. Al-Gaddal, "Tarīkh al-Sūdān al-Ḥadīth," p. 782.

126. Rahim, *Imperialism and Nationalism in the Sudan*, pp. 111–12.

127. Ibid., p. 785.

128. Ibid.

129. *Al-Latā'if al-Muṣawwara*, 25 August 1924.

130. *Al-Latā'if al-Muṣawwara*, 1 September 1924.

131. Kurita, *'Alī 'abd al-Laṭīf wa al-thawra 1924*, p. 80.

CONCLUSION

1. Roberts, *Civilization without Sexes*, p. 5.

2. Ibid.

3. Dagnino, *Bakhita Tells Her Story*, pp. 22–33. Dagnino was a Canossian missionary.

4. Mary Jane Malou, Blessed Josephine Bakhīta Women's Association, interview by author, Cairo, Egypt, 1 August 1997.

Works Cited

ARCHIVES

Archives of the Egyptian National Theater (AENT)
  'Abd al-Hamid Kamil, "Al-Hilāl," 1923
  Amīn Sidqī, "Al-Barbarī f-il-Jaysh," 1920

British and Foreign Anti-Slavery Society Papers (BFASSP),
Rhodes House, Oxford University, Boxes G25, G26, G29-A, G-30

Egyptian National Archives (ENA)
  Majlis al-Wuzara'/al-Sudan/al-thawra al-mahdīya/"z"/1/9
  Watha'iq al-thawra al-'urābīya (Documents of the 'Urābī rebellion),
  Muhafizah 1–26, Milaf 1–21

Public Record Office, London (PRO)
  Foreign Office (FO) 84 (Slavery)
  FO 141
  HD 3/67 (Confidential reports)
  407 (Confidential prints)

Sudan Archive, Durham University (SAD)
  630/8/1–33: Précis of Ibrahīm Fawzī Pasha
  630/8/49–51: Letters by and about Ibrahīm Fawzī Pasha

NEWSPAPERS

Egyptian National Library, Cairo
  Abū Nazzara Bayda

Abū Naẓẓara Zarqa
al-Ahrām
al-Fayūm
al-Jarīda
al-Kashkūl
al-Laṭā'if al-Muṣawwara
al-Liwā'
Miṣbaḥ al-sharq
al-Mu'ayīd
al-Muqaṭṭam
Riḥlat Abī Naẓẓara
al-Tankīt wa al-tabkīt
al-Ustādh

British Library, London

Anti-Slavery Reporter
Egyptian Gazette

BOOKS AND ARTICLES

al-'Abid, 'Abbas, trans. *Al-zubayr basha: Yirāwī 'an siratihi fi manfihi bi jabal tāriq* [Zubayr Pasha: In his own words from exile in Gibraltar]. Cairo: Center for Sudanese Studies, 1995.

al-Afghānī, Jamāl al-Dīn. *Al-'Urwa al-Wuthqa'* [Collected articles]. Cairo: Maktabah al-Ahliyya, 1927.

Ahmad, Ahmad Sayyid. *Rifa'ah Rafi' al-Ṭahṭawī fī-l-Sūdān.* Khartoum: al-Lajnat al-ta'alif w'al-tarjamah w'al-nashr, 1983.

Ahmad, Aijaz. *In Theory: Classes, Nations, Literatures.* London: Verso, 1992.

Ahmed, Leila. "Between Two Worlds: The Formation of a Turn-of-the-Century Egyptian Feminist." In *Life/Lines: Theorizing Women's Autobiography.* ed. Bella Brodzki and Celeste Schenk. Ithaca: Cornell University Press, 1988.

'Ali, Abbas Ibrahim Muhammad. *The British, the Slave Trade, and Slavery in the Sudan, 1820–1881.* Khartoum: Khartoum University Press, 1972.

'Alī, Mahmūd. *Saraqu al-sunduq ya Muḥammad: Min silsilah turāth 'Alī al-Kassār.* Cairo: al-Majlis al-'ala l-il thiqafah, 1992.

Altman, Israel. "The Political Thought of Rifa'ah Rafi' al-Ṭahṭawī, a Nineteenth-Century Egyptian Reformer." Ph.D. diss., University of California, 1976.

Amīn, Qāsim. *The Liberation of Women: A Document in the History of Egyptian Feminism.* Trans. Samiha Sidhom Peterson. Cairo: American University in Cairo Press, 1992.

Anderson, Benedict. *Imagined Communities: Reflections on the Origins and Spread of Nationalism.* Rev. ed. London: Verso, 1991.

Anūs, Najwa. *Al-La'bāt al-tiyatrīya ta'līf Ya'qūb Sanū'a, 1839–1912.* Cairo: al-Hi'ya al-miṣrīya al-'amma l-il-kitāb, 1987.

al-ʿAqad, ʿAmr. "Muḥammad Imām al-ʿAbd: Shakhṣiyatun la tunsa fī adābina al-ḥadīth." *Al-Faisal*, no. 104 (November 1985).

Badawi, El-Said, and Martin Hinds. *A Dictionary of Egyptian Arabic.* Beirut: Librairie du Liban, 1986.

Badawi, M. M. *Early Arabic Drama.* Cambridge: Cambridge University Press, 1988.

Baer, Gabriel. *Studies in the Social History of Modern Egypt.* Chicago: University of Chicago Press, 1969.

Baignières, Paul de. *L'Égypte satirique: L'Album d'Abou Naddara.* Paris: Imprimerie Lefebvre, 1886.

Baker, Sir Samuel W. *Ismailia: A Narrative of the Expedition to Central Africa for the Suppression of the Slave Trade.* London: Macmillan, 1879.

Bakhtin, M. M. *The Dialogic Imagination: Four Essays.* Ed. Michael Holquist, trans. Caryl Emerson and Michael Holquist. Austin: University of Texas Press, 1981.

Balibar, Etienne. "Racism and Nationalism." In *Race, Nation, Class: Ambiguous Identities,* ed. Etienne Balibar and Immanuel Wallerstein. New York: Verso, 1991.

Barbour, Neville. "The Arabic Theater in Egypt." *Bulletin of the Society of Oriental Studies* 8 (1935–1937).

Baron, Beth. "The Making and Breaking of Marital Bonds in Modern Egypt." In *Women in Middle Eastern History,* ed. Beth Baron and Nikki Keddie. New Haven: Yale University Press, 1991.

———. *The Women's Awakening in Egypt.* New Haven: Yale University Press, 1994.

Bashir, Muhammed ʿAmr. *Tārīkh al-ḥarakāt al-waṭanīya f-il-sūdān.* Khartoum: al-Dar al-sudaniyya l-il-kutub, 1980.

Bedri, Babikr. *The Memoirs of Babikr Bedri.* Vol. 1. Trans. Yusuf Bedri and George Scott. London: Oxford University Press, 1969.

———. *The Memoirs of Babikr Bedri.* Vol. 2. Trans. Yusuf Bedri and Peter Hogg. London: Ithaca Press, 1980.

Beinin, Joel. "Writing Class: Workers and Modern Egyptian Colloquial Poetry (Zajal)." *Poetics Today* 15, no. 2 (summer 1994).

Beinin, Joel, and Zachary Lockman. *Workers on the Nile.* Princeton: Princeton University Press, 1987.

Bell, Morag, Robin A. Butlin, and Michael Heffernan, eds. *Geography and Imperialism.* Manchester: Manchester University Press, 1995.

Berque, Jacques. *Egypt: Imperialism and Revolution.* London: Faber and Faber, 1973.

al-Bishri, ʿAbd al-ʿAziz. "Al-mudaʿabāt wa al-afakakiya (al-nukta al-miṣrīya fī al-ʿaṣr al-ḥadīth)." In *Mukhtar.* Vol. 2. Cairo: Dar al-Maʾarif, n.d.

Bjorkelo, Anders. *Prelude to the Mahdiyya: Peasants and Traders in the Shendi Region, 1821–1885.* Cambridge: Cambridge University Press, 1989.

Boddy, Janice. *Wombs and Alien Spirits: Women, Men, and the Zar Cult in Northern Sudan.* Madison: University of Wisconsin Press, 1989.

Bonola Bey, Dr. Frederic. *Sommaire historique des travaux géographiques exe-cutés en Égypte sous la dynastie de Mohammed Aly.* Cairo: Imprimerie Nationale, 1889.

Broadley, A. M. *How We Defended Arabi and His Friends: A Story of Egypt and the Egyptians.* London: Chapman and Hall, 1884; reprint, Cairo: Arab Research and Publishing Center, 1980.

Brunschvig, R. "Abd." In *The Encyclopedia of Islam.* 1st ed. London: Luzac and Company; Leiden: E. J. Brill, 1960.

al-Buheiry, Marwan, ed. *Intellectual Life in the Arab East, 1890–1939.* Beirut: American University in Beirut Press, 1981.

Cole, Juan R. I. *Colonialism and Revolution in the Middle East: Social and Cultural Origins of Egypt's Urabi Movement.* Princeton: Princeton University Press, 1993.

Collins, Robert O. "The Nilotic Slave Trade: Past and Present." *Slavery and Abolition* 8, no. 3 (December 1988).

———. *Shadows in the Grass: Britain in the Southern Sudan, 1918–1956.* New Haven: Yale University Press, 1983.

Cosgrove, Denis, and Stephen Daniels, eds. *The Iconography of Landscape.* Cambridge: Cambridge University Press, 1988.

Cromer, Lord [Evelyn Baring]. *Modern Egypt.* 2 vols. London: Macmillan and Company, 1908.

Dagnino, Maria Luisa. *Bakhita Tells Her Story.* Rome: General House, Canossian Daughters of Charity, 1992.

Darwish, Hassan. *Min Ajlī Abī Sayyid Darwīsh.* Cairo: al-Hi'ya al-miṣrīya al-'amma l-il-kitāb, 1990.

Davidson, Basil. *The African Slave Trade.* Rev. ed. Boston: Back Bay Books; New York: Little, Brown, and Company, 1980.

Daws, Madiha. "Al-'ammiya al-miṣrīya 'inda 'Abdallah al-Nadīm." In *Buḥuth nadwa al-ihtifāl bi dhikrī marūr miʾa 'am 'ala wafāh 'Abdallah al-Nadīm.* Cairo: al-Majlis al-'ala lil-thiqāfa, 1997.

Delanoue, Gilbert. "'Abd Allah Nadim (1845–1896): Les idées politiques et morales d'un journaliste égyptien." *Bulletin d'études orientale* 27 (1961–62).

———. *Moralistes et politiques Musulmans dans l'Égypte du XIXe siècle, 1798–1882, II.* Cairo: Institut Francais d'Archeologie Orientale du Caire, 1982.

Demolins, Edmond. *À quoi tient la supériorité des anglo-saxons?* Paris: F. Didot et cie., 1897.

de Moraes Farias, Paulo Fernando. "Models of the World and Categorical Models: The 'Enslaveable Barbarian' as a Mobile Classificatory Label." In *Islam and the Ideology of Enslavement.* Vol. 1 of *Slaves and Slavery in Muslim Africa.* London: Frank Cass and Company, 1985.

Douin, G. "L'Empire africain." Vol. 3, pt. 2 of *Histoire du regne du Khedive Ismail.* Cairo: Institut Francais d'Archeologie Orientale du Caire pour la Société Royale de Geographie d'Égypte, 1939.

Driver, Felix. "Geography's Empire: Histories of Geographical Knowledge." *Environment and Planning D: Society and Space* 10 (1992).

Fahmy, Khaled. *All the Pasha's Men: Mehmet Ali, His Army, and the Making of Modern Egypt.* Cambridge: Cambridge University Press, 1997.

Fawzī Pasha, Ibrahīm. *Kitāb al-sūdān bayna aydī Gordon wa Kitchener* [The Sudan under Gordon and Kitchener], 2 vols. Cairo: Idarah jaridah al-Mu'ayyad, 1901.

al-Gaddal, Muhammed Sa'id. "Tarīkh al-Sūdān al-Ḥadīth, 1820–1955." Manuscript, Beirut, 1993.

Gendzier, Irene. *The Practical Visions of Ya'qub Sanu'a.* Cambridge: Harvard Middle Eastern Monographs, Center for Middle Eastern Studies, 1966.

Gershoni, Israel, and James Jankowski. *Egypt, Islam, and the Arabs: The Search for Egyptian Nationhood, 1900–1930.* New York: Oxford University Press, 1986.

Godlewska, Anna, and Neil Smith, eds. *The Geography of Empire.* Oxford: Blackwell, 1994.

Gray, Richard. "The Origins and Organisation of the Nineteenth-Century Missionary Movement." *Tarikh* 3, no. 1 (1969): 19–21.

Greenblatt, Stephen. *Marvellous Possessions: The Wonder of the New World.* Chicago: University of Chicago Press, 1991.

Hafez, Sabry. *The Genesis of Arabic Narrative Discourse.* London: Saqi Press, 1993.

al-Hafna, Mahmud Aḥmad. *Sayyid Darwīsh.* Cairo: n.p., 1977.

Ḥamad, Salaḥ Hamdī. *Naḥnu wa al-Ruqī.* Cairo: Matba'ah Madrassa Walida Abbas al-Awal, 1906.

Hargay, Taj. "The Suppression of Slavery in the Sudan, 1898–1939." Thesis, St. Anthony's College, Oxford University, 1981.

Harley, J. B. "Maps, Knowledge, and Power." In *The Iconography of Landscape,* ed. Denis Cosgrove and Stephen Daniels. Cambridge: Cambridge University Press, 1988.

Hassan, Ibrahim Shahata. *Miṣr wa al-Sudan wa wajh al-thawra fi naṣīhat Aḥmad al-'Awam.* Cairo: n.p., 1981.

Helms, Mary W. *Ulysses' Sail: An Ethnographic Odyssey of Power, Knowledge, and Geographical Distance.* Princeton: Princeton University Press, 1987.

Hilāl, 'Umad Ahmad. *Al-raqīq fī miṣr fi-l-qarn al-tāsi' 'ashr.* Cairo: Matbu'at al-'Arabi, 1999.

Hill, Richard L. *A Biographical Dictionary of the Sudan.* 2d ed. London: Frank Cass and Company, 1967.

Hobsbawm, Eric. *The Age of Empire, 1875–1914.* New York: Vintage Books, 1989.

———. *Nations and Nationalism since 1789: Programme, Myth, Reality.* Cambridge: Cambridge University Press, 1990.

Holt, P. M., and M. W. Daly. *A History of the Sudan, from the Coming of Islam to the Present Day.* 4th ed. London: Longman Press, 1988.

————. *The Mahdist State in the Sudan, 1881–1898: A Study of Its Origins, Development, and Overthrow.* Nairobi: Oxford University Press, 1977.

Hourani, Albert. *Arabic Thought in the Liberal Age.* Cambridge: Cambridge University Press, 1983.

————. *A History of the Arab Peoples.* Cambridge: Harvard University Press, 1991.

Hunwick, J. O. "Black Slaves in the Mediterranean World: Introduction to a Neglected Aspect of the African Diaspora." *Slavery and Abolition* 13, no. 1 (April 1992).

Ibrahim, Abdullahi Ali. "Breaking the Pen of Harold MacMichael: The Ja'aliyyin Identity Revisited." *International Journal of African Historical Studies* 21, no. 2 (1988).

'Issa, Salaḥ. *Hikayāt min Daftār al-Waṭan* [Stories from the record of the homeland]. Cairo: Kitāb Dār al-ahālī, 1992.

Jacobs, Charles, and Mohamed Athie. "Bought and Sold." *New York Times,* July 13, 1994.

Johnson, Douglas. "Recruitment and Entrapment in Private Slave Armies: The Structure of the Zara'ib in the Southern Sudan." *Slavery and Abolition* 13, no. 1 (April 1992).

Kāmil, Muṣṭafa. *Al-khutub* [Speeches]. Ed. 'Abd al-'Azim Ramadan. Cairo: Matba'a al-miṣrīya al-'amma l-il-kitāb, 1986.

————. *Al-Maqalāt.* Ed. 'Abd al-'Azim Ramaḍan. Cairo: Matba'a al-miṣrīya al-'amma l-il-kitāb, 1987.

al-Kassar, Magid. *'Alī al-Kassār: Barbarī Miṣr al-waḥid.* Cairo: Dar Akhbar al-Yawm, 1991.

al-Khozai, Mohamed A. *The Development of Early Arab Drama (1847–1900).* London: Longman Press, 1984.

Kurita, Yoshiko. *'Alī 'abd al-Laṭīf wa al-thawra 1924: Baḥth fi maṣādir al-thawra al-sūdāniya.* Cairo: Markaz al-Dirasat al-Sudaniyya, 1997.

————. "The Concept of Nationalism in the White Flag League." In *The Nationalist Movement in the Sudan,* ed. Mahasin Abdel Gadir Haq al-Safi. Sudan Library Series no. 15. Khartoum: Institute of African and Asian Studies, University of Khartoum, 1989.

————. "The Role of the 'Negroid but Detribalized' People in Sudanese Society, 1920's–1940's." In *The Sudan: Environment and People.* Vol. 3 of *Second International Sudan Studies Conference Papers.* University of Durham, 8–11 April 1991.

Landau, Jacob M. "Prolegomena to a Study of Secret Societies in Modern Egypt." *Middle East Studies* 1, no. 2 (1965).

————. *Studies in Arab Theater and Cinema.* Philadelphia: University of Pennsylvania Press, 1958.

Lawson, Fred. *The Social Origins of Egyptian Expansionism during the Muhammad 'Ali Period.* New York: Columbia University Press, 1992.

Lockman, Zachary. "Imagining the Working Class: Culture, Nationalism, and

Class Formation in Egypt, 1899–1914." *Poetics Today* 15, no. 2 (summer 1994).

Loomba, Ania. *Colonialism/Postcolonialism.* London: Routledge Press, 1998.

Lorde, Audre. *Sister Outsider: Essays and Speeches.* Freedom, Calif.: Crossing Press, 1984.

Mackenzie, J. *Propaganda and Empire: The Manipulation of British Public Opinion, 1880–1960.* Manchester: Manchester University Press, 1984.

MacMichael, H. A. "Nubian Elements in Dar Fur." In *Sudan Notes and Records* 1 (1918).

Mansfield, Peter. *A History of the Middle East.* New York: Penguin Books, 1991.

Maqqar, Nissim. *Al-Bekbashī al-miṣri Selim Qapudan wa-al-kashf 'an manābi' al-nīl* [The Bekbashi Selim Qapudan and the discovery of the source of the Nile]. Cairo: al-Jina al-Bayyan al-'arabi, 1960.

Marqus, Joaqim Rizq. *Al-sūdān fī al-barlamān al-miṣrī, 1924–1936.* Cairo: al-Hi'ya al-miṣrīya al-'amma l-il-kitāb, 1989.

Marsot, Afaf Lutfi al-Sayyid. *Egypt in the Reign of Muhammad Ali.* Cambridge: Cambridge University Press, 1984.

McClintock, Anne. *Imperial Leather: Race, Gender, and Sexuality in the Colonial Context.* New York: Routledge Press, 1995.

al-Messady, Dr. Mohammed Gamal. "The Relations between 'Abbas Hilmī II and Lord Cromer." Ph.D. diss., University of London, 1966.

Miers, Suzanne, and Richard Roberts, eds. *The End of Slavery in Africa.* Madison, Wis.: University of Madison Press, 1988.

Milner, Lord. *Report of the Special Mission to Egypt.* London: n.p., 1921.

Mitchell, Timothy. *Colonising Egypt.* Cambridge: Cambridge University Press, 1990.

Montesquieu, *Persian Letters.* London: Routledge and Sons, 1891.

Moosa, Matti. *The Origins of Modern Arabic Fiction.* Boulder, Colo.: Lynne Rienner, 1997.

———. "Ya'qub Sanu' and the Rise of Arab Drama in Egypt." *International Journal of Middle East Studies* 5 (1974).

Morrison, Toni. *Playing in the Dark: Whiteness and the Literary Imagination.* Cambridge: Harvard University Press, 1992.

Mubārak, 'Alī Pasha. *'Alam al-Dīn.* Vol. 1. Cairo: al-Hi'ya al-miṣrīya al-'amma l-il-kitāb, 1993.

———. *Ḥayatī.* Ed. 'Abd al-Rahim Yusuf al-Jamal. Cairo: Maktabat al-adab, 1989.

Nachtigal, Gustav. *Sahara and Sudan.* New York: Barnes and Noble, 1971.

al-Nadīm, 'Abdallah. *'Abdallah al-Nadīm: al-'Adād al-kāmila li majallat al-ustādh.* Vols. 1 and 2. Cairo: al-Hi'ya al-'amma l-il-kitāb, 1994.

Najm, Dr. Mohammed Yusuf. *Al-masraḥ al-'arabī: Dirasāt wa nusūs, al-juz' al-thālith, Ya'qub Sanu'a (Abou Naddara).* Beirut: Dar al-Thaqafa, 1963.

Neufeld, Charles. *A Prisoner of the Khaleefa.* London: n.p., 1899.

O'Fahey, R. S. *State and Society in Dar Fur.* New York: St. Martin's Press, 1980.

Owen, Roger. *The Middle East in the World Economy*. London: Methuen Press, 1981.

Paule, Charles-Dominique, trans. and ed. *Voyageurs Arabes: Ibn Fadlan, Ibn Jubayr, Ibn Battuta*. Paris: Editions Gallimard, 1995.

al-Qadi, Wadad. "East and West in 'Ali Mubarak's *'Alam al-Din*." In *Intellectual Life in the Arab East*, ed. Marwan al-Buheiry. Beirut: American University in Beirut, 1981.

Qapudan, [al-Bakbasha] Selim. *Al-riḥla al-ūla lil-baḥth 'an yanābī al-baḥr al-abyaḍ (Al-jana al-bayān al-'arabī)*. Trans. Muhammad Masu' Rawad. Cairo: Ministry of the Interior, 1922. Selections from the official notes of the Geographic Society (1842).

al-Rafi'i, 'Abd al-Rahman. *Thawra al-sana 1919: Tārīkh Miṣr al-Qawmi min 1914–1921*. 4th ed. Cairo: Dār al-Ma'ārif, 1986.

Rahim, Muddathir 'Abdel. *Imperialism and Nationalism in the Sudan*. Khartoum: Khartoum University Press; London: Ithaca Press, 1986.

Ramadan, Dr. 'Abd al-'Azim Ramadan. *'Ukdhubat al-Ista'amar al-Miṣrī lil-Sudan*. Cairo: al-Hi'ya al-miṣrīya al-'amma l-il-kitāb, 1988.

———. *Al-jaysh al-miṣrī fī-l-siyāsa, 1882–1936*. Cairo: al-Hi'ya al-miṣrīya al-'amma l-il-kitāb, 1977.

Reid, Donald. "The Egyptian Geographical Society: From Foreign Laymen's Society to Indigenous Professional Association." *Poetics Today* 14, no. 3 (fall 1993).

Rizq, Younan Labib. "Al-Ahram: A Diwan of Contemporary Life, No. 186." In *al-Ahram Weekly* (June 19–25, 1997).

———. *Al-Sūdān fī 'ahd al-hukm al-thanā'ī al-Awwal*. Cairo: Jama'at al-Dawal al-'Arabiyya, 1976.

Roberts, Mary Louise. *Civilization without Sexes: Reconstructing Gender in Postwar France, 1917–1927*. Chicago: University of Chicago Press, 1994.

Robinson, Ronald, and John Gallagher. *Africa and the Victorians: The Official Mind of Imperialism*. 2d ed. London: Macmillan, 1981.

van Roosbeck, G. L. *Persian Letters before Montesquieu*. Reprint. New York: Burt Franklin, 1972.

Rushdie, Salman. *Midnight's Children*. New York: Alfred A. Knopf, 1981.

Said, Edward. *Orientalism*. New York: Vintage Books, 1978.

Sabry, M. *L'Empire égyptien sous Mohamed-Ali et la question d'Orient (1811–1849)*. Paris: Librairie Orientaliste Paul Geuthner, 1930.

———. *La revolution égyptienne*. Vol. 1. Paris: Librairie J. Vin, 1919.

———. *Le Soudan égyptien, 1821–1898*. Cairo: Imprimerie Nationale, 1947.

Salih, Sulayman. *Al-shaykh 'Alī Yusuf wa jarīdat al-Mu'ayid: Tārīkh al-ḥarakāt al-waṭaniya fī rub' qarn*. Cairo: al-Hi'ya al-miṣrīya al-'amma l-il-kitāb, 1990.

Santi, Paul, and Richard Hill, eds. *The Europeans in the Sudan, 1834–1878 (Some Manuscripts, Mostly Unpublished, Written by Traders and Missionaries, Officials and Others)*. Oxford: Clarendon Press, 1980.

Scholch, Alexander. *Egypt for the Egyptians! The Socio-Political Crisis in Egypt, 1878–1882*. London: Ithaca Press, 1981.

Shafīk, Aḥmad. "L'Esclavage au point de vue musulman." *Bulletin de la Société de Geographie de l'Égypte* 5 (1892).

———. *Ḥawliyāt Miṣr al-siyāsiya, Tamhid*. Cairo: Matba'ah Shafīk Pasha, 1926.

———. *Mudhakira fī niṣf qarn*. Cairo: al-Hi'ya al-miṣrīya al-'amma l-il-kitāb, 1994.

Sha'rawī, Huda. *Harem Years: The Memoirs of an Egyptian Feminist, 1879–1924*. Trans. and ed. Margot Badran. London: Virago Press, 1986.

———. *Mudhākirātī*. Cairo: Dar al-Hilal, 1981.

Sharkey, Heather J. "A Century in Print: Arabic Journalism and Nationalism in Sudan, 1899–1999." *International Journal of Middle East Studies* 31 (November 1999).

Shukry, M. F. *Equatoria under Egyptian Rule: The Unpublished Correspondence of Col. (afterwards Major-Gen.) C. G. Gordon with Ismail Khedive of Egypt and the Sudan during the Years 1874–1876*. Cairo: Cairo University Press, 1953.

Sikainga, Ahmad Alawad. *Slaves into Workers: Emancipation and Labor in Colonial Sudan*. Austin: University of Texas Press, 1996.

Slatin Pasha, Rudolph. *Fire and Sword in the Sudan*. Leipzig: n.p., 1899.

Smollett, Tobias, trans.. *The Adventures of Telemachus, the Son of Ulysses*. Athens: University of Georgia Press, 1997.

Socrates, Spiro. *A Dictionary of the Colloquial Arabic of Modern Egypt*. Beirut: Librairie du Liban, 1980. First published in Cairo in 1895.

Al-Sūdān al-miṣrī wa al-inklīz. Alexandria: Matba'a al-Ahrām, 1898.

al-Ṭahṭawī, Rifa'ah Bey Badawi Rafi'. *Manāhij al-albāb al-miṣriya fī mabāhij al-'adāb al-'asriya*. Cairo: Matba'ah shirkat al-ragha'ib, 1912.

———. *Mawāqi' al-aflak fī waqā'i' Telemaque*. Beirut: Matba'a al-suriyya, 1867.

Taylor, Bayard. *Journey to Central Africa; or, Life and Landscapes from Egypt to the Negro Kingdoms of the White Nile*. New York: Putnam and Company, 1854.

Taymūr, Muḥammad. *Ma tarāhu al-'uyūn* [What the eyes saw]. Cairo: Dar al-Salafiyya, 1927.

———. *Mu'alifāt Muḥammad Taymūr: Ḥayatunah al-tamthīlīya*. Vol. 2. Cairo: Matba'ah al-'Itimad, 1922.

———. *Mu'alifāt Muḥammad Taymūr: al-Masraḥ al-Miṣrīya*. Vol. 3. Cairo: al-Hi'ya al-miṣrīya al-'amma l-il-kitāb, 1973.

———. *Mu'alifāt Muḥammad Taymūr: Wamīd al-Ruḥ*. Vol. 1. Cairo: al-Hi'ya al-miṣrīya al-'amma l-il-kitāb, 1971.

Tignor, Robert L. *Modernization and British Colonial Rule in Egypt*. Princeton: Princeton University Press, 1966.

Toledano, Ehud. *The Ottoman Slave Trade and Its Suppression, 1840–1890*. Princeton: Princeton University Press, 1982.

———. "Slave Dealers, Women, Pregnancy, and Abortion: The Story of a Circassian Slave-Girl in Mid–Nineteenth Century Cairo." *Slavery and Abolition* 2, no. 1 (May 1981).

———. *Slavery and Abolition in the Ottoman Middle East* (Seattle: University of Washington Press, 1998.

———. *State and Society in Mid–Nineteenth Century Egypt.* Cambridge: Cambridge University Press, 1990.

Tucker, Judith. *Women in Nineteenth-Century Egypt.* Cambridge: Cambridge University Press, 1985.

al-Tunisī, Muḥammad ibn ʿUmar. *Tashḥīdh al-adhhān bi-sirat bilād al-ʿarab wal-sūdān* [Sharpening the intellect with travel in the country of the Arabs and the blacks]. Ed. Khalil Mahmud ʿAsakir and Mustafa Muhammad Musʿad. Cairo: n.p., 1965.

ʿUrābī Pasha, Ahmed. *Mudhākirāt ʿUrābī: Kashf al-sitār ʿan sirr al-asrār fi-l-nahḍa al-miṣriya al-mashhūra b-il-thawra al-ʿurābīya.* Cairo: Dar al-Hilal, 1953.

Walcott, Derek. *Omeros.* New York: Noonday Press, 1990.

Waller, Horace, ed. *The Last Journals of David Livingstone in Central Africa.* New York: Harper and Bros., 1875.

Walz, Terence. "Black Slavery in Nineteenth Century Egypt." In *Slaves and Slavery in Muslim Africa.* Vol. 2, ed. John Ralph Willis. London: Frank Cass and Company, 1985.

———. *Trade between Egypt and Bilad as-Sudan, 1700–1820.* Cairo: Institut Francais d'Archeologie Orientale, 1978.

Warburg, Gabriel R. *Egypt and the Sudan: Studies in History and Politics.* London: Frank Cass and Company, 1985.

———. *Historical Discord in the Nile Valley.* London: Hurst and Company, 1992.

Wendell, Charles. *The Evolution of the Egyptian National Image.* Berkeley: University of California Press, 1972.

Woodward, Peter. *Sudan, 1898–1989: The Unstable State.* Boulder, Colo.: Lynne Rienner; London: Lester Cook, 1990.

Young, Robert J. C. *Colonial Desire: Hybridity in Theory, Culture, and Race.* New York: Routledge Press, 1995.

Zaghlūl, Ahmad Fathī Pasha, trans. *Sirr al-taqaddum al-Anglo-Saxīyīn?* Translation of *À quoi tient la supériorité des anglo-saxons?* by Edmond Demolins. Alexandria: n.p., 1899.

Zaydan, Jurji. *Asir al-mutamahdī* [Prisoner of the False Mahdi]. Cairo: Matbaʿah al-Taʿalif, 1892.

Index

Text: 10/13 Aldus
Display: Aldus
Compositor: BookMatters, Berkeley
Printer: Thomson-Shore, Inc.